University of Michigan Studies

HUMANISTIC SERIES

VOLUME XIV

TWO STUDIES IN LATER ROMAN AND BYZANTINE ADMINISTRATION

THE MACMILLAN COMPANY
NEW YORK · BOSTON · CHICAGO · DALLAS
ATLANTA · SAN FRANCISCO

MACMILLAN & CO., LIMITED
LONDON · BOMBAY · CALCUTTA
MELBOURNE

THE MACMILLAN CO. OF CANADA, LTD.
TORONTO

TWO STUDIES IN LATER ROMAN AND BYZANTINE ADMINISTRATION

BY

ARTHUR E. R. BOAK

UNIVERSITY OF MICHIGAN

AND

JAMES E. DUNLAP

UNIVERSITY OF MICHIGAN

New York

THE MACMILLAN COMPANY

LONDON: MACMILLAN AND COMPANY

1924

PRINTED IN THE UNITED STATES OF AMERICA

Set up and electrotyped. Published February, 1924.

Norwood Press
J. S. Cushing Co. — Berwick & Smith Co.
Norwood, Mass., U.S.A.

Paperback ISBN: 978-0-472-75038-2

PART I

THE MASTER OF THE OFFICES IN THE LATER ROMAN AND BYZANTINE EMPIRES

The Index to Part I
will be found on pages 155–160

PREFATORY NOTE

THE following study of the Master of the Offices is an attempt to throw more light upon the intricate administrative system obtaining in the Later Roman and Byzantine Empires through a detailed treatment of the history and scope of one particular office. It is a development of work done in connection with a doctoral thesis on the *Roman Magistri*, some of the results of which are incorporated in the first chapter.

For directing his attention to the Late Roman and Byzantine field of historical research, as well as for constant guidance and suggestion in the preparation of this monograph, the writer's special acknowledgments are due to Professor W. S. Ferguson, of Harvard University. He is further under great obligation to Mr. William H. Murphy, of Detroit, whose generosity made the publication of this study possible.

A small edition of this study was published separately, in 1918. In reprinting it in the volume the writer has taken advantage of the opportunity to correct some typographical errors as well as to make additions to the lists of Masters given in Appendix B.

ARTHUR E. R. BOAK

ANN ARBOR, MICHIGAN
August, 1923

CONTENTS

THE MASTER OF THE OFFICES

INTRODUCTION

I. HISTORICAL SIGNIFICANCE OF THE MASTER OF THE OFFICES

THE Master of the Offices interests the student of the government of the Later Roman Empire, and invites his close attention, for various reasons.

First, no parallel to this officer can be found among the government ministers of modern states, and even among those of the Empire itself the Master of the Offices occupied a singular position; for while the other great officers of state controlled branches of the administration easily definable and possessing some essential unity, his sphere of activities was made up of an aggregation of various powers which brought him into touch with the most diverse functions of the government.

The Mastership of the Offices, too, had a long and interesting history, extending over the period from the reconstruction of Diocletian until the Latin conquest of Constantinople. From a comparatively inconspicuous beginning, by a series of additions to its competence, it became one of the most honorable and influential of the civil offices of the Empire. Then its power began to decline as it had arisen: one after the other its active functions were transferred to new offices, and, finally, it ceased altogether to be an administrative office, and remained solely as a title of honor. Thus arose the grade of dignitaries bearing the title of Master simply, no longer that of Master of the Offices. This was the final stage in the history of the Mastership.

Not only is the story of this office interesting in itself but the study of its development also illustrates, through a concrete example, many of the important changes that affected the character of the imperial Roman administrative system as a whole, and gives one an insight into the detailed working of that vast governmental machine.

II. SOURCES AND LITERATURE

The chief contemporary sources of information regarding the Master of the Offices are the Codes of Theodosius II and Justinian, with the *Novellae*[1] of Theodosius II, Valentinian III, Majorian and Justinian, which afford the best aid in reconstructing the historical development of that office up to about the middle of the sixth century A.D.

A list of the departments of the administration under the control of this Master at the end of the first quarter of the fifth century is preserved in the catalogue of the officials of the Empire known as the *Notitia Dignitatum*, compiled in its present form by about 425 A.D.[2] The *Notitia* also gives the organization of the Master's personal office at the same period. Equally important information regarding the Master of the Offices in the Gothic Kingdom of Theodoric in Italy in the first part of the sixth century is afforded by the *formula magisteriae dignitatis*, contained in the *Variae* of Cassiodorus, dating from 537 A.D. A brief and somewhat confused sketch of the growth of the Mastership up to the time of Justinian is given in the *De magistratibus imperii Romani* (περὶ ἀρχῶν τῆς Ῥωμαίων πολιτείας) of Johannes Lydus, written in 551 A.D. The *Kletorologion* of Philotheus, a list of the imperial dignitaries and functionaries at the end of the ninth century, prepared in 899, gives the position of the Masters, at that time forming an order of rank, among the dignitaries of the Empire, and the inaugural ceremony to this grade as well as its distinctive insignia. For the part played by these Masters in the various ceremonies of the Byzantine court in the tenth century, and also for considerable information regarding similar duties of the Master of earlier centuries, we are indebted to the *De Caerimoniis* (Ἔκθεσις τῆς βασιλείου τάξεως) of Constantine VII Porphyrogenitus (912–58).

[1] The editions of the *Novellae*, as of other works frequently cited, are indicated in the Bibliography, pp. 127–129.

[2] Mommsen, *Hermes*, vol. 36, pp. 544-47.

In addition, incidental references to Masters of the Offices, which are useful in throwing light upon the character and scope of the Mastership, are found throughout the literary material in general, chiefly, as might be expected, in that of a historical character, which has survived from the period between the opening of the fourth and the close of the twelfth century.

Of modern works which, directly or indirectly, are useful for the study of the Mastership of the Offices, the oldest is Gothofredus's edition of the Theodosian Code[1] with its learned commentaries. The work of other early commentators has been summed up and superseded by Böcking in extensive notes to his edition of the *Notitia Dignitatum* (1839–53).

Karlowa's *Römische Rechtsgeschichte* (vol. 1, 1880), Schiller in the second volume of his *Geschichte der römischen Kaiserzeit* (1887), and J. S. Reid's chapter on the "Reorganization of the Empire" in the *Cambridge Mediæval History* (vol. 1, 1911) offer the most satisfactory general surveys of the functions of the Master of the Offices at the height of his power. More valuable for the close study of this office are the contributions of Otto Seeck in his *Geschichte des Untergangs der antiken Welt* (vol. 2, 1901) and his article *comites* in the Pauly-Wissowa *Real-Encyclopädie der klassischen Altertumswissenschaft* (vol. 4, 1901). These have the merit of offering the most satisfactory view of the origin of the Master's office and of putting it in its proper relation to the general reorganization of the court and the administration at the opening of the fourth century.

Upon the position of the Mastership in the Gothic Kingdom of Italy and in the Eastern Empire at the close of the fifth and the first part of the sixth century much light is thrown by Mommsen's *Ostgothische Studien* (1889–90). As important for the later history of the Mastership as the works of Seeck for the earlier period is J. B. Bury's *Imperial Administration in the Ninth Century* (1911), which shows clearly the steps by which the Mastership was changed from an administrative office to an honorary title of rank, and indicates the general tendencies at work within the Empire which were responsible for this evolution.

What is still lacking is a complete history of the Mastership that will cover the whole period of its existence and trace clearly,

[1] First published at Paris, in 1549.

so far as is possible, in their proper chronological order, the various stages of its development and its decline, showing the connection between these changes and the general tendencies which affected the administration as a whole. Ancient as well as modern historians recognized that the powers of this office at its height were the result of a long period of growth, but the tendency has been to neglect the stages of the process and consider only its results. The works of Seeck and Bury supply the necessary corrective for two distinct epochs. It is the aim of this study to treat the entire history of the Mastership in the spirit of these historians.

CHAPTER I

THE ROMAN *MAGISTRI*

THE word *magister* contains the idea of superior power. It is probably a derivative from *magis*, and is applicable to that one of any group of individuals who has more authority than the rest.[1] Paulus [2] says that it was given as a title to persons "to whom is entrusted the special superintendence of affairs, and who, above the rest, owe diligence and care to the business of which they are in charge." The verb *magistrare* contains the same idea, being equivalent to *moderare* or *regere et temperare*.[3] *Magister* never had the force of *dominus*, 'lord,' which contains the idea of possession. It was this simple yet wide meaning of the word *magister*, so closely akin to that of our own Master, that permitted its adoption as an official title in practically all branches of Roman public and private life.

The office of a Master was called a *magistratus*, 'magistracy,' or, more usually, a *magisterium*, 'mastership.' [4] The antonym of *magister* is *minister*, and both have their corresponding feminine forms, *magistra*, 'Mistress,' and *ministra*.[5]

Under the Roman Republic, at least in historic times, *magister* was but sparingly used as a title of political officials, although its

[1] *Qui magis ceteris potest*, Varro, *De lingua latina*, 6, 83; *magister*, *maior in statione*, Isid. 10, 170; cf. Paul. *Epit.*, 126, 152 M. *Magister* is a Latin word not appearing in Greek until after the Roman conquest, and then as a borrowed term, in the forms μάγιστερ, μάγιστρος (the regular spelling), and μαγίστωρ; cf. Forcellini, *Lexicon*; Stephanus, *Thesaurus linguae Graecae*; Du Cange, *Glossarium mediae et infimae Graecitatis*. The older Latin form was *magester* (Quint. 1, 4, 18).

[2] *Digesta*, L, 16, 57.

[3] Paulus, *loc. cit.* It also appears in the form *magisterare*.

[4] *Magistratus*, *C.I.L.* I, p. 43, *epistula consulum de Bacchanalibus*; Paulus, *Epit.*, 126 M. *Magisteria*, *id.*, 152.

[5] *Minister*, Isid. 10, 170.

abstract *magistratus* was the regular term used to designate both the ordinary political office itself and the holder of such an office, who derived his power from popular election, or its substitute, co-optation.[1] Mommsen[2] thought that *magister* was not used of the public magistrates because the word originally denoted a single person endowed with superior authority and, consequently, was less suited than the abstract *magistratus* to officials organized on the collegiate principle. But the fact is that, as Mommsen admits, we find colleges of Masters in *vici*, *pagi*, *municipia* and other corporations, which shows that there is nothing inherent in the meaning of the word that conflicts with the idea of collegiality. Perhaps the explanation is that when Roman political thinking required a general term for magistrates, *magister* was already too commonly employed in other spheres to make its use convenient here. In the bureaucracy of the Empire the title Master appears much more frequently than under the Republican régime. However, in both periods the appellative Master, owing to the necessity of avoiding confusion in the case of a title capable of such wide application, was always accompanied by some qualifying epithet, as, for example, Master of the Horse (*magister equitum*) or Master of the Census (*magister census*); so that the whole phrase, and not the word Master alone, formed the title of the office. Only in the late Byzantine Empire, when the title of Master was restricted, first to one office, and then to members of an order of rank, did it dispense with such qualification.

In the other spheres of Roman life, social, religious, and commercial, Master as a title was in widespread usage. Festus[3] says that there were Masters, not only of the liberal arts, but also of rural districts, of associations, and of villages or city quarters. The various uses of the word "president" may offer an English analogy.

It will facilitate a survey of the Roman Masters to divide them into several groups, based upon the character of the offices which they held, and, to a certain degree, corresponding chronologically to the extension of the use of Master with an official significance. Therefore the following general classification is suggested:

[1] Paul. *Epit.*, 126 M.; Mommsen, *Römisches Staatsrecht*, vol. 1, p. 8.

[2] *Loc. cit.*, A. 1. Varro's explanation, *De ling. lat.* 5, 82, is impossible.

[3] Paul. *Epit.*, 126 M.: *Magistri non solum doctores artium sed etiam pagorum, societatum, vicorum, equitum dicuntur, quia hi magis ceteris possunt.*

Masters who were Magistrates of the Roman Republic.
Masters who were neither Public Officials nor Officers of Colleges, but who had a recognized position in Commercial and Social organizations.
Masters whose functions were primarily religious:
  Masters who were not Officers of Colleges, but who formed a College themselves, acting on behalf of a community in a public capacity.
  Masters who were Officers of Colleges.
Masters who were Imperial Officials in the Civil Service of the Roman Empire.
Masters who were Imperial Officials in the Military Service of the Roman Empire.

We shall now proceed to a dicussion of the Masters who fall within each of these categories and thus establish the relation of the title Master of the Offices to other official titles in which the word Master occurs.

I. Masters who were Magistrates of the Roman Republic

These Masters may be dismissed with a very brief mention. They were only two in number, namely, the Master of the People (*magister populi*) and the Master of the Horse (*magister equitum*). In historic times the name of Master of the People no longer appears, but has been supplanted by that of Dictator. On the contrary, the Master of the Horse persisted until the abolition of the Dictatorship in 44 B.C. These two titles, however, show that the use of Master to denote an official of state was probably as old as the Roman Republic itself.

II. Masters who were neither Public Officials, nor Officers of Colleges, but who had a Recognized Position in Commercial and Social Organizations

In this rather miscellaneous section have been grouped such Masters as were not civil or military authorities of the state or of municipalities, or religious officials bearing a public character or serving in private associations, but nevertheless occupied positions which, in common usage and in the eyes of the law, authorized them to bear that title.

All the titles of this class, with the possible exception of the Shopmaster (*magister tabernae*), were in current usage during the republican epoch and date from a period so far back of the earliest records which we have of their presence that it is impossible to determine just when they came to be generally employed. However, as can be seen by a glance at the appended list, the various titles represent a wide range of interests — legal, social, educational, commercial, and agricultural. And, since the presence of regular official titles indicates a certain degree of order and regularity in the conduct of affairs, one must place the introduction of these Masters at a time when Rome had attained a sufficient stage of material and cultural advancement to require the systematic organization of the various activities of her citizens. Thus the Master in Bankruptcy (*magister auctionis*) is the fruit of considerable legal experimenting with bankruptcy cases; the Schoolmasters (*ludimagistri*) presuppose a fairly widespread demand for elementary education; the Master of the Companies of *publicani* (*magister societatis*) is the product of a well-developed system of tax farming; the Master of the Herd (*magister pecoris*) and the Taskmaster (*magister operum*) can only have appeared with a well-organized and widely extended system of ranching and farming on a large scale, *i.e.* with a great territorial expansion of the state; while the Shipmaster (*magister navis*) is a figure which doubtless first arose after the appearance of Rome as a world power and mercantile factor in the Mediterranean basin, in a period subsequent to the unification of the Italian peninsula.

Thus the presence of each of these Masters indicates a considerable advance in the power and material resources of the Roman state and points to a period far removed from the origins of civic development, a fact not necessarily true of the public officials, the Master of the People and the Master of the Horse, who probably antedate all the Masters mentioned here.

The following are the Masters who may be included in this group:

1. *Magister auctionis*, Master in Bankruptcy.
2. *Magister bibendi*, Toastmaster.
3. *Ludimagistri*, Schoolmasters.
4. *Magister navis*, Shipmaster.
5. *Magister operum*, Taskmaster.
6. *Magister pecoris*, Master of the Herd.
7. *Magister societatis*, Company Master.
8. *Magister tabernae*, Shopmaster.

III. Masters whose Functions were Primarily Religious

This is by far the largest class of Masters. It includes all those whose chief duties were connected with the performance of certain religious rites, no matter what organization or combination of individuals they represented in this capacity, and who had, therefore, a priestly character.

However, the position occupied by these Masters will be seen more clearly if we distinguish two types of Masters within the general class under consideration. The organization of the various groups of Masters who fall within the class has been adopted as the basis of this subdivision, because the Masters themselves, and not the cults which they directed, interest us here. Therefore, they have been classified in two groups, Masters who, like the Roman magistrates, themselves formed a college, and Masters who were officers within larger colleges of which they were members. It happens that the Masters of the first subdivision, without exception, at the same time bore a public character as the representatives of political units recognized in the Roman governmental system; while the second group embraces Masters who, thanks to their presence in public priestly colleges, possessed in some measure this public character, and others, again, who lacked it entirely.

We shall now consider a little more closely the Masters of each of these subdivisions.

1. *Masters who were not Officers of Colleges, but who formed a College themselves, acting on Behalf of a Community in a Public Capacity*

Such Masters existed in Rome, in Italy, and throughout the provinces of the Roman Empire, and were present in the various *coloniae*, *municipia*, *vici*, *pagi*, *fora*, and *castella*, as well as in the *conventus* and *cannabae* of Roman citizens, which lay outside the Roman municipal system.

However, the Masters in these several political units were not all organized in like fashion nor possessed of identical powers. Indeed, in no two forms of communal organization do the colleges of Masters present exactly the same features, with the exception of the Masters of the Shrines (*magistri fani*) in the colonies and other municipalities. Two characteristics, nevertheless, were common to all and determine their place in this classification; namely, their collegiate organization and the religious nature of their functions. The latter might or might not be combined with duties of a purely secular character, which, however, did not overshadow the religious side of the office. Furthermore, these sacral functions were exercised by the Masters as representatives of the whole of the members of the body politic to which they belonged — their canton, village, ward, city, etc., — and in this sense the Masters were public officials.

The scope and importance of the secular powers of such Masters varied according to the stage of political development attained by the community to which they belonged; more definitely, according to the number and character of the magistrates officiating there. Thus we find Masters in a barrack village (*vicus cannabensis*), in the absence of regular magistrates, assuming the part of representatives of their community in all respects where it was called upon to act as a unity. A similar position was taken by the Masters in the Roman *conventus* on Delos, who were nothing more than Masters of Shrines,[1] while, in fully developed municipalities, such were merely the curators of particular shrines and, apparently, had no secular duties whatever. This latter type of Masters appeared also in cantons and villages, forming secondary colleges with strictly religious functions, even when other colleges of Masters stood at the head of the community.

The early development of such colleges of Masters is older than our records. We meet the system in operation in the second century B.C.; we see it adopted in the municipal organization of the following century, then in full bloom under the Principate; in some cases it persisted after the reforms of Diocletian and Constantine.

The following is the list of Masters of this group:

1. *Magistri pagi*, Masters of the Canton or District.
2. *Magistri vici*, Masters of the Village or Quarter.
3. *Magistri municipii*, Municipal Masters.
4. *Magistri castelli*, Masters of the Castellum.
5. *Magistri curiae*, Masters of the Curia.
6. *Magistri fani*, Masters of the Shrine.
7. *Magistri Fundi* and *Magistri Saltus*, Masters of the Estate and Masters of the Domain.

2. *Masters who were Members, and at the Same Time Officers, of Colleges, whose Membership included Others than the Masters themselves.*

These Masters differ from those of the preceding group in being the official representatives, not of some community organized on a political basis, or an administrative division of the same, but of a corporation or society, whether religious or secular. Here the

[1] Reference may be made to my article, *Magistri in Campania and Delos*, published in *Classical Philology*, vol. 10 (1915), pp. 25-45.

Masters themselves did not constitute the college, although often they may be said to have formed a college within a college, but were officers for the remaining members, whose number varied according to the character of the respective associations.

This class of Masters includes on the one hand Masters of colleges intrusted with the performance of public cults, and on the other Masters of other religious and secular colleges.

a. Masters of Colleges intrusted with the maintenance of Public Cults

Among the colleges which were responsible for the maintenance of the public cults (*sacra publica*), in Rome and elsewhere throughout the Empire, we have to distinguish priestly and non-priestly organizations. The priestly colleges were those in which all of the members were priests, as in the college of the pontiffs or that of the quindecemvirs. The non-priestly colleges included the remaining religious colleges of the group in question, in which the only true priests were those annually elected from among the ordinary lay members, as, for example, in the colleges of the Mercuriales.[1]

This difference in the constitution of the two sorts of colleges brought with it, as would naturally be expected, a corresponding difference in the position and functions of the Masters in the respective classes. Here, however, it will be sufficient to indicate the titles of the Masters belonging to the colleges of each sort.

The following Masters belong to the priestly colleges:

1. *Magister Fratrum Arvalium,* Master of the Arval Brothers.
2. *Magister Haruspicum,* Master of the Haruspices.
3. *Magister Collegii Lupercorum,* Master of the Lupercal College.
4. *Magister Pontificum,* Master of the Pontiffs.
5. *Magister Quindecemvirum Sacris Faciundis,* Master of the Quindecemvirs.
6. *Magister Saliorum,* Master of the Salii.
7. *Magister Sodalium Augustalium Claudialium,* Master of the Augustan and Claudian Sodales.

The Masters of the non-priestly colleges were:

1. *Magistri Augustales,* Masters of the Augustales.
2. *Magistri Capitolinorum,* Masters of the Capitolini.
3. *Magistri Ceriales,* Masters of the Ceriales.
4. *Magistri Martini,* Masters of the Martini.
5. *Magistri Mercuriales,* Masters of the Mercuriales.
6. *Magistri Collegii Minervae,* Masters of the College of Minerva.
7. *Magistri Herculanii,* Masters of the Herculanii.

[1] Cf. Wissowa, *Religion und Kultus der Römer*, p. 404, n. 7.

b. Masters of other Religious and Secular Colleges

Here are grouped in one section the Masters of all colleges, religious, funerary, social, professional, or of any other character, which differ from the religious colleges of the preceding class in not being charged with the maintenance of a public cult. It is not necessary to make separate categories for the Masters of the several varieties of colleges included in this section, because the organization of all these colleges was the same in its general features, and the position held by the Master was alike in each; and also because, in many cases, it is extremely difficult to determine under which category a particular college falls.[1] The designation of these colleges as *privata* has been avoided, following the example of San Nicolo,[2] who points out the inexactness of the use of this term with reference to many of the Roman corporations.

Mistresses, in place of Masters, are found in colleges whose members were women only, and in others where a considerable number of the female sex were enrolled they appear in company with Masters. In many colleges there were Ministers, *ministri*, who acted as the assistants of the Masters; also attendants of the other sex, *ministrae*, occupying a corresponding position with regard to the Mistresses.

In general, it may be said that, while the Masters of these colleges regularly acted as a board of annually or quinquennially elected Presidents exercising a general supervision over all the activities of their respective corporations, their most characteristic duties were in connection with the celebration of the particular cult which was the focus of the life of their institution. From this consideration they may justly be regarded as Masters whose functions were primarily religious.

For a list of these Masters and their colleges, which would be too long to be duplicated here, one may refer to Appendix A, or to the third volume of Waltzing's *Corporations Professionelles.*

[1] Cf. Mommsen, *De collegiis et sodaliciis Romanorum*; Schiess, *Die römischen collegia funeratica*; Liebenam, *Römisches Vereinswesen*; Waltzing, *Les corporations professionelles chez les Romains*; cf. also Ruggiero, *Dizionario Epigrafico*, vol. 2, pp. 340 ff.; Kornemann, Pauly-Wissowa *Real-Encycl.*, vol. 4, pp. 386–88.

[2] *Aegyptisches Vereinswesen*, vol. 1, p. 2 ff.

IV. Masters who were Officials in the Civil Service of the Roman Empire

The Masters who were officers in the civil service of the Roman Empire included: Masters who were in the service of the Financial Administration; Masters who were the chiefs of the Central Secretarial Departments; the Master of the Audiences and the Master of the Offices.

1. *Masters who were in the Service of the Financial Administration*

This group comprises Masters and Vicemasters (*promagistri*) who were imperial revenue officers in the period of the Early Principate, as well as Masters who were officials of the Fiscus and the Res Privata during the period of transition in the third century and after the reorganization of Diocletian and Constantine.

From the Early Principate we have record of the following Masters and Vicemasters: the Master and Vicemaster of the five per cent Inheritance Tax (*magister*, *promagister xx hereditatium*), the Vicemaster of the Inheritances (*promagister hereditatium*), the Vicemaster of the Port Dues (*promagister portuum*), and the Vicemaster of the Grain Rent (*promagister frumenti mancipalis*).

That branch of the imperial finances known as the Privy Purse (*res privata*), which from the time of Septimius Severus denoted the personal property of the Emperor, numbered among its officials several bearing the title of Master. These were the Master of the Privy Purse (*magister privatae rei*) and the Masters of the Privy Purse in the provinces (*magister privatae rei Africae*, *Aegypti et Libyae*, and the *magister aeris sive privatae rei* in Pontus and Asia).

The Fiscus, the treasury into which flowed the revenues that accrued to the Emperor in his official capacity as head of the state, also had some Masters in its service; namely, the Master of the Imperial Accounts (*magister summarum rationum*), the Masters of the Linen Wardrobe (*magistri lineae vestis*), and the Masters of the Private Wardrobe (*magistri privatae*).

2. *Masters who were the Chiefs of the Central Secretarial Departments*

Here belong the Masters of the Scrinia, or bureaus, through which the official correspondence of the central administration was conducted. The list of these Masters is as follows:

1. The Master of the *Memoria* (*magister memoriae*).
2. The Masters of the Latin and Greek Correspondence (*magistri epistularum latinarum et graecarum*).
3. The Master of the Petitions (*magister libellorum*).
4. The Master of the Sacred Inquests (*magister sacrarum cognitionum*).
5. The Master of the Imperial Schedules (*magister dispositionum*).

In addition to these Masters of the Scrinia, we must place here the Master of the Census (*magister censuum, census*) and the Master of the Records (*magister studiorum*).

3. *The Master of the Audiences and the Master of the Offices*

The Master of the Offices (*magister officiorum*), who forms the subject of this essay, will receive detailed consideration in the following chapters. The Master of the Audiences (*magister admissionum*) was one of his subordinates and had no independent sphere of action.

Among the civil officials of the Empire the title of Master makes its appearance towards the end of the first century A.D. It was then used as the title of certain officials employed in connection with the raising of the revenue, which at that time was being removed from the hands of private contractors and placed under imperial control. Other officials engaged in this same service had the title of Vicemaster. It seems clear that these titles were taken over into the imperial offices from the private corporations of tax-collectors, *societates publicanorum*, at the same time that the government assumed the responsibility for the raising of taxes. By the end of the second century these Masters and Vicemasters had disappeared, probably owing to a reorganization of the procuratorial system.

In the third century appears another group of Masters. The title was then used of the officials in charge of the various departments (*curae, officia, scrinia*) of the imperial administration centered at the capital. These Masters were not new officers, but merely the older *ab admissionibus*, *a censibus*, *a cognitionibus*, *ab epistulis*, *a libellis*, *a memoria*, and *a studiis* under new names. This can be seen at a glance from the transitional form of their titles, such as *magister ab admissione*, *magister a censibus*, and *magister a libellis*. It was probably under Diocletian, prior to 297 A.D., that these titles took their final forms.

It is perhaps impossible to say why the title of Master was

chosen for these bureau chiefs. One might think that the Masters of the priestly colleges, in which there was usually only one such official, furnished the model. But it was probably the general adaptability of this title, as indicating the one who assumed the direction or leadership in any field, that determined its adoption here.

Meanwhile the Masters had made their reappearance in the financial administration. In the course of the third century the director of the *res privata* became *magister (sacrae) privatae*, and the assistant of the chief of the fiscus was called *magister summarum rationum*. Both these titles disappeared before the close of the reign of Constantine I, and from then until towards 350 A.D. the supervisors of the *res privata* in the provinces enjoyed the title of *magistri (rei) privatae*. In this branch of the administration the title of Master was probably used in imitation of the practice in vogue in the secretarial departments.

In the course of the fourth century there were appointed in the Eastern Empire the minor officers known as the Masters of the Linen Wardrobe, *magistri lineae vestis*, and Masters of the Private Wardrobe, *magistri privatae (vestis)*. At the same time, in both East and West, the Master of the Sacred Inquests disappeared through the merging of his bureau with that of the Master of the Petitions. Contemporary, also, is the abolition of the office and Mastership of the Records (*magister studiorum*).

The Masters of the Scrinia disappeared in the West upon the establishment of the Gothic Kingdom in Italy, and, in the East, after the reign of Justinian they were known by their Greek titles only.

The date of the creation of the Mastership of the Offices and that of its disappearance will be discussed in the following pages.[1]

V. Masters who were Officials in the Military Service of the Empire

In the Roman armies of the Principate there were several officers of low rank who were called Masters. We know of a Master of Artillery (*magister ballistarius*), a Master of the Cohort (*magister cohortis*), a Master of the Horse (*magister equitum*), a

[1] Further details relative to the Masters in the Imperial Civil Service are given in *Roman Magistri in the Civil and Military Service of the Empire*, by A. E. R. Boak, in *Harvard Studies in Classical Philology*, Vol. XXVI (1915), pp. 73 ff.

Riding Master (*magister kampi*), and a Master of the Numerus (*magister numeri*). In the Later Empire we meet with another of these subordinate Masters, the Master of the Camp (*magister castrorum*).

However, it was during the Later Empire that the title Master came to denote once more, as in the republican epoch, officers clothed with the highest military command. This use of the Mastership was revived by Constantine I, probably in imitation of the Republican Mastership of the Horse. These military Masters at first had the specific titles of Master of the Foot (*magister peditum*) and Master of the Horse (*magister equitum*). But from the middle of the fourth century they began to be designated Masters of the Horse and Foot (*magistri equitum et peditum*), Masters of Both Services (*magistri utriusque militiae*), and finally as Masters of the Soldiers (*magistri militum*). In the East, from the time of Theodosius I, no further distinction between the infantry and cavalry commands was made, but in the West, officially at least, the difference was maintained.

Originally there were but two Masters of the Soldiers for the whole Empire. However, their number increased with the tendency of the rulers to divide the Imperial authority between two or more partners. Upon the definite separation of the Empire into two parts, in 395, there were five Masters of the Soldiers in the East and three in the West. Under Justinian at least two new Masterships were created.

These military Masterships disappeared by the end of the seventh century, owing to the loss of the Western part of the Empire to the barbarians, and the civil and military reorganization in the East.[1]

From this brief survey of the use of the title Master among the Romans, it will now be possible to approach the study of the Master of the Offices with a better understanding of the title itself and also of its position relatively to that of similar titles borne by both public and private officials.

[1] For a detailed treatment of these *magistri militum*, cf. the paper *Roman Magistri*, previously cited.

CHAPTER II

THE ADMINISTRATIVE SYSTEM OF THE ROMAN EMPIRE FROM THE TIME OF CONSTANTINE I: THE OFFICES OF THE PALACE

THE rivalry between the Senate and the Princeps for the control of the administration of the Roman world, which was the outgrowth of the dualism created by Augustus, and which persisted throughout nearly three centuries, by the fourth century A.D. had resulted in a complete victory for absolutism. The Senate had seen the spheres of government once under its control pass, one by one, into the hands of the Princeps and his officers, until finally, although it still continued to exist, that body, formerly so powerful, could claim no control whatever over the affairs of state.

Not only had the position of the senate as an organ of government completely changed, but its character also had been radically altered. The senatorial order was now a privileged class, comprising practically all the holders of important public offices, while the actual assemblies of the senate were composed chiefly of the highest officers of state. Thus the senate was made up of imperial officers and ex-officers. This development naturally removed all distinction between equestrian and senatorial offices; while the contrast between the equestrian and the senatorial *cursus honorum* gave place to one between the purely military and the purely civil careers.

The republican assemblies had long since ceased to be summoned, and such of the republican offices as still continued to be filled had lost all political power and had become merely honorary posts in the gift of the ruler.

The government of the Later Roman Empire was thus an undisguised absolutism. This conception of the position of the Emperor found formal expression at first in the deification of

Diocletian and his co-rulers, and later in the claim of his successors to govern by the will of God. The use of the diadem, and the attribution of the adjectives *sacer* and *divinus* not only to the imperial personage but to all that belonged to him, were further outward manifestations of absolute power.

The Emperor was the sole possessor of legislative and executive authority. Consequently, all the public officials were his servants, — appointed by him, owing allegiance to him alone, deriving from him their authority, existing to enforce his ordinances and responsible to him for the way in which they fulfilled their duties. The number and power of this official class are among the outstanding features of the governmental organization of the Later Roman Empire. The vast system of state officials, radiating from the administrative centres and permeating all the provinces, was a veritable millstone hung about the necks of the unhappy provincials, upon whom lay the double burden of supporting the army and the civil list.

The enormous increase in the number of the officials in the Later, over that in the Early, Empire was partly due to the desire of the emperors to prevent the rise of usurpers, and secure the peaceful succession to the imperial throne in a definitely settled fashion. Accordingly, no office was to be left so powerful that it could be made the basis of an attempt at an insurrection. The provinces, following a policy already initiated under the Principate, were divided and subdivided into smaller units until they numbered about one hundred and twenty, in place of the forty-five of Hadrian's time. No longer was civil and military authority held by the same officer, and accordingly a large number of purely military posts was created.

Besides the greater number of officials required for the new administrative districts and the new military commands, a further increase in the ranks of the civil service was due to the extension of the central administrative bureaus developed from those of the older régime, and to the creation of a series of household officers in charge of the imperial palace. The appointment of these latter officers was the result of the organization of the imperial court on a scale commensurate with the dignity of the autocratic sovereign, who thereby exalted himself above his subjects and by almost impenetrable barriers checked access to his person. The pomp and splendor of the court, its elaborate ceremonies and the employment of eunuchs in the personal service of the ruler, betray oriental, probably Persian, influences.

The administrative organization of the Roman Empire was essentially bureaucratic in character: that is to say, the greater part of the business of state was conducted through a series of departments controlled by offices or bureaus centred at the court and having representatives in the various administrative districts of the Empire. It was in these departments that the great army of government officers and their subordinates were employed. This bureaucratic organization, although the result of a development continuous throughout the first three centuries, received its definite form and dated its power from the reigns of Diocletian and Constantine, the two Emperors who cast the Roman system of government into the form which it kept from the beginning of the fourth to the end of the sixth century.

To secure efficiency in the working of this complicated government machine the minor officials in the several departments were regularly placed under the orders (*sub dispositione*) of those having wider spheres of action. Thus a system of graded subordination was established, whereby the control was ultimately concentrated in the hands of a group of the highest civil and military officials, about ten in number, who were directly in touch with the Emperor and responsible to him alone. These were the heads of the army and of the administrative, judicial, and financial organs of the state; and alongside of them, because of their position at the head of similarly organized departments, may be placed the officers in control of the management of the imperial estates and of the imperial household.

True to the principle of mistrust towards its servants, however, the imperial government did not always clearly define the spheres of competence of the several official groups, believing that from this cause rivalries and jealousies would arise, through the officials spying upon and hampering one another, to the advantage of the throne. Further, direct communication between the subordinates of the great ministers and the Emperor was often provided for, and, finally, by a highly developed system of state espionage the ruler kept watch upon the actions of his officers. However, in spite of the precautions taken to insure an honest and efficient administration, the actual result of the development of this elaborate bureaucratic system was the erection of an almost impassable obstacle between the Emperor and his subjects. Neither did their complaints reach his ears, nor were his ordinances for their relief effective, because the officials coöperated with one another to conceal their misdemeanors and to enrich themselves at the expense of the provincials.

Within official circles, in addition to the administrative subordination, there was established a strict hierarchy of rank, based upon the classification, into a number of grades, of all the official posts in the imperial service. This gradation was due, on the one hand, to the development of an oriental court life with its elaborate ceremonial demanding a fixed order of precedence among those present at imperial audiences, and, on the other, to the growth in the number and importance of the public officials, which of itself necessitated a classification of the various official posts from the point of view of rank. All officials occupying posts of sufficient importance became members of the senatorial order and were styled *clarissimi*. Among these a narrower circle of higher officials formed the class of the *spectabiles*, and a still more exclusive order, comprising only the heads of the various departments of government, was that of the *illustres*. Subsequently, under Justinian, a still higher grade, that of *gloriosus*, was created.

Among the different offices belonging to the same class a definite order of precedence was established. The official positions which conferred such titles of rank upon their holders were called *dignitates*. The great demand for admission to these rank classes, which entitled their members to various privileges, caused the conferment of honorary *dignitates;* the titles of official posts with their appropriate rank but without the duties of office. These honorary dignities were conferred as rewards for past services, as indications of favor, or even in return for a monetary consideration.

Besides these classes, defined in terms of official rank, there existed two orders or titles of rank, which were of a somewhat different character from the preceding as they were not altogether dependent upon any fixed office. These were the Patriciate and the Comitiva. The former, created by Constantine I in imitation of the older Patrician order, although not attached to any definite official post, was granted solely to the highest dignitaries; it was conferred for life, and gave precedence over all officials except the functioning consuls. The latter order, which was given a new meaning by Constantine, became a title of honor attached to some public offices, or conferred as a reward for service or for favor. In certain cases, with a suitable adjunct, it designated a definite office, such as 'Count of the Sacred Largesses,' or Minister of the Treasury, *comes sacrarum largitionum*. There were three grades of Counts (*comites*) — Counts of the First, Second, and Third orders — distinguished according to the importance of their official position.

The sharp distinction, already referred to, made between the civil and the military careers, gave rise to a division of the offices of state into the two classes of *militares* and *civiles*. The functions of these two classes were strictly separated. Thus in the provinces where troops were stationed the civil and the military authority were no longer united in the hands of the provincial governor (*praeses*, *corrector*, *iudex*); he was now restricted to the oversight of the civil administration, while the military command was exercised by a *dux* or *comes rei militaris*. On the one hand, the civil governors were subordinated to the Vicars (*vicarii*) of the thirteen dioceses into which the provinces were grouped, and to the Pretorian Prefects, who presided over the highest appellate jurisdiction, with the exception of that of the court of the Emperor himself, and who likewise controlled the raising and distribution of the taxes paid in natural products. On the other hand, the military governors were under the Masters of the Soldiers (*magistri militum*), the newly-created commanders-in-chief, who were themselves subject to the Emperor alone.

The centralization of the administration, which has been briefly outlined above, was intimately bound up with the working of the *consistorium*, the Imperial Consistory or Council of State. This was mainly composed of the Ministers at the head of the various departments of the administration. These were the Minister of Finance, known as the Count of the Sacred Largesses (*comes sacrarum largitionum*), who controlled the revenues of state apart from those which passed into the hands of the Prefects: the Minister of Crown Lands, called the Count of the Privy Purse (*comes rerum privatarum*), who administered the imperial property and who was now a public official, since the importance of the imperial domains and the almost complete identification of the ruler with the state had made the management of his revenues a matter of public business: the Quæstor, who was the Emperor's adviser in legal and judicial matters: and the Master of the Offices (*magister officiorum*), the subject of this study.

In attendance upon the Consistory were also without doubt the Prefect whose seat of government was at the Capital, and the Grand Chamberlain (*praepositus sacri cubiculi*). Since they were permanently attached to the court, the administrative center of the Empire, these offices were called *dignitates palatinae*, to distinguish them from those official posts which kept their holders in the provinces. Other *dignitates palatinae* were the Counts of the Body Guard (*comes domesticorum equitum* and *comes domesticorum peditum*), the Steward of the Household (*castrensis sacri palatii*), and the Chief Eunuch of the Bed-chamber (*primicerius sacri cubiculi*), who was a subordinate of the Grand Chamberlain. To these must be added the four imperial Secretaries — the First Secretary (*magister memoriae*), the Secretary for Correspondence (*magister epistularum, magister epistularum graecarum*), the Secretary for Petitions (*magister libellorum*), all of whom were engaged in receiving or transmitting the correspondence of the central government; and, from the middle of the fourth century, the Secretary of the Imperial Schedules (*magister*, later *comes, dispositionum*).

In addition to the holders of these important posts, there was attached to the court a great host of subordinates employed in the civil administration of the Empire or in the management of the palace. These functionaries in general were known as *officiales*. Among them must be reckoned the Corps, or *schola*, of the *agentes in rebus*, who served in various capacities as imperial messengers or secret service men; also the *tribuni* and *notarii*, clerks employed in the Consistory, and the *advocati*, lawyers assigned to the various tribunals.

Moreover, each one of the palace dignitaries mentioned above was aided in the performance of his duties by a staff of clerks, who constituted his *officium*. Under the Principate, such clerks had been freedmen or slaves. Now, however, they were freemen, for as in the new régime the person of the Emperor was exalted above the persons of his subjects, so those engaged in his service were no longer upon the same level as the servants of other men, but the very fact of their presence in the imperial offices was a guarantee of their freedom.

Since Diocletian had virtually transformed his palace into a moving camp, these clerks and all others in the palace service had been given a military organization, with a system of promotion, insignia, and special privileges copied from those of the army. Their service itself was called a *militia*. Serving for long periods in the one office they made possible regularity and continuity in the routine administration of their department in spite of the frequent change of their chief. The lowest grades of these palace servants included such as performed menial service at the court, from the ushers (*admissionales*) to the torchbearers (*lampadarii*), grooms, and others whose duties were of the same general character.

Nor did the palace lack its regular soldiery. These were the Palace Guards, the seven *scholae scutariorum et gentilium*, 3500 strong, who had been established by Constantine to take the place of the disbanded Pretorian Guard. These Scholarians belonged to the regular army, the *militia armata*, but, as a rule, did not serve away from the court.

Such were the officials and servants who were attached to the imperial court, which served as the administrative centre of the Empire. And it was at this court, among the *dignitates palatinae*, that the Master of the Offices played his rôle.[1]

[1] Surveys of the official positions in the Empire are to be found in the *Notitia Dignitatum*, the *Variae* of Cassiodorus, and the *De Magistratibus* of Lydus.

For a detailed treatment of the governmental organization of the Later Empire, cf. Grenier, *L'empire byzantin*, vol. 2; Hodgkin, *Italy and her Invaders*, vol. 1, pt. 2, chap. 12; Karlowa, *Römische Rechtsgeschichte*, vol. 1, pp. 828 ff.; Reid, *Cambridge Medieval History*, vol. 1, chap. 2; Schiller, *Geschichte der römischen Kaiserzeit*, vol. 2, p. 101 ff.; Seeck, *Geschichte des Untergangs der antiken Welt*, vol. 2, pp. 52–109, *Hof und Provinzen*.

CHAPTER III

THE HISTORY OF THE MASTERSHIP OF THE OFFICES

THE history of the Mastership of the Offices may be divided conveniently into three periods: the establishment of the office under Diocletian and Constantine; the period from the death of Constantine, in 337 A.D., to the close of the sixth century; and the Byzantine period, to the Latin conquest in 1204 A.D.

I. THE ESTABLISHMENT OF THE OFFICE

The date of the establishment of the office of *magister officiorum* is unknown, and the record thereof, as well as the names of its first holders, had passed into oblivion when Johannes Lydus wrote his *De Magistratibus Populi Romani*, about the middle of the sixth century.[1] The earliest Master of the Offices then known was Martinianus, who held that post under Licinius at the close of the latter's reign (307–324 A.D).[2] This Martinianus was evidently the one called by Zosimus[3] the chief of the palace *officia*, with the explanation that the Romans styled this personage the Master of the Offices. During his final struggle with Constantine, Licinius created Martinianus Caesar, but the latter, upon the defeat of Licinius in 324 A.D.,[4] was captured and executed.[5]

However, constitutions of the Theodosian Code record that at this time there were Masters of the Offices under Constantine in the West, where Heraclianus was *tribunus et magister officiorum*

[1] Περὶ ἀρχῶν τῆς Ῥωμαίων πολιτείας, written in 551 A.D. When the title *magister officiorum* is used in the *Historia Augusta* it refers to the *magistri scriniorum* of the third century.

[2] Lydus, *De Mag.*, 2, 25.

[3] Zosimus, 2, 25: ἡγεμόνα τῶν ἐν τῇ αὐλῇ τάξεων ὄντα μάγιστρον τοῦτον ὀφφικίων καλοῦσι Ῥωμαῖοι.

[4] For the date of the battle of Chrysopolis, September 18, 324, see Jouguet, *Séances de l'Académie des Inscriptions, Bulletin*, 1906, pp. 231–236.

[5] Zosimus, 2, 28.

in 321,[1] and Proculianus likewise *tribunus et magister officiorum* in 323.[2] Upon his victory over Licinius, Constantine appointed Palladius as his Master of the Offices, and the list of his successors in this office down to the time of Lydus was found by the latter in the work of Petrus upon this *magisterium*.[3]

The earliest epigraphic record of a Master of the Offices is much later; it is found in an inscription in honour of Flavius Eugenius, who had been *magister officiorum* under Constans in 346 A.D.[4]

Now from these notices we see that there were Masters of the Offices at the court of each of the two Augusti, Licinius and Constantine, before the latter reunited the Roman world under one ruler, and, consequently, it does not seem likely that Constantine was the creator of this office. And further, when we consider that it was Diocletian who effected the organization of the palace service on a military basis, as a *militia*, and that the title *tribunus*, which the early Masters of the Offices bore, is of a purely military character at this period, the evidence seems to point to his having established the office in question.[5]

The precise character of this office at the time of its creation is just as uncertain as the date of its establishment. Naturally, therefore, various views have been advanced on this point.

Mommsen[6] thought that possibly Diocletian or Constantine had appointed an official to preside over the *consistorium* and had given him a *vicarius* in the person of the *vicarius a consiliis sacris*, and that these two offices subsequently developed into those of the *Quaestor Sacri Palatii* and the Master of the Offices,

[1] *Codex Theodosianus*, XVI, 10, 1.

[2] *Codex Theodosianus*, XI, 9, 1.

[3] Lydus, *De Mag.*, 2, 25: Παλλάδιον μάγιστρον τῆς αὐλῆς ἐχειροτόνησεν. τοῖς δὲ ἱμειρομένοις τοὺς ἐφεξῆς μὴ ἀγνοῆσαι μαγίστρους ἄχρις ἡμῶν ἀρέσκει πρὸς διδασκαλίαν Πέτρος . . ., δι' ὧν αὐτὸς ἐπὶ τοῦ λεγομένου μαγιστηρίου ἀνεγράψατο. The reference is probably to a part of the Περὶ πολιτικῆς καταστάσεως of Petrus the Patrician, a work of which only fragments have survived; cf. Krumbacher, *Geschichte der byzantinischen Literatur*, p. 236.

[4] Dessau, *Inscriptiones Latinae Selectae*, 1244: FL(avio) EUGENIO V(iro) C(larissimo), EX PRAEFECTO PRAETORIO, CONSULI ORDINARIO DESIGNATO, MAGISTRO OFFICIORUM OMNIUM, COMITI DOMESTICO ORDINIS PRIMI OMNIBUSQUE PALATINIS DIGNITATIBUS FUNCTO, OB EGREGIA EIUS IN REM PUBLICAM MERITA; etc. For the date of his mastership, cf. Athanasius, *Apologia ad Constantinum*, c. 3; cf. also *C. I. L.* VI, 1721.

[5] Seeck, *Geschichte des Untergangs der antiken Welt*, vol. 2, pp. 89–90.

[6] *De C. Caelii Saturnini titulo, Memorie dell' Instituto di corrispondenza archeologica*, 1865, p. 298 ff. The suggestion here made is followed by Cosenza, *Official Positions after Constantine*, p. 55.

respectively. The objection to this view is that it does not afford an adequate explanation of the early character of the Master's office, as will appear later; and, further, that the nature of the duties of the *vicarius a consiliis sacris* is too hypothetical for any connection to be evident between them and the duties subsequently performed by the Master of the Offices. Moreover, the title of the latter does not suggest a development from that of the *vicarius*.

Schiller[1] has advanced the view that the Mastership of the Offices developed out of a superintendency of the four palace *scrinia*, presided over by the *magistri memoriae*, *magistri libellorum*, *magistri epistularum* and *magistri dispositionum*. With this suggestion Karlowa[2] agrees, arguing that the close connection between the spheres of duty of the several *scrinia* would necessitate a common chief to supervise their activities. The title *magister officiorum* (*palatinorum*) naturally, then, would be given to the chief of these *officia palatina*. This explanation of the origin of the office obviously contains a certain element of truth; for the supervision of the work of these secretarial departments was among the earliest of the duties of the Master of the Offices. However, it is evident that no theory on this subject will be adequate which does not account for the whole of the early title *tribunus et magister officiorum*.

Accordingly Schiller's alternative explanation[3] is preferable, in which he derives the Mastership of the Offices from the senior tribunate of the *cohortes praetorianae*. This is substantially the opinion of Seeck,[4] who believes that the Master of the Offices had the title of *tribunus* because he was placed by Diocletian over the several corps of the court attendants who were given a military organization (*militia*) and was himself an officer of the soldiers attached to the palace. As these various divisions of the palace servants were styled *officia*, the origin and meaning of the title *magister officiorum* are apparent.

Accepting this explanation as the one that best accords with what little is known of the early development of the office, we may picture to ourselves the establishment of the Mastership of

[1] *Geschichte der römischen Kaiserzeit*, vol. 2, p. 101.

[2] *Römische Rechtsgeschichte*, vol. 1, p. 831.

[3] *Op. cit.*, vol. 2, p. 101.

[4] *Geschichte des Untergangs der antiken Welt*, vol. 2, pp. 89–90.

the Offices as having taken place in the following way. Diocletian, having effected his reorganization of the *officiales* of the palace on a military basis, found it advisable to have a single officer in control of and responsible for their discipline, their *matriculae* or rolls, admission to and dismissal from service, order of seniority, regular promotion, uniform, and the like. Accordingly, he nominated to this post the senior tribune of the Pretorian Guard and gave him the additional title of *magister officiorum* to express his powers of supervision over the subordinates in the several *officia*. It is not clear why the term *magister* was employed in the new title, but it has already been noted that the heads of the *scrinia* were called Masters and it was, in fact, under Diocletian that their titles became fixed in the forms *magister memoriae*, *magister libellorum*, etc., which correspond exactly with that of *magister officiorum*. At this time, too, there were numerous other *magistri* at the court, for the title was one which, with an appropriate qualification, could be employed readily for officials with widely differing functions.[1] When, after the battle of Saxa Rubra in 312 A.D., Constantine disbanded the remnant of the Pretorians,[2] and formed in their place the new palace guards,[3] known as the Scholarians, each of the *scholae* was commanded by a *tribunus*,[4] and the senior officer of this rank probably was the Master of the Offices.

However, one cannot claim for the Master of the Offices authority over all the *officiales* of the palace, for it is fairly certain that those immediately under the orders of the *Praepositus Sacri Cubiculi* or Grand Chamberlain, — namely the *cubicularii* and *silentiarii*, as well as those at the disposal of his subordinate the *Castrensis*, the cooks, bakers, and pages, and those engaged in works of construction and repair at the court, — did not come under the Master's control in any way until a later date.[5] The same holds true of the *officiales* in the departments of the Sacred Largesses and the Private Accounts, who were at all times subject only to the Counts at the head of these branches of the

[1] *Harvard Studies in Classical Philology*, vol. XXVI, 1915, pp. 112–114.

[2] Zosimus, 2, 17.

[3] Seeck, *op. cit.*, vol. 2, p. 42.

[4] Ammianus Marcellinus, 20, 2, 5.

[5] That part of the *Notitia Dignitatum* which dealt with these offices unfortunately has not been preserved. For a reconstruction see Böcking, *Notitia Dignitatum*, vol. 2, pp. 293–301. On the *castrensiani* cf. Seeck, Pauly-Wissowa *Real-Encyclopädie der klass. Altertumswissenschaft*, vol. 3, p. 1774 ff.

financial administration.[1] But we may attribute to the Master authority over those *officia* which we know from the *Notitia Dignitatum* to have been *sub dispositione eius* at the beginning of the fifth century, except in so far as they can be shown to have been placed in his charge at a date subsequent to the establishment of this office.

Thus, at this early period, in the opening years of the reign of Constantine I, the Master of the Offices was in command of the seven *scholae* of the palace guards, supervised the work of the chiefs of the secretarial bureaus (*scrinia*) and the discipline of those employed there, was in charge of the court ushers or *officium admissionum*, and likewise had under his orders various corps of palace servants, such as the *mensores*, 'quarterers,' and *lampadarii*, 'torchbearers.' But attention must be called to the fact that many of the palace *officia* were not subject to the orders of only one of the great officers of the court. It was quite possible for them in the execution of one part of their duties to be directed by one, in performing another part to be supervised by a second, of these functionaries. Thus from constitutions of 321[2] and 323[3] which refer to the Master's receiving correspondence relating to the damage of a public building and a report which gave rise to a legal decision, we may safely assume that at this time he was in charge of the general correspondence conducted by the *scrinia*. Yet it is probable that the Quaestor also in certain cases could command the services of the employees of the *scrinia*, for he subsequently had this right.[4] However, the relations between the Master of the Offices and other officials, whose spheres of action touched his own, will be considered in detail in a following chapter. The Master of the Offices himself, whose position, as we have seen, was in the beginning a comparatively humble one, did not from the first have charge of an independent department of the administration, under the supervision of the Emperor alone. Certainly, so far as the command

[1] *Codex Theodosianus*, VI. 30, 4, 379 = *Codex Justinianus*, XII. 23, 4; *id.* 23, 12, (Theodosius and Valentinian).

[2] *Codex Theodosianus*, XVI, 10, 1, . . . *de tactu amphitheatri* . . ., *de qua ad Heraclianum tribunum et mag(istrum) officiorum scribseras.*

[3] *Codex Theodosianus*, XI, 9, 1: *litterae missae ad Proculianum tribunum et mag(istrum) officiorum continent quorundam provincialium mancipia abducta pro pignore sub officio retineri*, . . ., *atque haec mancipia neque dominos solutis debitis recepisse neque alios comparasse, veritos ne haec rescinderetur distractio.*

[4] *Notitia Dignitatum or.* XII, *occ.* X.

of the palace guards is concerned, he was subordinate to the Pretorian Prefect, and it is fairly safe to assume that in general the Master was under the orders of the latter.[1]

Although, as we are warranted in believing, the foundations of this office were laid by Diocletian, it remained for Constantine to make it a great and influential position. Such development is to be explained in connection with radical changes made by Constantine in the organization of the administration. One of the results of these innovations, as Seeck[2] has pointed out, was the appearance of two groups of officials, the one military and the other civil, caused by the assignment of definite and permanent spheres of action to certain *comites*, who bore the general title of *comes*, with a specific title derived from the duties which they performed. The new military offices were those of *comes et magister equitum*, *comes et magister peditum*, *comes domesticorum equitum*, and *comes domesticorum peditum.* The civil *comites* were the *comes et quaestor sacri palatii*, the *comes et magister officiorum*, the *comes sacrarum largitionum*, and the *comes rerum privatarum.*

The reason for this creation of new offices, and change in the rank and competence of offices already existing, was the change made in the Pretorian Prefecture. Up to this time the Prefects had functioned for the Empire as a whole, and had been the chief military as well as the highest administrative and judicial officers. But when Constantine appointed his sons Caesars and placed them in authority over parts of the Empire while they were yet children, he had to entrust the actual work of administration to Prefects, who accompanied each of the young Caesars.[3] Thus the way was paved for the creation of the four Prefectures, of Gaul, Italy, Illyricum, and the Orient, with definite boundaries; an arrangement which was completed under Constantine's successors. This resulted in the separation of the office of Pretorian Prefect from the person of the ruler, and its association with specific administrative districts. At the same time the Prefects were deprived of military authority, lest those who administered the districts of the young princes should be tempted to use their powers to secure the

[1] Cf. Lydus, *De Mag.*, 2, 10: *ἀνάγκη γέγονε τόν ὕπαρχον μηκέτι μὲν τῆς αὐλῆς . . . ἄρχειν.*

[2] Pauly-Wissowa, *Real-Encyclopädie*, vol. 4, p. 632, s. v. *comites.*

[3] Seeck, *op. cit.*, vol. 2, pp. 64 ff., 83.

throne for themselves. The command over the military forces of the Empire was divided among the new group of military *comites*, who were directly under the orders of the Emperor.[1]

Not only was the Prefecture thus weakened by division and the loss of the right of military command; it was also at this time shorn of considerable civil authority. The fundamental reason for this, as in the case of the deprivation of military power, was doubtless the desire to lessen the Prefect's influence. A contributory cause may have been that the assignment of Prefects to those portions of the Empire which were allotted to the Caesars permanently separated the former from the centre of the administration, the court of the Augustus,[2] and therefore the supervision of the *officia palatina* was no longer regarded as an essential part of a Prefect's duties. Consequently, a successor to his functions in this sphere had to be found. Under such circumstances, it was only natural that the Master of the Offices should become independent of the Prefect's supervision and receive control of the branches of the administration which were conducted directly through those *officia palatina* that were already in part under his charge.

Accordingly, Lydus quite correctly connects the great increase in the power of the Master of the Offices with the weakening of the Prefecture, in saying that the control of the court passed into the hands of the Master at the same time that the *magistri militum* succeeded to the military command of the Prefects.[3] It is true that Lydus mentions only one Prefecture, that of the Orient, and misunderstands the reason for the Prefect's presence there, which was that the Orient formed one of the administrative divisions of the Empire which Constantine entrusted to his young Caesars, in this case to Constantius.[4] However, he justly emphasizes the rise of the *magistri militum* and the Master of the Offices at the expense of the Prefect; and also it seems that he believed that, as has been suggested, the separation of the Prefect from the person

[1] Zosimus, 2, 33; Lydus, *De Mag.*, 2, 10; 3, 40; Seeck, *op. cit.*, 83 ff.

[2] Evidence for this is that, from 318 A.D., the Pretorian Prefects begin to appear as frequent recipients of imperial constitutions. Seeck, *Rheinisches Museum*, vol. 49, p. 213.

[3] *De Mag.*, 2, 10 . . . ἀνάγκη γέγονε τὸν ὕπαρχον μηκέτι μὲν τῆς αὐλῆς καὶ τῶν ἐν ὅπλοις ἄρχειν δυνάμεων, τῆς μὲν τῷ λεγομένῳ μαγίστρῳ παραδοθείσης, τῶν δὲ τοῖς ἄρτι κατασταθεῖσι στρατηγοῖς ἐκτεθεισῶν, τὴν δὲ ἀνατολὴν πρὸς τῇ κάτω Ἀσίᾳ, καὶ ὅσα ταύτης, διοικοῦντα τὸ λοιπὸν τῆς ἀνατολῆς χρημτίζειν ὕπαρχον; cf. 3, 40.

[4] Seeck, *op. cit.*, vol. 2, p. 69; Pauly-Wissowa, vol. 4, p. 1045 f.

of the Augustus had to do with his loss of control over the palace administration.

The greater importance of the Master's office caused a corresponding elevation in the rank of its holder, who was now no longer *tribunus* but *comes et magister officiorum.* That is to say, the position of Master of the Offices became one of the regular and definite spheres of competence assigned to a *comes*, as was the case with the *magisterium militum.* This change in title also marks the transformation of the office from one of a semi-military character, expressed in the title *tribunus*, to an essentially civil post.[1]

The date of the enlargement of the Master's functions, and his elevation to the rank of *comes*, is not recorded but may be fixed with considerable certainty. The earliest record of a Master who was a *comes* dates from 346 A.D.[2] and the combination *comes et magister officiorum* first appears in a constitution of 357 A.D.[3] However, as we have pointed out, there are good reasons for believing that these changes were accomplished by 325 A.D. The Master of the Offices in 362 appears as one of the *comites* who were permanent members of the *consistorium*, together with the Quaestor, the Count of the Sacred Largesses and the Count of the Privy Purse, with whom he was equal in rank, although taking precedence over the two Counts.[4] Since *comites* with the functions, although not with the ultimate titles, of these other officials can be traced back to 325, it is only reasonable to suppose that the Master of the Offices ranked with them at that date. As the latter, however, was still a *tribunus* in 323,[5] it must have been between this date and 325 that he was made a *comes*, for which change a convenient opportunity would have been afforded by the reorganization of the

[1] Seeck, Pauly-Wissowa, vol. 4, p. 632; *Geschichte des Untergangs der antiken Welt*, vol. 2, pp. 77, 90. There is a certain parallel between the change of title in the case of the Master of the Offices and of the *comes sacri stabuli.* The latter was first *tribunus s. s.*, ranking as a *tribunus* of a *schola palatina* (Amm. 14, 10, 8; 20, 2, 5), later he received the *comitiva ordinis primi* (*Codex Theodosianus*, VI, 13, 1, 413) and was indifferently *comes* or *tribunus s. s.* (Dessau, Inscr. Sel. 1277, 1278), until finally the title of *tribunus* was discarded (*Codex Just.* XII, 11, 1), cf. Pauly-Wissowa, vol. 4, p. 632. The parallel is not perfect, for the change in the Master's case was much more rapid and indicative of an important accession of power.

[2] Dessau, *Inscriptiones Selectae*, 1244: *magistro officiorum, comiti domestico ordinis primi.*

[3] *Codex Theodosianus*, VIII, 5, 8: *et ad Musonium clarissimum virum comitem et magistrum officiorum referri.*

[4] *Codex Theodosianus*, XI, 39, 5; VI, 9, 1; VI, 30, 1; 4; IX, 14, 3, etc.

[5] *Codex Theodosianus*, XI, 9, 1.

Empire following the defeat of Licinius on September 18, 324 A.D.[1] If this hypothesis is accepted, the first *comes* to fill the office of *magister officiorum* would be the Palladius whom Constantine made his Master of the Offices after reuniting the Empire.[2] This Palladius had acted as Roman ambassador on a diplomatic mission to the Persian court in the time of Galerius Maximian, and was therefore a person of considerable importance, worthy to be a member of the consistory and hold the Mastership of the Offices with its newly extended sphere of competence.

For the Master of the Offices now ceased to be dependent in any way upon the Pretorian Prefect, and became one of the eight great ministers whose administration was under imperial supervision only. Accordingly, the Master becomes the commander-in-chief of the *scholae palatinae*, no longer subject to the Prefect's orders. In like manner, in his control of the secretarial bureaus he is free from the latter's authority. It was probably at this time, too, that the corps of imperial despatch bearers, the *schola agentum in rebus*, came under the immediate direction of the Master of the Offices.[3] Seeck[4] believes that it was under Constantine that the Master of the Offices also assumed control of the government arsenals (*fabricae*), which had previously been centred at the court in the hands of a subordinate of the Prefect, the *praepositus fabricarum* (?). However, the first clear proof that the Master directed the administration of the arsenals comes from the year 390 A.D.,[5] although it must be admitted that in the interval we have no indication that the Prefect was active in this sphere. On the other hand nothing marks the transfer of this power to the Master.

Thus, at the close of the reign of Constantine the Great, the office of the *magister officiorum* was constituted essentially as it was at the time of the compilation of the *Notitia Dignitatum*, shortly before 425 A.D.[6] Perhaps the sole important extension of the powers of the Master in the meantime was the supervision of the use of the *cursus publicus* or State Post, although his authority in various respects required, and underwent, further definition in relation to that of other officers of state.

[1] Cf. p. 24, n. 4. [2] Lydus, *De Mag.*, 2, 35.
[3] Lydus, *De Mag.*, 2, 25; cf. *Codex Theodosianus*, I, 9, 1.
[4] Pauly-Wissowa, vol. 6, p. 1928, s. v. *fabricae*; cf. Lydus, *l. c.*
[5] *Codex Theodosianus*, X, 22, 3. [6] See p. 2.

It only remains to say a few words with regard to the number of *magistri officiorum* in the Empire up to the end of the reign of Constantine I. We have seen already that in 324 A.D., when two Augusti, Constantine and Licinius, ruled the Empire, each had his Master of the Offices.[1] We may, therefore, consider it most probable that this was the arrangement from the establishment of the office, and that the number of the Masters of the Offices corresponded to that of the Augusti. So when Constantine became sole ruler in 324 there was but one Master, who was at his court.[2] Nor when Constantine appointed his sons as Caesars is there any evidence that they had Masters of the Offices in their immediate service.

II. The Mastership from 337 to 600 A.D.

From the time of Constantine until the end of the reign of Justinian the Master of the Offices continued to be one of the important administrative officials of the Empire, and the character of his office remained essentially the same, although his sphere of activity was considerably enlarged.

As we have seen, before the concentration of the imperial power in the hands of Constantine the Great the number of Masters of the Offices in the Empire probably was equal to the number of Augusti, and from this time until the death of Constantine there was, accordingly, only one Master. However, upon his decease, in 337 A.D., the imperial authority was again divided, this time among three Augusti. Each of these had his own administrative functionaries, among them his Master of the Offices, if we may draw this inference from the previous custom and the fact that Magnentius, who overthrew Constans and took the title of Augustus in 350 A.D., appointed his own Master of the Offices. His choice was Marcellinus, who had been Count of the Sacred Largesses under Constans and had actively supported the usurper.[3] But in 353 A.D. there was again but a single ruler of the Roman world, Constantius, and the officials of his former partners and rivals in power had disappeared. However, in 351 Constantius himself had raised his nephew Gallus to the dignity of a Caesar and appointed him to govern the Orient, with

[1] *Codex Theodosianus*, XVI, 10, 1; XI, 9, 1; Lydus, *De Mag.*, 2, 25; Zosimus, 2, 25.
[2] Lydus, *De Mag.*, 2, 25.
[3] Zosimus, 2, 42; 43 fin.; 46, 3.

residence at Antioch.[1] There Gallus had his own court and palace officers, among whom was a Master of the Offices.[2] In 354 Gallus fell a victim to the suspicions of Constantius and his establishment was consequently dissolved.[3] Not much later, in 355, his brother Julian was made Caesar and sent to Gaul,[4] where he too had his own Master of the Offices. Pentadius, who held that post when Julian assumed the title of Augustus in 360, was despatched by him to announce this usurpation to Constantius,[5] and a little later the latter nominated a certain Felix as Julian's Master of the Offices, only to find that Julian had already promoted to this office Anatolius, who had been his *magister libellorum*.[6]

From 361 to 364 there was a brief period with only one Augustus for the whole Empire, and no Caesar to share in the administration. But from 364 to 395 there were regularly two Augusti, one governing the East and the other the West. In 364 the two were Valentinian and Valens, and each had a Master of the Offices under his orders, Ursatius under Valentinian in the West and Euphrasius with Valens in the East.[7] The same conditions prevailed under their successors until, with the practical division of the Roman Empire in 395, the duplication of the whole administrative system, as it appears in the *Notitia Dignitatum*, became permanent, and henceforth the presence of a Master of the Offices in each half was a necessity.

Turning now to consider the functions which the Master of the Offices exercised during the period in question, we find that the first extension of his powers occurred during the rule of Constantius and Constans (340–50 A.D.). Then it was that the Overseers of the State Post (*curiosi cursus publici*) were appointed from the corps of the *agentes in rebus*, instead of from the *memoriales* and other *palatini* as previously.[8] Thus the control of the use of the *cursus publicus* was transferred from the Prefects to the Master of the Offices. This change was accomplished before

[1] Zosimus, 2, 45.

[2] Ammianus, 22, 3, 3: *et Palladium primum ex magistro officiorum in Britannos exterminarunt suspicione tenus insimulatum quaedam in Gallum composuisse apud Constantium, dum sub eodem Caesare officiorum esset magister.*

[3] Zosimus, 2, 55.

[4] Ammianus, 15, 8, 1; 13; Zosimus, 3, 2.

[5] Ammianus, 20, 8, 19.

[6] Ammianus, 20, 9, 5; 8.

[7] Ammianus, 26, 4, 4; 5, 7; 26, 7, 4; 10, 8.

[8] *Codex Theodosianus,* VI. 35, 2 (319); Gothofredus, *Paratit.* to *Codex Theodosianus,* VI, 29.

350, as we learn from an inscription from Thermae Selinuntiae, which dates between 340 and 350 and records a *ducenarius agens in reb(us) et p(rae)p(ositus) cursus publici.*[1] However, the respective powers of the Prefects and the Master in regard to the Post, especially relative to the right of issuing passes (*evectiones*), were not clearly defined until the end of the century.[2]

It was likewise under Constans that the inscription to Flavius Eugenius[3] was set up, which attributes to him the title of *magister officiorum omnium. Omnium* seems here to be an exaggeration, for, as has been pointed out, at this time the Master of the Offices did not have under his authority those classes of palace attendants which were under the orders of the Praepositus Sacri Cubiculi or the Castrensis. As we shall see, the Master acquired jurisdiction over them in the next century.

It was likewise somewhere about the middle of the fourth century that the Master of the Offices became practically a Minister for Foreign Affairs; that is to say, his office was the regular medium of communication between the Roman Emperor and foreign potentates. The origin of this development of the Master's functions was his direction of the court audiences, through his subordinates the *admissionales.* All admissions to the imperial presence, even in the case of Roman senators, were in this way controlled by him.[4] So it was naturally the Master of the Offices who received the ambassadors from other peoples, and it was through him that they were able to communicate with the Emperor or obtain an audience. In 365 the ambassadors of the Alemanni were greatly offended by their treatment at the hands of the Master, and, magnifying the insult, withdrew to stir up war.[5] Proofs of the Master's activities in this sphere are more

[1] *C.I.L.* X, 7200; cf. *Codex Theodosianus*, VI, 29, 1 (355); 2 (357).

[2] Lydus, *De Mag.*, 2, 10; Seeck, Pauly-Wissowa, vol. 4, p. 1859.

[3] Dessau, *Inscr. Sel.* 1244: FL(avio) EUGENIO V(iro) C(larissimo), EX PRAEFECTO PRAETORIO, CONSULI ORDINARIO DESIGNATO, MAGISTRO OFFICIORUM OMNIUM, COMITI DOMESTICO ORDINIS PRIMI OMNIBUSQUE PALATINIS DIGNITATIBUS FUNCTO, OB EGREGIA EIUS IN REM PUBLICAM MERITA: HUIC DD. NN. CONSTANTIUS VICTOR AC TRIUMFATOR SEMPER AUGUSTUS ET JULIANUS NOBILISSIMUS CAESAR STATUAM SUB AURO IN FORO DIVI TRAIANI, QUAM ANTE SUB DIVO CONSTANTE VITAE ET FIDELISSIMAE DEVOTIONIS GRATIA MERUIT, ADPROBANTE AMPLISSIMO SENATU SUMPTU PUBLICO LOCO SUO RESTITUENDAM CENSUERUNT.

[4] *Notitia Dignitatum or.* XI, *occ.* IX; Ammianus, 15, 5, 18; Athanasius, *Apologia ad Constantium*, c. 3; Cassiodorus, *Variae*, 6, 6; Seeck, Pauly-Wissowa, vol. 1, p. 382, s. v. *admissionales.*

[5] Ammianus, 26, 5, 7.

numerous from the succeeding centuries,[1] but there is no reason to doubt that by this time the Roman precedent had been established, in virtue of which their ambassadors to the Persian court in 579 A.D. declined to declare their business to any one but the official who corresponded to the Roman Master of the Offices.[2] Such duties as these necessarily involved the handling of considerable correspondence in foreign languages and consequently the staff of the Master included a number of official interpreters, the *interpretes diversarum gentium* of the *Notitia*.[3]

In the history of the relations between the Prefect of the Orient and the Master of the Offices at Constantinople the prefecture of Rufinus deserves especial mention. Lydus[4] says that "the power of the prefecture was diminished until the time of Arcadius, the father of Theodosius the Younger, under whom it happened that Rufinus, called the Insatiate, who was his Prefect, aimed at a tyranny, but failed in his purpose to benefit the state, and utterly ruined his office. For the Emperor thereupon deprived it of its military authority, then of the supervision of the arsenals, and of the State Post, and all the rest of the powers, of which the so-called Mastership is composed."

Taken literally, this statement implies that it was after the fall of Rufinus, in 395 A.D., that the Master of the Offices received the command of the Scholarians, with the control of the arsenals and of the State Post. However, we have already seen that the Master exercised all these powers by the middle of the fourth century; hence the statement of Lydus is, to say the least, confusing. But there must have been some reason why he connected the career of Rufinus with the dissolution of the Prefect's power, and the corresponding growth of the power of the Masters. Rufinus

[1] Priscus, *Frag.* 7, *Fragmenta Historicorum Graecorum*, vol. 4, p. 77; Cassiodorus, *Var.* 6, 6; Lydus, *De Mag.*, 2, 26; Corippus, *In laudem Justini*, 3, 233.

[2] Menander, *Fr.* 52, *Fragmenta Historicorum Graecorum*, vol. 4, p. 256: μαγίστρῳ, καθὰ τοῦτον καλοῦσι Ῥωμαῖοι.

[3] *Notitia Dignitatum or.* XI; *occ.* IX, *omnium gentium*; Priscus, *loc. cit.*, οἷα δὴ τῶν τε ἀγγελιαφόρων καὶ ἑρμηνέων καὶ στρατιωτῶν τῶν ἀμφὶ τὴν βασιλείαν φυλακὴν ὑπ᾽ αὐτὸν ταττομένων.

[4] *De Mag.*, 2, 10–3, 40: διεσύρη δὲ οὐδὲν ἧττον ἡ τῆς ἀρχῆς δυναστεία ἄχρι τῶν Ἀρκαδίου τοῦ πατρὸς Θεοδοσίου τοῦ νέου καιρῶν, ἐφ᾽ οὗ συμβέβηκε Ρουφῖνον τὸν ἐπίκλην ἀκόρεστον, ὃς ἦν ὕπαρχος αὐτῷ, τυραννίδα μελετήσαντα τοῦ μὲν σκοποῦ ὑπὲρ λυσιτελείας τῶν κοινῶν ἐκπεσεῖν, εἰς βάραθρον δὲ τὴν ἀρχὴν καταρρῖψαι. αὐτίκα μὲν γὰρ ὁ βασιλεὺς τῆς ἐκ τῶν ὅπλων ἰσχύος ἀφαιρεῖται τὴν ἀρχήν, εἶτα τῆς τῶν λεγομένων φαβρικῶν οἱονεὶ ὁπλοποιῶν φροντίδος τῆς τε τοῦ δημοσίου δρόμου καὶ πάσης ἑτέρας, δι᾽ ὧν τὸ λεγόμενον συνέστη μαγιστέριον.

had been Master of the Offices under Theodosius I,[1] was promoted by him to the Prefecture in 392,[2] and, upon the death of that Emperor in 395, as *praefectus praetorio Orientis* was left in practical control of the government in the eastern half of the Empire where the young Arcadius was but a nominal ruler. However, his rivalry with Stilicho, the western regent, and the jealousy of others at the court of Arcadius, led to his murder in that very year.[3] It is possible that Rufinus, aiming to establish his influence more firmly, subordinated the Mastership to the Prefecture, giving to the latter the powers which it had exercised before the reforms of Constantine I. Naturally, upon his fall the Master's Office would have regained its independence and the Prefecture would have been again reduced to the position which it had prior to 395, while its holders would be regarded with greater suspicion because it had formed the basis of the power of the late Minister. This is a possible explanation for the view of Lydus that at this date there was a sudden increase of the Master's sphere of duties, to the detriment of the Prefecture.

Towards the end of the fourth century the corps of the *decani* was added to the list of *officia* of palace servants. They were servitors of very low rank, being door-keepers and messengers in the service of the women of the imperial household.[4] These *decani*, like other brigades of court attendants of similar character, were placed under the orders of the Master of the Offices.[5]

From a consideration of the *Notitia Dignitatum* it is evident that up to about 425 A.D. the Masters of the Offices in both halves of the Empire exercised practically the same administrative functions.[6] The *Notitia* of the Occident, however, mentions the *cancellarii*, as one of the *officia* under the Master's authority, whereas they do not appear in that of the Orient. The *cancellarii* were attendants performing services in connection with the exercise of judicial functions by the higher magistrates in whose service they stood. However, those mentioned here were in the immedi-

[1] *Codex Theodosianus*, X, 22, 3 (390); Zosimus, 4, 51: μάγιστρος τῶν ἐν τῇ αὐλῇ τάξεων καταστάς.

[2] *Codex Theodosianus*, VIII, 6, 2; Ambrosius, *Ep.* 53, *Rufinus ex magistro officiorum factus est in consulatu praefectus praetorio.*

[3] Zosimus, 5, 1; 7; Seeck, *Geschichte*, vol. 5, pp. 267–9, 273–9.

[4] Seeck, Pauly-Wissowa, vol. 4, p. 2246.

[5] *Codex Theodosianus*, VI, 31, 1 (year 416).

[6] *Notitia Dignitatum*, *or.* XI; *occ.* IX.

ate service of the Emperor, and so were classed with the other *palatini*. This corps of imperial *cancellarii* was probably established early in the fifth century. A possible explanation why they appear in the Western and not in the Eastern *Notitia* is that the former may here, as in some other instances, present a somewhat later phase of the administrative organization than the latter.[1] However, it may be that there was really no corresponding body of imperial *cancellarii* in the East, since there is no reference to them, although such officials were found in the office of the Prefects, and other high functionaries.[2]

As the list of those who were *sub dispositione magistri officiorum* in the East makes no mention of the *cancellarii*, so that in the West lacks the *mensores* and *lampadarii* which the former contains. This discrepancy can only be explained as an error of omission, for *lampadarii* were found at the Western court and were under the Master of the Offices.[3]

In the year 443 A.D. the Master of the Offices in the Orient received an addition to his sphere of duties that did not fall to the lot of the Western Master. This was the inspection of the condition of the troops and defences on the frontiers of the Orient and the preparation of an annual report thereon.[4] The Master of the Offices was selected for this purpose in the hope that a more accurate report on such matters would be presented by one who was not a military officer and who would, therefore, have little personal interest in the *duces*; for the *duces* were responsible for the condition of the *limites*. And the Master was the most logical civil official for this duty, as the corps of the *agentes in rebus*, or the imperial secret service, was under his orders, and, as a permanent member of the *consistorium*, he came directly into contact with the Emperor himself.

It was also during the fifth century that the Master of the Offices acquired considerable judicial authority, so that eventually his jurisdiction extended over practically all the *officiales* of the palace and over others who had not the same intimate connection with the Master as an administrative officer. A characteristic of the organization of the Later Roman Empire was that the magistrate was the general judge of his *officiales* in both civil and crimi-

[1] Seeck, Pauly-Wissowa, vol. 3, pp. 1457–8.

[2] *Codex Justinianus*, I, 51: *de adsessoribus et domesticis et cancellariis iudicum*; Lydus, *De Mag.*, 3, 36.

[3] *Novellae Valentiniani*, III, 30 (450).

[4] *Novellae Theodosii*, 24.

nal cases, and that from his decisions there was no appeal.[1] There was, consequently, nothing unusual in the Master exercising jurisdiction over all those to whom he sustained the relation of administrative chief. However, the full judicial powers of the Master of the Offices were acquired more slowly than his civil authority and did not always coincide with the latter. It is probable that the Master began to exercise some jurisdiction over the various *officia* which stood under his orders as soon as they passed under his control. Nevertheless, at first, their members could be compelled to answer charges in other courts than that presided over by the Master. But gradually the privilege was granted them of defending themselves in his court only; and the other tribunals ceased to have jurisdiction over them.

The first notice of the exercise of judicial functions by the Master of the Offices occurs in a report of Symmachus, then Urban Prefect, dating from 384 or 385,[2] from which it is evident that at that time the Master had some judicial authority over the *stratores*, and hence, we may infer, over all the *officia palatina*. However, the Master's jurisdiction does not seem to have been exclusive at that early date.

Apparently the Master first exercised this exclusive judicial authority over the Scholarians, whose commander he was, and who could be summoned before no other tribunal than his, as is implied in a constitution of 443.[3] By this same constitution the *decani*, whom we have met already as the Master's subordinates in other respects, were placed in similar fashion entirely under his jurisdiction.[4]

However it was not until the reign of Leo I (457–74) and his successors Zeno (474–91) and Anastasius (491–518) that there was a marked extension of the Master's judicial functions. During this period he became sole judge of other classes of functionaries who had long been under his authority and also of the employees in various departments which, up to this time, had been free from his control. In addition, military officers and their subordinates,

[1] Bethmann-Hollweg, *Der römische Civilprozess*, vol. 3, 139.

[2] Symmachus, *Relationes*, [10], 38.

[3] *Codex Justinianus*, XII, 26, 2: *Ad exemplum itaque devotissimorum scholarium nulli licere memoratos* (i.e. *decanos*) *ad aliud judicium trahere . . . praecipimus.*

[4] *Nostrae pietatis famulationibus adhaerentes decanos non oportet pro desiderio pulsantium ad alia protrahi judicia, sed viri illustris tantum magistri officiorum observare examen.*

and, in some cases, ex-officials of high rank came under the jurisdiction of the Master of the Offices. Leo and Anthemius (467–72) extended the Master's exclusive jurisdiction over the *cubicularii*,[1] the *fabricenses* in Constantinople,[2] and the *schola sacrae vestis*,[3] to whom were soon afterward added the *agentes in rebus*[4] and the *duces*, with their subordinates, *apparitores*, *limitanei*, and *castrorum praepositi*,[5] on the frontier of the Empire in the East. Under Leo II (Nov. 473–Nov. 474) and Zeno certain *officia* of *ministeriani* were given the protection of the court of the Master of the Offices,[6] and Zeno granted the *silentiarii* the same privilege.[7] This latter Emperor also placed the honorary *viri illustres*, resident in Constantinople, in special instances under the Master's judicial authority.[8] Finally, Anastasius put the members of the four *scrinia*[9] in possession of the same judicial privileges as the *ministeriani*, and from constitutions of Justinus and Justinian[10] it may be inferred that the *adjutores* of the Quaestor were upon an equal footing with the *scriniarii*.

Among these various classes of *officiales*, who are thus expressly mentioned as subject to the jurisdiction of the Master of the Offices, the *scholares*, *decani*, *fabricenses*, *agentes in rebus* and *scriniarii* were his subordinates in an administrative sense also, and this was the basis of his judicial authority over them. However, the *cubicularii*, *silentiarii*, and *schola sacrae vestis*[11] were under the orders of the Praepositus Sacri Cubiculi, while the *ministeriani* were the subordinates of the Castrensis, and hence in other respects beyond the control of the Master of the Offices. Why, in spite of this, they were placed under his jurisdiction, is best explained by the constitution dealing with the *silentiarii*.[12]

1 *Codex Justinianus*, XII, 5, 3.

2 *Op. cit.*, XI, 10, 6: *Eos, qui inter fabricenses sacrae fabricae sociati sunt*, etc.

3 *Op. cit.* XII, 25, 3.

4 *Op. cit.* XII, 20, 4 (Leo).

5 *Op. cit.* XII, 59, 8 (Leo).

6 *Op. cit.* XII, 25, 4: *sacro ministerio nostro deputatos, quorum officia singillatim brevis subter adnexus continet.* The *brevis* is unfortunately lost.

7 *Op. cit.* XII, 16, 4.

8 *Codex Justinianus*, III, 24, 3 (485–86).

9 *Codex Justinianus*, XII, 19, 12.

10 *Codex Justinianus*, XII, 19, 13; 14.

11 This *schola* is to be distinguished from the officials of the *sacra vestis* who were under the *comes sacrarum largitionum*; cf. Böcking, *Notitia Dignitatum*, vol. 2, pp. 298, 337.

12 *Codex Justinianus*, XII, 16, 4: *Ne ad diversa tracti viri devoti silentiarii judicia sacris abstrahi videantur obsequiis, jubemus eos, qui quemlibet devotissimorum silentiariorum scholae vel ejus uxorem civiliter vel etiam criminaliter pulsare maluerint, minime eum ex cuiuslibet alterius judicio nisi ex judicio tantummodo viri excellentissimi magistri officiorum conveniri.*

From this we learn that the *officiales* of the Praepositus and the Castrensis were liable to prosecution in the court of the Master only, because the former functionaries lacked judicial authority and if summoned to appear before outside tribunals their subordinates were liable to be withdrawn for too long a time from the performance of their duties at the palace.

The same reason may have been partially responsible for granting the Master exclusive jurisdiction over his own subordinates. Such arrangements were of course very much to the advantage of the members of the various departments affected by them, and these included practically all the *palatini*, with the exception of the subordinates of the Count of the Sacred Largesses and the Count of the Privy Purse, who by a constitution of Theodosius II and Valentinian III (425–50) were granted the privilege of answering charges, except in a few specified cases, in the courts of these *comites* alone.[1]

In the case of the *duces* and their office staff and orderlies (*apparitores*), as well as the commanders of garrisons (*castrorum praepositi*) and border militia (*limitanei*) under their orders, the exercise of judicial powers by the Master of the Offices obviously grew out of his duty of inspecting the Eastern frontiers. For the *limites* under his supervision, which are mentioned specifically in the constitution of 443, are described in Justinian's Codex in general terms as those subject to his jurisdiction.[2] This was contrary to the practice that military officers should not exercise jurisdiction over civilians, nor the ordinary civil judges over *viros militares*,[3] and the Master was thus an exception in that members of both services were under his authority in this respect. Previously these *duces* and *limitanei* had been under the jurisdiction of their military superiors, the *magistri militum*,[4] and the latter still retained some judicial power over them, although the nature of this power is not clear.[5] This extension of the jurisdiction of the

[1] *Codex Justinianus*, XII, 23, 12: *Viros devotos palatinos non oportere in hac regia urbe apud virum illustrem praefectum urbis litigare compelli, nisi de aedificatione domorum et servitutibus et annonis orta videatur causa; in aliis vero causis tam pecuniariis quam criminalibus apud viros illustres tantummodo comites suos respondere.*

[2] *Codex Justinianus*, I, 31, 4: *super omni limite sub tua jurisdictione constituto;* cf. *Novellae Theodosii*, 24.

[3] *Codex Justinianus*, I, 29, 1 (386–7).

[4] Cf. *Harvard Studies in Classical Philology*, vol. XXVI, p. 148.

[5] *Op. cit.*; *Codex Justinianus*, XII, 59, 8: *illustribus scilicet ac magnificis viris magistris militum consuetudine ac potestate, si qua ad limites aliquos Orientis Thraciarum et Illyrici ex longo tempore hactenus obtinuit, reservata.*

Master of the Offices may, therefore, be regarded as an encroachment upon that of the Masters of the Soldiers, with the aim of bringing the control of the frontiers and their garrisons more strictly under the supervision of the court. Later, under Anastasius, when the *duces* were placed in command of the detachments of the central field army (*praesentales numeri*) in the diocese of the Orient, these troops remained under the jurisdiction of the *magistri militum praesentales*, which was exercised directly or through the courts of the *duces*.[1] However, Justinian ordered that all appeals coming from the court of a *dux* (*ducianum judicium*) should be decided by the Master of the Offices and the Quaestor of the Palace, acting conjointly.[2]

The *illustres* in Constantinople, who at times were subject to the Master's jurisdiction, were those known as the *honorarii*, i.e. those who had received the patents (*codicilli*) of an office entitling them to the Illustrissimate without their actually having filled such a post. Ordinarily, such *illustres* were under the jurisdiction of the Pretorian and Urban Prefects, but by a special order of the Emperor they could be brought before the court of the Master of the Offices.[3]

The Master of the Offices in the Occident certainly did not exercise jurisdiction over the *duces* of the Western Empire, owing to the strict subordination of these to the *magister peditum praesentalis*,[4] and perhaps his office remained unaffected by the enactments regarding this sphere of the Master's duties subsequent to the death of Anthemius, although in other respects his jurisdiction in the Ostrogothic Kingdom probably was the same as that of the Master in the Orient.[5]

Indeed, since the organization of the court and the administration of Theoderic was thoroughly Roman in character — for the Romans the Empire might still be said to be in existence in the West — it is not surprising to find the officials at the Ostrogothic court in Ravenna holding the same titles and exercising the same functions as those who formerly officiated under the Roman Emperors in the West and were still functioning in the

[1] *Codex Justinianus*, XII, 35, 18 (492).

[2] *Codex Justinianus*, VII, 62, 38 (529).

[3] *Codex Justinianus*, III, 24, 3, par. 2: *quotiens tamen ad eius judicium specialis nostrae pietatis emanaverit jussio.*

[4] Mommsen, *Aetius*, in *Hermes*, vol. XXXVI, pp. 537 ff.

[5] To be inferred from Cassiodorus, *Variae*, 6, 6.

East.[1] Thus we see that the Master of the Offices under Theoderic holds a position almost identical with that of the officials bearing the same name at the courts of Anastasius, Justin, and Justinian.[2]

Only in a few points has the sphere of the Master's activities undergone any change. The control of the arsenals and their employees in Italy had been restored to the office of the Pretorian Prefect,[3] perhaps with the object of obtaining more efficient control by a better concentration of authority. To offset this loss of power the Master of the Offices might point to an extension of his authority in regard to the State Post, of which the maintenance, as well as the use, was under his supervision in the West.[4] Further, the Master of the Offices under the Ostrogoths had the power to appoint at his discretion *peraequatores victualium* for Ravenna.[5] These were officers whose duty it was to fix the price for articles of consumption offered for sale in the city.[6] The Master likewise named a judge to settle disputes arising in connection with their activities.[7] It seems probable that this phase of municipal administration was placed in the hands of the Master because at Ravenna there were no officials corresponding to the *praefecti annonae*, or even the Urban Prefects, of Rome and Constantinople, who would have had such matters under their care. Furthermore, when the seat of the Mastership, along with the centre of the administration, was transferred from Rome to Ravenna, the Master of the Offices at times appointed a deputy with the title of *vices agens* to represent him in Rome.[8] Such an official is attested for the year 533.[9]

From this historical survey it will be clear that the office of *magister officiorum* remained essentially the same in character

[1] Cassiodorus, *Var.*, *passim;* Mommsen, *Ostgothische Studier*, *Neues Archiv*, vol. 14. 1899; Dumoulin, *Cambridge Medieval History*, vol. 1, pp. 441–5. Cf. *Anonymus Valesii*, 60: (*Theodoricus*) *militiam Romanis sicut sub principes esse praecepit.*

[2] Casssiodorus, *Variae*, 6, 6.

[3] *Op. cit.*, 7, 18, 19.

[4] Cassiodorus, *Variae*, 6, 6, 3; 5, 5.

[5] *Op. cit.*, 6, 6: *Peraequatores victualium rerum in urbe regia propria voluntate constituit.*

[6] Defined by DuCange, *Glossarium mediae et infimae Latinitatis: qui rebus venalibus pretium indunt ac indicunt.*

[7] Cassiodorus, *loc. cit.: et tam necessariae rei iudicem facit. Ipse enim gaudium populi, ipse nostris temporibus praestet ornatum quando tales viros copiae publicae praeficit, ut plebs querula seditionem nesciat habere satiata.*

[8] Mommsen, *Neues Archiv*, vol. XIV, p. 463.

[9] Cassiodorus, *Variae*, 11, 4; 11, 5; 12, 25.

from Constantine to Justinian, although its sphere of administrative duties was slightly enlarged and it acquired new powers in the exercise of judicial functions. The Master of the Offices likewise maintained his rank among the *dignitates palatinae* and the other high officials of the empire. This will be apparent from a consideration of the several classes of dignitaries to which the Master was successively admitted. And in this connection there should be borne in mind the dominant tendency in the organization of the hierarchy of rank of the Later Empire. This was to extend previously established grades of rank to include ever wider circles of officials and thus depreciate their worth, while, in compensation, new and more exclusive classes with fresh titles of rank were created for the higher offices.

The Master of the Offices as one of the *comites consistoriani*, or standing members of the imperial *consistorium*,[1] was a *comes primi ordinis*[2] and consequently authorized to bear the title of *comes*, so that his full official designation was, as we have seen, *comes et magister officiorum*. This form appears frequently in imperial constitutions and elsewhere throughout the fourth and the greater part of the fifth century.[3] However, as the word *comes* was merely a personal designation of rank and did not form an integral part of the Master's official title, as came to be the case with the *comes sacrarum largitionum*, and because the holder of the Mastership was *ipso facto* a *comes*, the *comitiva* was frequently ignored, even in official documents.[4] This neglect of the *comitiva* extended to all similar offices, and became more frequent as that dignity was rapidly extended to officials of very low rank; and, finally, to practically all who were exempt from the municipal *munera*, although it long continued in vogue for high military officials in the West.[5] From the last quarter of the fifth century it is no longer found among the titles of the Master of the Offices.

It is probable that the first of the graded classes of the digni-

[1] Ammianus, 15, 5, 12; *Codex Theodosianus*, VI, 30, 1, and 4; VII, 8, 3, cf. VI, 9, 1; and IX, 14, 3; Cassiodorus, *Var.*, 6, 6, 2; Mommsen, *Neues Archiv*, vol. 14, p. 445; Seeck, Pauly-Wissowa, vol. 4, p. 645.

[2] Dessau, *Inscr. Select.*, 1244; Mommsen, *loc. cit.*; Seeck, *loc. cit.*

[3] The earliest instance of this full title is *Codex Theodosianus*, VIII, 5, 8, (357); the latest, *Codex Justinianus*, XII, 55, 4 (474).

[4] Thus Hilarianus appears as *comes et magister* in *Codex Justinianus*, XII, 19, 10 (470) and XII, 55, 4 (474), but as *magister* only in I. 23, 6 (470) and XII, 59, 9 (id?); Mommsen, *Neues Archiv*, vol. 14, pp. 510 f.

[5] Seeck, Pauly-Wissowa, vol. 4, pp. 635–6.

taries to which the Master belonged was the Perfectissimate, which in the early years of the reign of Constantine I still included civil officials of high rank. At least a *comes*, evidently in charge of the administration of the *res privata*, was a *perfectissimus* in 319,[1] and, as we shall see, the Master of the Offices, although taking precedence over the Counts of the financial administration, regularly belonged to the same order of rank. However, when the equestrian career was abolished, presumably after the defeat of Licinius in 323, the Perfectissimate was conferred upon lower grades of officials, and the Clarissimate was for a long time the sole order of rank for the highest officers.[2] Consequently the Master became a *vir clarissimus*.[3] In 372, the Master of the Offices, along with the Quaestor and the Counts of the Sacred Largesses and the Privy Purse, was given precedence over the proconsuls,[4] evidently because of the increasing importance of these *comites consistoriani*, owing to their close proximity to the Emperor. By 378 the Master had become a *vir spectabilis*,[5] and not long afterwards, by 385 at the latest,[6] had attained the highest of the orders of rank existing at that time, the Illustrissimate, to which the other *comites consistoriani* were admitted at about the same time.[7]

Shortly before this, in 380, a constitution of Gratian and Theodosius granted to the ex-Masters, together with the ex-Quaestors and the ex-Counts of the Sacred Largesses and the Privy Purse, the same honorable reception on official occasions that the ex-Prefects enjoyed.[8]

[1] *Codex Theodosianus*, X, 8, 2; *virum perfectissimum comitem et amicum nostrum*. The Nemesianus, *v. p. com. larg.* of XI, 7, 5 (345), is a subordinate official, and not the chief of the *sacrae largitiones*. Hirschfeld, *Die Rangtitel der römischen Kaiserzeit*, *Sitzungsbericht der Berliner Akad.*, 1901, p. 593; Mommsen u. Meyer, *Codex Theodosianus*, vol. I, pp. CLXXXVIII, CCII.

[2] Hirschfeld, *op. cit.*, 588, 593.

[3] The earliest instance of a Master with this title is in 357, *Codex Theodosianus*, VIII, 5, 8; but references to *magistri officiorum* prior to 350 are very rare and the first constitution addressed to one dates from 362 (*Codex Theodosianus*, XI, 39, 5).

[4] *Codex Theodosianus*, VI, 9, 1; *Eorum honores, qui sacrario n(os)tro explorata sedulitate oboediunt, hac volumus o(bser)vatione distingui, ut quaestor atque officiorum m(agis)ter nec non duo largitionum comites proconsula(rium) honoribus praeferantur.*

[5] *Codex Theodosianus*, VIII, 5, 35: *spectabilis viri officiorum magistri.*

[6] Symmachus, *Relationes*, 34, 8; 38, 4; 43, 2.

[7] Hirschfeld, *op. cit.*, p. 599 f., who rightly refuses to accept *Codex Theodosianus*, VI, 9, 2 as implying that these officials were *viri illustres* in 380. The attribution of *illustris* to a Master in *Codex Theodosianus*, VIII, 5, 22 (365) is certainly an error.

[8] *Codex Theodosianus*, VI, 9, 2: *Qui exquaesturae honore aut efficaci magis(te)rio aut comitiva utriusque aerarii nostri attonito sp(len)dore viguerunt, adclamatione*

Whenever the Master of the Offices is given the combined title of *vir clarissimus et illustris*,[1] the *clarissimus* is to be regarded as the general title of rank of the senatorial order to which the bearer belonged, while the *illustris* denotes the special grade of rank conferred by the particular office, the Mastership.[2]

Within the order of the Illustrissimate there were several grades. Of these the first was composed of the Prefects, the Magistri Militum and the Grand Chamberlain; the second comprised the Master of the Offices and the other *comites consistoriani*.[3] Under Valentinian III and Marcian (450–55) the Master of the Offices and the Quaestor seem to have formed a second class of *illustres* by themselves, while the Counts of the Treasury made up a third grade.[4] However, under Zeno[5] (474–91) and Anastasius[6] (491–518) the latter were again in the same class as the Master. In another constitution of Zeno a Master was designated as *excellentissimus*,[7] and before the middle of the fifth century the title *magnificus*[8] began to be applied to the holders of this office. However, these new titles do not imply new orders of rank, for *excellentissimus* was applied quite generally to the highest officials without special reference to a grade of dignity, and *magnificus* was only used of *illustres*, either alone or in the *illustris et magnificus*.[9]

In 535 the Master of the Offices appears as a member of the recently established order of the *gloriosissimi*, a higher rank than the *illustres*, along with the Prefects, Magistri Militum, Quaestor, and Grand Chamberlain.[10] This was the last and highest grade of dignitaries created before the Byzantine period. At this time also the adjective *sacer* was employed with greater frequency to

excipiantur solita, n(ec) praetereantur ut incogniti atque, ut non aequand(i) (il)lis, qui gesserint praefecturas, sed eo observentur c(ul)tu omni coetu omnique conventu.

1 Symmachus, *Relationes*, [10], 34; 34, 8; 38, 4; 43, 2.

2 Koch, *Die byzantinischen Beamtentitel von* 400 *bis* 700, p. 12.

3 *Codex Theodosianus*, VI, 7, 8; VI, 8, 1; VI, 9, 1; Jullian, Daremberg et Saglio, *Dictionnaire des Antiquités grecques et romaines*, vol. 3, p. 385 f.

4 *Codex Justinianus*, XII, 40, 10.

5 *Op. cit.*, X., 32, 64.

6 *Op. cit.*, X, 32, 66 (497–499).

7 *Op. cit.*, XII, 16, 4.

8 *Novellae Theodosii*, 6, (438), *viri inlustris atque magnifici magistri officiorum*; *Codex Justinianus*, XII, 20, 4: (Leo) *viri magnifici magistri officiorum*; *op. cit.* III, 24, 3 (485–86), *viri magnifici*.

9 Cf. Koch, *Byzantinische Beamtentitel*, 43, 51.

10 *Novellae Justiniani*, 2, (535); 14, *fin.* (535); *Edictum Justiniani*, 8, 1 (548); Jullian, Daremberg et Saglio, vol. 3, p. 388; Koch, *op. cit.*, pp. 43, 65.

designate persons or things immediately connected with the Emperor; a usage that applied to the officia of the palace. Hence the full title of the Master of the Offices was *gloriosissimus magister sacrorum officiorum*, in Greek, ἐνδοξότατος μάγιστρος τῶν θειῶν ὀφφικίων.[1]

Moreover, the Masters of the Offices, who were actually exercising, or had exercised, the functions of this office, like the Consuls, Prefects, and Magistri Militum, might receive the patriciate, the most coveted honorary title of the Empire.[2]

The order of precedence among the great ministers of the Empire, as established in the course of the fourth century, is preserved in the *Notitia Dignitatum*, and was maintained with but little alteration while these offices themselves endured. Naturally those offices forming the higher took precedence over those forming the lower grades of rank. Thus in the *Notitia* the Master of the Offices is ranked below the Prefects, the Magistri Militum, and the Grand Chamberlain, yet he is placed above others in the same grade as himself, namely the Quaestor and the Counts of the Sacred Largesses and the Privy Purse.[3] However, there was practically no distinction in the ranking of the Master and the Quaestor, as will be seen at once from the way in which now one and now the other took precedence.[4] In the constitutions of 362,[5] 372,[6] and 380[7] the Quaestor is given the priority, but in others of 409[8] and 415[9] this order is reversed. However, in 416[10] the Quaestor again takes precedence; and, although in the *Notitia* he stands below the Master, he retains this precedence at the time of the compilation of the Theodosian Code (438).[11] The

[1] *Novellae Justiniani*, 2 (535); 85 (539); *Edictum Justiniani*, 8, 1 (548).

[2] *Codex Justinianus*, XII, 3, 3: *Nemini ad sublimem patriciatus honorem, qui ceteris omnibus anteponitur, adscendere liceat, nisi prius aut cousulatus honore potiatur aut praefecturae praetorio vel Illyrici vel urbis administrationem aut magistri militum aut magistri officiorum, in actu videlicet positus, gessisse noscatur, ut huiusmodi tantum personis sive adhuc administrationem gerendo seu postea liceat (quando hoc nostrae sederit maiestati) patriciam consequi dignitatem* (Zeno); an example is Hermogenes, *magister sacrorum officiorum et patricius, Novellae Justiniani*, 10 (535).

[3] *Notitia Dignitatum or.* 1, *occ.* 1; Hirschfeld, *Rangtitel der römischen Kaiserzeit*, p. 599, thinks that the high position of the Grand Chamberlain was due to the influence of Eutropius, who held that post under Arcadius.

[4] Cf. Mommsen, *Neues Archiv*, vol. 14, p. 454.

[5] *Codex Theodosianus*, XI, 39, 5.

[6] *Codex Theodosianus*, VI, 9, 1.

[7] *Codex Theodosianus*, VI, 9, 2 = *Codex Justinianus*, XII, 6, 1.

[8] *Codex Theodosianus*, XI, 18, 1.

[9] *Codex Theodosianus*, I, 8, 1.

[10] *Codex Theodosianus*, VI, 26, 17.

[11] *Codex Theodosianus*, I, *tit.* 18, 9; cf. VI, 9 rubric = *Codex Justinianus*, XII, 6.

same situation prevails in 440–41,[1] but in 485–86[2] the Master has the seniority. In the West under Theoderic both Eugenites[3] and Cassiodorus[4] were promoted from the Quaestorship to the Mastership, but yet in his *Formulae* Cassiodorus gives the precedence to the former office.[5] In the East under Justinian, Trebonian held both offices at once[6] and under Justinus II Anastasius had the same twofold powers.[7]

The examples cited show how slight was the distinction in rank between the two offices in question. Seeck[8] has sought to prove that at the beginning of the fifth century there was a definite period during which the Master took precedence over his fellow-official, but Mommsen[9] has pointed out that the evidence does not support his contention. However, from the fact that, as has been noticed, the Mastership and not the Quaestorship qualified its holder for the patrician dignity,[10] we may conclude that towards the end of the fifth century the former had come to be regarded as the more honorable office. This view is supported by the mention, in Justinian's Edict of 548, of the Mastership immediately after the Prefecture and before the *magisterium militum*,[11] although there is no proof that it had permanently gained precedence over the latter. On the other hand, both the Master and the Quaestor now ranked above the Grand Chamberlain,[12] who in the *Notitia* stood next to the Magistri Militum.

The Master of the Offices, as *clarissimus*, *spectabilis* or *illustris*, was of senatorial rank, but it was only after the expiration of his term of office that he took his place as a member of that order.[13]

And so, at the middle of the sixth century, the Master of the Offices not only held one of the most influential positions in the imperial administration, but also in rank was one of the highest dignitaries of Roman officialdom.

[1] *Codex Justinianus*, XII, 8, 2.

[2] *Codex Justinianus*, III, 24, 3; so also XII, 40, 10 (450–5).

[3] Cassiodorus, *Variae*, 1, 12; 13.

[4] *Op. cit.*, 9, 24.

[5] *Op. cit.*, 6, 5; 6.

[6] *Novellae Justiniani*, 33: *illustris magister officiorum et quaestor sacri palatii* (536).

[7] Corippus, *Panegyr. in Justinum, pr.: gemino honore quaestor et magister*.

[8] *Quaestiones de notitia dignitatum*, p. 12.

[9] *Neues Archiv*, vol. 14, p. 464.

[10] *Codex Justinianus*, XII, 3, 3.

[11] *Edictum Justiniani*, 8, 1.

[12] *Codex Justinianus*, III, 24, 3 (485–6).

[13] Id., *qui magistri officiorum vel quaestoris officio functus aut sacri nostrae pietatis cubiculi praepositus post depositam administrationem senatorio ordini sociatus est*; cf. Lécrivain, *Le sénat romain*, p. 63.

III. The Mastership in the Byzantine Empire to the Latin Conquest, in 1204 A.D.

Granted that the division of history into periods is an arbitrary convention and that there is an unbroken line of continuity in the constitutional development of the Roman Empire from Augustus until the Latin conquest of Constantinople in 1204 A.D., and perhaps even longer, it must nevertheless be acknowledged that the period between the death of Justinian (565) and the accession of Heraclius (610) wrought changes of such importance in the Roman Empire of the East that afterwards it bore a decidedly new character. This fact will justify the use of the term Byzantine to designate that period of its history which extends from the revival following the collapse of the Justinian organization to the final dissolution of the Empire.[1]

Partly responsible for the altered tone of the new epoch was the loss of almost all the Latin-speaking provinces, which earlier had been under the imperial authority, and the consequent overwhelming preponderance of the Greek element in the Empire. As a result of this, Latin by the end of the sixth century had ceased to be the official imperial language;[2] and although the citizens of the Empire continued to be called *Romaioi*, this title had lost its original significance.[3]

The change in the official language brought about a corresponding change in the titles of the offices of state which had been created while Latin was yet the imperial tongue, and which, consequently, had Latin names. These titles had now to be expressed in Greek. For this purpose a Greek word, which in significance corresponded to the original Latin title, was often employed. Frequently, however, when such an equivalent was not ready to hand, the Latin form was simply written in Greek characters. Thus, while the Prefect was henceforth ὁ ἔπαρχος, the Master of the Offices became ὁ *μάγιστρος τῶν βασιλικῶν ὀφφικίων*[4]; or, more simply, ὁ *μάγιστρος*, '*the* master,' since the

[1] Gelzer, *Abrisz der byzantinischen Kaisergeschichte*, in Müller's *Handbuch der klassischen Altertumswissenschaft*, vol. IX, 1, pp. 909, 946; Bury, *Later Roman Empire*, vol. 2, pp. 67–68; Baynes, *Cambridge Medieval History*, vol. 2, p. 263; Pernice, *L'imperatore Eraclio*, p. 222.

[2] Bury, *Later Roman Empire*, vol. 2, p. 166.

[3] *Op. cit.*, p. 171.

[4] Mansi, *Sacrorum conciliorum collectio*, vol. XI, pp. 209, 217.

titles of the other *magistri* were not merely transliterated, but translated, in the new official terminology.

Moreover, not only were the titles of officials altered in this way, but the administrative system itself was fundamentally changed. The older system, with its small group of "great ministers," who were directly responsible to the Emperor and under whom the other administrative officers were ranged in a system of graded subordination," was definitely abandoned under the Heraclid dynasty in the seventh century. In its place arose a new order, perfected by the ninth century, in which there was practically no hierarchy of office, only one of rank; in which, moreover, the administration was entrusted to some sixty officials, each of whom was directly responsible to the sovereign. This change had been made possible by the great diminution of the territorial extent of the Empire, and had been carried out, (1) by a reorganization of the provincial administration, whereby the older dioceses and provinces gave place to new units of organization called *themes* — a change which was accompanied by the disappearance of the *magistri militum* and the Pretorian Prefects; and (2), by the breaking up of the great central ministries into the various departments of which they had been composed, so that each of these now became an independent office.[1]

For a time, however, the Master of the Offices remained unaffected by these changes; he appears with unaltered title, and apparently in the full enjoyment of his former powers, as late as the reign of Constantine IV (668–85).[2] But before the end of the reign of Leo III, the Isaurian (717–40), the greater part of the administrative functions of the Master had been transferred to several officials, some of whom had once been subordinates of the Master but had later been given an independent sphere of administration.[3] The chief of those among whom the functions of the Master were divided were the Logothete of the Post (*λογοθέτης τοῦ δρομοῦ*), the Domesticus of the Guard (*δομεστικὸς τῶν σχολῶν*), the Quaestor, the Secretary of Petitions, *ὁ ἐπὶ τῶν δεήσεων*, and the Master of Ceremonies, *ὁ ἐπὶ τῆς καταστάσεως*.

The office of the Logothete of the Post originated in that of

[1] Bury, *Imperial Administration in the Ninth Century, British Academy Supplementary Papers*, I (1911), pp. 19–20.

[2] *Op. cit.*, p. 91, where there is a list of references to Masters of the seventh century.

[3] Bury, *op. cit.*, p. 32. Bury also (pp. 29–31) gives a list of the known instances of the occurrence of the title *magistros* from 718–9 to 886–8 A.D.

the *curiosus cursus publici praesentalis*, a member of the Master's *officium*, who first acquired the title of Logothete in the eighth century. This official now took charge of the State Post, and, with it, of the diplomatic duties which the Master had exercised, such as the correspondence with foreign powers and the reception of ambassadors.[1]

The Domesticus of the Guard probably developed from the *domesticus* who appears earlier in the service of the Master of the Offices.[2] The title δομεστικὸς τῶν σχολῶν appears as early as 759,[3] and its bearer may possibly have been in command of the Scholarians, as the subordinate of the Master of the Offices, by 624.[4] However, in the eighth century the Domesticus was the chief in command of these guards, free from any subordination to the Master.

The Quaestor, to some extent at least, had always controlled the activities of the *scrinia*. It is not surprising therefore to find that when the Master of the Offices ceased to supervise the Secretaries, ἀντιγραφεῖς, who were the *magister epistolarum* and *magister libellorum* in Greek guise,[5] these should have been finally placed under the Quaestor alone.[6]

The Secretary for Petitions, ὁ ἐπὶ τῶν δεήσεων, however, who was formerly the *magister memoriae*, the highest in rank among the Masters of the *scrinia*, had had his charge raised to the dignity of an independent administrative bureau.[7]

Finally, the Master of Ceremonies, ὁ ἐπὶ τῆς καταστάσεως, whose function is defined by his title and whose office seems to have originated in that of the *comes* (once *magister*) *dispositionum*, chief of the *scrinium dispositionum* and a subordinate of the Master of the Offices,[8] likewise had been freed from the control of a superior official and had acquired the direction of the court ushers (*officium admissionum*), who had been at one time also *sub dispositione magistri officiorum*.[9] Possibly the functions involv-

[1] Bury, *op. cit.*, p. 91.

[2] Ammianus, 30, 2, 10–11 (374). Bury, *op. cit.*, p. 50, thinks that the *domesticus* was possibly the same as the *adjutor* who was at the head of the Master's *officium* (*Notitia Dignitatum or*. XI, 41; *occ*. IX, 41). This may ultimately have been the case, but originally the two offices were quite distinct; cf. Seeck, Pauly-Wissowa, vol. 5, pp. 1296 ff.

[3] Theophanes, 684.

[4] *Chronicon Paschale*; Bury, *op. cit.*, p. 50.

[5] Bury, *Harvard Studies in Classical Philology*, vol. XXI, pp. 23–9; *Imperial Administration*, pp. 74–5.

[6] Bury, *Imperial Administration*, p. 76.

[7] *Op. cit.*, pp. 76–7.

[8] Cf. *Harvard Studies*, vol. XXVI, p. 99 f.

[9] *Notitia Dignitatum or*. XI, 16, 17; Bury, *op. cit.*, pp. 118–19.

ing the supervision of the court ceremonial were among those which remained longest with the Master of the Offices.

Nevertheless, although the *magistros* of the eighth century, without administrative and judicial functions, presents such a different appearance from the *magister officiorum* of the sixth, this is not due to the creation of a new Mastership but to the radical changes which have altered the character of the old office. This Bury[1] has proved by pointing out that, first, the *magistri militum* and the *magistri scriniorum* did not have the title *magistros* in Greek, while the Master of the Offices of earlier times appears in Theophanes usually simply as ὁ μάγιστρος; secondly, the part which the Master plays in the eighth century is that of the Master of the Offices in his rôle of "Master of Ceremonies"; thirdly, in the court functions described in the *De Caerimoniis*,[2] and dating from an earlier period, the *magistros* acts as a Master of Ceremonies, which fact seems to supply the link between the Master of the Offices of the seventh and the Master of the eighth century; and fourthly, in the old ceremonial at the appointment of a Master,[3] the latter was placed "at the head of the σέκρετον," which seems to imply that he held the highest rank at the imperial audiences. This ceremony dates from the time when there was only one Master, whose position thus seems to accord with that of the earlier official of the same name. Finally, in the Novels of Leo VI (886–912), Stylianos, father-in-law and minister of that Emperor, is expressly called Master of the Offices.[4]

However, in the eighth century this Master, whose title regularly lacked the addition τῶν ὀφφικίων, since he had lost control of the *officia* of the palace, was also known as the First Master ὁ πρῶτος μάγιστρος.[5] This usage implies that at that time there was more than one Master at the Byzantine court, and indeed, such was the case. For there had appeared a second Master, whose presence is first clearly noticed in the account of the elevation of the sons of Constantine V to the rank of Caesar in 768 A.D.,[6] where Magistri are mentioned in the plural and form a rank (*velum*, βῆλον) distinct from the Patricians. Of these Masters

[1] *Op. cit.*, pp. 30–1.

[2] *De Caer.*, I, 68, 70.

[3] *De Caer.*, I, 46, 233: καὶ ἵστησιν αὐτὸν ὁ πραιπόσιτος εἰς κεφαλὴν τοῦ σεκρέτου ἐπάνω πάντων τῶν πατρικίων. Σέκρετον corresponds to the older *consistorium*.

[4] Στυλιανῷ τῷ περιφανεστάτῳ (or ὑπερφανεστάτῳ) μαγίστρῳ τῶν θείων ὀφφικίων (*Nov.* I, 18, etc. Cf. Bury, *op. cit.*, p. 31).

[5] *De Caer.*, I, 43, 224.

[6] *De Caer.*, I, 43.

the one who was called ὁ μάγιστρος,[1] or ὁ πρῶτος μάγιστρος,[2] had a more elevated position than his associate.

The reason for the establishment of a second Mastership, according to Bury,[3] may possibly be found in the imperial absences from the capital. The presence of the original Master was required, as we shall see, in the city, and as the Emperor probably desired to have a Master in his moving court a second Master was appointed. Originally, this latter position may not have been a permanent office, but one created for special occasions only. Later, however, the two Masters were in office at the same time. The second Master, Bury[4] would identify with the μάγιστρος ἐκ προσώπου mentioned by Theophanes in connection with the rebellion of Artavasdos in 741.[5] However, I am inclined to think that this is an erroneous conclusion. Bury clearly intimates that it was the second Master who accompanied the Emperor during his absences from the city. But the term ἐκ προσώπου, which corresponds to the Latin *vices agens*, implies that the Master thus described was the deputy of the Emperor, and, therefore, the one left in Constantinople to direct affairs there. This duty, as we shall see, was later performed by the official known as ὁ μάγιστρος. And, as a matter of fact, Theophanes, μάγιστρος ἐκ προσώπου in 741, had been left in the capital when the Emperor Constantine V went to Asia.[6] Consequently, we must conclude that ἐκ προσώπου was a term applied to the First Master, who acted as a sort of Viceroy, or that it was the First Master who accompanied the Emperor, while the other remained in the city, a conclusion which would conflict with the custom of the following century.[7]

In the eighth century the Mastership was no longer an annual office but was conferred for life upon holders of the patrician dignity.[8] But it had not yet become a mere title of rank, for it involved the performance of certain duties. The Master who was at the head of σέκρετον,[9] *i. e.*, the πρωτομάγιστρος, was the leading

[1] *De Caer.*, 219, 9; 220, 4.

[2] *De Caer.*, 224, 5–13. This appears as πρωτομάγιστρος in Philotheos, 781, 11.

[3] *Imperial Administration*, p. 32. [4] *Loc. cit.*

[5] Theophanes, 639, 3. For the chronology, cf. Bury, *Later Roman Empire*, vol. 2, pp. 425, 451. Bury here makes the Master in question a *magister militum in praesenti*, but in his *Imperial Administration* he has apparently abandoned this interpretation as incorrect.

[6] Theophanes, 639: Ἀρταβάδος δὲ γράφει πρὸς Θεοφάνην τὸν πατρίκιον καὶ μάγιστρον ἐκπροσώπω ὄντα ἐν τῇ πόλει. [7] Περὶ τάξεων, 504, 506 (831 A.D.). [8] *De Caer.*, 1, 46, 235.

[9] *De Caer.*, 233, 13; cf. Genesius, 83, 17: ὁ πρῶτα φέρων Μανουὴλ ἐν μαγίστροις (under Theophilus).

member of the senate.[1] During the absence of the Emperor from the capital, as late as the ninth century he shared in the direction of the government with the Chamberlain and the Urban Prefect, as we learn from the document called *περὶ τῶν βασιλικῶν ταξειδίων*.[2] Upon such occasions the administration was entrusted to a committee of three, of whom the Chamberlain acted as the representative or vicar of the Emperor (*ὁ διέπων*), officiating wherever the presence of the latter or his *alter ego* was necessary, while the Master and the Prefect supervised the administration in general. At this time it was the Chamberlain who held the Emperor's power *ἐκ προσώπου*, as the Master had done in the previous century.

This arrangement, usual in the ninth century, had apparently been discarded in the tenth, since it is described as *τὸ παλαιὸν ἔθος* in the work just referred to. Recollecting the ceremonial duties of this Master, which have been noted previously, we may say that the position which he held was more honorable, although less onerous, than that of the earlier Master of the Offices.

The second Master shared in the ceremonial duties of the first, as is evidenced in the account of the ceremonial at the creation of a Patrician, probably dating from the time of Michael III (842–67),[3] and when the Emperor made offerings in St. Sophia,[4] he also had administrative duties to perform.[5] This additional Mastership was created before 768,[6] and its establishment, as has been noted, was the cause of the employment of the title *πρῶτος μάγιστρος* to designate the senior office.

The number of Masters continued to be limited to two during

[1] Theodore of Studion, *Epistulæ*, 76 (A.D. 821?): *τῆς συγκλήτου πρωτόβαθρον*.

[2] Appendix to *De Caer.*, 1 (Bekker), 504, 4: *ἐξῆλθεν ἡ Αὐγούστα ἀπὸ τῆς πόλεως καὶ ὁ διέπων σὺν τῷ μαγίστρῳ καὶ τῷ ἐπάρχῳ τῆς πόλεως καὶ ἐν τῇ πόλει σύγκλητος ἅπασα*; 506, 1; *ὁ μάγιστρος καὶ ὁ διέπων καὶ ὁ ἔπαρχος τῆς πολέως*, 831 A. D.; 503, 6; *ὁ τοίνυν ἐναπομείνας μετὰ τοῦ μαγίστρου καὶ τοῦ ἐπάρχου, ὁ καὶ διέπων τὴν ἐκ προσώπου τοῦ βασιλέως δουλείας ἀρχὴν Βαάνης ἦν, ὁ πατρίκιος πραιπόσιτος καὶ σακελλάριος, καθὼς τὸ παλαιὸν ἐκράτει τοῖς βασιλεῦσιν ἔθος, ἐξερχομένου τοῦ βασιλέως ἐπὶ φοσσάτον τὸν πραιπόσιτον παρεᾶν τὴν ἑαυτοῦ ἀρχῆς ἐπικράτειαν, καὶ τῷ μαγίστρῳ καὶ τῷ ἐπάρχῳ τὴν τῆς πολιτέιας καὶ τοῦ κοινοῦ τὴν διοίκησιν*; at the time of the expedition of Basil I against Tephrike, 871. On the title of this work, cf. Bury, *English Historical Review*, 1907, p. 439.

[3] *De Caer.*, 1, 48, 245, 17–20; 248, 16, 21, 24; 249, 7; Bury, *Imperial Administration*, p. 31.

[4] *De Caer.*, 2, 31.

[5] Theophanes Continuatus, 347, see below. This passage does not refer to ceremonial duties; cf. Bury, *Imperial Administration*, p. 31.

[6] *De Caer.*, 1, 43, see above.

the rest of the eighth and the first decades of the ninth century.[1] But in the reign of Michael III (842–67), their number seems to have been increased. For a time, indeed, even under this Emperor, they were apparently still restricted to two,[2] but it is possible to trace at least three, and possibly six Masters appointed by him.[3] These, with the Manuel who was Master after 842,[4] make a total of seven during this reign, more than two of whom certainly held the title of Master at the same time. Furthermore, in one of the ceremonies dating from this epoch, Masters are mentioned in such a way as to point unmistakably to the possibility of creating several at once.[5] For these reasons we may conclude that it was Michael III who first transformed the Mastership into an order of rank like the patrician dignity;[6] whereas the honorary Master of the Roman period had been *illustris*, with the specific title of *magister officiorum.*

This conversion of the Mastership into an order of rank is to be connected with the creation of the class of the ἀνθύπατοι, higher than that of the Patricians, likewise effected under Michael III;[7] the change marks important innovations in the grades of dignities made by that Emperor. Of these Masters two, the successors of the earlier pair, apparently continued to have official duties. Under Basil I, successor of Michael III, these were known as "the two Masters of State" and were entrusted with the execution of extraordinary missions.[8] One of them also, as we have seen, shared in the direction of the administration during the absence of the Emperor from Constantinople.[9] Stylianos, father-in-law of Leo VI, who appears under the title of μάγιστρος τῶν θείων ὀφφικίων,[10] was one of these Masters, enjoying the old title of the Mastership, and, at the same time, the senior in rank of all the Masters,

[1] Bury, *op. cit.*, pp. 29 ff., with a list of the references to Masters of these centuries. Also Philotheos, 727, 3: ὁ μάγιστρος, ὁ μάγιστρος. Cf. Bury, *op. cit.*, p. 32. See n. 7, p. 58.

[2] *De Caer.*, 2, 31: ἀναμεταξὺ τῶν δύο μαγίστρων.

[3] Certain are Petronas, Genesius, 97, 8: Basil, Genesius, 111, 19: and Leo Theodatakes, Nicetas, *vita Ignatii*, in Mansi, vol. XVI, p. 237. Possible are Arsaber, Theophanes Continuatus, 175; and Stephen and Bardas, *ibid.*

[4] Theophanes Continuatus, 148, 13,

[5] *De Caer.*, 1, 26, 143: εἰ μὲν κελεύει ὁ βασιλεὺς ποιῆσαι μαγίστρους, etc.; cf. Bury, *op. cit.*, p. 30.

[6] In the ceremonies of the time of Michael III the Masters appear as an order like the Patricians; cf. Bury, *op. cit.*, p. 30.

[7] Bury, *op. cit.*, p. 28.

[8] Theophanes Continuatus, 347, 6: τοῖς δυσὶ τῆς πολιτείας μαγίστροις, 347, 20, παραιτοῦνται δὲ τὴν ὑπουργίαν καὶ οἱ λαμπρότατοι μάγιστροι.

[9] περὶ τάξεων, 503, 6.

[10] *Novellae Leonis*, VI. 1, 18, etc.

as is indicated by application to him of πρωτομάγιστρος,[1] which here has the same connotation as πρωτοπατρίκιος.[2]

For the early years of the reign of Constantine VII (912–58) we know of four Masters,[3] and of five in the later period of the same Emperor's rule, all of them apparently in enjoyment of this rank at the same time.[4] Still, the total number of Masters at this epoch seems to have been less than twelve, for there were not enough of them to wear the twelve golden λῶροι at one of the ceremonies dating from this period,[5] and some of the ἀνθύπατοι had to be associated with them for this purpose. Luitprand [6] says that there were twenty-four Masters in Constantinople during his visit there in 968, but that seems an almost incredible number and his report arouses suspicion.[7]

In the tenth century there is no further evidence that any of these Masters, as such, performed active administrative duties. However, the Mastership was regularly conferred upon holders of important offices, such as Leo and Bardas Phokas, who were δομεστικοὶ σχολῶν,[8] and Romanos Saronites and Romanos Mousele, who seem to have been Strategoi.[9] Those honored with the Mastership are found, indeed, playing an active part in the administrative and military spheres, but this is due to the various offices or the special authority which they held in addition to the Mastership, and not because the title of Master involved any special services of this nature, or qualified its holder for them. It was therefore purely a dignity, and no longer an office.

Among the eighteen titles of honor conferred by the Byzantine Emperors at the close of the ninth century that of Master ranked fourteenth in the ascending order, and the Masters formed the highest class of dignitaries; the more honorable titles of Zōstē Patricia, Curopalates, Nobelissimus, and Caesar were rarely conferred upon more than one individual at the same time; in the case of the last, three at least, were usually reserved for

[1] *Vita Euthymii*, 3, 6.

[2] Theophanes, 380, 291; cf. Bury, *op. cit.*, p. 28.

[3] Theophanes Continuatus, 380, 381, 385, 388, 390; Stephanos, Johannes Eladas, Leo Phokas; 413, and 417, Nicetas.

[4] Theophanes Continuatus, 436, 459, Bardas Phokas; 443, Johannes Kurkuas, Kosmas, Romanos Saronites, Romanos Mousele.

[5] *De Caer.*, I, 24.

[6] *Antapodosis*, 6, 10.

[7] So, too, with Bury, *op. cit.*, p. 33.

[8] Theophanes Continuatus, 388: 436.

[9] Theophanes Continuatus, 443; Bury, *op. cit.*, p. 32.

members of the imperial family.[1] This remained the status of the Masters so far as we can trace the existence of this dignity.

By the tenth century the Mastership had become an hereditary dignity in certain princely families who were vassals of the Byzantine Empire. Such were the families of the princes of Armenia[2] and of Taran or Daran.[3] Says Rambaud,[4] "the court of Byzantium distributed the brevets of its court dignities in the valley of the Caucasus and Armenia, as later the court of St. Petersburg has distributed the cordons of its orders." This was a species of diplomatic flattery, destined to secure the loyalty of the local chieftains to the Byzantine throne. The title of Master, however, was only conferred upon sovereign princes and members of their families. This conferment of the Mastership was accomplished by the decoration with the Master's robe of rank, as we learn from the procedure in the case of Curcenios the Iberian, who received his title from the Emperor Romanus.[5]

From the ninth and tenth centuries we have the names of the following princes who received the Mastership in this way: Pancratios, Curcenios, a second Pancratios, grandson of the former, and Adranse, princes of Iberia;[6] George, prince of Abasgia;[7] Apasacios, son of Symbatius, prince of Apachume;[8] and Cricoricios or Gregory, prince of Taran.[9]

The same custom was followed in the eleventh century; in this period the title of Master was often conferred upon foreign princes as a reward for their submission to the authority of the Emperor. Among those who received the Mastership for this reason were Prusianos, the Bulgar, in 1017;[10] the son of George, the prince of Abasgia mentioned above, in 1022;[11] Jobanesices, ruler of Anium, under Constantine Monomachos,[12] and Karikios. under the same Emperor.[13]

1 Philotheos, 708–12; Bury, *op. cit.*, pp. 20–36.

2 Schlumberger, *Sigillographie de l'empire byzantin*, p. 532.

3 *De Caer.*, I, 24, 138; Schlumberger, *op. cit.*, p. 533; Rambaud, *L'empire grec au dixième siècle*, p. 514.

4 *Op. cit.*, p. 513.

5 Constantine Porphyrogenitus, *De administrando imperio*, 46, 208. Constans, *drungarius* of the fleet, was appointed to bestow the ἱμάτιον μαγιστράτου.

6 *De adm. imp.*, 46, 206–7.

7 *De adm. imp.*, 46, 206.

8 *De adm. imp.*, 44, 191.

9 *De adm. imp.*, 43, 185.

10 Cedrenus, II, 469, 24: (Basil II) τοῦτον μὲν μάγιστρον ἐτίμησεν; cf. 483, 6; 487, 12.

11 Cedrenus, II, 478: ὃν μάγιστρον ποιήσας ὁ βασιλεὺς ὑπέτρεψεν.

12 Cedrenus, II, 557, 8: ὁ δὲ τῆς συνέσεως τοῦτον ἀποδεξάμενος μάγιστρόν τε τιμᾷ.

13 Cedrenus, II, 559, 6: ὁ μὲν ἐς τὸν βασιλέα ἐλθὼν καὶ μάγιστρος τιμηθείς.

The purely honorary character of the Mastership at this period is clearly shown in the elevation to this dignity in 1028 of a certain Romanos, whom the Emperor Constantine VIII had caused to be deprived of his sight.[1] Nevertheless it was an honor eagerly sought for, to judge from the persistency that Erbebios, or Hervè, the Frankish mercenary in the Byzantine service, displayed in trying to secure it from the Emperor Michael VI (1056–57).[2]

The last notices of the Mastership that I have been able to discover date from the dynasty of the Comnenoi (1081–1185). Anna Comnena mentions an Alan who was a Master under her father, Alexis (1081–1118),[3] while two seals of the Magistrissa Maria,[4] and one of the Magister Christophoros,[5] belong to the late eleventh or early twelfth century. After the restoration of the Byzantine power in the new kingdom of the Paleologoi (1265–1453), the title does not appear among those of the court dignitaries.[6] It is, however, probable that the title continued to be used throughout the period between the death of Alexis Comnenos and the capture of Constantinople by the Latins in 1204.[7]

[1] Cedrenus, II, 487: *ἀνήγαγε δὲ καὶ εἰς τὸ λαμπρὸν τῶν μαγίστρων ἀξίωμα . . . ʻΡωμανὸν, ὃν ὁ Κονστάντινος . . . ἀπετύφλωσεν.*

[2] Cedrenus, II, 617, 2. Michael refused him, *παρακαλοῦντα γὰρ καὶ ἱκετεύοντα τῆς τῶν μαγίστρων τιμῆς τυχεῖν.*

[3] *Alexias*, 95: *ἠκροᾶτό τις τῶν λεγομένων, Ἄλανας τὸ γένος, μάγιστρος τὴν ἀξίαν.*

[4] Schlumberger, *Sigillographie de l'empire byzantin*, p. 532, nos. 8 and 9.

[5] Schlumberger, *op. cit.*, p. 463, no. 1.

[6] Codinus, *De officiis*, 7.

[7] The continuator of Theophanes relates (p. 72), it is true, that Michael II, about 823 A.D., unsuccessfully tried to bribe two Anatolian chieftains by offering them the rank of *magistros* (*τιμὰς μεγάλας τὰς τῶν μαγίστρων*). This would seem to indicate that it had already become a purely honorary title of rank. Such a view is not, however, supported by the evidence from Constantinople.

CHAPTER IV

THE COMPETENCE OF THE MASTER OF THE OFFICES

AFTER following the history of the Masters of the Offices through eight centuries, from the time of their establishment until their disappearance, the next step is to consider, in somewhat greater detail, the part which they played in the administration of the Empire.

As we have seen, this Office was formed by the association, in the hands of one minister, of various powers which brought under his control most widely separated branches of the administration. Consequently it is not easy to group these various functions and powers into categories. It might be possible to classify them under the heads "administrative" and "judicial," for the reason that the Master's judicial powers were but an outgrowth from, and an adjunct to, his administrative; yet it is not practicable to make such a distinction. We may freely grant that the administrative functions of the Master of the Offices fell into two general groups, according as they were concerned with the organization of the palace or with the governance of the Empire as a whole; nevertheless, the line between these two spheres of action cannot be drawn too sharply, for a great deal of the business of imperial administration was conducted through the *officia palatina*. For example, in the cases of the *scriniarii* and the *agentes in rebus*, it would be difficult to distinguish between the authority which the Master exercised over them as the person responsible for the maintaining of order and discipline among the *officiales* of the court, and the use to which he put them as his agents in fulfilling his duties as an imperial minister. Therefore, it seems most convenient to study the Master's activities so far as possible in connection with the various *officia*, or departments of the administration, over which he, in any respect whatever, exercised control.

I. The Master of the Offices and the Palace Guards

The essentially military character of the Mastership of the Offices at the time of its creation has been previously emphasized; and although the military side of his functions was soon overshadowed by the civil, the Master preserved traces of the origin of his office in retaining for a long period the command of the palace guards.

It is probable that the Master of the Offices was in command of the Scholarians from the time when they were instituted by Constantine[1] to take the place of the Pretorian Guard, which he had disbanded after the battle of Saxa Rubra (312).[2] As *tribunus et magister* the Master of the Offices was probably for some time under the orders of the Pretorian Prefect, but with the reorganization of his office and its elevation to the *comitiva* (c. 325), in this respect as elsewhere the Master was subject to none but the Emperor himself.[3]

These new palace guards comprised various corps or *scholae;* they were so called because there was assigned to them a hall, or *schola*, where they were to hold themselves in perpetual readiness for service. They were distinguished from one another by differences in equipment and personnel.[4] At first there were probably five of these corps,[5] but by the opening of the fifth century there were seven in Constantinople and five in Rome.[6] Each of the corps numbered 500 men, so that the total strength of the Scholarians at Rome was 2500, and at Constantinople 3500,[7] until Justinian, when co-Emperor with Justinus, raised the number of those at the Eastern capital by the addition of four new *scholae*, or 2000 men.[8] These latter were called supernumeraries (ὑπερ-

[1] *Codex Theodosianus*, XIV, 17, 9; Mommsen, *Hermes*, vol. 24, p. 222.

[2] Zosimus, 2, 17.

[3] See above, pp. 29, 32; Lydus, *De Mag.*, 2, 10; 3; 40.

[4] Mommsen, *Hermes*, vol. 24, pp. 222 f.

[5] Mommsen, *op. cit.*, 224.

[6] *Notitia Dignitatum or.* XI: *Scola scutariorum prima, scola scutariorum secunda, scola gentilium seniorum, scola scutariorum sagittariorum, scola scutariorum clibanariorum, scola armaturarum iuniorum, scola gentilium iuniorum*; *occ.* IX: *scolae scutariorum prima* and *secunda, armaturarum seniorum, gentilium seniorum, scutariorum tertia.*

[7] Procopius, *Historia Arcana*, 24: Ἕτεροι στρατιῶται οὐχ ἧσσους ἢ πεντακόσιοι καὶ τρισχίλιοι τὰ ἐξ ἀρχῆς ἐπὶ φυλακῇ τοῦ παλατίου κατέστησαν, οὕσπερ σχολαρίους καλοῦσιν; cf. Suidas, s. v. Σχολάριοι.

[8] *Codex Justinianus*, IV, 65, 35: *in undecim devotissimis scholis*; Procopius, *Historia Arcana*, 24: ἡνίκα τοίνυν Ἰουστῖνος τὴν βασιλείαν παρέλαβεν, οὗτος Ἰουστινίανος πολλοὺς εἰς τὴν τιμὴν κατεστήσατο ταύτην, . . . ἐπεὶ δὲ τούτοις καταλόγοις οὐδένα ἐνδεῖν τὸ λοιπὸν ᾔσθετο, ἑτέρους αὐτοῖς ἐς δισχιλίους ἐντέθεικεν, οὕσπερ ὑπεραρίθμους ἐκάλουν.

ἀριθμοι), and were afterwards disbanded by Justinian himself.[1] However, it may be that the ranks of the Palace Guards were again enlarged, for Lydus[2] gives their strength as ten thousand horse and foot.

The Scholarians were classed as regular soldiers, belonging to the *armata militia*,[3] and had all the privileges of such, but received higher pay than the rest.[4] Hence enrollment in their ranks was an honor highly esteemed and was at first granted only to soldiers who had seen actual service, preferably to Germans[5] and, later, Armenians.[6] However, from the time of Zeno the Isaurian, admission to these scholae was obtained no longer as a reward of merit, but by favor, and finally by open purchase.[7]

This brought about a complete change in the character of the guards, who were now merely an ornamental body, the members of which had secured for themselves an easy berth for life.[8] They had never been called upon to serve outside the capital, and were so utterly unqualified to take the field that, as it is reported, when Justinian threatened to send them on foreign service, they voluntarily secured exemption by a surrender of their pay.[9] At first they had been in a real sense the guards of the palace, being on duty day and night,[10] but Leo seems to have transferred a large share of these actual services to a corps of three hundred *excubi-*

[1] Procopius, *ibid.*

[2] *De Mag.*, 2, 24: τὸ γὰρ μάγιστρος ὀφφικίων ὄνομα οὐδὲν ἧττον ἡγούμενον τῶν αὐλικῶν καταλόγων σημαίνει, ἐν οἷς ἥ τε ἱππικὴ καὶ ἡ πεζομάχος δύναμις τῆς βασιλείας θεωρεῖται, εἰς μυρίους συναγομένη πολεμιστάς. This number seems suspiciously large, and lacks confirmation.

[3] *Codex Justinianus*, IV, 65, 35: *milites autem appellamus eos, qui tam sub excelsis magistris militum tolerare noscuntur militiam quam in undecim devotissimis scholis*, etc.; Agathias, 5, 15: οὗτοι δὲ στρατιῶται μὲν ὀνομάζονται, καὶ ἐγγεγράφαται τοῖς τῶν καλόγων βιβλίοις.

[4] Procopius, *Historia Arcana*, 24; cf. Suidas, *s. v.* Σχολάριοι.

[5] Mommsen, *Hermes*, vol. 24, p. 223.

[6] Agathias, 5, 15; Procopius, *Historia Arcana*, 24: τούτους οἱ πρότερον μὲν ἀριστίνδην ἀπολέξαντες ἐξ Ἀρμενίων ἐς ταύτην δὴ τὴν τιμὴν ἦγον; cf. Suidas, *loc. cit.*

[7] *Loc. cit.*

[8] Agathias, 5, 15: εἰσὶ δὲ οἱ πολλοὶ ἀστικοί τε καὶ φαιδροείμονες, καὶ μόνον, οἶμαι, ὄγκου τοῦ βασιλείου ἕνεκα καὶ τῆς ἐν ταῖς προόδοις μεγαλαυχίας ἐξευρημένοι; Mommsen, *op. cit.*, p. 225.

[9] Procopius, *Historia Arcana*, 24.

[10] Agathias, 5, 15: ἐκ τῶν ταγμάτων ἐκείνων, οἳ ἐς τὸ διημερεύειν τε καὶ διανυκτερεύειν ἐν τῇ αὐλῇ ἀπεκέκριντο, οὓς δὴ σχολαρίους ἀποκαλοῦσιν; Procopius, *De Bello Gothico*, 4, 27: τῶν ἐπὶ τοῦ παλατίου φυλακῆς τεταγμένων λόχων, οὕσπερ σχολὰς ὀνομάζουσιν; *Historia Arcana*, 24; cf. Suidas, *l.c.*; Rutilius Namatianus, *Itinerarium*, I, 563: *Officiis regerem cum regia tecta magister Armigerasque pii principis excubias.*

tores, which he created.[1] It was because the Scholarians had thus ceased to be soldiers in the true sense of the word that they were permitted to exist under the command of the Master of the Offices at the Ostrogothic court at Ravenna,[2] although under Theoderic the Romans were excluded from the profession of arms, which became a prerogative of the Gothic conquerors.

As commander of the Scholarians the Master had control over their enrollment,[3] discipline,[4] and promotion.[5] Enrollment in the *scholae* was made by the Master, but only such recruits were received as had been able to secure the imperial sanction in the form of a warrant (*probatoria*), and the Master had to see to the preparation of quarterly lists of the Scholarians, which were to be placed on file so that their *notitia* might be kept up to date and definitely known.[6]

The Master also exercised judicial authority over the Scholarians, their wives or widows, their widowed mothers, their children, in so far as the latter were not under some other judicial authority, and even their slaves, in both civil and criminal cases.[7] The Scholarians, on the other hand, enjoyed exemption from prosecution before any other than the Master's tribunal.[8] This same privilege was accorded in civil cases for the rest of their lives to Scholarians who at the end of their time of service had obtained the rank of *primicerius* and the dignity of *viri clarissimi comites*.[9] However, in criminal cases, or those in which the revenues of state were affected, these latter were subject to the jurisdiction of the provincial governors, that the plea of special privilege

[1] Lydus, *De Mag.*, I, 16: καὶ ὁ Λέων δὲ ὁ βασιλεὺς πρῶτος τοὺς λεγομένους ἐκσκουβίτωρας τῶν παρεξόδων τοῦ παλατίου φύλακας προστησάμενος τριακοσίους μόνους ἐστράτευσε; Mommsen, *Hermes*, vol. 24, p. 225.

[2] Cassiodorus, *Variae*, 6, 6: *ipse insolentium scholarum mores procellos moderationis suae terminis prospere disserenat.*

[3] *Codex Justinianus*, XII, 33, 5; I, 31, 5 (527).

[4] Cassiodorus, *Variae*, 6, 6; *Codex Justinianus*, XII, 29, 1.

[5] *Codex Theodosianus*, VII, 1, 14 (394); this can only refer to the Scholarians, as they alone among the *viri militares* were subject to the orders of the Master.

[6] *Codex Justinianus*, I, 31, 5.

[7] *Codex Justinianus*, XII, 29, 3 (Zeno): *Quotiens super causa civili vel etiam criminali ex sententia videlicet iudicii tui culminis, scholares vel eorum conjuges, sive adhuc vivent mariti sive post mortem eorum in viduitate constitutae sunt, matresve eorum in viduitate permanentes aut liberi, qui non specialiter alterius iudicis iurisdictioni subiectam conditionem sortiti sunt, et servi ad eos pertinentes conveniuntur.*

[8] *Codex Justinianus*, XII, 26, 2 (443–4): *Ad exemplum itaque devotissimorum scholariorum nulli licere memoratos ad aliud iudicium trahere.*

[9] *Codex Justinianus*, XII, 29, 2 (474).

might not result in danger to the public interest.[1] At all times the Master might delegate his judicial authority over the Scholarians to other officials, such as the judges in the provinces.[2]

Each of the *scholae* had its own commander, at first a *tribunus*, later regularly a *comes*,[3] who was naturally subordinate to the Master of the Offices. Theophanes, for 554 A.D., mentions that in that year the Scholarians mutinied against a *comes* who was in authority over the whole guard.[4] Such an officer would at that time have been a second in command to the Master of the Offices. However, as there is elsewhere no trace whatever of the presence of this *comes*, we are obliged to agree with Bury[5] that Theophanes misunderstood his source and that under the Master were no *comites* except those in command of the separate *scholae*.

By the middle of the eighth century the Master had been relieved of his military authority over the Scholarians; a new commander had been given them, the δομεστικὸς τῶν σχολῶν, whose office had originated in that of the Domesticus of the Master.[6]

II. The Master of the Offices and the *Officia Palatina*

The term *officia palatina*, in its widest sense, covers all persons employed in the various branches of the court service, *qui in sacro palatio militant*.[7] Of these, such as were members of the departments of the Counts of the Sacred Largesses and the Privy Purse were in no way subject to the Master of the Offices.[8]

Among the rest, those who were engaged in rendering menial services about the imperial person, *i.e.* all included under the general name *cubicularii*, were the subordinates of the Grand Chamberlain;[9] while those who performed similar duties in con-

[1] *Codex Justinianus*, XII, 29, 2 (474).

[2] *Codex Justinianus*, XII, 29, 3, 3: *Quotiens sane apud viros clarissimos provinciarum moderatores, ex delegatione scilicet sententiae tuae magnitudinis, contra viros fortissimos vel eorum coniuges vel liberos vel servos cognitio celebretur.*

[3] *Codex Theodosianus*, VI, 13, 1 = *Codex Justinianus*, XII, 11, 1: *de comitibus et tribunis scholarum; Codex Justinianus*, XII, 29, 1; Constantine Porphyrogenitus, *De Caer.*, 1, 84.

[4] Theophanes, 366, 3: ἐπανέστησαν αἱ σχολαὶ τῷ κόμητι αὐτῶν.

[5] *Imperial Administration*, p. 50, n. 2.

[6] Theophanes, 684 (767 A.D.); cf. p. 105 below.

[7] *Codex Justinianus*, XII, 28, 1; 2.

[8] *Codex Justinianus*, XII, 23.

[9] In later times Chamberlains, for the Augusta as well as the Augustus, had a *praepositus sacri cubiculi*. *Codex Justinianus*, XII, 5, 5 (Anastasius).

nection with the maintenance of the imperial household, *i.e.*, the so-called *castrensiani* and *ministeriani*, were at the disposal of the Castrensis or Steward of the Palace, later known as the Curopalates.[1] In the execution of their duties therefore the *cubicularii* were subject to the orders of the Grand Chamberlain and the *castrensiani* to the Steward, while neither were in this respect under the authority of the Master of the Offices. However, in so far as matters of discipline were concerned, and also in questions relating to the organization of their *officia*, both these classes of *officiales palatini* appear to have come under the Master's supervision.[2] It was for this reason that the Master had judicial authority over them. As we have seen, in the course of the fifth century this jurisdiction became exclusive; the members of these *officia* receiving, like the Scholarians, the privilege of answering all charges in the Master's court alone, to prevent any long interference with the performance of their regular duties which would result from their being haled before outside tribunals. This privilege was also extended in various cases to the families of these *officiales*. Leo and Anthemius decreed that the *cubicularii* of both the Emperor and the Empress should be prosecuted only in the Master's court,[3] and the same rulers bestowed a like privilege upon the members of the *schola sacrae vestis*, their mothers and their wives, in both civil and criminal suits.[4] In 474 this right was extended to the *ministeriani* in general,[5] and later Zeno

1 *Notitia Dignitatum or.* XVII; *occ.* XV. The title *curopalates* gradually supplanted that of *castrensis* in the course of the fifth century; cf. Hartmann, Pauly-Wissowa, vol. 3, pp. 1770–1.

2 Cassiodorus, *Variae*, 6, 6: *Ad eum nimirum palatii pertinet disciplina;* Rutilius Namatianus, 1, 563: *officiis regerem cum regia tecta magister; Codex Justinianus*, XII, 33, 5, where the Master is instructed to prevent the same persons serving in several *officia* or *scrinia*, the duties of which were not closely related; cf. the title *magister officiorum omnium*, Dessau, *Inscriptiones Selectae*, 1244.

3 *Codex Justinianus*, XII, 5, 3: *Cubicularios tam sacri cubiculi mei quam venerabilis Augustae, quos utrosque certum est obsequiis occupatos et aulae penetralibus inhaerentes diversa iudicia obire non posse, ab observatione aliorum tribunalium liberamus, ut in sublimitatis solummodo tuae iudicio propositas adversus se excipiant actiones.*

4 *Codex Justinianus*, XII, 25, 3: *Ii qui in schola vestis sacrae militant vel matres eorum vel uxores criminalem vel civilem litem contra se commovendam in nullo alio nisi in sublimitatis tuae suscipiant examine.*

5 *Codex Justinianus*, XII, 25, 4: *Ante omnia nullius penitus alterius iudicis minoris vel maioris sacro ministerio nostro deputatos, quorum officia singillatim brevis subter adnexus continet, nisi a tuae dumtaxat magnitudinis sententiis conveniri, ut in nullo penitus alterius iudicis foro pulsantium nisi in tuae tantummodo amplitudinis examine praebeant aliquando responsum.*

forbade the prosecution of a *silentiarius* or his wife on civil or criminal charges before any other judicial authority.[1]

It seems that the *notarii*, or court stenographers and secretaries, whose duties included the keeping of the record of proceedings in the *consistorium* and the care of the *notitia dignitatum et administrationum tam militarium quam civilium*,[2] formed another group of officials whose activities did not fall under the direction of the Master, but whose *matricula* came under his supervision. At least such appears to be the implication of a constitution of Zeno,[3] addressed to a Master of the Offices, containing regulations for the length of service of the *notarii*, their order of seniority, and the honors bestowed on them at the expiration of their term of service.

Further, the *referendarii*, who were appointed from the *tribuni notarii*,[4] and whose duties it was to present petitions to the Emperor, to transmit imperial answers to the requests of officials and to convey unwritten orders of the Emperor to judges both in the capital and in the provinces,[5] came under the supervision of the Master to the same extent as the *notarii* themselves.[6]

A similar relation with the Master of the Offices may be claimed for the *schola* of the *stratores*, whose services were employed in connection with the selection of horses for the imperial stables.[7] The services of the *stratores* were also under the Master's judicial authority, as we learn from a letter of Symmachus,[8] dating from 384–85, dealing with a case where a Master had claimed for his jurisdiction a *strator*, whose appeal from the court of the governor of Apulia was brought before the Urban Prefect. This is the earliest reference to the exercise of judicial functions by the Master of the Offices.

[1] *Codex Justinianus*, XII, 16, 4: *Ne ad diversa tracti viri devoti silentiarii iudicia sacris abstrahi videantur obsequiis, iubemus eos qui quemlibet devotissimorum silentiariorum scholae vel eius uxorem civiliter vel etiam criminaliter pulsare maluerint, minime eum ex cuiuslibet alterius iudicio nisi ex iudicio tantummodo viri excellentissimi magistri officiorum conveniri.*

[2] Karlowa, *Römische Rechtsgeschichte*, vol. 1, p. 845.

[3] *Codex Justinianus*, XII, 7, 2.

[4] *De Caer.*, 1, 86.

[5] Bury, *Magistri scriniorum*, ἀντιγραφῆς and ῥεφερενδάριοι, *Harvard Studies in Classical Philology*, vol. XXI, pp. 27–9.

[6] *Novellae Justiniani*, 10 (535).

[7] *Codex Theodosianus*, VI, 31, 1 (365–73?) = *Codex Justinianus*, XII, 24, 1; *Cod. Theod.*, VIII, 8, 4 = *Cod. Just.* XII, 59, 3; Ammianus, 30, 5; Gothofredus, *Cod. Theod.*, vol. 2, p. 224.

[8] *Relationes*, [10], 38, 4: *Venatium, quem v. c. et inlustris officiorum magister iusserat exhiberi, censui agenti in rebus, Decentio, quo prosequente venerat, esse reddendum.*

We now come to those *officia* which, not only in matters pertaining to organization, discipline, and jurisdiction, but also in the active execution of their duties, came to a greater or less extent under the Master's direction. These *officia* comprised the *agentes in rebus*, the *admissionales*, the *cancellarii*, the *decani*, the *lampadarii*, the *mensores*, and the *scrinium memoriae*, *scrinium epistularum*, *scrinium libellorum*, and *scrinium dispositionum*.

The *admissionales*, or *officium admissionum*, are placed at the Master's disposal in the *Notitia Dignitatum*.[1] They were a corps of court ushers, which had developed under the Principate and had been carried over into the Empire, where its importance was enhanced owing to the increased attention paid to the details of court ceremonial.[2] Its immediate chief was at first the *magister admissionum*,[3] who by the sixth century had acquired the title of *comes admissionum*.[4] This *officium* assisted the Master of the Offices in the direction of the receptions and audiences, and must have been subject to his jurisdiction as well as to his orders in general.

The *cancellarii* in the immediate service of the Emperor are mentioned only in the *Notitia* for the Occident, as being under the Master's orders.[5] However, as has been noted,[6] it is altogether likely that there was a similar body under the Eastern Master.

The *decani* do not appear in either *Notitia* but their *schola* was under the Master's supervision as early as 416,[7] and in 434[8] (?) they were made subject to the sole jurisdiction of his court.

The *lampadarii* are named in the oriental *Notitia*[9] only, but a constitution of Valentinian III,[10] 450 A.D., shows that in the West their *schola* was wholly under the Master's control and that regulations affecting its organization were issued in accordance with his recommendations.

All these *officia* performed duties of so humble a character that it would be impossible to expect a greater amount of information regarding them in their relation to the Master of the Offices. However, from the few notices that occur it is quite

[1] *Notitia Dignitatum or.* XI, 17: *occ.* IX, 14.

[2] *Codex Theodosianus*, VI, 35, 3 (319); cf. *Codex Justinianus*, XII, 1, 3; Seeck, Pauly-Wissowa, vol. 1, p. 382; *Harvard Studies in Classical Philology*, vol. XXVI, pp. 110 ff.

[3] Ammianus, 15, 5, 18; *Codex Theodosianus*, VI, 2, 23.

[4] *De Caer.*, 1, 84: κόμης ἀδμηνσιόνων.

[5] *Notitia Dignitatum occ.* IX, 15.

[6] P. 38.

[7] *Codex Theodosianus*, VI, 33, 1; cf. *Codex Justinianus*, XII, 26, 1.

[8] *Codex Justinianus*, XII, 26, 2.

[9] *Notitia Dignitatum, or.* XI, 12.

[10] *Novellae Valentiniani*, 30.

evident that both administratively and judicially they were entirely under his control.

The *scrinium dispositionum* differed widely from the other three *scrinia* both in the character of its activities and with regard to the officials who directed them. Consequently it can be given separate consideration. This bureau was organized about the middle of the fourth century,[1] and from its establishment was probably under the control of the Master of the Offices, as were the older *scrinia* at that time. In the *Notitia*[2] it appears *sub dispositione eius*, and, like the other *scrinia*, was subject to his disciplinary and judicial authority.[3] The immediate chief of this *scrinium* was originally called the *magister dispositionum*,[4] later the *comes dispositionum*,[5] but in rank he was only the equal of the *proximi* of the other *scrinia*.[6] There is no trace of this official having an independent sphere of action, or of his being under the authority of any other than the Master of the Offices.

The duty of the *scrinium dispositionum* was to prepare the program of imperial business and engagements, especially that part of it which concerned the number and routes of the imperial journeys, and possibly the lists of those to be summoned to court receptions of various kinds.[7] In the Byzantine period, the official known as the ὁ ἐπὶ τῆς καταστάσεως, who from the ninth century played the part of a Master of Ceremonies at the court, seems to have been the older *comes dispositionum* with a new title, emancipated from the Master's control.[8] He was at that time the superior of the ἀδμηνσουνάλιος,[9] who was probably the same as the κόμης ἀδμηνσιόνων,[10] formerly also, as head of the *officium admissionum*, under the Master's orders.

There remain for consideration the *agentes in rebus*, the *mensores*, and the *scrinia sacrae memoriae*, *epistularum*, and *libellorum*. The question of their connection with the Master of

[1] The first mention is in *Codex Theodosianus*, VI, 21, 6 (362).

[2] *Notitia Dignitatum or.* XI. 16; *occ.* IX, 11.

[3] *Codex Justinianus*, XII, 19, 11 (Anastasius), cf. XII, 19, 7 (443–44), and other constitutions concerning all the *scrinia*.

[4] *Codex Theodosianus*, VI, 26, 2 (381).

[5] *Codex Theodosianus*, VI, 2, 23 (414).

[6] *Codex Theodosianus*, VI, 26, 2 (381).

[7] Gothofredus on *Cod. Theod.*, VI, 26, 1; Schiller, *Geschichte der römischen Kaiserzeit*, vol. 2, p. 103; Karlowa, *Romische Rechtsgeschichte*, vol. 1, p. 836; Seeck, Pauly-Wissowa, vol. 4, p. 647.

[8] Bury, *Imperial Administration*, pp. 118–9.

[9] *De Caer.*, 800, 8; 805, 4.

[10] *De Caer.*, 386, 25. It is perhaps this *comes* who appears in Lydus, *De Mag.*, 2, 17, under the name of ἀδμισσιονάλιος.

the Offices involves a somewhat lengthy discussion; separate sections have therefore been assigned to them in this chapter. In general, the Master's authority over these *officia* was very similar to that which he exercised over those just mentioned, including disciplinary and judicial powers as well as the direction of a considerable part of their active duties.

We are now in a position to appreciate the meaning of Cassiodorus, when in his Formula of the Master's office [1] he wrote with reference to the latter's control of the *officia palatina* : *Tam multi ordines sine confusione aliqua componuntur, et ipse sustinet onus omnium quod habet turba discretum ;* adding, in allusion to his judicial authority over them, as well as over others, *causarum praeterea maximum pondus in eius audientiae finibus optima securitate reponimus.*

With the gradual diminution of his power in the course of the seventh and eighth centuries [2] the Master saw the control of the *officia palatina* transferred to other hands, until in the ninth century he exercised no authority whatever over them.

III. The Master of the Offices and the *Agentes in Rebus*

The *schola* of the *agentes in rebus* was probably established by Diocletian [3] to take the place of the so-called *frumentarii* of the Principate, whom he had abolished,[4] although the earliest notice of the Agentes occurs in a constitution of Constantine I, dating from 319.[5] The *frumentarii* were originally soldiers sent into the provinces to supervise the transportation of grain for the provisioning of the army (*frumentum militare*), but had developed into secret agents of the imperial administration, having also under their care the *cursus publicus* or State Post.[6] These latter were the duties that fell to the lot of the Agentes.

The *schola* of the Agentes was a large one. At first, apparently, their number was not definitely limited, but could be augmented at the pleasure of those in control as administrative needs

[1] *Variae*, 6, 6.

[2] See pp. 50–53.

[3] Hirschfeld, *Die Agentes in Rebus, Sitzungsberichte der Berliner Akademie*, 1893, p. 422.

[4] Aurelius Victor, *Caesares*, 39, 44 : *remoto pestilenti frumentariorum genere, quorum nunc agentes rerum simillimi sunt ;* Hieronymus, *in Abdiam*, 1, *Eos enim quos nunc agentes in rebus vel veredarios appellant, veteres frumentarios nominabant ;* Lydus, *De Mag.*, 2, 26.

[5] *Codex Theodosianus*, VI, 35, 3 fin.

[6] Fiebiger, Pauly-Wissowa, vol. 7, pp. 122 f.

might require. However, the Emperor Julian, in the interests of the provincials,[1] reduced their number to seventeen. This restriction probably was effective only until the end of his reign, for in 430 the authorized number, *statuti*, of Agentes on the roll of the *schola* was eleven hundred and seventy-four.[2] In the time of Leo[3] it had been increased to twelve hundred and forty-eight, and besides these there was a long waiting list of *supernumerarii* ready to fill any vacancies that might occur in the ranks of the regulars. The Agentes were looked upon as soldiers; they were dressed and organized as a military corps, and were divided into five grades, with regular promotion from the lowest to the highest.[4]

The supervision and direction of the Agentes at the outset was certainly in the hands of the Pretorian Prefect, but under Constantine it was transferred to the Master of the Offices,[5] whose connection with this *schola* was maintained so long as he continued to be an active administrative official. According to the *Notitia Dignitatum* the Master had under his control both the *schola* at the court and its deputies on special service elsewhere.[6]

At first, apparently, the Master controlled admissions to the *schola*;[7] but in 399[8] the sanction of the Emperor, which probably had been ordinarily obtained before, became an essential requisite for those who desired to be enrolled among the Agentes, and, once granted, this permit could not be cancelled. However, the right of nominating to the *schola* had been granted to certain officials and to Agentes who had obtained the rank of *princeps*.[9] This privilege was not expressly revoked, but the nominations thus made had now to receive the imperial approval. Neglect of the regulation put into force in 399 probably caused Leo to reaffirm the necessity of securing an imperial *probatoria* for admission to service with the Agentes.[10]

[1] Seeck, *Geschichte des Untergangs der antiken Welt*, vol. 2, p. 103.

[2] *Codex Theodosianus*, VI, 27, 23.

[3] *Codex Justinianus*, XII, 20, 3.

[4] Hirschfeld, *op. cit.*, pp. 422 f.; Seeck, Pauly-Wissowa, vol. 1, pp. 776 f.

[5] Lydus, *De Mag.*, 2, 10; 26; cf. pp. 29–34. The earliest proof of the Master's control dates from 359; *Codex Theodosianus*, I, 9, 1.

[6] *Schola agentum in rebus et deputati eiusdem scholae*, *Notitia Dignitatum or.* XI, *occ.* IX.

[7] *Cod. Theod.*, I, 9, 1 (359); VI, 27, 3 (380); Seeck, Pauly-Wissowa, vol. 1, p. 776.

[8] *Cod. Theod.*, VI, 27, 11: *Consultissima definitione statuimus, ut executionem agentis in rebus inconsultis nobis nemo mereatur, concessam vero quispiam revocare non audeat.*

[9] *Codex Theodosianus*, VI, 27, 8 (396), not repeated in *Codex Justinianus*.

[10] *Cod. Just.*, XII, 20, 3 fin.: *Nemo autem sine divali probatoria, quam codices in sacro nostro scrinio memoriae positi debeant inserendam accipere, militaribus eiusdem devotissimae scholae stipendiis vel privilegiis potiatur.*

The task of removing from the roll of the Agentes the names of such persons as had illegally succeeded in having themselves entered thereon, was upon several occasions undertaken by the Master at the Emperor's orders.[1] Such purgings involved the right of dismissal by the Master, and apparently he possessed such power until 415, when this privilege was withdrawn,[2] and the right of sanctioning dismissals as well as admissions was reserved for the Emperor alone, and the Master required a special warrant before removing any one from the *schola*.[3]

The *matricula*, or accredited roll of the Agentes, was placed by an imperial warrant under the care of the Master, whose duty it likewise was to inquire into the degree of efficiency and assiduity possessed by the various members of the *schola*, so that in conferring promotions and honors the preference might be given to those who had exhibited the greatest industry and capacity.[4] Promotion within the *schola* was thus under his supervision; although advancement was regularly made on the basis of seniority,[5] there was an opportunity for preferment upon the Master's recommendation. In exceptional cases promotion out of the regular order might be made by special sanction of the Emperor,[6] which was usually granted on the recommendation of a majority of the *schola*.[7] Such a recommendation was originally required in the appointment of the *adiutor* of the Master, who was regarded as the head of the *schola*, but later the Master was left freedom of choice subject to the imperial confirmation.[8]

[1] *Cod. Theod.*, I, 9, 1 (359): *Universi, qui indignis natalibus et conversatione deterrima ad scholam agentum in rebus adspiraverunt vel translati sunt, cognoscente v. c. comite et magistro officiorum vestro consortio secernantur.* Cf. also VI, 27, 17 (415); 18 (416); 23, 1 (430).

[2] *Cod. Theod.*, VI, 27, 17: *Merito magnificentia tua concessam sibi pridem a nostra maiestate licentiam pro removendis his, quorum consortio agentum in rebus schola laborabat, ad nostram denuo auctoritatem credidit revocandam. Nulli igitur posthac sine nostrae maiestatis auctoritate discingendi agentem in rebus, nulli eximendi pateat copia*; cf. *Cod. Just.*, XII, 20, 2. Seeck thinks that this constitution applied to the East only, and that the Master had lost the right of dismissal in the West in 399 (Pauly-Wissowa, I, 777 on *Cod. Theod.*, VI, 27, 11). However, in that year it was only ordered that the Master could not reject a candidate for admission who had secured an imperial *probatoria*.

[3] *Codex Theodosianus*, VI, 27, 18.

[4] *Cod. Theod.*, I, 9, 3 (405): *Magnificentia tua matriculam scholae agentum in rebus ex nostra auctoritate tractabit atque perficiet*; VI, 27, 23; *Cod. Just.*, XII, 20, 3 (Leo).

[5] *Cod. Theod.*, I, 9, 1 = *Cod. Just.*, I, 31, 1; *Cod. Theod.*, I, 9, 2 = *Cod. Just.*, I, 31, 2; *Cod. Theod.*, VI, 27, 20; 21; 14 = *Cod. Just.*, XII, 20, 1.

[6] *Codex Theodosianus*, VI, 27, 3; 7; 9; 19.

[7] *Codex Theodosianus*, VI, 27, 4; 28, 8; 29, 4.

[8] Compare *Codex Theodosianus*, I, 9, 1 and *Codex Justinianus*, I, 31, 1.

There was evidently a considerable tendency to attempt to gain undeserved promotion by the use of influence or other illegitimate means, for numerous constitutions were published to check this evil.[1]

The Master, being in control of the *deputati* of the *schola*, had to see that the Agentes despatched on public business to the provinces, or granted leave of absence for a fixed period, did not overstay their time limit.[2]

The general supervision of the *schola*, with the duty of enforcing the imperial regulations regarding it and of making suggestions for a more efficient administration, rested with the Master.[3] His *adiutor* and *subadiuvae* might also be held responsible in case of transgression of the rules of the *schola*.[4] These rules were not always very strictly observed if we may judge from the necessity which the Emperors felt of issuing edicts at frequent intervals to enforce obedience to them. The honors and privileges of the Agentes were likewise safeguarded by the Master of the Offices.[5]

He also exercised judicial authority over them, and, from the time of Leo,[6] all Agentes of the rank of *ducenarius* or *centenarius*, while in the city of Constantinople, had the privilege of answering all civil and criminal charges in the court of the Master or his representative. This right was also extended to the *subadiuvae*, who, however, lost it on the expiry of their term of office unless they had attained the rank of *centenarii*. But all *centenarii* while in the provinces were subject to the regular judicial authorities, unless they were entrusted with the performance of public business.

Turning from the organization of the *schola* to consider its activities, we find that a great part of these consisted in the execution of the Emperor's commands, the delivery of imperial documents, and the providing of escorts at the imperial pleasure. In short, the Agentes might be called upon to undertake any service that the Emperor desired to be performed. From their duties as

[1] *Codex Theodosianus*, I, 9, 1 and 2; VI, 29, 4; VI, 27, 14 = *Codex Justinianus*, XII, 20, 1, etc.

[2] *Codex Theodosianus*, VI, 27, 15 (412).

[3] *Codex Theodosianus*, VI, 27, 23 (430): *Cuncta, quae super agentum in rebus militia ordine loco numero statuisti, amplectimur; Cod. Just.*, XII, 20, 3 (Leo).

[4] *Codex Theodosianus*, VI, 27, 3.

[5] *Codex Theodosianus*, VI, 27, 20 (426); *Codex Justinianus*, XII, 20, 5 (Leo); 9 (Anastasius).

[6] *Codex Justinianus*, XII, 20, 4.

despatch-riders they were sometimes called in Greek ἀγγελιαφόροι. They had further to bring in reports on whatever occurrences or conditions in the provinces appeared to them to be worth while making known to the central government, thus playing the part of an imperial secret service.[1]

It was also the Agentes who supplied the annual inspectors of the public post, who, as *deputati* of this *schola*, came under the immediate supervision of the Master of the Offices.[2] The relation of these inspectors to the Master will be discussed in greater detail in a subsequent section. The Agentes likewise provided the Master with his special staff or *officium*, which will also be given separate consideration.

From the highest grade of the Agentes, the *ducenarii*, were selected the *principes* or heads of the *officia* both of the Prefects and the most important civil governors in both the Orient and the Occident, as well as of the military governors in the Orient.[3] In the Gothic kingdom of Theoderic in Italy the *comites* and *duces* also received their *principes officii* from the *officium* of the Master of the Offices,[4] in obvious imitation of the practice in the Orient. In the case of officials of the rank of *illustris*, the *principes* ceased to be members of the *schola* of the Agentes and came completely under the authority of the officers over whose bureaus they were placed. With the *spectabiles*, however, the *principes* continued to be regarded merely as *deputati* of the *schola* and remained to a certain extent under the supervision of the Master of the Offices.[5] Through these *principes* the court could keep a strict watch over the actions of the provincial governors and had an official spy permanently in attendance upon each.[6]

Finally, the Agentes were at the Master's disposal for employment on any special mission which he desired to have undertaken. An instance of this character was the despatch, in 384 A.D., of an Agens by the Master of the Offices to the Urban Prefect to

[1] Seeck, Pauly-Wissowa, vol. 1, pp. 778–9; *Geschichte des Untergangs der antiken Welt*, vol. 2, pp. 102–4.

[2] *Codex Theodosianus*, VI, 29, 2; Lydus, *De Mag.*, 2, 10.

[3] *Notitia Dignitatum or.* XXI–XXIX, XXXI–XXXVI; *occ.* XVIII–XXIII; *Cod. Theod.*, VI, 28 = *Cod. Just.*, XII, 21, *de principibus agentum in rebus; Novellae Valentiniani*, 28; Karlowa, *Römische Rechtsgeschichte*, vol. 1, p. 882.

[4] Cassiodorus, *Variae*, 7, 24; 25; Mommsen, *Neues Archiv*, vol. 14, p. 504.

[5] *Novellae Valentiniani*, 28 (449); *Cod. Just.*, XII, 21, 4; 6; 8 (484): *viros clarissimos eiusdem scholae principes;* Mommsen, *op. cit.*, pp. 475 ff.

[6] Seeck, *op. cit.*, vol. 2, p. 96.

demand the person of a *strator* who had been brought before an ordinary court but who was claimed for the Master's jurisdiction.[1]

Thus it was through his position as chief of the Agentes that the Master became in a certain sense the head of the imperial intelligence office and, owing to his consequent possession of the secrets of state, one of the most influential personages at the court.

The peculiarly close relation between the Master and the Agentes is evidenced by the name *magisteriani*, which was given to the members of this *schola*,[2] and which appears frequently in Greek as *μαγιστριανοί*.[3] It would seem as though the whole *schola* was regarded as forming a larger *officium* of the Master of the Offices.[4]

It is questionable whether the Agentes were in existence in the Ostrogothic Kingdom in Italy. Mommsen[5] identified with them the *comitiaci* or *comitiani*, who appear there as a special corps for the execution of royal orders of various kinds. However, Seeck[6] has advanced good reasons for believing that these *comitiaci* had their origin in the *officiales* of the *comites et magistri militum* rather than in the Agentes of the Master of the Offices. He points out that the title *comes* in the fifth century was employed with ever increasing rarity by the *magister officiorum*, whereas it continued to be a favorite designation of the *magistri militum*, and the important position which these Masters of the Soldiery occupied at that time in the Empire of the West would warrant their *officiales* assuming a position very similar to that held by the Agentes in the East. If this latter view is accepted, we must admit that the Agentes had been displaced altogether by these *comitiaci*, as indeed seems probable, for the *comitiaci* were in direct dependence upon the royal authority and not under the Master's orders.[7] Further, the creation of the distinctly Gothic corps of the *saiones*, whose duties also corresponded to those of the Agentes, might have removed the necessity for the continuance of that *schola*.

[1] Symmachus, *Relationes*, [10], 38.

[2] Du Cange, *Glossarium*, s. v.; Seeck, Pauly-Wissowa, vol. 1, p. 776.

[3] Lydus, *De Mag.*, 3, 7; 12, etc.; Du Cange, *op. cit.*, *loc. cit.*

[4] Evidence lies in the regulations affecting the Agentes in the title *de officio magistri officiorum*, *Cod. Theod.*, I, 9, 1; 2; 3; *Cod. Just.*, I, 31, 1; 2.

[5] *Neues Archiv*, vol. 14, pp. 469–72.

[6] Pauly-Wissowa, vol. 4, pp. 715–6.

[7] Seeck, *op. cit.*, *loc. cit.*

In the Empire of the East the Agentes continued in the same relations with the Master of the Offices until the eighth century,[1] but with his loss of control over the post and other branches of the administration in that and the following century, his need of an *officium* ceased, and his connection with the Agentes had no further warrant. And the *schola* of the Agentes, at least under its old name and organization, does not appear either in the *Kletorologion* of Philotheos of the ninth century, or in the list of Byzantine Court Offices compiled by Codinus Curopalates in the twelfth.

IV. The Master of the Offices and the *Cursus Publicus*

Up to the time of Constantine the Great, the *cursus publicus*, or state post, an establishment created under the Principate for the rapid conveyance of imperial despatches and persons travelling on state business throughout the Empire, had been under the supervision of officers called *praefecti vehiculorum*,[2] roughly 'Superintendents of stage service,' subject to the control of the Pretorian Prefects. These *praefecti vehiculorum* were chosen from among the *memoriales* and other *palatini*.[3] But as early as the reign of Constantius[4] they had been supplanted by *praepositi cursus publici*, who from the first were popularly known as *curagendarii* or *curiosi*,[5] so called, Lydus[6] explains, because it was their duty to inspect the *evectiones*, or passes, which entitled their holders to make use of the post service. This popular designation, *curiosi*, had, by 381 at least, been adopted as an official title.[7]

Now the *praefecti vehiculorum* had been subordinates of the Pretorian Prefects, but the *curiosi* were sent out from the corps of the *agentes in rebus*,[8] and the members of any other *officia* were

[1] Cf. the use of μαγιστριανός as late as 705 A.D., by Constantine Porphyrogenitus, *De adm. imp.*, c. 32. Cf. Hirschfeld, *Sitzungsberichte der Berliner Akademie*, 1893, p. 440.

[2] *Codex Theodosianus*, VIII, 5, 4, 1 (326); Seeck, Pauly-Wissowa, vol. 4, p. 1859.

[3] Gothofredus, *Paratit.* to *Cod. Theod.*, VI, 29.

[4] *C. I. L.*, X, 7200: DUCENARIUS AGENS IN REB(us) ET P(rae)P(ositus) CURSUS PUBLICI (340–50); cf. Hirschfeld, *op. cit.*, 1893, p. 432; *Cod. Theod.*, VI, 29, 9.

[5] *Ii, quos curagenda(ri)os sive curiosos provincialium consuetudo appellat*, *Cod. Theod.*, VI, 29, 1 (355).

[6] *De Mag.*, 2, 10; cf. *Cod. Theod.*, VI, 29, 2 (357); 29, 8 = *Just.*, XII, 22, 2.

[7] *Codex Theodosianus*, VI, 29, 6; cf. VI, 29, 10 (412); 11 (414).

[8] *C. I. L.*, X, 7200, quoted above; *Cod. Theod.*, VI, 29, 2 (357): *Agentes in rebus in curis agendis et evectionibus publici cursus inspiciendis*; 29, 6; 29, 8: *Agentes in rebus singulos per singulas provincias mi(tten)dos esse censemus.*

strictly forbidden to attempt to act in this capacity.[1] And since, as we have seen, the Agentes were under the direction of the Master of the Offices, it followed that the supervision of the use of the passes was now transferred from the Prefects' to the Master's sphere of duties.[2]

The selection of the *curiosi* to be sent into the provinces was directed by the Master of the Offices.[3] They were chosen according to seniority within the ranks of their *schola* and with the approval of their fellows,[4] were appointed on the anniversary of the Emperor's birthday, and remained in this service for one year only.[5] During this time they acted under the Master's order.[6] In 357, two of these inspectors were despatched to each province,[7] but later one was considered sufficient.[8] However, this restriction, which had been imposed in 395, was cancelled in 412,[9] and an older custom was once more adopted, whereby an indefinite number of *curiosi* could be sent into the various districts where their presence was required. But finally a return was made to the provision of the edict of 395 limiting the number to one inspector for every province,[10] although it is uncertain at what date it was again enforced.

This limitation upon the number of the inspectors was probably intended to safeguard the interests of the provincials, whose oppression by *curiosi* from the *schola* of the Agentes caused the exclusion of the latter from Africa[11] and Dalmatia.[12] However, it may well be that the *curiosi* thus excluded from the provinces mentioned were not *curiosi cursus publici* but *curiosi litorum*,[13] members of the corps of the Agentes sent on special service to various ports and harbors, for the name *curiosi* was used for Agentes in other business than the supervision of the post.[14] In

[1] *Codex Theodosianus*, VI, 29, 2 = *Justinianus*, XII, 22, 2: *ideoque solos agentes in rebus in hoc genere iussimus obsequium adhibere et non ab alio penitus officio.*

[2] Cf. Lydus, *De Mag.*, 2, 10; 26; 3, 40; also pp. 34–35 above.

[3] *Codex Theodosianus*, VI, 29, 6; 8.

[4] *Codex Theodosianus*, VI, 29, 4 (359).

[5] *Op. cit.*, VI, 29, 6 (381).

[6] *Codex Theodosianus*, VI, 29, 10 (412): *curiosis ex viri inl(ustris) comitis et magistri officiorum iudicio dirigendis.*

[7] *Codex Theodosianus*, VI, 29, 2, 1 (357).

[8] *Codex Theodosianus*, VI, 29, 8 (395): *Agentes in rebus singulos per singulas provincias mi(tten)dos esse censemus.*

[9] *Codex Theodosianus*, VI, 29, 10.

[10] *Codex Justinianus*, XII, 22, 4.

[11] *Codex Theodosianus*, VI, 29, 11 (414), extended by *Novellae Valentiniani*, 13, 7 (445) to Numidia and Mauretania Sitifensis.

[12] *Codex Theodosianus*, XII, (415).

[13] So in *Novellae Valentiniani*, 13, 7.

[14] Hirschfeld, *Sitzungsberichte der Berliner Akademie*, 1893, p. 440. Hudemann. *Geschichte des römischen Postwesens*, p. 95, holds that they were *curiosi cursus publici*.

support of this view it may be urged that the exactions which caused the exclusion of the *curiosi* in question are hardly in accord with the powers of those engaged in the service of the state post, which since 395 [1] had been strictly limited to the inspection of passes.

The burden of supporting the establishment of the *cursus publicus* fell upon the provincials of the districts which it traversed; in consequence, the oversight of its maintenance rested with the provincial governors and their superior, the Pretorian Prefect, and not with the Master of the Offices.[2] In the Eastern Empire this arrangement was still in force under Justinian,[3] but in the Ostrogothic Kingdom of Theoderic the Master of the Offices had been made responsible for the condition of the postal establishments,[4] and the money paid in fines for the abuse of privileges in using the state conveyances was expended on their maintenance through the *officium* of the Master.[5] This new system was rendered feasible by the comparatively small extent of territory controlled by the Gothic Kings.

There was also another change introduced in the Gothic Kingdom in connection with the control of the state post. As was previously noted, it is highly probable that the Agentes no longer existed in Italy at this date, and that the duty of inspecting the passes had been transferred to royal *saiones*,[6] with due reservation of the customary rights of certain *praefecti*, who may have been deputed from the Master's office, although their position is not clearly defined.

The right to make use of the state post, as has been said, was granted by the issuing of *evectiones* or passes. In order to prevent too heavy a burden being laid upon the provinces responsible for the upkeep of the *cursus publicus*, by allowing an unduly great number to make use of this convenience, a limi-

[1] *Codex Theodosianus*, VI, 29, 8; cf. *Codex Justinianus*, XII, 22, 4.

[2] Cf. *Codex Theodosianus*, VIII, 5, and *Codex Justinianus*, XII, 50.

[3] Lydus, *De Mag.*, 2, 10; 3, 40; *Codex Justinianus*, XII, 50.

[4] Cassiodorus, *Variae*, 6, 6, 3: *Veredorum quin etiam opportunam velocitatem, quorum status semper in cursu est, diligentiae suae districtione custodit, ut sollicitudines nostras, quas consilio iuvat, beneficio celeritatis expediat.*

[5] Cassiodorus, *Variae*, 5, 5, 4 (523–26): *quam summam protinus exactam, sicut iam anterioribus edictis constitutum est, per officium magisteriae dignitatis cursui proficere debere censemus.* The formula for the Pretorian Prefect has nothing relative to the upkeep of the *cursus publicus* (Cass., *op. cit.*, 6, 3, 511).

[6] Cassiodorus, *Variae*, 5, 5 (523–526).

tation of the right to issue passes was necessary. This right was a privilege highly prized, and the imperial government found great difficulty in restricting it to reasonable limits, while yet allowing those really justified in using the postal service to have the power to do so. Not until the fifth century was the privilege of granting passes definitely regulated.

The right to issue such passes was, of course, ultimately an imperial prerogative. However, under Constantine I, it seems to have been exercised independently by the Pretorian Prefect [1] and other officials. Among the latter were the provincial governors, who lost the privilege in 354.[2] By 357 the Master of the Offices was also in possession of this right,[3] but, owing to the abuse of the privilege, Julian, in 362, deprived all officials, except the Pretorian Prefect, of the right to issue *evectiones*, although giving to certain others the right to dispose of a definite number signed by himself.[4]

Under the successors of Julian, however, there was once more an extension of this privilege. In 364 the Urban Prefect was given authority to issue passes in matters of state business,[5] a right which he had lost again by 382 A.D.;[6] and in 371 the Senate obtained a like privilege for delegations proceeding to and from the Emperor.[7] By 365 the Master of the Offices was acting as the imperial representative in granting *evectiones*,[8] and in 378, along with the Prefect, he had the power in certain cases of adding to the privileges in making use of the state post which were specified in the individual passes.[9] Still in 382 the Emperor and the Prefect alone possessed the right to issue

[1] *Codex Theodosianus*, VIII, 5, 3 (326).

[2] *Codex Theodosianus*, VIII, 5, 5; cf. VIII, 5, 40 (382).

[3] *Codex Theodosianus*, VIII, 5, 9: *sufficere namque posse confidimus, quae isdem a nobis vel magistri officiorum comitatus nostri jussis necessaria habita ratione praebentur.*

[4] *Codex Theodosianus*, VIII, 5, 12 (362).

[5] *Codex Theodosianus*, VII, 5, 19.

[6] *Codex Theodosianus*, VIII, 5, 40; more explicitly in *Codex Justinianus*, XII, 50, 9.

[7] *Cod. Theod.* VIII, 5, 32; cf. *Just.* XII, 50, 6.

[8] *Codex Theodosianus*, VIII, 5, 22: *Praeterea illud adiungimus, ut parhippum vel avertarium nullus accipiat, nullus inpune praesumat, nisi eum nostrae serenitatis arbitrio aliqua necessitate cogente vir inl(ustris) magister officiorum textui evectionis addiderit*; cf. Seeck, Pauly-Wissowa, vol. 4, p. 1859.

[9] *Codex Theodosianus*, VIII, 5, 35, 1: *Si tamen necessitas maior coegerit, super sollemnem numerum iubemus admitti quos aut sacras litteras ferre constiterit aut habere in evectionibus adnotatum, ut aliqua de causa instantius ire iubeantur, quod vel spectabilis viri officiorum magistri vel sinceritatis tuae litteris oportet adscribi.*

such passes,[1] although it was not very long after this that the Master of the Offices acquired the same authority as the Prefect, which he enjoyed at the opening of the fifth century[2] and retained for the future.

By this time, following the system inaugurated by Julian, a definite number of passes had been granted to certain other high officials to dispose of during their term of office.[3] This was the ultimate settlement of the question, and under Justinian the right to give extra passes was limited to the sovereign, to the Prefect, and to the Master of the Offices.[4] The same condition prevailed in Italy under Theoderic, where the Master acted as the representative of the sovereign in this matter.[5]

The relations of the Pretorian Prefect and the Master of the Offices in respect to the *evectiones* require further definition. It seems that from 395 in the Eastern Empire the Prefect, although possessed of the right to issue these passes, had to submit them for approval to a representative of the Master of the Offices. Says Lydus,[6] speaking of the time of Rufinus:

"Since it was impracticable that the Prefect should have the burden of maintaining the state horses and those in charge of them throughout the provinces, while the control over and the administration of these was in the hands of others, a law was promulgated to the effect that the Prefect should indeed retain the care of the *cursus publicus*, but that the senior of the *frumentarii* (*i.e.* Agentes), who is at present called *princeps*, should continually be present in the office of the Pretorian Prefect, and should actively scrutinize and inquire into the reasons why many used the state post on the authority of passes provided by the prefecture (for which reason he was called *curiosus*, equivalent to περίεργος, and not he alone, but all those who superintended the state horses in the provinces), while the so-called Master appended his signature to these *evecti-*

[1] *Codex Theodosianus*, VIII, 5, 40.

[2] *Notitia Dignitatum or.* XI, *magister officiorum ipse emittit;* omitted in *occ.* IX.

[3] *Notitia Dignitatum*, passim; Seeck, Pauly-Wissowa, vol. 4, p. 1860.

[4] *Codex Justinianus*, XII, 50, 9: *Iudicibus faciendae evectionis copiam denegamus, cum id tantum nostro numini et tuae sedi nec non viro illustri magistro officiorum sit reservandum, cum neque praefecto urbis neque magistris militum neque ducibus neque vicariis nec cuiquam alii praeter memoratas duas potestates hoc a nobis concessum sit.*

[5] According to Cassiodorus (*Variae*, 6, 3, 3), the Pretorian Prefect *evectiones simili potestate* (i.e. *pro sua deliberatione*) *distribuit;* id. ibid., 6, 6, *per eum* (the Master of the Offices) *nominis nostri destinatur evectio, et isti principaliter creditur quam tam necessarium esse creditur;* cf. also 5, 5, 2.

[6] *De Mag.*, 2, 10; 3, 40; cf. 3, 23.

ones. And that this is so, one may learn from the constitution itself, which although incorporated in the old Codex of Theodosius, has been omitted in the new code."

This account agrees with what the same author has to say regarding the *regendarii* in the Prefect's *officium* in the sixth century:[1]

"The *regendarius* is still said to be placed in charge of the *evectiones* for the state post, but his functions are purely nominal, for the Master of the Offices has taken over the full control of the business."

This testimony must be credited for the time at which Lydus wrote, and there seems to be no adequate reason for disbelieving his statements with regard to the arrangements in force after 395, even if the constitution to which he refers is not found in our text of the Theodosian Code.[2] We may attribute to this period a reorganization of the post service with stricter centralization of control,[3] as a result of which the *evectiones* that the Prefect issued had to be passed by a *princeps* from the Agentes and countersigned by the Master of the Offices. This *princeps* was the *princeps* of the Prefect's *officium*, who was advanced to that post from the *schola* of the Agentes.[4] Although Lydus calls him variously πρῶτος τῶν φρουμενταρίων,[5] κουρίωσος,[6] πρίγκιψ τῆς τάξεως τοῦ μαγίστρου,[7] and πρίγκιψ τῶν μαγιστριανῶν,[8] this identification is clear from the use of the title *princeps*, which was not applied to any member of the Master's *officium*, and the account of his relation to the *cornicularius* of the Prefect's office.[9] It was probably about the close of the fourth century also that the number of the passes annually allotted to the various administrative posts was defined as in the *Notitia*.

[1] *De Mag.*, 3, 4: ῥεγενδάριοι δύο οἱ τὸν δημόσιον δρόμον ἰθύνοντες; 21: ὁ ῥεγενδάριος ἐπὶ τῆς φροντίδος τῶν συνθημάτων τοῦ δημοσίου δρόμου τεταγμένος ἔτι καὶ νῦν λέγεται μέν, πράττει δὲ οὐδέν, τοῦ μαγίστρου τῆς αὐλῆς τὴν ὅλην ὑφελομένου τοῦ πράγματος ἐξουσίαν; cf. *Notitia Dignitatum or.* II, *regerendarius*, III *id.*

[2] So Hirschfeld, *Sitzungsberichte der Berliner Akademie*, 1893, p. 439, n. 7, against Mommsen, *Ostgothische Studien, Neues Archiv*, vol. 14, p. 475, n. 1. *Codex Theodosianus*, VIII, 5, 35 (378), which Mommsen, in his edition of the Code, suggests is the constitution mentioned by Lydus, does not agree in date or substance with the latter, and, further, appears in part in *Codex Justinianus*, XII, 50, 8.

[3] Hirschfeld, *op. cit.*, *l.c.*, would attribute this reform to Rufinus. But it is more likely that this restriction upon the Prefect's power would come after his fall, as Lydus says, *De Mag.*, 3, 23.

[4] Cf. p. 72, above.

[5] *De Mag.*, 2, 10; 3, 40.

[6] *De Mag.*, loc. cit.

[7] *De Mag.*, 3, 23.

[8] *De Mag.*, 3, 24.

[9] *De Mag.*, 3, 23–4.

Evidence is not lacking of conflicts arising between the Pretorian Prefects and the Master of the Offices with regard to their respective spheres of competence in connection with the *cursus publicus*. As early as 357 a special constitution prohibited the Prefect from granting passes to the Agentes, who were henceforth to receive them only from the Emperor or the Master.[1] And two years later protection was given the Agentes, when serving as *curiosi*, from the judicial power of the Prefect, provided that they acted as befitted their office.[2] This division of control is further emphasized by the requirement that persons using the post service without a pass, or exceeding the privileges granted therein, should be detained and reported both to the Prefect and to the Master.[3] Under Justinian this provision was so far modified that only offenders of rank were thus reported to the Master, while the Prefect was empowered to deal alone with those of inferior status.[4] In the *officium* of the Master, in addition to the *curiosus cursus publici praesentalis* already mentioned, there were included, in the inspectors of the state post throughout the provinces, the *curiosi omnium provinciarum*.[5] Through these again, as well as through the other Agentes, the Master of the Offices was the centre of an espionage system stretching out from the capital to the furthest corners of the Empire.

The Master continued to control the use of the state post until the creation of the Logothete of the Post (λογοθέτης τοῦ δρόμου), whose office arose from that of the *curiosus cursus publici praesentalis*, and who became the head of an independent department of the administration in charge of this portion of the Master's duties during the eighth century.[6]

V. The Master of the Offices and the *Mensores*

From the time of Constantine I, the quartering of officers and soldiers, on their way to and from the scene of active service, upon

[1] *Codex Theodosianus*, VIII, 5, 9.

[2] *Codex Theodosianus*, VI, 29, 3; cf. *Justinianus*, XII, 22, 3.

[3] *Codex Theodosianus*, VIII, 5, 8 (357).

[4] *Codex Justinianus*, XII, 50, 3: *Si quidem dignitate praeditus sit, de eius nomine ac prudentiam tuam et ad illustrem virum comitem et magistrum officiorum referri.*

[5] *Notitia Dignitatum or.* XI, *occ.* IX.

[6] Bury, *Imperial Administration*, p. 91. The state post was not abolished by Justinian, but merely restricted in the Orient; cf. Hirschfeld, *Sitzungsberichte der Berliner Akademie*, 1893, p. 440, n. 1, against Hudemann, *Geschichte des romischen Postwesens*, 95, on Procopius, *Anecdota*, 30; Lydus, *De Mag.* 3, 61.

the inhabitants of the towns and districts through which they passed, became a regularly established system. The same method was used in obtaining quarters for the Emperor and his suite, whenever he undertook a journey from his capital. This obligatory reception of public servants by householders was called *hospitium*, or *hospitalitas*, and the quarters furnished were known as *metata*. The officials whose duty it was to prepare such quarters for the Emperor and to indicate lodgings for the individual *palatini* accompanying him, as well as for other persons, were the *mensores* or *metatores*,[1] 'Quartermasters.'

The *mensores* formed a *schola* at the palace, headed by a *primicerius* who, after two years' service, was placed on the list of the Agentes at the foot of the register.[2] It is most likely that the Master of the Offices was placed in charge of these Quartermasters by Constantine I, at the time when his office received its great increase of power. However, the earliest direct evidence of any connection between them and the Master is found in a constitution of 368 or 373,[3] instructing the Master to see that synagogues were not occupied by those who had the right of *hospitium*. From a constitution of 405,[4] we see that the organization of the schola of the *mensores* was under the Master's supervision, and the *Notitia* of the Orient[5] places it among the *officia* which were subject to his commands. Although the occidental *Notitia* fails to mention them, their status in the West was undoubtedly the same as in the East.

As with other officials under his orders, the Master probably exercised exclusive jurisdiction over the Quartermasters. His authority over them remained undiminished in the Eastern Empire under Justinian,[6] but there is no trace of them in Italy under the Gothic régime.

In supervising the work of the *mensores*, the chief care of the Master of the Offices was to see that they did not demand more than was authorized by law in making their assignments of *hospitia*, and that they had regard for the exemptions that were granted to certain officials, to the *illustres*, and to those engaged in specific

[1] Gothofredus *ad Cod. Theod.* VI, 34, 1; *Paratit. ad Cod. Theod.* VII; Cagnat, in Daremberg et Saglio, vol. 3, pp. 302–303, s. v. *hospitium*.

[2] *Codex Theodosianus*, VI, 34, 1 (405).

[3] *Codex Theodosianus*, VII, 8, 2; cf. *Codex Justinianus*, I, 9, 4.

[4] *Codex Theodosianus*, VI, 34, 1; cf. *Codex Justinianus*, XII, 59, 10.

[5] *Notitia Dignitatum or.* XI, 12.

[6] *Codex Justinianus*, I, 9, 4; XII, 40, 1, etc.

occupations.[1] In this connection we may note that it was upon the recommendation of the Master Aemilianus that in 400 A.D. the *fabricenses* were relieved of the burden of *hospitium*.[2]

In addition to his direction of the *mensores*, it was the Master's duty to exercise a general oversight of the whole system of *metata*, preventing, on the one hand, any unwarranted exactions on the part of those entitled to the privileges of *hospitium*, and, on the other, forcing those who were subject to this service to fulfil their obligations.[3] The authority which the Master of the Offices exercised over the *mensores* formed a part of his general powers as head of the *officia palatina*, while the placing in his hands of the supervision of the whole system of quartering gave the central executive a further check upon the abuse of their power by civil and military officials to the detriment of the provincials.

VI. The Master of the Offices and the *Scrinia*

The three secretarial bureaus, known as the *scrinia memoriae, epistularum*, and *libellorum*, which, in the *Notitia*,[4] are placed *sub dispositione magistri officiorum*, were most probably under the oversight of the Master from the time of the establishment of his office, certainly from the date of the enlargement of its competence under Constantine I.[5]

The Master exercised full authority over the organization and administration of the *scrinia*. The number of the clerks in each bureau, both of the *statuti* or regular employees and the *supernumerarii*, the admission to the service among the *statuti*, and the character of the duties to be performed by each of the latter, were under his supervision.[6] The roll of each *scrinium*, with the order of rank of its members, and all promotions were likewise under his care.[7] The Master also maintained the privileges and exemptions, judicial and otherwise, which the *scriniarii* enjoyed.[8]

[1] *Codex Theodosianus*, VII, 8, 3 (384); VII, 8, 14 (427); VII, 8, 16 (435); *Codex Justinianus*, XII, 40, 2 (398); XII, 40, 8 (400); XII, 40, 9 (444); XII, 40, 10 (Valentinian and Marcian); XII, 40, 11 (Zeno).

[2] *Codex Justinianus*, XII, 40, 4.

[3] *Codex Theodosianus*, VII, 8, *de metatis*; *Codex Justinianus*, XII, 40, id.

[4] *Notitia Dignitatum or.* XI, *occ.* IX.

[5] Cf. Chapter III, pp. 26–28.

[6] *Codex Theodosianus*, I, 30, 3 (392); *Codex Justinianus*, XII, 19, 7 (443–4); 9; (470); 10 (Leo); 11 (Athanasius).

[7] *Codex Theodosianus*, VI, 26, 6 (396); 11 (397); 17 (416); cf. *Codex Justinianus*, XII, 19, 6.

[8] *Codex Justinianus*, XII, 19, 9 (Leo); 12 (Anastasius); 14 (Justinus).

He also exercised judicial authority over those serving in the *scrinia;* at least from the time of Anastasius, neither they themselves, nor their parents, wives, children, nor even their slaves and *coloni* residing in Constantinople, could be prosecuted on civil or criminal charges except in accordance with a decision of the Master.[1]

From among those serving in these *scrinia* the Quaestor selected his aides (*adiutores*).[2] In the East the number of these *adiutores* had become fixed at twelve from the *scrinium memoriae* and seven from each of the *scrinia epistularum* and *libellorum,* whereas the total number in each of these bureaus was sixty-two, thirty-four, and thirty-four respectively.[3] However, this restriction had been disregarded and the number of the Quaestor's aides was threatening to equal the total number of the employees in each department, when Justinus took steps to reduce them to the former number.[4] The Master had to supervise this reduction and prevent the recurrence of similar circumstances in the future.[5] These *adiutores* of the Quaestor remained under the jurisdiction of the Master.[6]

Unlike the *scrinium dispositionum,* which, as we have seen, was entirely at the disposal of the Master of the Offices, the *scrinia memoriae, epistularum,* and *libellorum* performed only part of their functions under his orders. The direction of their services he shared with the Quaestor and the Magistri Scriniorum.

The titular head of each of the *scrinia* was a *magister* (ἀντιγραφεύς), who took his title from that department with which he was associated, as *magister memoriae, magister epistularum,* or *magister libellorum;* these officials were known collectively as the Magistri Scriniorum.[7] The Masters of the Scrinia had formerly been the active heads of their several departments, but after the Principate had passed into the Empire they had lost control over the personnel of these bureaus, having been in this respect super-

[1] *Codex Justinianus,* XII, 19, 12 (Anastasius): *In sacris scriniis militantes et parentes atque uxores eorum nec non liberos ex sententia tantummodo tuae celsitudinis criminales et civiles intentiones agentium excipere iubemus, insuper etiam colonos seu adscripticios et servos eorum in hac regia urbe degentes eodem beneficio potiri.*

[2] *Notitia Dignitatum or.* XII, *Officium non habet, sed adiutores de scriniis quos voluerit; occ.* X, *habet subaudientes adiutores memoriales de scriniis diversis.*

[3] *Codex Justinianus,* XII, 19, 10 (Leo).

[4] *Codex Justinianus,* XII, 19, 13, cf. 15, § 1 (527).

[5] *Codex Justinianus,* XII, 19, 15.

[6] *Codex Justinianus,* XII, 19, 14 (Justinus).

[7] *Notitia Dignitatum or.* XIX, *occ.* XVII; *Codex Justinianus,* XII, 9.

seded by the Master of the Offices, and therefore merely commanding their services for certain purposes. However, unlike the *scriniarii* themselves, the Masters of the Scrinia were not subordinates of the Master of the Offices.[1]

As the Quaestor, the Master of the Offices, and the Masters of the Scrinia divided among them the control of the activities of the *scriniarii*, it remains to see for what purposes each could employ them.

First, then, let us consider the powers of the Masters of the Scrinia. These had no private *officium* but, like the Quaestor, had the right to draw aides from the *scrinia* to execute their orders.[2] With regard to the number of these aides we have no information. The *magister memoriae*, says the *Notitia*,[3] *adnotationes omnes dictat et emittit, et precibus respondet;* that is to say, he saw to the putting into proper form the verbal comments of the Emperor, which he despatched without the imperial signature. He also answered requests, *preces*, from individuals, and himself prepared these answers for the imperial approval, until Justinian[4] put an end to his independent action in judicial questions and placed him in this respect under the Quaestor's supervision. In view of the lack of an exact modern equipment for the title *magister memoriae*, on the basis of function and relation to the other Secretaries, we may venture to translate it as First Secretary.

The *magister epistularum*, or Secretary for Correspondence, dealt with the communications of legations from foreign states and from *civitates* within the Empire, with requests for advice from officials, and with certain petitions.[5] In the case of the legations the *magister epistularum* was doubtless subject to the supervision of the Master of the Offices, otherwise to that of the Quaestor.

[1] Karlowa, *Römische Rechtsgeschichte*, vol. 1, pp. 833 ff.; Bury, *Harvard Studies in Classical Philology*, vol. XXI, p. 24; cf. *id.* vol. XXVI, pp. 101 ff.

[2] *Notitia Dignitatum or.* XIX: *officium autem de ipsis nemo habet, sed adiutores electos de scriniis.* In the *N. D. occ.* XVII this is lacking, perhaps accidentally.

[3] *Or.* XIX; *occ.* XVII: *respondet tamen et precibus.*

[4] *Novellae Justiniani*, 114, 1.

[5] *Notitia Dignitatum or.* XIX: *legationes civitatum, consultationes et preces tractat;* cf. *occ.* XVII. The activity of the *magister epistularum graecarum*, who existed only in the East, and who *eas epistolas, quae graece solent emitti, aut ipse dictat aut latine dictatas transfert in graecum* (*Notitia Dignitatum or.* XIX), does not require separate comment here. For the work of the *magister epistularum* see further *Codex Justinianus*, VII, 62, 32, 2 (440); 37 (529); 38 (*id.*); 63, 3 (518); *Novellae Justiniani*, 20 pr., where the *epistulares* act under his directions.

The Secretary for Petitions, *magister libellorum*, handled the cases, *cognitiones*, which were brought before the Emperor himself, and formulated independent rescripts in answer to petitions entered in other courts.[1] Here his work was subject to the Quaestor's revision.

The Quaestor was the official through whom the Emperor gave expression to his power as the source of law. The Quaestor consequently formulated laws and edicts, as well as answers to supplications requiring the imperial signature.[2] In dealing with supplications the Magistri Scriniorum, as we have seen, did most of the preparatory work, which was subject to the Quaestor's revision. The Quaestor had also the control of the *laterculum minus* or register of the subordinate officials of the Empire. For some time previous to 424 the *magistri militum* had usurped this right, but in that year the preparation of the list, which included the *praepositi*, *tribuni*, and the *praefecti castrorum*, was restored to the Quaestor.[3] Appointments to these offices were issued through the *scrinium memoriae*, which for this purpose was at the disposal of the Quaestor. This arrangement apparently concerned the East only, while in the West the *magister peditum praesentalis* continued to control the appointment of a great number of such officials, as at the time of the compilation of the *Notitia*.[4] For the preparation of the documents involved in the performance of his other duties the Quaestor, as we have seen, had in his service assistants drawn from the three *scrinia*.

The task of issuing the *probatoriae*, or imperial warrants entitling persons to be admitted to service in the various *officia*, both at the capital and throughout the provinces, was distributed among these three bureaus.[5] In this field the supervision of their activities fell to the lot of the Master of the Offices.[6] It was through the *scrinia* also that the notices of appointment were

[1] *Notitia Dignitatum or., occ., cognitiones et preces tractat;* cf. *Codex Justinianus*, III, 24, 3 pr.; VII, 62, 32, 4; *Novellae Justiniani*, 20, c. 9.

[2] *Notitia Dignitatum or.* XII, *occ.* X, *leges dictandae, preces;* cf. Karlowa, *Römische Rechtsgeschichte*, vol. 1, p. 833.

[3] *Codex Theodosianus*, I, 8, 2 = *Codex Justinianus*, I, 30, 1: *Totius minoris laterculi curam scias ad tuae sublimitatis solicitudinem pertinere, ita ut tuo arbitrio ex scrinio memoriae totius minoris laterculi dignitates, hoc est praeposituræ omnes, tribunatus et praefecturae castrorum iuxta consuetudinem priscam clementiae meae auctoritate deinceps emittantur; Codex Theodosianus*, I, 8, 3 = *Codex Justinianus*, I, 30, 2.

[4] *Notitia Dignitatum occ.* XLII.

[5] *Codex Justinianus*, XII, 59, 10 (Leo).

[6] *Codex Justinianus*, XII, 59, 9 (Leo).

issued to the higher officials in the government service, and here, too, the Master was their superintendent, so that Cassiodorus [1] could say that no provincial judge was able to assume office without the sanction of the Master of the Offices.

In summary, then, the Master of the Offices had charge of the organization of the *scrinia*, and also of a part of their functions: the Masters of the Scrinia only commanded the services of selected *scriniarii* for specific purposes in which their work was generally subject to a revision by the Quaestor or the Master of the Offices: while the Quaestor on the one hand monopolized the services of a definite number of the clerks in each of these bureaus, and on the other, in connection with the care of the *laterculum minus*, directed the action of the *scrinium memoriae*. From this definition of the respective powers of these officers in connection with the *scrinia* it is now clear why the Master of the Offices was the recipient of imperial edicts regulating the relations of the Quaestor to the *scriniarii*,[2] and why it was at times found convenient to unite these two offices in the hands of one person.[3]

The connection of the Master and the *scrinia* was severed during the reorganization of the administration in the Eastern Empire in the seventh and following centuries. In the ninth century the *scrinia epistularum* and *libellorum* with their *magistri* or ἀντιγραφεῖς appear to be completely under the control of the Quaestor, while the *magister memoriae*, as the ὁ ἐπὶ τῶν δεήσεων, had attained an independent sphere of action in the matter of petitions.[4]

VII. The Master of the Offices and the State Arsenals

Under Diocletian the control of the manufacture and distribution of weapons made in the state arsenals (*fabricae*) was centred at the court under an official called the *praepositus fabricarum* (?), a subordinate of the Pretorian Prefect.[5] Apparently

[1] Cassiodorus, *Variae*, 6, 6: *His enim laboribus aestimatis potestatem maximam huic decrevit antiquitas, ut nemo iudicum per provincias fasces assumeret, nisi hoc et ipse fieri decrevisset.*

[2] As *Codex Justinianus*, I, 30, 2 = *Codex Theodosianus*, I, 8, 3; *Codex Theodosianus*, I, 30, 3; *Codex Justinianus*, XII, 19, 15.

[3] As Trebonianus in 536, *Novellae Justiniani*, 33; Anastasius under Justinus II, Corippus, *Panegyr. pr.* 30.

[4] Bury, *Imperial Administration*, pp. 75–77.

[5] Seeck, *Pauly-Wissowa*, vol. 6, p. 1978.

under Constantine I this office disappeared, and the direction of the arsenals was placed in the hands of the Master of the Offices.[1] Lydus[2] connects this transfer with the fall of Rufinus in 395, although it had certainly taken place at an earlier date.[3] The correct interpretation of his statement probably is that Rufinus, following the example of various pretenders to the imperial throne,[4] during his brief period of power brought the *fabricae* under his control by restoring the control over them to the prefecture which he himself occupied, and that after his death they were put once more under the Master's supervision.[5] The earliest constitution that points to the Master's exercise of authority in this sphere dates from 390 A.D.[6]

This edict deals with the retirement and rank of the *primicerii fabricarum*, the seniors among the employees of the several arsenals, while subsequent constitutions of 398[7] and 404,[8] as well as one of Leo and Anthemius,[9] likewise show that the Master of the Offices had authority over the *corpus fabricensium*, or hereditary guild of armorers laboring in these *fabricae*. Matters of discipline, restrictions upon their freedom of movement, their relations with persons outside of their guild, and punishments for engaging in forbidden occupations, were under the Master's oversight. Consequently we find that it was upon the suggestion of the Master of the Offices that the guild of the *fabricenses* was held in corporate liability for the delinquencies of one of their number.[10]

Also, under Leo and Anthemius,[11] his jurisdiction over the *fabricenses*, their wives, and their sons, who were considered as serving in the ranks of the corporation, was made exclusive and they could be prosecuted in his court alone.

This power the Master continued to enjoy in the East under

[1] Seeck, *op. cit.;* see chap. III, p. 32. [2] *De Mag.*, 2, 10; 3, 40.

[3] *Codex Theodosianus*, X, 22, 3 (390). [4] Seeck, *Pauly-Wissowa*, vol. 6, p. 1926.

[5] Seeck, *op. cit.*, p. 1928; cf. chap. III, p. 36.

[6] *Codex Theodosianus*, X, 22, 3 = *Codex Justinianus*, XI, 10, 2.

[7] *Codex Theodosianus*, X, 22, 4 = *Codex Justinianus*, XI, 10, 3.

[8] *Codex Theodosianus*, X, 22, 5. [9] *Codex Justinianus*, XI, 10, 7.

[10] *Novellae Theodosii*, 6, 2 (438); cf. *Codex Justinianus*, XI, 10, 5: *Universi itaque velut in corpore uniformi uni decoctioni, si ita res tulerit, respondere coguntur, ut viri inlustris et magnifici magistri officiorum suggestio nostrae clementiae patefecit.*

[11] *Codex Justinianus*, XI, 10, 6: *Eos, qui inter fabricenses sacrae fabricae sociati sunt vel eorum uxores aut filios, qui itidem inter fabricenses militare dicentur, non alibi pulsare volentibus respondere praecipimis, nisi in iudicio tuae sublimitatis, ad cuius iurisdictionem potestatemque pertinent.*

Justinian,[1] but in the Ostrogothic Kingdom it was restored to the Pretorian Prefect.[2]

To assist him in the supervision of the arsenals and armorers the Master had in his *officium* officials called *subadiuvae fabricarum*. Of these there were three in the East,[3] and in the West an indefinite number,[4] in the early part of the fifth century. In the East, under Leo, these *subadiuvae* constituted a separate bureau, or *scrinium*, within the *officium*, to which there were annually admitted for one year's service four Agentes of the rank of *princeps*.[5] This is evidently the same as the *scrinium fabricensium* which appears under Justinian.[6]

In the Orient there were sixteen state arsenals for the manufacture of weapons of various kinds, of which four were in the diocese of the Orient, three in the Pontic, one in the Asian, two in the Thracian, and four in the Illyrian diocese.[7] The Master in the Occident, at the same period of the fifth century, controlled twenty of these factories. They were located, five in Illyricum, six in Italy, and nine in Gaul.[8]

However, the manufacture of arms was not made an imperial monopoly until the time of Justinian, who in 539[9] absolutely prohibited the making of weapons by, or their sale to, civilians. This regulation was to be enforced by the Master of the Offices. It was his duty to appoint *cartularii*, or 'keepers of records' of the *scrinium fabricensium*, for whom five *priores* of the *scrinium* were responsible; to take depositions from *iudices* and their *officia*, and from *defensores* and *patres civitatis*, that they would not aid any one to do what was prohibited by this law; and personally to investigate contraventions thereof. The Master, furthermore, had the duty of making this edict known in the capital and throughout the provinces.[10]

The transport of the manufactured weapons from the arsenals to various points was also under the Master's care.[11] He notified

[1] *Codex Justinianus*, VI, 10, *de fabricensibus; Novellae Justiniani*, 85, 3.

[2] Cassiodorus, *Variae*, 7, 18, 9.

[3] *Notitia Dignitatum, or.* XI, 34.

[4] *Notitia Dignitatum, occ.* IX, 43.

[5] *Codex Justinianus*, XII, 20, 5: *Agentes in rebus, qui per ordinem consequi solent principatus insignia, in unoquoque scrinio fabricarum et barbarorum quarternos subadiuvarum solicitudinem per annum dumtaxat integrum procedentes gradatim subire hac in aeternum valitura lege decernimus.*

[6] *Novellae Justiniani*, 85, 3.

[7] *Notitia Dignitatum, or.* XI, 18–39.

[8] *Notitia Dignitatum, occ.* IX, 16–39.

[9] *Novellae Justiniani*, 39, 3.

[10] *Novellae Justiniani*, 3; 4.

[11] *Codex Justinianus*, XI, 10, 7.

the Prefect's office of the quantity to be transported, and the point of delivery, whereupon due provision had to be made by that office for the conveyance of the material specified, by land or sea, without delay, upon pain of a heavy penalty.[1]

The various *fabricae* were each under the immediate supervision of an official styled either *praepositus* or *tribunus*,[2] who was evidently a subordinate of the Master of the Offices, but whose relations to the latter are nowhere defined. These *praepositi* and *tribuni* were among those who made up the *laterculum minus*, which was under the care of the Quaestor;[3] they may have been nominated by him, or by the Master of the Offices, subject, in any case, to the imperial approval.[4]

In connection with the *fabricae* for the manufacture of weapons we have to consider imperial factories of another sort, those that were engaged in the production of goods interwoven with gold, pearls, and precious stones, which were reserved for the use of the imperial family. Such manufactures were a state monopoly from the time of Diocletian. The employees in these factories were called *barbaricarii*.[5] Under Valens, in the East, they were given the duty of decorating with gold and silver the helmets and shields of the soldiers,[6] and for this reason they, like the *fabricenses*, were placed under the control of the Master of the Offices.[7] In the West this transfer did not take place. To aid in the management of the factories served by the *barbaricarii*, the Master of the Offices had in his officium four assistants, called *subadiuvae barbaricariorum*.[8]

VIII. The Master of the Offices, the *Limites*, and the *Duces*

In the year 443 A.D. the Master of the Offices in the Eastern Empire was intrusted with the duty of preparing an annual report on the number of the soldiers (*limitanei*) on duty on certain of the frontiers (*limites*), as well as on the condition of the fortified camps and of the guard boats, which patrolled the river bound-

[1] *Codex Justinianus*, XI, 10, 7.

[2] Seeck, Pauly-Wissowa, vol. 6, pp. 1927–8.

[3] *Codex Justinianus*, I, 30, 1 (424); cf. p. 85, above.

[4] They do not appear among the *praepositi* and *tribuni* nominated by the *magister peditum praesentalis* in the West, *Notitia Dignitatum*, *occ.* XLII.

[5] Seeck, Pauly-Wissowa, vol. 2, pp. 2856–7.

[6] *Codex Theodosianus*, X, 22, 1 (324).

[7] Seeck, *op. cit.*

[8] *Notitia Dignitatum*, *or.* IX, 45.

aries. The *limites* specified were those of Thrace, Illyricum, the Orient, Pontus, Egypt, Thebes, and Libya; that is, practically all the borders of the Eastern Empire.[1] The report was to be delivered in the imperial *consistorium* during the month of January on the Master's own initiative.[2]

Under Justinian this duty was still performed by the Master. However, the frontiers which he then inspected are not specified, but are simply referred to as all those placed under his jurisdiction; and the report is not assigned to any definite time nor place, being given solely upon the Master's initiative.[3] Still, the actual care and repair of the fortified camps and guardboats, and the command of the *limitanei*, remained in the hands of the *duces limitum*, who were under the supervision of the *magistri militum*.[4]

The reason which caused this inspection of the frontier defences to be intrusted to the Master of the Offices may be gathered from the general content of the edict of Theodosius II.[5] It was evidently the desire to obtain a credible report on the condition of the defences of the Empire through an official who was not directly concerned with their construction, maintenance, and garrisoning. This involved the use of an official of the civil administration as a check upon military officers; and for the performance of this task there was none more suitable than the Master of the Offices, the director of the *agentes in rebus*. The Master of the Offices in the Occident did not receive this power, probably on account of the exceptional influence of the *magister peditum praesentalis* at Rome.[6]

The right of the Master to inspect the *limites* led to the con-

[1] *Novellae Theodosii*, 24, 5: *Id autem curae perpetuae tui culminis credimus iniungendum, ut tam Thracici quam Inlyrici nec non etiam Orientalis ac Pontici limitis, Aegyptiaci insuper Thebaici Libyci quemadmodum se militum numerus habeat castrorumque ac lusoriarum cura procedat, quotannis mense Ianuario in sacro consistorio significare nobis propria suggestione procures.*

[2] *Novellae Theodosii*, 24, 5.

[3] *Codex Justinianus*, I, 31, 4: *Curae perpetuae tui culminis credimus iniungendum, ut super omni limite sub tua iurisdictione constituto, quemadmodum se militum numerus habeat castrorumque ac clusurarum cura procedat, quotannis significare nobis propria suggestione procuret.*

[4] *Novellae Theodosii*, 24, 1 (cf. *Codex Justinianus*, I, 46, 4): *Imprimis itaque duces limitum et praecipue, quibus gentes quae maxime cavendae sunt adpropinquant, in ipsis limitibus commorari et milites ad proprium redigere numerum, inminentibus magisteriis potestatibus diuturnisque eorum exercitationibus inhaerere praecipimus.*

[5] *Novellae Theodosii* 24, 5: *ut uniuscuiusque tam industria quam desidia nostris auribus intimata, et strenui digna praemia consequantur et in dissimulatores competens indignatio proferatur.*

[6] Cf. *Harvard Studies in Classical Philology*, vol. XXVI, pp. 124 f, 144 f.

ferring upon him of judicial authority over their defenders. This jurisdiction Leo made exclusive, removing the *duces* and their *apparitores*, the *limitanei* and the *praepositi castrorum* from the jurisdiction of any other than the Master,[1] subject only to the respecting of certain indefinite privileges previously enjoyed by the *magistri militum* in relation to the frontiers of the Orient, Thrace, and Illyricum.

Justinian directed that all appeals coming from the court of a *dux*, no matter what the rank of the judge officiating there, should be settled by the Master of the Offices and the Quaestor acting together.[2] For this reason the code of Justinian speaks of the *limites* under the Master's jurisdiction.[3]

The Master's supervision of the frontiers did not survive the reform of the military organization of the Empire and the creation of the *themes* in the seventh century.

IX. The Master of the Offices and the Imperial Consistory

From about the year 325 A.D. the Master of the Offices was a *comes consistorianus*,[4] that is to say a standing member of the *consistorium*, or Imperial Privy Council, which was composed of a select number of the high administrative officers of the Empire, in addition to extraordinary members summoned from time to time as the occasion demanded; this consistory acted as a council of state for the settlement of questions of policy beyond the competence of the various individual officials and as a high court of justice on special occasions.[5] This participation in the highest councils of the state added to the prestige and influence of the Master's office, and the part which he played there reflected the character of the various departments of the administration which were under his control.

We have already made mention of one of the Master's duties in connection with the *consistorium*, namely the obligation to

[1] *Codex Justinianus*, XII, 59, 8: *Viros spectabiles duces eorumque apparitores nec non limitaneos castrorumque praepositos tantummodo ex sublimis tui iudicii sententia conveniri nec aliis subiacere iudicibus praecipimus: illustribus scilicet ac magnificis viris magistris militum consuetudine ac potestate, si qua ad limites aliquos Orientis Thraciarum et Illyrici ex longo tempore hactenus obtinuit, reservata.*

[2] *Codex Justinianus*, VII, 62, 38 (529). [3] *Codex Justinianus*, I, 31, 4.

[4] Cf. p. 31.

[5] Karlowa, *Roemische Rechtsgeschichte*, vol. 1, pp. 848 ff.; Seeck, Pauly-Wissowa, vol. 4, p. 931; Reid, *Cambridge Medieval History*, vol. 1, p. 48.

present there his annual report upon the condition of the frontier defences of the provinces.[1] Further interesting evidence regarding the presence of the Master at the sessions of this Council is afforded by the record of part of the proceedings of a meeting called by the Emperor Julian, contained in a constitution of 362, the prelude of which contains the words *in consistorio, adstante Jovio, viro clarissimo, quaestore, Anatolio, magistro officioru(m), Felice, com(iti) sacrarum largitionum.*[2]

The Master of the Offices arranged all the imperial audiences, both of private persons, of officials, and of ambassadors from foreign states, which were usually held in the *consistorium.* In this he was assisted by the *officium admissionum*, the corps of court ushers (*admissionales*) with the *magister admissionum* at their head, who were subject to his orders.[3]

Cassiodorus, whose *formula* of the Master's office[4] lays special stress upon this aspect of his duties, informs us that it was he who introduced the senators to the royal presence, and directed them in their deportment and speech.[5] It was the Master who promised an audience, who granted admission to the *consistorium*, and, as the morning star foretold the coming day, so he heralded the prospect of seeing the royal countenance.[6]

Persons to be presented might be actually introduced by an ordinary *admissionalis*, or by the *magister admissionum.*[7] In the case of men of eminence, such as senators, the Master himself might stand before the curtain (*velum*) of the council chamber and usher in the favored individuals.[8] In this latter fashion the Bishop Athanasius seems to have been brought before the Emperor Constans in 346,[9] and the monk Constantius before Theodosius II in 449.[10]

[1] *Novellae Theodosii*, 24, 1; 5; cf. *Codex Justinianus*, I, 31, 4.

[2] *Codex Theodosianus*, XI, 39, 5.

[3] *Notitia Dignitatum*, *or.* XI, 17; *occ.* IX, 14; sect. 2 above.

[4] *Variae*, 6, 6.

[5] Cassiodorus, *loc. cit.*: *Per eum senator veniens nostris praesentatur obtutibus; admonet trepidum; componit loquentem; sua quin etiam verba solet inserere, ut nos decenter omnia debeamus audire.*

[6] Cassiodorus, *loc. cit.*: *Aspectus regi haud irritus, promissor collocutionis nostrae, gloriosus donator aulici consistorii, quasi quidem lucifer; nam sicut ille venturum diem promittit, sic iste desiderantibus vultus nostrae serenitatis attribuit.*

[7] Ammianus, 15, 5, 8: *per magistrum admissionum, qui mos est honoratior, accito.*

[8] Valesius on Ammianus 26, 5, 7; Cassiodorus, *Variae*, 6, 6; *De Caer.*, 1, 87.

[9] *Apolog. ad Constantinum*, 3: δύναται καὶ Εὐγένιος ὁ γενόμενος μάγιστρος μαρτυρῆσαι· αὐτὸς γὰρ εἱστήκει πρὸ τοῦ βήλου καὶ ἤκουεν ἅπερ ἠξιοῦμεν αὐτόν, καὶ ἅπερ αὐτὸς κατηξίου λέγειν ἡμᾶς.

[10] Mansi, vol. 6, p. 821.

Representatives of foreign countries were under the care of the Master of the Offices from the time they crossed the Roman borders. He provided their escort, received and entertained them, introduced them to the Emperor, gave them suitable presents, and upon their departure provided them with a safe-conduct.[1] Ammianus[2] records that in 365 the ambassadors of the Alemanni, having rejected as unworthy the gifts offered to them, were treated with asperity by Ursatius, then Master of the Offices, and withdrew to stir up war.

The poet Corippus[3] has left a description of the introduction of the ambassadors of the Avars into the presence of Justin II by the Master in 566; and the Roman usage that legates should declare the object of their mission to the Master of the Offices first of all is indicated by the refusal of the Roman representatives sent to the Persian court in 579 to deliver their message to any one except that official whom the Romans styled the Master.[4] Further, Priscus[5] relates that when, in 448, Theodosius II was party to a plot to assassinate Attila, after corrupting one of the latter's ambassadors, he sent for Martinalius, his Master of the Offices, and informed him of the arrangements; the latter was entitled, through his official position, to know them. The Master, he says, "shared in all the Emperor's counsels, because he had at his orders the Agentes, the interpreters, and the soldiers of the palace guard," thus giving the grounds for the Master's presence in the consistory, and his connection with the diplomatic relations of the Empire.

The *Ceremonial Book* of Constantine Porphyrogenitus has preserved an account of the procedure customary in the fifth century at the court of Constantinople in the reception of embassies from an Emperor in the Occident, who had not yet

[1] As Cassiodorus (*Variae*, 6, 6) phrases it: *Per eum exteris gentibus ad laudem rei publicae nostrae ordinatur humanitas, et nolentes redeunt quos merentes exceperit: per eum quippe nobis legatorum quamvis festinantium praenuntiatur adventus.*

[2] Ammianus, 26, 5, 7.

[3] *In laudem Justini*, III, 231 ff.:

Legatos Avarum jussos intrare magister
  Ante fores sacras divinae nuntiat aulae
Orantes sese vestigia sacra videre
  Clementis domini, quos voce et mente benigna
Imperat admissi.

[4] Menander Protector, *Fragmenta Historicorum Graecorum*, vol. 4, p. 257, fr. 55.

[5] *Fragmenta Historicorum Graecorum*, vol. 4, p. 77, fr. 7.

been acknowledged by the Emperor in the Orient; it also sets forth the custom followed in the case of embassies from the Persian court.

On occasions of the former sort,[1] the Master had to provide for the entertainment of the legates, receive them, and arrange for their audience. If the legate were himself a Master of the Offices, he was brought to the palace by the *adiutor* of the Master at the court of Constantinople; otherwise by members of the *officium admissionum.* The legate or legates attended in the hall of the Master (*σχολὴ τοῦ μαγίστρου*) in the palace until the time of their reception. After the Eastern Emperor had confirmed the appointment of his Western colleague, legates of the rank of Prefect were placed upon an equal footing with the Prefects in Constantinople, but those who were Masters gave precedence to the Master in the East.[2] This procedure was also followed in the case of similar delegations from the Gothic Kings of Italy.[3]

Prior to their farewell reception the Master of the Offices had to prepare a list of presents for the legates and their attendants, which, when approved by the Emperor, he turned over to the Count of the Sacred Largesses to make ready. Finally, the Master took any letters from the Eastern to the Western Emperor and handed them over to the ambassadors, when they came to take leave of him.[4]

When a Persian legate visited Constantinople, the Master's duties were still more onerous.[5] He had to send a representative to the border city of the Empire, Nisibis, to greet him, to present a written or oral invitation to visit the capital, and to convoy him on his way thither. The *officiales* of the *duces* in the provinces traversed had to provide the requisites for the journey and a record of these expenditures was kept in the bureau of foreigners, *scrinium barbarorum,* which formed a part of the Master's *officium.* As the legate approached Antioch he was met by one of the Agentes sent by the Master to exchange courtesies. Again, at Chalcedon, the Master had to have quarters ready for him and his retinue, to send him an adjutant from the *scrinium*

[1] *De Caer.*, I, 87; 88.

[2] *De Caer.*, I, 87: ὃ ἔπαρχος τῶν πραιτωρίων καὶ ὁ ἔπαρχος τῆς πόλεως, λοιπὸν οὕτως δέχονται ὡς ἐνταῦθα ὄντες ἔπαρχοι, . . ., καὶ ὁ μάγιστρος μετὰ τὸν μαγίστρον τὸν ἐνταῦθα περιπατεῖ.

[3] *De Caer.*, I, 87 fin.

[4] *De Caer.*, I, 88.

[5] *De Caer.*, I, 89, 90.

barbarorum (ὀπτίων τῶν βαρβάρων), to furnish the cost of his sojourn there and offer him presents, and to send others to greet him again and to inquire whether his journey had been made pleasantly and without annoyance. A residence with due furnishings had to be provided for the ambassador in Constantinople, to the preparation of which the Count of the Private Purse or the Saccellarius of the Emperor and the Urban Prefect made contributions according to a written order from the Master.

To meet the legate on his arrival at the European shore the Master sent horses from the imperial stables under the direction of the Emperor's *spatharius*. When he reached his quarters the Master again sent him greetings and presents. This greeting was returned by a representative of the legate. The legate next visited the Master himself, who received him with polite formalities and later notified him through a *subadiuva* of his office of the date set for his audience with the Emperor. In preparing for the reception, the *magister admissionum* ascertained the Master's pleasure with regard to the standard-bearers (λαβαρήσιοι) and gave them their orders. The Master then received the legate in his audience hall, asked about the number of presents that the latter brought, and took a list of them, which he presented to the Emperor. The *candidati* and their attendants, the *admissionales*, the *cartularii* of the *scrinium barbarorum*, and the interpreters took up their respective posts and executed their duties at the Master's command. It was the Master who summoned the legate to the *consistorium*. Later an evaluation of the presents brought by the legate was made and given to the Master, who used it in advising the Emperor as to the gifts to be made in return.

At the Master's word the guard of the *candidati* was dismissed and the legate awaited the Master in the latter's hall until he came to close the interview. Subsequently, the Emperor signified to the Master of the Offices that he was ready to grant another audience, whereupon the latter notified the legate, received him, and introduced him as before. Upon this occasion private gifts of the legate were received through the Master, who also dismissed the former at the close of the ceremony. Further, as the Emperor thought best, he allowed the Master alone to discuss business of state with the legate, or permitted other officials to do the same.

On account of his duties in connection with such embassies,

and likewise for the purpose of handling diplomatic correspondence with foreign peoples, the Master of the Offices had in his *officium* a body of interpreters, known as *interpretes diversarum gentium*.[1] However, correspondence with legations coming from within the Empire was transacted through the *scrinium epistularum*.[2]

The Master of the Offices himself was sometimes employed as a Roman legate to foreign nations; his position in the confidence of the Emperor, and the influence which his office lent him in the conduct of foreign affairs, rendered him well suited for such missions. Thus, in 456, Euphemius, Master under Marcian, went on an embassy to Gobazes, King of the Lazi in the Caucasus, and persuaded him to make peace with the Romans.[3] In 522, Hermogenes, another Master, was a Roman representative at the Persian court;[4] and ten years later Celer, also a Master, concluded a peace for seven years with the same foe.[5] In 555 and 562 Petrus, Master under Justinian, likewise negotiated treaties with the Persians.[6] In 579, Tiberius sent his Master of the Offices, Theodorus, as a legate to Chosroes II,[7] and as late as 774 A.D. a Master named Petrus, in company with the Logothete of the Post and the Domesticus, went on an embassy to make terms with the Arabs.[8]

In addition to representing the imperial interests on diplomatic missions, the Master of the Offices was appointed to undertake other extraordinary services, for which his position in the consistorium particularly fitted him. For example, in 360, Florentius, Master under Constantius, was nominated one of the two officials forming a commission to investigate the loss of Amida.[9] A little later, Julian sent his Master, Pentadius, on a confidential mission to Constantius.[10] In exceptional cases a Master of the Offices was even intrusted with a high military command, as when Justinian,

1 *Notitia Dignitatum*, *or*. XI, 52; *omnium gentium*, *occ*. X, 46; cf. Priscus, *Fragmenta Historicorum Graecorum*, vol. 4, p. 77, fr. 7; *De Caer*., 1, 89.

2 Cf. p. 84 above.

3 Priscus, c. 12, p. 155, Bonn: ὥστε δὲ θάτερον βασιλεύειν, Γοβάζην, ἢ τὸν αὐτοῦ παῖδα, τῆς Κολχίδος, καὶ τῇδε λυθῆναι τὸν πόλεμον, Εὐφήμιος ἐσηγήσατο, τὴν τοῦ μαγίστρου διέπων ἀρχήν.

4 Theophanes, 276 Bonn.

5 Procopius, *De bello Persico*, 1, 8.

6 Theophanes, 370, Bonn: cf. Procopius, *De bello Gothico*, 4, 11; Menander Protector, *Fragmenta Historicorum Graecorum*, vol. 4, p. 207, fr. 11.

7 Menander Protector, *Frag. Hist. Graec*., vol. 4, p. 257, fr. 55; Theophylactus, 3, 15.

8 Theophanes, 706, Bonn.

9 Ammianus, 20, 2, 2.

10 Ammianus, 20, 8, 19.

in 532, sent his Master Celer as one of the four generals in command of the forces destined for the relief of Amida,[1] and later appointed Hermogenes to a joint command with Belisarius.[2]

It is also probable that the exercise of judicial functions by the Master in special cases, where honorary *illustres* resident in Constantinople were concerned,[3] was due to his presence in the *consistorium*.

The importance and influence, in the state, of the position occupied by the Master of the Offices, are further illustrated by the prominent rôle that he carried at the accession and inauguration of the Emperors Leo I (457), Leo II (474), Anastasius (491), and Justin I (518), accounts of which are to be found in the Ceremonial Book.[4] In the latter instance,[5] upon the death of Anastasius, who did not leave an Empress surviving to nominate a successor, and who had neglected to make such a nomination himself or to take a colleague during his lifetime, the first persons notified were the Master, Celer, and the Commander of the *excubitores*, Justinus. The former convened the Scholarians and the *candidati;* the latter the regular soldiers, tribunes, *vicarii* and officers of the *excubitores*, and each announced the need of choosing a new Emperor. In the meeting of the senate which followed Celer played a leading part; his exhortation to the dignitaries is the only one preserved, and it was this body that finally nominated Justinus.

Even after the Master's office had lost its immediate control over the various departments of the administration, it continued to be one of the great offices of state, whose holder assisted in the imperial councils and in the general government of the Empire. In such capacity under Theophilus and Basil I the Master officiated as one of the three dignitaries who conducted the government during the absence of the Emperor from the capital. His associates upon such occasions were the Viceroy (ὁ διέπων), who was regularly the Praepositus, and the Urban Prefect.[6] These duties remained the longest with the Mastership; even after it had become an order of rank, as late as the reign of Basil I, the two Masters, who still performed some duties as the

[1] Procopius, *De bello Persico*, 1, 8.

[2] Procopius, *op. cit.*, 1, 13: ξυνδιακομήσων τὸν στρατόν; cf. Müller, *Philologus*, 1912, p. 107.

[3] *Codex Justinianus*, III, 24, 3.

[4] *De Caer.*, 1, 91; 92; 93; 94.

[5] *De Caer.*, 1, 93.

[6] *De Caer.*, appendix (περὶ τάξεων) 503, 504, 506, Bonn; cf. p. 54 above.

Emperor's advisers, were accordingly known as the "Masters of the State." [1]

The duties of the Master in connection with the introduction of officials to the imperial presence, as well as in receiving and presenting foreign ambassadors, passed to the Logothete of the Post, whom we find performing them in the tenth century.[2]

X. The Ceremonial Duties of the Master of the Offices

The position of the Master of the Offices as commander of the Palace Guards and director of the various corps of palace servants, especially that of the court ushers, who, as we have seen, were under his orders, naturally rendered him responsible for the part which they played at the various court ceremonies where their presence was required. Hence he came to assume control over the ceremonial on such occasions, and to take over the function of a Master of Ceremonies. This is clearly indicated in the account given by Corippus [3] of an audience in the palace where, upon the Emperor's command, the various corps of *officiales palatini* took up their respective positions according to the Master's orders.

A large part of the ceremonial duties fell to the lot of the Master in connection with the audiences held in the council chamber (*consistorium*), where delegates from foreign peoples, senators, and other persons, who for various reasons were accorded an official interview with the Emperor, were received. The Master's share in such proceedings has been amply illustrated in the discussion of his duties in connection with the *Consistory* and requires no further comment here.

There were other official ceremonies, however, at which the Master had a similar part to play. One of these was the inaugu-

[1] Theophanes Continuatus, 5, 99: τοῖς δυσὶ τῆς πολιτείας μαγίστροις, whom the Emperor desired to intrust with the direction of the survey of lands which had become ownerless, and their reassignment.

[2] *De Caer.*, 1, 24, 138 Bonn; 2, 3; 2, 15; 2, 47; Luitprand, *Historia*, 6, 2: *imperator non voce sua, sed per logothetam, cum legatis loquitur.*

[3] *In laudem Justini*, III, 162 ff.:

> Ornata est Augusta domus, iussuque regentis
> Acciti proceres omnes, schola quaeque palati est
> Iussa suis adstare locis. Iamque ordine certo
> Turba decanorum, cursorum, in rebus agentum,
> Cumque palatinis stans candida turba tribunis
> Et protectorum numerus mandante magistro.

ration of a new Emperor, regarding which the book *On Ceremonies* has preserved several notices. From it we learn that at the induction of Leo I the Master of the Offices, Martialius, and the archbishop of Constantinople, Anatolius, were the two chief personages.[1] At the coronation of Leo II, also, the Master had a prominent part; with the assistance of certain Patricians, he introduced the Caesar who was to be crowned.[2] The Master, likewise, had charge of the introduction of Anastasius upon the occasion of his assumption of the imperial title.[3]

The prominent rôle assumed by the Master Celer in connection with the choice of a successor to Anastasius, in 518, has already been discussed.[4] We know further that at Justin's inauguration it was the duty of the Quaestor, or of Celer himself, to read the address of the new Emperor to the people; but the former was absent from the ceremony, and the latter had in the meantime suffered an attack of gout, so that some member of the Bureau of Petitions, *scrinium libellorum*, had to take his place.[5] In the account given of the coronation of Leo II the Master of the Offices is mentioned along with the *consul ordinarius* as an eponymous official;[6] in that of the coronation of Justinian he is the only official mentioned in connection with the dating of the event.[7]

Further, in the sixth century the Master had important ceremonial duties to perform at the appointment of officers to higher posts, or at their admission to the imperial service, especially when they were under the orders of the Master himself, as in the case of the *comes admissionum*[8] or *candidati*.[9]

The general functions of the Master of the Offices as a Master of Ceremonies gradually passed to the Praepositus and to the officer known as the ὁ ἐπὶ τῆς καταστάσεως, or Master of Ceremonies. To the transitional stage of this process is to be attributed the procedure recorded for three functions in the *De Caerimoniis*.

[1] *De Caer.*, 1, 91; they alone, of all the dignitaries, are mentioned by name.

[2] *De Caer.*, 1, 94.

[3] *De Caer.*, 1, 92.

[4] See p. 97 ff. above.

[5] *De Caer.* 1, 93.

[6] *De Caer.*, 1, 94: τῇ οὖν πρὸ δεκαπέντε καλανδῶν Δεκεμβρίων ἐν ὑπατίᾳ Λέοντος τοῦ μικροῦ, μαγίστρου ὄντος Εὐσεβίου.

[7] *De Caer.*, 1, 95: τῇ οὖν τετάρτῃ τοῦ Ἀπριλίου μηνὸς ἰνδέ, μαγίστρου ὄντος Τατιανοῦ. The prominent position thus given to the Mastership may be due to the partiality of the Master Petrus with whom these accounts originated, and whose work on this office has been referred to before; cf. Lydus, *De Mag.*, 2, 25.

[8] *De Caer.*, 1, 84.

[9] *De Caer.*, 1, 86.

The first of these is the appointment of a Caesar,[1] and dates from a time when there were several Masters, forming a grade of dignitaries.[2] Here the Praepositus and the First Master (ὁ πρῶτος μάγιστρος) are charged with the duty of introducing the future Caesar. The second case is that of celebrations held in the Golden Hippodrome,[3] and the third that of the races held on the anniversary of the foundation of Constantinople.[4] The rôle of the Master is the same in both cases. In admitting the senate and the ex-Prefect to their places the Emperor gave the signal to the Praepositus, who nodded to the Master, who in turn signalled to the Master of Ceremonies, ἐπὶ τῆς καταστάσεως, who summoned the dignitaries. In these latter instances, however, it was the Praepositus and the Master of Ceremonies who really had charge of the arrangements of the celebrations; the share of the Master of Offices was now purely nominal, a relic of his former importance.

In later ceremonies of the ninth and tenth centuries the Masters take no active part whatever.

XI. The *Officium* of the Master of the Offices

The Master of the Offices, like the other important administrative officials, had his *officium*. This was an office staff of clerks, secretaries, and the like, who kept the Master in touch with the various departments of the palace and the administration that were under his control, aiding him in the work of supervision; they also assisted him in the performance of the general duties that fell to his lot.

According to the *Notitia*[5] the *officium* of the Master in the Orient was composed of the following officials, who were chosen from the *schola* of the Agentes in Rebus:

An Aide, *adiutor*.

Two Assistant Aides, *subadiuvae adiutores*.

Three Deputies for the Arsenals, *subadiuvae fabricarum*.

Four Deputies for the Textile Factories, *subadiuvae barbaricariorum*.

A Resident Inspector of the State Post, *curiosus cursus publici praesentalis*.

[1] *De Caer.*, I, 43.

[2] βῆλον ά, τοὺς μαγίστρους.

[3] *De Caer.*, I, 68.

[4] *De Caer.*, I, 70.

[5] *Notitia Dignitatum or.* XI, 40: *Officium autem suprascripti viri illustris magistri officiorum de scola agentum in rebus est ita.*

Inspectors, *curiosi*, throughout all the provinces.

Interpreters of various nations.

The same source gives the *officium* of the Master in the Occident, likewise recruited from among the Agentes, as follows:[1]

An Aide, *adiutor*.

Assistants to the Aide, *subadiuvae adiutoris*.

Deputies for the different Arsenals, *subadiuvae fabricarum diversarum*.

One Resident Inspector of the State Post, *curiosus cursus publici in praesenti*.

Inspectors, *curiosi*, for all the provinces.

Interpreters of all nations.

In addition to the above-mentioned officials each *officium* had a number of clerks for the performance of office work of various kinds, who were under the direction of the *adiutor* and *subadiuvae*.

The *adiutor*, or Master's aide, was in control of the *officium*, and likewise of the whole *schola* of the Agentes,[2] which in a certain sense might be regarded as a larger *officium*. His position corresponded to that of the *principes* in the other *officia*. The *adiutor* was selected among the Agentes of the rank of *ducenarius*,[3] by the Master himself, but his appointment was subject to the imperial confirmation.[4] Originally, the whole *schola* of the Agentes was called upon to testify as to his fitness for the post, but later this formality was dispensed with.[5] Upon his retirement he took rank with the *vicarii*,[6] and at the end of the fifth century was a *clarissimus*[7] when in the active service.

The *scrinium* of the *adiutor*, that is the body of clerks at his disposal, is also mentioned, and in such terms as to indicate that

[1] *Notitia Dignitatum occ.* IX, 40.

[2] *Codex Theodosianus*, I, 9, 1 (359): *Adiutor praeterea, in quo totius scholae status et magistri securitas constituta est.*

[3] *Codex Justinianus*, XII, 21, 5 (440–441).

[4] *Codex Theodosianus*, I, 9, 1: *Adiutor praeterea, . . . , omni schola testimonium praebente, idoneus probitate morum ac bonis artibus praeditus nostris per magistrum obtutibus offeratur, ut nostro ordinetur arbitrio;* cf. *Cod. Just.* 1, 31, 1; Cass. *var.* 6, 6, 8.

[5] Compare *Codex Theodosianus*, I, 9, 1 with *Codex Justinianus*, I, 31, 1, where the phrase *omni schola* etc. is omitted.

[6] *Codex Justinianus*, XII, 21, 5: *Eos, qui ordine transcursa militia post ducenam ad desideratum principis pervenerint gradum aut adiutores viri illustris magistri officiorum extiterint, cum inter honoratos coeperint numerari, vicarianae dignitatis titulis decorari censemus.*

[7] *Codex Justinianus*, XII, 19, 12 (Zeno); XII, 29, 2 (474); *C. I. L.* VIII, 989.

it had charge of the documents relating to cases brought against the *scriniarii* who were under the Master's jurisdiction.[1]

It was the *adiutor* who, as Bury[2] thinks, subsequently developed into the *domesticus scholarum*, the officer that later superseded the Master as commander of the Scholarians. However, this point will be discussed more fully in connection with the *domesticus* of the Master.

The *subadiuvae adiutores*,[3] or *adiutoris*,[4] were the aides of the *adiutor* and probably assisted him in the general direction of the office. In the ceremonial followed in connection with the reception of a Persian ambassador at Constantinople it was one of these *subadiuvae* whom the Master sent to notify the legate of the time set for his audience.[5]

The *subadiuvae fabricarum*, as their name indicates, were occupied with the business arising from the Master's control of the arsenals. In the early fifth century there were three of them in the office of the Eastern Master,[6] but apparently a greater number in the West.[7] Later, however, the number in the East was increased; for under Leo[8] four *subadiuvae* from the highest class of the Agentes were annually chosen for a year's service in the *scrinium fabricarum*. Evidently the *scrinium fabricarum* consisted of these *subadiuvae* and the clerks under their orders. In 539 it still formed part of the Master's *officium*, and the latter was then directed to appoint *chartularii* therefrom to investigate contraventions of the edict forbidding the manufacture of arms by private persons, while five seniors (*priores*) of the *scrinium* were responsible for the acts of these deputies.[9]

The four *subadiuvae barbaricariorum* in the Orient occupied a position closely corresponding to that held by the *subadiuvae fabricarum*. They assisted the Master in the supervision of the imperial factories for the making of goods interwoven with gold, pearls, and precious stones, in which the workmen were styled *barbaricarii*. From the time of Valens such factories in the

[1] *Codex Justinianus*, XII, 19, 12, 3.

[2] *Imperial Administration*, p. 50.

[3] *Notitia Dignitatum or.* XI, 42–3.

[4] *Notitia Dignitatum or.* IX, 42.

[5] *De Caer.*, I, 89.

[6] *Notitia Dignitatum or.* XI, 44.

[7] *Notitia Dignitatum occ.* IX, 43.

[8] *Codex Justinianus*, XII, 20, 5: *Agentes in rebus, qui per ordinem consequi solent principatus insignia, in unoquoque scrinio fabricarum et barbarorum quaternos subadiuvarum sollicitudinem per annum dumtaxat integrum procedentes gradatim subire hac in aeternum valitura lege decernimus.*

[9] *Novellae Justiniani*, 85, c. 3; cf. p. 88 above.

Orient had been under the direction of the Master of the Offices along with the arsenals.[1] One of these *subadiuvae* acted for the diocese of the Orient, one for Asia, one for Pontus, and the fourth for Thrace and Illyricum.[2] Under Leo there was a Bureau of Foreigners, *scrinium barbarorum*, to which four *subadiuvae* were annually detached from the Agentes in the same way as to the *scrinium fabricarum*.[3] It is a question whether these are to be identified with the *subadiuvae barbaricariorum*. This problem is not simplified by the fact that there is considerable confusion in the texts between *barbari* and *barbaricarii*.[4]

There is little further information with regard to the *scrinium barbarorum*. An edict of Theodosius II,[5] addressed to a Master of the Offices, ordained that the *scrinium barbarorum* should pay a fine of ten pounds of gold if it permitted senators, *ducenarii* or *centenarii* of the Agentes to become *domestici* of the *comites scholarum*, or if it failed to give information regarding any attempt on their part to gain such an appointment. Further, it was the *scrinium barbarorum* which preserved the accounts of the expenditures made for the conveyance of a Persian legate and his suite from the eastern frontier to Constantinople,[6] and it was also this *scrinium* that furnished the *optio* or adjutant to the Persian legate upon his arrival at Chalcedon.[7] Finally, *cartularii* of the *scrinium barbarorum* were in attendance under the Master's orders at the audience granted the legate,[8] where they acted in conjunction with the *magister admissionum* and the interpreters.

From this I think we may conclude that, owing to the close connection between the *scrinium barbarorum* and the Master of the Offices, evidenced by the passages cited, and the appointment of the *subadiuvae* of this *scrinium* from the Agentes in the same way as those of the *scrinium fabricarum*, the *scrinium barbarorum* formed a part of the Master's *officium*. However, in view of the fact that this *scrinium* does not appear to have anything to do with the work of the *barbaricarii*, but rather acts as a bureau of records for various statistics, we cannot identify the *subadiuvae barbaricariorum* of the *Notitia* with members of this *scrinium*,[9]

[1] See above, p. 89.
[2] *Notitia Dignitatum or*. XI, 45–49.
[3] *Codex Justinianus*, XII, 20, 5.
[4] Cf. Böcking, *Notitia Dignitatum*, vol. 1, p. 245.
[5] *Novellae Theodosii*, XXI, 2 (441).
[6] *De Caer.*, 1, 89, 400 Bonn.
[7] *De Caer.*, 1, 89, 401.
[8] *De Caer.*, 1, 89, 404, 405.
[9] Cf. Seeck, Pauly-Wissowa, vol. 2, p. 2857.

unless we suppose that they had later received a sphere of duties differing widely from those which they originally performed. The probabilities are, therefore, that some time after the compilation of the *Notitia* a new *scrinium*, that in question, was added to the *officium* of the Master.

The Inspector of the Post at the Court — the *curiosus cursus publici praesentalis*,[1] or *in praesenti*[2] — evidently had charge of the passes for the State Post issued in the Master's *officium*, and probably of those issued in the name of the Emperor also; for the title *praesentalis* seems to suggest his connection with the imperial person. The other Inspectors of the Post, those despatched throughout the provinces, the *curiosi per omnes provincias*[3] or *omnium provinciarum*,[4] whose duties have been explained elsewhere,[5] were likewise reckoned as forming part of the Master's office.

Lastly, there were the interpreters for the foreign peoples with whom the Empire entered into official contact,[6] who were of assistance to the Master in his conduct of diplomatic correspondence or personal negotiations with foreign governments or their representatives.[7]

The members of the Master's *officium*, upon the expiration of their term of service, were accorded the rank of *princeps*, taking precedence over those from the offices of the Pretorian and the Urban Prefects.[8] This general statement is exclusive of the *adiutor*, whose special honors have been mentioned.

This office staff gradually broke up, as the various departments, in the direction of which they had assisted the Master, passed from his hands into those of others; it disappeared entirely when the Master ceased to be an active administrative official.

XII. The *Domesticus* of the Master of the Offices

Besides the members of his Staff, *officium*, the Master of the Offices had in his service an officer called a *domesticus*. Such

[1] *Notitia Dignitatum or.* XI, 50.
[2] *Notitia Dignitatum occ.* IX, 44.
[3] *Notitia Dignitatum or.* XI, 51.
[4] *Notitia Dignitatum occ.* IX, 45.
[5] See p. 74 ff. above.
[6] *Notitia Dignitatum or.* XI, 52: *interpretes diversarum gentium; occ.* IX, 46: *omnium gentium.*
[7] Priscus, *Fragmenta Historicorum Graecorum*, vol. 4, p. 77, fr. 7; *De Caer.*, 1, 89.
[8] Cassiodorus, *Variae*, 6, 6, 7: *Officium vero eius tanta genii praerogativa decoratur, ut militiae perfunctus muneribus ornetur nomine principatus miroque modo inter praetorianas cohortes et urbanae praefecturae milites videantur invenisse primatum.*

domestici were found in the staff of practically all the high civil and military officials. In the *Notitia* these *domestici* are not given a place in the offices of their chiefs nor are they mentioned at all, probably because, being appointed at the pleasure of their superiors, they were regarded theoretically as holding no official position, but as acting in an entirely personal relation to the official who employed them.[1] However, by the reign of Valentinian I the *domestici* had attained an official status, and subsequently considerable legislation was required to regulate their position and powers; and their failure to appear in the *Notitia* may be due to the fact that the *cancellarius* or some other member of the *officia* filled the position of *domesticus*.[2]

The first mention of the *domesticus* of the Master of the Offices is for the year 374,[3] when he appears as the confidential agent of the Master. In the Orient, we can trace this official well into the seventh century,[4] now with the Greek title *δομεστικὸς τοῦ μαγίστρου*. This Domesticus accompanied the Emperor Heraclius on an expedition to the East, and Bury[5] plausibly infers that the Scholarians went along under his command, while the Master remained in Constantinople. Consequently, when we find that in the eighth century the Scholarians were under the command of an officer called the *δομεστικὸς τῶν σχολῶν*,[6] who was not a subordinate of the Master of the Offices, the natural conclusion seems to be that when the latter lost control of the palace guard this command was transferred to his *domesticus*, who received a corresponding elevation in rank.[7]

XIII. Characteristics of the Mastership

Our examination of the various spheres of competence which went to make up the Mastership of the Offices reveals the power and influence of that office, but at the same time makes clear the difficulty of comparing it with any administrative office in other states, ancient or modern. The view of Lydus,[8] who, looking at the power of the Master of the Offices as commander of the palace guards, saw in him a revival of the Master of the Horse of the

[1] Seeck, Pauly-Wissowa, vol. 5, p. 1296.
[2] Seeck, *op. cit.*, pp. 1296–7.
[3] Ammianus, 30, 2, 10–11.
[4] 624 A.D., *Chronicon Paschale*, 724 Bonn.
[5] *Imperial Administration*, p. 50.
[6] Theophanes, 684 (767 A.D.).
[7] Bury suggests (*op. cit.*, p. 50) that the Domesticus may have been the same as the *adiutor* of the Master. Originally these two positions were quite distinct, but later it is possible that they were filled by the same individual.
[8] *De Mag.*, 2, 24.

early regal period of Rome, is pure fantasy; and the difficulty which modern writers find in choosing a title to translate that of the Master is further proof of the uniqueness of his position.

A few of these attempts at correlation may be mentioned. Hodgkin [1] thinks that a combination of the offices of the principal Secretaries of State of Great Britain, united with that of a Private Secretary to the Sovereign, would correspond closely with the functions of the Master of the Offices. Serrigny [2] views him as a *ministre de la police générale*, acting as a guard over the other ministers. Again, Bouché-Leclercq [3] translates Master of the Offices by *prévôt de palais*, and Schiller [4] uses a corresponding term, Oberhofmarschall, which, in turn, is not very different from Madvig's Reichshofmeister.[5]

Although there does not seem to have been any definitely established *cursus honorum* necessarily preceding the holding of the Mastership of the Offices, still from the official careers of some of the Masters known to us, which may be regarded as typical examples, one can infer the general nature of the official training which was a prelude to the appointment. Naturally this was of a civil and not of a military character, as may be clearly seen from the list of offices filled by the two Masters whose careers are most fully known, Flavius Eugenius, Master in 346, and Cassiodorus, Master between 523 and 527. Prior to his Mastership, Eugenius, as an inscription [6] shows, had been employed in the various subordinate offices about the palace; Cassiodorus held in succession the following posts: Conciliarius of the Pretorian Prefect, Quaestor, Corrector of Apulia and Bruttium, Consul Ordinarius, Master of the Offices, and Pretorian Prefect.[7]

In the fourth century Masters of the Offices were often chosen among those who had filled secretaryships and clerkships, even as members of the staff of other officials. Thus Anatolius [8] was promoted from the Secretaryship of the Petitions, Felix,[9] Leo,[10]

[1] *Italy and her Invaders*, Vol. I, 2, p. 610. [2] *Droit public romain*, p. 87.

[3] *Manuel des Institutions romaines*, p. 165.

[4] *Geschichte der römischen Kaiserzeit*, Vol. 2, p. 101.

[5] *Verfassung des römischen Staates*, vol. I, 1, p. 587.

[6] Dessae, *Inscriptiones Selectae*, 1244; FL(avio) EUGENIO, V(iro) C(larissimo), EX PRAEFECTO PRAETORIO, CONSULI ORDINARIO DESIGNATO, MAGISTRO OFFICIORUM OMNIUM, COMITI DOMESTICO ORDINIS PRIMI OMNIBUSQUE PALATINIS DIGNITATIBUS FUNCTO, etc.

[7] *Monumenta Germaniae Historica, Auctores Antiquissimi*, vol. XII, pp. x–xi.

[8] Ammianus, 20, 9, 8 (360), *libellis respondens*. [9] Ammianus, 20, 9, 5 (360).

[10] Ammianus, 28, 1, 12 (368).

Syagrius[1] and Johannes[2] from *notarii;* and Remigius[3] from a clerkship in the office of a *magister militum.*

At this time the Mastership might be a step to a provincial governorship of the highest rank, as in the case of Ampelius,[4] who was advanced from it to become Proconsul of Asia, Proconsul of Africa, and Pretorian Prefect. Later, however, probably from the time that the *comites consistoriani* were given equal rank with the proconsuls,[5] any such appointments preceded the Mastership, as we have seen in the case of Cassiodorus.

Frequently Masters were promoted from the Ministry of Finance, as in the case of Hadrianus,[6] Macedonius,[7] and Palladius,[8] who had been Counts of the Sacred Largesses before being made Masters of the Offices. It is also true that the reverse order was sometimes followed, and that ex-Masters were made Counts of the Sacred Largesses,[9] but this was not at all usual and doubtless ceased as the mastership became increasingly important.

In the fourth and fifth centuries the Consulate usually followed the Mastership, if we may judge from the following instances: Eugenius, Master in 346, and then *consul ordinarius designatus;*[10] Rufinus, Master in 390, and Consul in 392;[11] Nomus, Master in 443–4, Consul in 445;[12] Opilio, Master in 449–50, Consul in 453;[13] and Vincomalus, Master and *consul designatus* in 452.[14] But even at this time the Consulship sometimes preceded the Mastership,[15] and in the following century it was, as a rule, held first, as for example, by Cassiodorus[16] and Hermogenes.[17]

[1] Ammianus, 28, 2, 5; 9: *Cod. Theod.* I, 15, 10 (379). [2] Zosimus, 5, 40; Sozomenus, 9, 8.

[3] *Rationalis adparitoris armorum magistri,* Ammianus, 15, 5, 36; 27, 6, 36; 27, 9, 2 (368). [4] Ammianus, 28, 4, 3 (before 369).

[5] *Codex Theodosianus,* VI, 12, 1 (399).

[6] *Codex Theodosianus,* V, 14, 35; VI, 26, 11.

[7] *Codex Theodosianus,* XI, 30, 39; Severus, *Sacra Historia,* 2, 48.

[8] *Codex Theodosianus,* IV, 13, 8, 9; X, 24, 3.

[9] So Felix under Julian, as recorded by Ammianus, 20, 9, 5; 23, 1, 5.

[10] Dessau, *Inscriptiones Selectae,* 1244; see above.

[11] *Codex Theodosianus,* X, 22, 3; I, 29, 7 and 8; cf. Seeck, *Geschichte des Untergangs der antiken Welt,* vol. 5, p. 268.

[12] *Codex Justinianus,* I, 31, 4; *Novellae Theodosii,* 24, 25.

[13] *Novellae Valentiniani,* 28, 30. [14] Mansi, vol. 7, p. 497; 505.

[15] An example is that of Valerius, *magister* and *ex consule ordinarius; Codex Theodosianus,* VII, 8, 16 (435). [16] See above, p. 106.

[17] Master and ex-Consul in 535, *Novellae Justiniani,* 2. However, if this is the same Hermogenes who was Master in 533 (*Codex Justinianus,* V, 17, 11), he may have been Consul and Master at the same time.

As the Quaestorship and the Mastership were offices of practically equal rank in the hierarchy of Roman officials, the holding of the one was not a preliminary step to holding the other. In the sixth century, indeed, these two offices were at times placed in the hands of one person, as we have seen in the cases of Trebonian[1] and Anastasius.[2] However, at the same epoch, in the Gothic Kingdom in Italy, Eugenes[3] and Cassiodorus[4] both held the Quaestorship before the Mastership of the Offices.

Once the Mastership had been put in possession of the greater part of the power that it eventually wielded, it tended to become the regular prelude to a Prefecture; promotions were made directly from the former to the latter office as early as the middle of the fourth century. So it was with Florentius,[5] Siburius,[6] Syagrius,[7] Hadrianus,[8] Anthemius,[9] and Cassiodorus,[10] Pretorian Prefects, and Theodotus[11] and Aemilianus,[12] Urban Prefects. With Eugenius[13] and Rufinus,[14] the Consulate intervened between Mastership and Prefecture.

As a rule, then, we may conclude that a Master of the Offices had had a considerable official experience previous to attaining this position, and might reasonably look forward to a still higher office. Nevertheless it is probable that in many cases no strict rules for promotion were observed, and influence and ability had much to do with obtaining the Mastership. So when Cassiodorus[3] boasted that he had obtained his position by merit and not through the influence of wealth, he implied that the opposite sometimes occurred. And we know that Petrus, a lawyer of Constantinople, without official position, was rewarded

[1] *Novellae Justiniani*, 23 (536). Trebonian's career is instructive. He was an *illustris* with the rank of a Master in active service in 528 (*Codex Justinianus, de novo codice*, 1); in 530 he was Quaestor (*id.*, I, 17, 1); in 533 he was Master and ex-Quaestor (*id.*, I, 17, 2 *pr.*); finally, in 536, he held both Mastership and Quaestorship (*Novellae Justiniani*, 23).

[2] Corippus, *Panegyr. Pr.*, 30 (565).

[3] Cassiodorus, *Variae*, 1, 12 and 13.

[4] See p. 106.

[5] Ammianus, 20, 2, 2 (360).

[6] *Codex Theodosianus*, XI, 31, 7; cf. *Monumenta Germaniae Historica*, vol. VI, *auctores antiquissimi*, p. cxxxi.

[7] *Codex Theodosianus*, I, 15, 10; XI, 30, 38 (380).

[8] *Codex Theodosianus*, VI, 27, 11; II, 8, 24 (400).

[9] *Codex Theodosianus*, XVI, 4, 4; VII, 10, 1 (405).

[10] Cassiodorus, *Variae*, 9, 24, 25 (533).

[11] *Codex Theodosianus*, VII, 1, 14; VI, 28, 5 (395).

[12] *Codex Theodosianus*, I, 9, 3; XV, 1, 44 (406).

[13] Dessau, *op. cit.*, 1244.

[14] *Codex Theodosianus*, I, 29, 7; VIII, 6, 2; see above.

[15] *Variae*, 9, 24.

by Justinian with this office, in recognition of his astuteness displayed on a diplomatic mission to Italy.[1]

The Mastership, like the Quaestorship, was, strictly speaking, an annual charge,[2] but apparently there was no limit placed upon the number of times that it could be held by the same person.[3]

[1] Procopius, *De bello Goth.*, 1, 3, 6–8; 2, 22: *Historia Arcana*, 16.

[2] Lécrevain, *Le Sénat Romain*, p. 67; cf. Appendix B.

[3] Hadrianus was Master from 397 to 399 (*Codex Theodosianus*, VI, 26, 11; 27, 11); Helio was Master from 414 (*Codex Theodosianus*, XIII, 3, 17) to 427 (*Cod. Theod.*, XIII, 3, 18), and, notably, Peter the Patrician was Master from 539 to 565 (Procopius, *Historia Arcana*, c. 16; *De Bello Gothico*, 4, 11; *Novellae Justiniani*, 123; 137). See Appendix B.

CHAPTER V

THE TITLES, HONORS, AND PRIVILEGES OF THE MASTER OF THE OFFICES

I. The Roman Period

We have seen how, during the first three centuries following its establishment, the Mastership of the Offices gradually increased in influence and dignity, with the result that it successively entitled its holders to higher and more exclusive titles of rank, until they had passed through all the gradations of rank in the Later Empire, from the Perfectissimate to the Gloriosissimate. And we have found that, during the first two of these centuries, the Masters of the Offices received the distinction of the *comitiva*, which in the highest of its three grades had become attached to this, as well as to other imperial dignities. In a preceding chapter[1] we traced the different stages in the elevation of the Mastership through the various grades of rank, and it will be unnecessary to review the same facts again here; it will be sufficient, after a consideration of the privileges and honors that at various times fell to the lot of the Masters, to append lists of the known examples of the use of the several titles pertaining to these classes, which furnish the basis for the conclusions already presented. The same plan will be adopted in regard to the *comitiva*, the connection of which with the Mastership has been amply discussed.[2]

The incumbents of the magisterial dignity, *tot titulis claram, tot insignibus opulentam*,[3] enjoyed the right to use the title and insignia of the special order of rank to which their office at any time gave admission. Likewise they were in possession of the numerous privileges and exemptions to which the members of these orders were entitled.

The emblems of the Master of the Offices, *insignia viri illustris magistri officiorum*, which appear in the *Notitia Dignitatum*[4] and which may be called the Master's official seal, were

[1] Chapter III, pp. 44–47.
[2] Pp. 29, 31, 44.
[3] Cassiodorus, *Variae*, 6, 6, 8.
[4] *Or.* XI, *occ.* IX.

inscribed on the codicils containing his appointment,[1] which was couched in the language of Cassiodorus's *formula magisteriae dignitatis*. These emblems consist of the following parts arranged within a square border. At the top, a draped table, upon which is depicted a *liber mandatorum*, adorned with the portrait (*imago*) of the Emperor or Emperors. Below is the word FABRICAE, underneath which are grouped seven [2] round shields; alongside of and beneath these were various types of offensive and defensive weapons and armor. The legend FABRICAE and the weapons have obvious reference to the Master's control of the arsenals, while the seven shields with their varied blazonry represent the seven *scholae* of the palace guards.

Along with the codicils there was given to the Master of the Offices an official guide or set of instructions (*mandata*) issued by the Emperor to guide him in the conduct of the business of his office. This constituted the *liber mandatorum* represented in the Master's insignia.[3]

For the issuance of his diploma of appointment and his *mandata*, in all probability the Master of the Offices, like other officials,[4] had to make a donation (*consuetudo*, *sportula*), at first voluntary, but later obligatory, and of a definite amount, to the clerks of the bureau whose duty it was to prepare such documents. In the case of the Master, the recipients of these gratuities were probably the *cartularii sacri cubiculi*, the *primicerius notariorum*, his *adiutor* and his *laterculenses*.[5] Further, upon the receipt of such an appointment it was the custom for the beneficiary to express his gratitude by suitable gifts to the Emperor and Empress.[6]

We have no information regarding any special robes of office

[1] Cf. Böcking, *Über die Notitia Dignitatum utriusque imperii*, p. 97. Justinian translated *insignia* by σύμβολα or παρασήματα τῆς ἀρχῆς ἐν τοῖς καλουμένοις κωδικέλλοις.

[2] The *Notitia Dignitatum or*. has only six shields, but one is obviously lacking; cf. Böcking, *Notitia Dignitatum*, vol. 1, p. 234. Further differences between the oriental and occidental insignia are that the former has the *imago* of one Emperor only, while the latter has the *imagines* of two, and that the weapons depicted in each are not of the same types, nor arranged in the same way.

[3] Karlowa, *Römische Rechtsgeschichte*, vol. 1, p. 869; cf. *Novellae Justiniani*, 17 *pr.*; 24, 6 (referring to the appointment of provincial *iudices*): *non solum eis praebere magistratus insignia in his qui vocantur codicilli, sed etiam inscribere modum secundum quem regant administrationem, quae ante nos legislatores mandata principis appellabant.*

[4] *Codex Justinianus*, I, 27, 1, 19; 2, 36; *Novellae Justiniani*, 8, *notitia*; 24 *fin.*

[5] Böcking, *Über die Notitia Dignitatum*, p. 97; Karlowa, *Römische Rechtsgeschichte*, vol. 1, p. 869.

[6] Karlowa, *op. cit.*, p. 870; Böcking, *op. cit.*

which the Master wore during this period. Still we know that upon the occasion of the procession of the Emperor Heraclius to the church of St. Sophia on January 1, 639 A.D., a function described in the *De Caerimoniis*,[1] the Master Eustathius and four patricians wore the *toga*, which, from being the characteristic dress of Roman citizens, had evidently become the robe of state of certain high officials and dignitaries of the Eastern court. In any case an essential part of the Master's official regalia was the *cingulum*.

The conferment of the *cingulum*, or belt of office, was of greater significance in promotions to the Mastership, as to other official posts, than the granting of the codicils. The *cingulum* had originally been the symbol of military service, but under the Later Empire it denoted employment in the civil administration as well. The conferment of this *cingulum* was so essential a feature in the investiture of such officials, and its use was so characteristic of the tenure of office, that eventually *cingulum* came to be employed in official language as synonymous with *magistratus* or ἀρχή.[2]

From 441 A.D.,[3] and probably from the time the Master's office admitted its occupant to the class of the *illustres*, it was the custom to elevate a deserving official to the Illustrissimate by the conferment of an honorary Mastership, which did not involve the performance of the duties appertaining to that position. This honorary Mastership, again, might be conferred in two grades, distinguished by the possession of the right to wear the *cingulum*, or the lack of it.

In consequence, all the *illustres* who had the title of Master of the Offices were not of the same rank. The highest was the Master *pro tempore* in office. He was classed with the *illustres in actu positi*, or *administratores*, officials like himself in active service. Next in order came those who had gone into retirement after having held the Mastership. Such were called *illustres honorati*.

Then came those who had been awarded both the *cingulum* and the codicils of the Mastership without being called upon to undertake its burdens. Such appointments were really retirements, with the rank of the office that the recipient might have next

[1] *De Caer.*, 2, 28.

[2] *Novellae Justiniani*, 24, 2; etc.

[3] *Codex Justinianus*, XII, 8, 2.

attained if he had remained in active service. The Mastership was thus awarded to *primicerii* of the *tribuni notarii*,[1] but with the special provision that they should rank as if they had actually held the Mastership; that is, as *honorati*. Usually, however, Masters of this type belonged to the *illustres vacantes*, who might, if called upon subsequently to undertake the active administration of the Mastership, be classed among the *administratores*.

Finally, there were Masters who received the codicils without the *cingulum*. These too were on the retired list, and belonged to the class of *illustres honorarii*. In each of the last two classes a distinction was made between those who had received the insignia, or diploma, of their rank at the hand of the Emperor, and those to whom these emblems had been merely despatched. The former in each case were ranked above the latter. Within each of these classes of *illustres* the Masters ranked according to the position which, as we have seen, the Masters *in actu positi* took among the high officials of the Empire. Those who were in active service took precedence over all *honorati*, and these in turn over all *vacantes* and *honorarii*. However, *illustres vacantes* with the title of Master did not take rank above all *honorarii*, but only above such as had attained the same or a lower dignity. Among Masters of the same class the seniority was decided according to the time of their respective appointments.[2]

The Masters of the Offices as *clarissimi*, *spectabiles*, or *illustres* were members of the senatorial order,[3] and enjoyed all the special privileges and exemptions which were accorded to senators as a body, as well as to the members of these classes of rank. The most important of such advantages fell to the lot of the Masters in connection with the Illustrissimate. These included freedom from certain obligations to the fiscus; exemption from the necessity of furnishing recruits and horses to the army, of performing curial *munera* in provincial towns, and of furnishing the regular *hospitium* to officers and soldiers; and also the right

[1] *Codex Justinianus*, XII, 7, 2, 5 (Zeno): *Hoc etiam adiciendo, ut primicerius post depositam publicam numerorum sollicitudinem, ac si ipsam gessisset administrationem, cuius consequitur dignitatem, magistri officiorum pro antiqua consuetudine infulas sortiatur, omnibus vacantibus quamvis tempore praecedentibus praeponendus.*

[2] *Codex Justinianus*, XII, 8, 2. Cf. Jullian in Daremberg et Saglio, vol. 3, pp. 386 f.; Karlowa, *op. cit.*, vol. 1, pp. 870 f.

[3] Lécrevain in Daremberg et Saglio, vol. 4, p. 1197, s. v. *senatus*.

to pass on their titles and privileges to their wives and children, as well as an exceptional position before the law both in the matter of the courts before which they could be summoned and in the penalties to which they were subject. Furthermore, when the *clarissimi* and the *spectabiles* were relieved of the necessity of residing at the capital, active membership in the senate was practically confined to the *illustres*.[1] In regard to the obligation of furnishing quarters to troops, we are told specifically that the Masters of the Offices, and the Quaestors, were allowed to have one residence and the half of another immune from this burden during their lifetime, and that their heirs could claim exemption for one house.[2]

In addition to the title of his office and that of his order of rank, the Master of the Offices received many other honorable and complimentary appellations. Conspicuous among these was the term *frater amantissime*, used as a form of address to their Masters by the Western Emperors about the middle of the fifth century.[3] Along with other notables in the fifth and early sixth centuries, the Master of the Offices was sometimes accorded the titles of *excellentissimus*,[4] *vir excelsus*,[5] and *sublimissimus*,[6] which did not denote any definite rank but were attributed to high officials in general. Again, titles suitable to the Master himself were used with reference to his office, as in the phrase *illustris summitas magistri*,[7] or to the place where his authority was exercised, as in the application of *sublimis* to his *iudicium*.[8]

Furthermore, in official communications from the Emperor, the Masters were entitled to a series of substantive forms of address, which were very much the same as those used towards other officials of the rank of *illustres*.[9] These forms are arranged below in alphabetical order.

[1] Jullian in Daremberg et Saglio, vol. 3, pp. 387 f., s. v. *illustres.*

[2] *Codex Justinianus*, XII, 40, 10 (Valentinian and Marcian): *Magistri vero officiorum vel quaestores unam semis domum suam quoad vixerint habeant hospitium onere libertam: heredes vero eorum praedicti unam ab hospitibus iure defendant.*

[3] *Flegeti f(rater) a(mantissime)*, *Novellae Theodosii*, 21 (441); Nomus, id. 24 (443), 25 (444); Opilio, *Novellae Valentiniani*, 28 (449), 30 (450).

[4] *Codex Justinianus*, XII, 16, 4 (Zeno); I, 31, 5 (527).

[5] *Codex Justinianus*, I, 17, 2 (533).

[6] *Codex Justinianus*, VII, 62, 38 (529).

[7] *Codex Theodosianus*, VI, 10, 4 (425).

[8] *Codex Justinianus*, XII, 59, 9.

[9] Cf. Karlowa, *Römische Rechtsgeschichte*, vol. I, p. 871; Koch, *Byzantinische Beamtentitel*, p. 124; *Harvard Studies in Classical Philology*, vol. XXVI, pp. 139 f.

1. **Amplitudo**, "Your Greatness"

Amplitudo tua appears twice in constitutions of the fifth century.

Novellae Valentiniani, 30 (year 450).
Codex Justinianus, XII, 25, 4 (474).

2. **Auctoritas**, "Your Worthiness"

Illustris auctoritas tua is used with considerable frequency, especially in the West, towards the end of the first half of the fifth century. The Greek form, ἡ ὑπερλαμπροτάτη καὶ μεγαλοφύης αὐθεντία σή (*illustrissima et magnifica auctoritas tua*) appears in the *acta* of the Council of Chalcedon.[1]

Codex Theodosianus, VI, 27, 23 (year 430).
Novellae Theodosii, 24 (443); 25 (444).
Novellae Valentiniani, 28 (449); 30 (450).

3. **Celsitudo**, "Your Highness"

Tua celsitudo (ἡ σὴ ὑπεροχή) is employed from about the middle of the fifth century until well into the sixth.

Novellae Theodosii, 21 (year 441).
Codex Justinianus, XII, 19, 12 (Leo); XII, 20, 3 (id.); XII, 29, 2 (474).
Novellae Justiniani, 85 (539).

4. **Culmen**, "Your Eminence"

Culmen tuum (ἡ σὴ ὑπεροχή) is in use during the same period as *tua celsitudo.*

Novellae Theodosii, 21 (year 441), cf. *Codex Justinianus*, I, 31, 3; 24 (443); cf. *Codex Justinianus*, I, 31, 4.
Codex Justinianus, XII, 29, 3 (Zeno); XII, 19, 12 (Anastasius); I, 31, 5 (527).

5. **Eminentia**, "Your Eminency"

Eminentia tua appears in the early sixth century.

Codex Justinianus, XII, 19, 12 (Anastasius).
Novellae Justiniani, 10 ep. (535).

6. **Gloria**, "Your Glory"

The Greek equivalent of *tua gloria*, ἡ σὴ ἐνδοξότης, is found in a constitution of 565.

Novellae Justiniani, 137 ep.

7. **Magnificentia**, "Your Magnificence"

Magnificentia tua is used at the opening of the fifth century.

Codex Theodosianus, I, 9, 3 (year 405); VI, 27, 17 (415).

8. **Magnitudo**, "Your Grandeur"

Magnitudo tua occurs throughout the fifth and early in the sixth centuries.

Novellae Theodosii, 25 (year 444).
Codex Justinianus, XII, 25, 4 (474); XII, 29, 3 (Zeno); XII, 19, 12 (Anastasius); XII, 19, 15 (527).

[1] Mansi, vol. 7, p. 500; p. 505 (year 451).

9. **Sinceritas,** "Your Honor"

One example of *sinceritas tua* comes from the fourth century.

Codex Theodosianus, VIII, 5, 22 (year 365).

10. **Sublimitas,** "Your Loftiness"

Sublimitas tua is the most common of these designations in constitutions addressed to the Master of the Offices, being used throughout the whole of the fifth and the early part of the sixth centuries. In Greek, like *celsitudo* and *culmen*, it is rendered by ὑπεροχή, which also translates *eminentia* and seems to have no preferred Latin equivalent.[1]

Codex Theodosianus, VI, 27, 18 (year 416).
Novellae Theodosiani, 21 (441); cf. *Codex Justinianus*, I, 31, 3.
Novellae Valentiniani, 28 (449).
Codex Justinianus, XI, 10, 6 (Leo and Anthemius); XI, 10, 7 (id.); XII, 5, 3 (id.); XII, 20, 3 (Leo); XII, 25, 4 (474); I, 31, 5 (527); XII, 19, 15 (527).
Novellae Justiniani, 2 ep. (535); 14 ep. (id.)

It remains to present in chronological order the examples of the use of the titles of the several orders of rank to which the Mastership of the Offices at various times admitted its holders. These titles were *comes*, *vir clarissimus*, *vir spectabilis*, *vir magnificus* or *magnificentissimus*, and *vir gloriosus* or *gloriosissimus*.

1. **Comes,** "Count"

Dessau, *Inscriptiones Latinae Selectae*, no. 1244, *magister officiorum omnium comes domesticus ordinis primi* (year 346).
Codex Theodosianus, VIII, 5, 8 (357); I, 9, 1 (359); IX, 38, 11 (410); VI, 29, 10 (412); VI, 33, 1, cf. *Codex Justinianus*, XII, 26, 1 (416); I, 8, 3, cf. *Codex Justinianus*, I, 30, 2 (424); VII, 8, 15 (430).
Novellae Theodosii, 21, cf. *Codex Justinianus*, I, 31, 3; XII, 29, 1 (441).
Codex Justinianus, I, 24, 4 (444).
Mansi, vol. 6, p. 821 (449).
Codex Justinianus, XII, 5, 3; XII, 25, 3 (Leo and Anthemius); XII, 19, 10 (Leo); XII, 25, 4 (474).

2. **Vir Clarissimus,** "The Honorable"

Codex Theodosianus, VIII, 5, 8 (year 357); I, 9, 1 (359).

3. **Vir Spectabilis,** "The Respectable"

Codex Theodosianus, VIII, 5, 35 (year 378).

4. **Vir Illustris,** "The Illustrious"

Symmachus, *Relationes*, 34, 8 *v. c. et inlustris;* 38, 4; 43, 2 (year 384–5).
Marcellus, *De medicamentis*, *tit.* (*post* 395).
Codex Justinianus, I, 55, 8 (409).
Codex Theodosianus, VI, 29, 10 (412); VI, 26, 17 (416); VI, 27, 20 (427).

[1] Koch, *Byzantinische Beamtentitel*, p. 124.

Novellae Theodosii, 6, *illustris et magnificus* (438).
Codex Justinianus, VII, 63, 4 (440); XII, 21, 5 (440–1); XII, 26, 2 (443–4?); I, 51, 11 (444).
Marini, *Papiri*, 82, *illustris et magnificus* (489).
Corpus Inscriptionum Latinarum, VIII, 989 (V–VI cent.).
Cassiodorus, *Variae*, 1, 12 (507–11); 1, 13 (507–11).
Codex Justinianus, XII, 50, 3 (Justinian); XII, 50, 9 (id.).
Novellae Justiniani, 23 (536).
Mansi, vol. 8, p. 1118 (536).

5. **Vir Magnificus** or **Magnificentissmus** (μεγαλοπρεπέστατος), "The Magnificent"

Mansi, vol. 6, p. 821 (year 449); vol. 6, p. 564; p. 940; p. 993; vol. 7, p. 97, pp. 185 ff., *magnificentissimus et gloriosissimus*, Greek μεγαλοπρεπέστατος καὶ ἐνδοξότατος (451).
Codex Justinianus, XII, 20, 4 (Leo); III, 24, 3, 2 (485–6); I, *de novo codice* (528).

The use of *gloriosissimus* in conjunction with *magnificentissimus* in 451 antedates the creation of the special class of the *gloriosissimi*, and occurs only in the *acta* of the Council of Chalcedon.

6. **Vir Gloriosus** or **Gloriosissimus** (ἐνδοξότατος), "The Glorious"

Mansi, vol. 6, pp. 564, 940, 993; vol. 7, pp. 97, 185 ff. (year 451); on the use of *gloriosissimus* at this date, see above.
Novellae Justiniani, 2 pr. (535), 10 pr. (id.).
Mansi, vol. 8, p. 817 (531).
Mansi, vol. 8, p. 1118, p. 1119 (536).
Novellae Justiniani, 79, ep. (539); 82, 1 (id.), 85 pr. (id.); 123 pr. (546).
Historiens des Gaules et de le France (*Boquet*), vol. IV, p. 85 (588).
Chronicon Paschale, year 626.
Mansi, vol. 11, p. 209, p. 217, pp. 221 ff. (680).

II. The Byzantine Period

Besides the administrative changes that mark the transition from the Roman to the Byzantine Period, there are also changes in the character and organization of the court ceremonial which reflect the current interpretation of the constitutional position of the Emperor. Justinian succeeded in reëstablishing the cult of the deified Emperor, a revival of the old emperor worship disguised under a Christian name; he instituted, and the Byzantine Emperors further elaborated, the ceremonial which accorded with such an assertion of absolutism. In this theory of state, justly called "Caesaropapism," of which the motto was "a single God, a single Empire," the Emperor was the vicar of God upon Earth, the equal of the Apostles and the head of the Church, who governed for Christ and with Christ.[1]

[1] Hesseling, *Essai sur la civilization byzantine*, 1907, pp. 174 ff.

As a natural consequence, the Emperor became the centre, not only of the political, but also of the religious, life at the capital. Herein we find the explanation of the peculiar character of the court ceremonies of this epoch, described for us in so great detail in the *De Caerimoniis* of Constantine Porphyrogenitus. It was a truly "pontifical" life that the rulers of Constantinople led in the midst of chants, processions, parades, and rhythmic acclamations, which, in the palace "guarded of God," constituted the order of ceremonies that regulated each of their acts and the countless changes of their gorgeous costume.[1]

In the performance of these ritual obligations the Emperor was accompanied by the dignitaries and officials resident in the capital, marshalled in a fixed order according to their titles of rank. Their raiment, position, and actions upon each public occasion were as rigorously prescribed as those of the Sovereign himself. Under such conditions it will be readily seen that during the Byzantine Period the honors and privileges of the Mastership were chiefly connected with the part which those of this grade of dignity played in the ceremonial life of the palace.

In the course of the ninth century the Mastership became one of the dignities bestowed for life by the conferment of certain insignia (αἱ διὰ βραβείων ἀξίαι).[2] On account of the high rank of the Mastership among the dignities of the Empire, holders of this title naturally belonged to the senatorial order (οἱ συγκλητικοί) in its wide sense, in contrast with the senate as a small body of officials actively assisting in the counsels of state.[3] They also belonged to the smaller group of senatorial dignitaries known as οἱ προελευσιμαῖοι,[4] those entitled to appear in the imperial *cortège* on the occasion of public processions.[5] And with these latter, they, in company with certain other court officials, formed the group of dignitaries known as the ἄρχοντες τοῦ Λαυσιακοῦ.[6] The Masters also belonged to the οἱ ὑπὸ καμπάγιον, the wearers of the

[1] Diehl, *Études byzantines*, pp. 108 ff.

[2] Philotheos, 707: οἵτινες ἅπαξ διδόμεναι οὐδαμῶς ἀναστρέφονται.

[3] *De Caer.*, 1, 1: οἱ δὲ μάγιστροι καὶ ἀνθύπατοι καὶ οἱ λοιποὶ συγκλητικοί; 20; 24; 2, 6: μετὰ τε τῶν μαγίστρων καὶ πατρικίων καὶ τῶν λοιπῶν τῆς συγκλήτου: Bury, *Imperial Administration*, 37 ff.

[4] Philotheos, 707.

[5] Bury, *Imperial Administration*, p. 23.

[6] Philotheos, 787: καὶ γίνεται ἡ διανομὴ εἰς μόνους τοὺς ἄρχοντας τοῦ Λαυσιακοῦ, οἷον εἰς μαγίστρους, πραιποσίτους, ἀνθυπάτους, etc. The Lausiakon was one of the edifices of the palace, Bury, *op. cit.*, p. 23.

kampagion, which included practically all the high dignitaries and many of the officers of the court, that is, all entitled to wear this particular style of shoe as part of their official uniform.[1] Classes like these, as may be readily seen from their designations, existed for ceremonial purposes only.

We have seen how the rank gradations of the *illustres*, *gloriosissimi*, and the like, of the later Roman period disappeared before the new honorary orders of the Byzantine epoch. Hence we no longer find in use the older adjectival titles of rank, which the Masters had previously enjoyed. The changed position of the Mastership itself, which from an office had become one of the honorary orders, would have prevented their employment even if they had not fallen into disuse. However, as late as the reign of Leo VI, the Masters were called ἐνδοξότατοι (*gloriosissimi*),[2] without any special degree of rank being thereby indicated, and at the same time Stylianos was addressed as ὁ περιφανέστατος, or ὁ ὑπερφυέστατος μάγιστρος,[3] phrases in which the adjectives are purely personal compliments.

The *De Caerimoniis* has preserved accounts of two types of ceremonies for the conferment of the dignity (ἀξία, τιμή) of the Mastership. The earlier of these dates from the time when there was only one Master, and is, therefore, prior to the middle of the eighth century.[4] Here we have the procedure followed in case the Emperor ordered that a Master be appointed on the occasion of a procession to St. Sophia. At the palace, in the presence of the Patricians and the whole senate, the Praepositus conducted before the Emperor the Patrician chosen for elevation to the Mastership. Upon him the ruler conferred an embroidered robe (στιχάριον) and a belt (βαλτίδιον). He was then led away, to be reintroduced shortly afterwards, clad in his new insignia, and then placed "at the head of the *sekreton*, above all the Patricians."

The latter type of ceremony,[5] of a time when the Mastership had become an order of rank, was probably that in use in the

[1] Philotheos, 757: φίλους τοὺς ὑπὸ καμπάγιν ἅπαντας, ἄρχοντας τῆς συγκλήτου, ἀπό τε μαγίστρων, etc.; 759, τοὺς ὑπὸ καμπάγιν πάντας, οἷον μαγίστρους, etc.; cf. 769, 1. Cf. Bury, *op. cit.*, pp. 38 f. On the *kampagion*, see *De Caer.*, 2, 40, 639.

[2] Philotheos, 710: ἡ τῶν ἐνδοξοτάτων μαγίστρων ἀξία. The Patricians were called περίβλεπτοι (*spectabiles*), id.

[3] *Novellae, Leonis VI*, 1, 18, etc.; cf. Bury, *op. cit.*, p. 31.

[4] *De Caer.*, 1, 46, 231–33.

[5] *De Caer.*, 1, 46, 234–5; 1, 26.

tenth century. An appointment in this fashion might be made on any ordinary Sunday (κυριακὴ παγανή), and then it took place in the *consistorium*.[1] There, in the presence of the whole body of senators, arranged according to their orders of rank, the Praepositus presented the Patrician selected for promotion, and the Emperor conferred upon him the robe and belt of his new rank. As in the older ceremony, the newly appointed Master was then led away by the Praepositus, soon to reappear wearing his new decorations, and to take his place at the head of the *sekreton* of the Patricians. At the conclusion of the ceremony the Master went to the apartment of the palace called the Indoi, put on a purple cloak (σαγίον ἀληθινόν) over his robe and departed for his own house, as far as which, if it happened to be in the neighborhood of the palace, he was escorted by the various grades of dignitaries, the Foot Guards of the Domestici and the Scholarians, the soldiers of the Watch, the διαιτάριοι, and the Decani. If he lived at a distance the dignitaries were excused from this exhibition of respect, which, however, the others were still obliged to manifest.

A similar promotion to the Mastership might also occur on the occasion of a festival, as, for example, Candlemas.[2] Here the procedure was practically the same as that just described, except that the Master of Ceremonies, ὁ ἐπὶ τῆς καταστάσεως, played the rôle of the Praepositus in introducing the candidate for promotion. The escort to the Master's house was also the same as in the preceding ceremony. These promotions might take place elsewhere than in the *consistorium*, for, in connection with the account of the reception of a foreign envoy,[3] mention is made of a *triclinium* (τρίκλινος) in which appointments to the Mastership were made.[4]

In all of these ceremonies the essential feature was the conferment of the insignia of the Mastership — the robe and the belt. These insignia were called βραβεῖα, and hence the Mastership was classed among the αἱ διὰ βραβείων ἀξίαι. Philotheos[5] gives the insigne (βραβεῖον) of this rank as follows: a white tunic

[1] *De Caer.*, 1, 46. [2] *De Caer.*, 1, 26. [3] *De Caer.*, 2, 15, 573; 578.

[4] *De Caer.*, *loc. cit.*: ὁ τρίκλινος, ἐν ᾧ καὶ τὸ καμελαύκιον ἵσταται καὶ οἱ μάγιστροι γίγνονται.

[5] Philotheos, 710–11: χιτὼν λευκὸς ὢν χρυσοῦφαντος, καὶ ἐπωμὶς χρυσόταβλος, καὶ ζώνη δερματίνη κόκκινος ἐκ λίθων τιμίων κεκοσμημένη, ἥτις λέγεται βαλτίδιν, ἐπὶ τοῦ κονσιστορίου ἐκ βασιλικῆς χειρὸς ἐπιδίδοται.

embroidered with gold, a cloak with a golden border, and a scarlet leather belt studded with precious stones: all conferred by the Emperor's hand in the consistory. The whole ceremony is evidently a development from that of the conferment of the cingulum in the preceding period. However, as the Mastership is no longer an office, the codicils and the *liber mandatorum* do not now accompany the outward badge of rank.

In addition to this, their regular uniform on official occasions, at certain specified ceremonies the Masters were required to wear special attire. Thus we find regulations laid down for their dress at the audiences held at the daily opening of the palace on Sundays and on week-days, and for the occasion of their return to court after an absence on public or private business.[1] Probably at the functions where they appeared with the so-called loroi (λῶροι) the Masters presented their most gorgeous appearance. These loroi were golden scarfs, twelve in number, worn by the Masters, or, if there were fewer than twelve Masters, by them and by a number of Proconsuls or other dignitaries and officials sufficient to bring the total up to twelve, on particularly solemn occasions. Such occasions were the procession to St. Sophia,[2] Christmas,[3] and Easter.[4] However, the loroi might also be worn on extraordinary occasions, as at the reception of the envoys of Amerimnes, who had come from Tarsus in 917 to negotiate for the exchange of captives and the conclusion of peace.[5]

The explanation of this custom of the wearing of the loroi is given in the *De Caerimoniis* in connection with the description of the Easter ceremonial,[6] and also alluded to in Philotheos.[7] The loroi worn by the Masters and the Patricians symbolized the entombment of Christ; their golden decoration suggested the glory of his resurrection. Thus arrayed, the Masters and the

[1] *De Caer.*, 2, 1.

[2] *De Caer.*, 1, 1, 24: καὶ εἰσέρχεται ὁ πραιπόσιτος, προπορευόμενος τῇ τάξει τῶν μαγίστρων καὶ ἀνθυπάτων, ἤγουν τῶν φορούντων τοὺς δώδεκα χρυσοϋφάντους λώρους.

[3] Philotheos, 742: μαγίστρους δύο, ἀνθυπάτους πατρικίους στρατηγοὺς ἕξ, βουλγάρους φίλους δύο, ὀφφικιαλίους ἀπὸ τῆς τοῦ στρατιωτικοῦ λογοθέτου τάξεως καὶ κατωτέρου δύο, πρὸς τὸ συνανακληθῆναι τῷ βασιλεῖ εἰς τύπον τῆς ἀποστολικῆς δωδεκάδος.

[4] *De Caer.*, 2, 40, 637 ff.: τὸ μὲν περιβεβλῆσθαι λώρους τοὺς μαγίστρους καὶ πατρικίους ἐν τῇ ἑορτασίμῳ ἡμέρᾳ τῆς ἀναστάσεως Χριστοῦ τοῦ Θεοῦ ἡμῶν; Philotheos, 766: τοὺς μὲν μαγίστρους, ἀνθυπάτους καὶ πατρικίους, τοὺς λώρους ἠμφιεσμένους μετὰ τῶν χρυσέων αὐτῶν θωρακίων καὶ μόνον. Loroi, probably differing in some respects from those now under consideration, were sometimes carried by other dignitaries and officials; cf. *De Caer.*, 1, 50; 2, 28.

[5] *De Caer.*, 2, 15, 574.

[6] *De Caer.*, 2, 40.

[7] Philotheos, 742, see above.

Patricians represented the twelve Apostles; the Emperor, as far as was humanly possible, represented the Lord. Upon these occasions, in addition to the loroi, the Masters and Patricians carried staffs (*σκεπαῖα*) in the form of a cross, to symbolize the triumph of Christ over death, and also what were popularly called *τόμοι ἀνεξικακίας*, parchments inscribed with the Christian doctrines, which they, in the character of disciples, bore before the Emperor. Further, the wrapping of their legs in linen and their wearing of golden sandals were emblematic of the death and glorification of Christ. All these insignia were believed to have had their origin in those of the victorious Roman proconsul when rendering an account of his achievements to the consuls upon his return to the city.[1]

The loroi, and the other vestments that the Masters wore with them, apparently did not belong to these dignitaries, like the insignia of their order, but were supplied to them for the particular ceremonies. These articles were kept in store in the Church of the Lord,[2] where, in the time of Constantine VII, there were stored fifteen loroi woven with gold, an equal number of short-sleeved tunics of the same material to match, and twelve breastpieces (*θωράκια*) to go with the loroi.[3] Besides these there were twenty-five colored cloaks with tassels and a golden border,[4] to be worn by Masters, Proconsuls, and Patricians.

Upon their inauguration into their new order of rank it was customary for the Masters to distribute various gratuities (*συνήθειαι*).[5] The Master of Ceremonies, *ὁ ἐπὶ τῆς καταστάσεως*, received the *καμίσιον*, a sort of cloak, from the new Master of the Offices, who also had to entertain the Praepositi and the other Masters; to all of them he made gifts in the form of articles of apparel. Furthermore, he was obliged to make a monetary donative to these dignitaries and to various court officers, the total of which was double that distributed by a Patrician on

[1] *De Caer.*, 2, 40, 638–9.

[2] *ὁ ναὸς τοῦ Κυρίου*, *De Caer.*, 2, 40; *fin.*, 41.

[3] *De Caer.*, 2, 41: *Λῶροι χρυσοῦφαντοι ιε'. κοντομανίκια χρυσοῦφαντα τῶν αὐτῶν λώρων ιβ'. Θωράκια τῶν αὐτῶν λώρων ιβ'.* One is tempted to see in the gold pectorals, published and described by Mr. Walter Dennison in vol. XII of this Series of Studies (pp. 109–117, 121–127 with plates I, VI, VII, XII, XIII) an example of these *θωράκια*. However, on the basis of the evidence at hand, this identification cannot be maintained.

[4] *χλανίδια φουνδάτα χροαμὰ χρυσόταβλα.*

[5] Philotheos, 711: *δίδωσι συνήθειαν τῷ τῆς καταστάσεως τὸ καμίσιν αὐτοῦ, τοῖς δὲ πραιποσίτοις καὶ μαγίστροις συνεστιᾶται παρέχων αὐτοῖς καὶ δόματα ἱματίων. συνήθειαν δὲ τοῖς πραιποσίτοις καὶ μαγίστροις καὶ λοιποῖς τὴν τοῦ πατρικίου διπλὴν συνήθειαν παρέχει.*

similar occasions.[1] The ἀτρικλίναι, or officers in charge of the *kletorologion*, the court invitation list, were entitled to receive a gratuity of twenty-four milaresia from the newly decorated Master.[2] These obligatory presents, distributed among the Praepositi, the Master of Ceremonies and the other officials who functioned at the ceremony of the Master's inauguration, in addition to the older members of the same order, are a development of the *consuetudines* which, as we have seen, magistrates and dignitaries of the Later Roman period regularly donated to the various officials through whose hands the documents relative to their appointments passed. However, we have no mention of gifts presented at this time to the Emperor and Empress as a token of gratitude for the honor conferred.

On the other hand the Masters themselves were entitled to a number of largesses and perquisites, such as we have noted already upon the appointment of a new Master. At the annual celebration of the festival of the Brumalia in the month of November a generous purse (ἀποκόμβιον), part of which fell to the share of the Masters, was distributed by the rulers among their dignitaries and officials. In the time of Leo VI,[3] and earlier, the donations were as follows: on the day of the Senior Augustus, twenty pounds of gold; on the day of the Junior Augustus, ten pounds; and on the day of the Augusta, another eight pounds.

Later, under Constantine VII, a single largess of fifty pounds was made on the day of the Senior Augustus in the name of his partner on the throne, and of the Empress.[4] The largest shares of these donations were received by the Masters individually, and by the few dignitaries and officers who were classed with them for this occasion:[5] their portions were twice as large as those allotted to the Proconsuls.[6] In addition, at the same festival, each of the Masters who were guests at the imperial table received from the Emperor's hands a second largess of one hundred and sixty milaresia, and some silk goods of a special make.[7]

Similarly, on the anniversaries of the coronation of the Augusti (στέψιμον), and of their advancement to Autocratores or

[1] Cf. Philotheos, 710.

[2] Philotheos, 787: περὶ συνηθείας τῶν ἀτρικλινῶν. προβαλλομένης γὰρ ζῶστης ἢ μαγίστρου, δίδοται αὐτοῖς ἐξ ἑκάστου αὐτῶν καθάπαξ, κδ'.

[3] Philotheos, 782; *De Caer.*, 2, 18, 606.

[4] *De Caer.*, 2, 18, 607.

[5] Philotheos, 784.

[6] Philotheos, 785.

[7] *De Caer.*, 2, 18, 607.

Senior Augusti (αὐτοκρατορία),[1] largesses were distributed. On these occasions the beneficiaries were the so-called ἄρχοντες τοῦ Λαυσιακοῦ, to whom, as has been pointed out previously, the Masters belonged.[2] Further, whenever the Masters accompanied the Emperor on his journeys from the capital, they, along with the others of his retinue, were entitled to a definite allowance of wine, supplied by the imperial Apothecarius.[3] Then, too, they and the Patricians together with the Praepositi and other officials, ate at the imperial table.[4]

Whenever it was the custom for the Emperor to entertain at banquets the prominent officials and dignitaries present at the capital, the order according to which these should be invited and seated was determined by a guest list, or Kletorologion.[5] Such a guest list is that compiled in 899 A.D. by Philotheos, the imperial *atriklines*, whose duty it was to supervise "the ceremony of imperial banquets in the palace, to receive guests and arrange them in order of precedence."[6] From this Kletorologion we see that at such banquets the Masters were accorded a place corresponding with the dignity of their position among the orders of rank of the Empire.

As a rule, the Masters were not included among those who were actually seated at the same table with the Emperor,[7] but headed the list of the other guests who sat at the general table.[8] However, on the second day of the celebration of the Brumalia, in the time of Leo VI, Masters who were relatives of the Emperor sat at the table of the Senior Augustus, while the rest were assigned to that of his colleague.[9] Under Constantine VII the Masters, with other dignitaries and officers, were placed with the Emperors at a table prepared for about sixteen persons.[10]

The various festivals, the celebration of which involved the entertainment of the Masters and other official guests at the palace, are enumerated in the Kletorologion.[11] The most important of these were Christmas, Candlemas, Easter, and the Brumalia.

It was a privilege as well as an obligation for all the Masters, like those enjoying other similar titles of honor, when in Constan-

[1] Cf. Reiske, *Ad De Caer.*, 2, 33.
[2] Philotheos, 787.
[3] περὶ τάξεων, 364, 484–5.
[4] περὶ τάξεων, 472.
[5] *De Caer.*, 2, 18, 603.
[6] Bury, *Imperial Administration*, p. 11.
[7] Philotheos, 727–8.
[8] Philotheos, 730.
[9] *De Caer.*, 2, 18, 604.
[10] *De Caer.*, 2, 18, 603.
[11] Philotheos, 741–754; 782: cf. *De Caer.*, 2, 18, 602 ff.

tinople to appear in the insignia of their rank at all the public ceremonies in which the Emperor and his retinue participated. These ceremonies included coronations and anniversaries of the Emperors, promotions of ministers, officers, and dignitaries, and festivals and processions in commemoration of various events of religious or political importance. The list of these functions, with the order of ceremonial at each, is given in the *De Caerimoniis* of Constantine Porphyrogenitus. Here it will be sufficient to refer briefly to the part taken by the Masters on such occasions.

When the dignitaries of the court were arranged in order of precedence, the Masters regularly formed the first rank or *velum* (Βῆλον α´),[1] as they were the holders of the highest title of honor enjoyed by several persons at the same time. Sometimes, however, it might happen that the bearer of one of the higher titles participated in the procession of dignitaries. In that case he formed the first *velum*, as did the Curopalates at the elevation of a Nobilissimus, while the Masters made up the second.[2] Again, it was at times convenient to arrange the cortège in larger groups, and for this purpose the Masters were united with those of inferior rank in one *velum*.[3]

An inevitable result of the establishment of the several grades of dignity, such as the Mastership, the Proconsulship, and the like, was that the distinctions in rank thus created should not be confined to men alone but should be extended also to the wives of those who attained the respective titles. Accordingly we find the wives of officials and dignitaries ranked in various groups corresponding to the grades that their husbands had attained, and receiving titles derived from those conferred upon the men. In this way arose the titles of μαγίστρισσαι, πατρίκιαι, and other derivatives of the same character. The bearers of these titles were in a different position from the πατρίκιαι ζωσταί, who had this dignity conferred upon them directly, whereas the former depended for their position upon the rank of their husbands.

When the Empress participated in any of the public functions and was attended by the ladies of the court, these latter were arranged in ranks corresponding with those of the Emperor's cortège. The first *velum* was made up of the πατρίκιαι ζωσταί, while

[1] *De Caer.*, 47, 48, 49, 50, 51, etc.
[2] *De Caer.*, I, 44: βῆλον α´, κουροπαλάτην; βῆλον β´, μαγίστρους.
[3] *De Caer.*, I, 9, 66.

the Magistrissai formed the second.[1] The celebration of the Feast of Pentecost,[2] that on the occasion of the birth of a son to the Emperor,[3] and certain irregular occurrences, such as the reception of Elga, Princess of Russia,[4] were functions at which the ladies of the court formally participated, forming a *sekreton*, graded like that of the officials and dignitaries.

As was to be expected, the ladies who owed the rank which they held to the position of their husbands, lost their honorary title upon the death of the latter, although they still continued to have an honorable recognition at court; upon official occasions they were placed after all those whose husbands were of senatorial rank.[5]

[1] *De Caer.*, 1, 9, 67, βῆλον α′, πατρικίας ζωστάς: βῆλον β′, μαγιστρίσας.
[2] *De Caer.*, 1, 9. [3] *De Caer.*, 2, 21, 216. [4] *De Caer.*, 2, 15, 596.
[5] *De Caer.*, 2, 21.

BIBLIOGRAPHY

For the convenience of the reader the editions of ancient authors cited, and of the modern works most frequently referred to, are here noted.

I. Greek and Latin Texts

Agathias, *Historiae*. *Corpus Scriptorum Historiae Byzantinae*. Recensuit B. G. Niebuhr. Bonn, 1828.

Athanasius, *Apologia ad imperatorem Constantinum*. *Patrologia Graeca*, vol. 25. Edidit J.-P. Migne. Paris, 1857.

Ammianus Marcellinus, *Rerum Gestarum libri qui supersunt*. Edidit V. Gardthausen. Leipzig, 1874. Edidit C. U. Clark, vol. 1, Berlin, 1910.

Cassiodorus Senator, *Variae*. *Monumenta Germaniae Historica*. *Auctores antiquissimi*, vol. 12. Recensuit Th. Mommsen. Berlin, 1894.

Georgius Cedrenus, *Compendium historiarum a mundo condito usque ad imperatorem Isaacum Comnenum*. *Corpus Scriptorum Historiae Byzantinae*. Recensuit Bekker. Bonn, 1838.

Chronicon Paschale, *Corpus Scriptorum Historiae Byzantinae*. Recensuit Dindorf. Bonn, 1832.

Collections, *Codex Theodosianus*. Edidit Gothofredus-Ritter. Leipzig, 1736.

Theodosiani libri XVI cum constitutionibus Sirmondianis et leges novellae ad Theodosianum pertinentes. Ediderunt Th. Mommsen et P. Meyer. Berlin, 1905.

Corpus Juris Civilis. II. *Codex Justinianus*. Recognovit P. Krüger. Berlin, 1906. III. *Novellae*. Recognovit Schöll-Kroll. 1895.

Fragmenta Historicorum Graecorum. Edidit C. Müller. Paris, 1841–83.

Leonis VI Novellae: Jus Graeco-Romanum, vol. III. Edidit Zachariae von Lingenthal. 1857.

Papiri Diplomatici. Edidit G. Marini. Rome, 1805.

Sacrorum Conciliorum Collectio. Evulgavit J. D. Mansi. Vols. I–XV, Florence, 1759 ff.; vol. XVI, Venice, 1798.

Anna Comnena, *Alexias*. *Corpus Scriptorum Historiae Byzantinae*. Recensuit Schopen. Bonn, 1839.

Constantinus Porphyrogenitus, *De Caerimoniis aulae Byzantinae*. *Corpus Scriptorum Historiae Byzantinae*. Recensuit Bekker. Bonn, 1829.

De administrando imperio. Id. 1840.

Corippus, *Libri qui supersunt*. *Monumenta Germaniae Historica*. *Auctores antiquissimi*, vol. 3, 2. Recensuit Partsch. Berlin, 1879.

Inscriptions, *Corpus Inscriptionum Latinarum*. Berlin, 1863 ff.

Inscriptiones Latinae Selectae. Edidit Dessau. Berlin, 1892 ff.

Joannes Lydus, *De magistratibus populi Romani*. Edidit R. Wünsch. Leipzig, 1903.

Michael Attaliota, *Historia*. Recognovit Bekker. Bonn, 1853.

Notitia Dignitatum. Edidit E. Böcking. With notes. Bonn, 1839–53. Edidit O. Seeck. Berlin, 1876.

Philotheos, *Kletorologion.* Edidit J. B. Bury. *British Academy Supplemental Papers*, I. London, 1911.

Procopius Caesariensis, *Opera Omnia.* Edidit Haury. Leipzig, 1905.

Psellus (Michael), *Historia.* Edidit C. Sathas. Leipzig, 1899.

Rutilius Claudius Namatianus, *De reditu suo.* Edidit Müller. Leipzig, 1870.

Symmachus, *Q. Aurelii Symmachi quae supersunt. Monumenta Germaniae Historica. Auctores antiquissimi*, vol. VI. Edidit O. Seeck. Berlin, 1883.

Theophanes, *Chronographia. Corpus Scriptorum Historiae Byzantinae.* Recensuit J. Classen. Bonn, 1839.

Theophanes Continuatus, *Chronographia.* Id. Recensuit Bekker. Bonn, 1838.

Theophylactus Simocatta, *Historiae.* Id. Recognovit Bekker. Bonn, 1834.

Zonaras, *Chronicon.* Id. Vols. 1 and 2. Recensuit M. Pinder. Bonn, 1834. Vol. 3. Recensuit Büttner-Wobst. 1897.

Zosimus, *Historia Romana.* Edidit L. Mendelssohn. Leipzig, 1887.

II. Modern Works

Bethmann-Hollweg, M. A., *Der römische Civilprozess.* 3 vols. Bonn, 1865–66.

Bury, J. B., *A History of the Later Roman Empire from Arcadius to Irene.* 2 vols. London, 1889.

Imperial Administration in the Ninth Century. British Academy Supplemental Papers, I. London, 1911.

Magistri scriniorum, ἀντιγραφῆς and ῥεφερενδάριοι. Harvard Studies in Classical Philology, vol. XXI, 1910.

Cagnat, R., *Hospitium militare*, in Daremberg et Saglio, *Dictionnaire des Antiquités grecques et romaines*, vol. 3, pp. 302 f.

Cosenza, M. E., *Official Positions after Constantine.* Columbia University Dissertation. 1907.

Diehl, Ch., *Études byzantines.* Paris, 1895.

Gelzer, M., *Abrisz der byzantinischen Kaisergeschichte.* I. Müller's *Handbuch der klassischen Altertumswissenschaft*, vol. IX, pt. 1. München, 1897.

Grenier, P., *L'empire byzantine: son évolution sociale et politique.* Paris, 1904.

Hesseling, D. C., *Essai sur la civilisation byzantine.* Paris, 1907.

Hirschfeld, Otto, *Die Agentes in Rebus. Sitzungsberichte der Berliner Akademie der Wissenschaft*, 1893 = *Kleine Schriften*, pp. 624 ff. Berlin, 1913.

Die Rangtitel der römischen Kaiserzeit. Sitzungsberichte der Berliner Akademie der Wissenschaft, 1901 = *Kleine Schriften*, pp. 646 ff.

Hodgkin, T., *Italy and her Invaders.* Vol. 1. Oxford, 1892.

Jullian, C., *Illustres*, in Daremberg et Saglio, *Dictionnaire*, vol. 3, pp. 385 f.

Karlowa, O., *Römische Rechtsgeschichte.* Bd. I. *Staatsrecht und Rechtsquellen.* Leipzig, 1885.

Koch, P., *Die byzantinischen Beamtentitel von 400 bis 700.* Jena, 1903.

Lécrevain, Ch., *Le sénat romain depuis Diocletien. Bibliothèque des écoles françaises d'Athènes et de Rome*, vol. 28. Paris, 1888.

Mommsen, Th., *Aetius. Hermes*, vol. XXXVI, 1901, pp. 516 ff.

Das römische Militärwesen seit Diocletian. Hermes, vol. XXIV, 1889, pp. 195 ff. = *Gesammelte Schriften*, vol. 6 (*Historische Schriften*, 3), pp. 206 ff.

Ostgotische Studien. Neues Archiv, vol. XIV, 1889, pp. 225 ff., 453 ff.; vol. XV, 1890, 181 ff. = *Historische Schriften*, vol. 3, pp. 362 ff.

Pernice, A., *L'imperatore Eraclio.* Firenze, 1905.

Reid, J. S., *The Reorganization of the Empire. Cambridge Medieval History*, vol. 1, chap. 2. 1911.

Schiller, H., *Geschichte der römischen Kaiserzeit.* 3 vols. Gotha, 1883–87.

Schlumberger, G., *Sigillographie de l'empire byzantin.* Paris, 1884.

Seeck, O., *Geschichte des Untergangs der antiken Welt.* 5 vols. Berlin, 1895–1911.

Quaestiones de Notitia Dignitatum. Berlin, 1872.

Pauly-Wissowa, *Real-Encyclopädie der klassischen Altertumswissenschaft.* Stuttgart, 1894 ff.: Articles on *Admissionales*, *Barbaricarii*, *Castrensiani*, *Comites*, *Domesticus*, *Fabricae*.

APPENDIX A

REFERENCES TO THE TITLE *MAGISTER* IN INSCRIPTIONS AND IN LITERATURE

For the convenience of those who may wish to pursue the subject further, the references to the *Magistri* in both the literature and the inscriptions are here brought together in a classified list.

MAGISTER POPULI

Cicero, *De finibus*, 3, 75; *De legibus*, 3, 9, and 3, 10; *De republica*, 1, 63.
Paulus Diaconus, *Epitome Festi*, p. 198 M.
Seneca, *Epistulae*, 108, 31.
Varro, *De lingua latina*, 5, 82.
Velius Longus, *De orthographia*, p. 2234 P.

MAGISTER EQUITUM

C.I.L. I, 197 (133–118 B.C.); 198 (122 B.C.);
p. 287, *xxvii* (after 309 B.C.);
p. 288, *xxix* (after 296 B.C.); p. 448, *anno* 707 (47 B.C.);
p. 425 ff. = I^2, part 1, p. 16 ff. (*Fasti Consulares Capitolini*);
pp. 633 ff. = I^2, part 1, pp. 345 ff. Here may be found a list of eponymous and other magistrates, arranged by Mommsen; cf. the list of the *magistri equitum* given by Daremberg et Saglio, *Dictionnaire des Antiquités grecques et romaines*, vol. 3, p. 1524.
Notizie degli Scavi di Antichità, 1904, p. 9 (320–319 B.C.).

MAGISTER AUCTIONIS

Cicero, *Ad Atticum*, 1, 1, 3, and 6, 1, 15; *Ad familiares*, 12, 30; *Pro Quinctio*, 15, 50.
C.I.L. I, 200, v. 57 (*Lex Agraria* of 111 B.C.).
Digesta, XLVI, 8, 9 (here styled *magister universitatis*).
Gaius, *Institutiones*, 3, 79.
Quintilian, *Institutiones oratoriae*, 6, 3, 51.

MAGISTER BIBENDI

Apuleius, *Apologia*, 98.
Cicero, *De Senectute*, 14, 46: *magisteria*.
Martial, *Epigrammata*, 12, 48, 15 (*magistri cenarum*).
Varro, *De lingua latina*, 5, 122; *Rerum humanarum liber*, XX, *apud Nonium Marcellum*, 142, 8.

Other designations of the *magister bibendi* are:

arbiter, Horace, *Carmina*, 2, 7, 25;
rex, *op. cit.*, 1, 4, 18, and Macrobius, *Saturnalia*, 2, 1, 3;
modiperator, Nonius Marcellus, p. 142, 8;
strategus, Plautus, *Stichus*, 5, 4, 20.

LUDIMAGISTRI

Under this head are cited references to *magistri ludi* and other *magistri* acting as professional instructors in any art or science. Figurative usages of the title *magister* have not been included.

(Pseudo-) Asconius, *On Cicero*, *De divinatione*, 14: *magistri ludi*.
Augustine, *Confessiones*, 1, 3, 1: *primi magistri*.
Ausonius, *Epigrammata*, 28, 1; *magister* (*philosophiae*); 138, 1 and 3: *magister* (*grammaticus*).
Epistolae, 4, 95: *magister* (*praeceptor*).
Gratiarum Actio pro consulatu, §§ 31 and 32: *magister* (*praeceptor*).
Idyllia, 4, 3 and 26, and 5, 2: *magister* (*ludi*); 4, 87: *magister* (*praeceptor*).
Professores, 3, 1: *magister* (*rhetor*); 8, 9: *magister* (*grammaticus*).
Praefatiunculae, 2, 29: *magistri* (*rhetores*).
Boethius, *Ars geometrica*, *de ratione abaci*: *magister* (*philosophiae*).
De institutione musica, 1, 33: *magister* (*id.*).
Bulletin de la Société nationale des Antiquaires de France, 1891, p. 266: *magister* (*eloquentiae*), Hippo Diarrytus.
Cicero, *De inventione*, 1, 25, 35: *magistri artium liberalium*.
De oratore, 3, 23, 86: *magister* (*armorum*.)
De senectute, 5, 13: *magistri* (*eloquentiae*).
9, 29, *magistri bonarum artium*.
De Senectute Philippicae, 2, 17, 43: *magister* (*ludi*).
Codex Theodosianus, XIII, 3, 5 (362 A.D.) = *Codex Justinianus*, X, 53, 7: *magistri studiorum*.
Columella, *De re rustica*, 1, *pr.*, 3, *magister* (*placitae disciplinae*).
4, 28, 2, *magistri* (*rerum rusticarum*).
12, 2, *magister* (*chori canentium*).
Corpus Glossariorum Latinorum, V, 604, 42 and 635, 54: *magister ludi*.
II, 126, 6 and 276, 12; also III, 25, 21, and 352, 4, and 455, 31, and 410, 57, and 514, 55; *magister* (*ludi*, διδάσκαλος).
III, 277, 30: *magister* (ἐξηγήτης, *praeceptor*).
C.I.L. II, 5181, l. 57, Metallum Vepascense (first century A.D.): *ludi magistri*.
III, p. 831, 7, l. 66 (*Edictum Diocletiani de pretiis rerum*, 301 A.D.): *magistri litterarum*.
VI, 9529, Rome: *m*]*agister ludi litt*(*erarii*).
VI, 9530, Rome: *ma*]*gister ludi*.
VI, 9858, Rome (after 425 A.D.): *magister eloquentiae*.
VI, 10,008, 10,012, 10,013, 10,015, 10,017, Rome: *magister* (*ludi* or *artium liberalium*).
VIII, 12,418, Aquaeductus Carthaginiensis: *magister iuris*.
IX, 4226, Amiternum, *mag*(*ister*) *ludi*.

X, 3969, Capua, *magister ludi litterarii.*
X, 8387, Frusino, *magister iuris.*
Digesta, L, 13, 1 : *magistri ludi litterarii.*
L, 5, 2, 8 : *magistri* (*ludi*).
Festus, *Epitome Pauli*, 126 M : *magistri* (*doctores artium*).
Florus, *Epitome*, 4, 2, 60 : *magister* (*artium liberalium*).
Aulus Gellius, *Noctes Atticae*, 19, 9, 2 : *magister* (*docendis publice iuvenibus*).
Historia Augusta, *Vita Aureliani*, 30, 3 : *magister ad graecas litteras.*
Vita Caracallae, 1, 8 : *magistri* (*praeceptores*).
Vita Commodi, 1, 7 : *magistri disciplinarum.*
Vita Diadumeni, 8, *magister* (*praeceptor*).
Vita Heliogabali, 16, 4 : *magister* (*praeceptor*).
Vita Marci, 2, 2 : *magistri ad prima elementa;*
2, 7 : *magister* (*praeceptor*) ;
3, 5 : *magistri* (*artium liberalium*) ;
4, 9 : *magister* (*pingendi*) ;
16, 5 : *magistri* (*philosophiae*).
Vita Maximianorum Duorum, 27, 3 : *magister ad primam disciplinam.*
Vita Taciti, 6, 5 : *magistri litterarii.*
Horace, *Carmina*, 1, 18, 13 : *magister* (*ludi*) ;
1, 1, 14 and *Sermones*, 2, 3, 257 : *magister* (*philosophiae*).
Ars Poetica, 415 : *magister* (*musicae*).
Justin, *Trogi Pompei, Historiarum Philippicarum Epitoma*, 16, 5, 13 : *magister* (*philosophiae*).
Juvenal, *Satirae*, 5, 122 : *magister* (*ludi*).
Martial, *Epigrammata*, 7, 64, 7 and 9, 68, 1, and 10, 62, 1 : *ludi magister.*
1, 35, 2, and 5, 56, 1 and 84, 2, and 8, 3, 15 and 9, 29, 7 : *magister* (*ludi*).
14, 80, 1 : *magistri* (*ludi*) ;
7, 67, 8 : *magister* (*palaestrae*) ;
1, 104, 10 and 2, 75, 1 : *magister* (*exercitator*) ;
1, 42, 12 : *magister* (*saltandi*).
Persius, *Satirae*, 3, 46 : *magister* (*ludi*) ;
4, 1 : *magister* (*philosophiae*).
Petronius, *Satyricon*, 3, 4 : *magister eloquentiae ;*
29 : *magister* (*palaestrae*) ;
99 : *magister bonarum artium.*
Plautus, *Bacchides*, ll. 152, 404, 439 and 566 : *magister* (*praeceptor*).
Prudentius, *Peristephanon*, 9, 40 : *magister* (*ludi*) ;
10, 89, 822 and 13, 2 : *magister* (*doctrinae christianae*).
Quintilian, *Institutiones oratoriae*, 2, 1, 13 ; 2, 8, 7 and 10, 3, 1 : *magister dicendi ;*
2, 1, 3 : *magister declamandi ;*
2, 5, 5 : *magister eloquentiae ;*
5, 11, 17 ; 5, 14, 32, and 12, 6, 7 : *magister* (*eloquentiae*) ;
1, 2, 11 and 2, 4, 8 : *magister* (*praeceptor*) ;
2, 17, 33 : *magister* (*armorum*) ;
12, 1, 36 : *magister* (*sapientiae*) ;
10, 2, 6 : *magister* (*cuiusquam rei*).

Seneca, *Dialogi*, 2, 11, 3 : *magister* (*ludi*) ;
De beneficiis, 5, 25, 6 : *ludi magister*.
Suetonius, *De grammaticis*, 23.
Tacitus, *Annales*, 12, 8 and 14, 52 : *magister* (*praeceptor*) ;
13, 66 : *magistri* (*praeceptores*) ;
6, 20 : *magister* (*artis Chaldaeorum*).
Historiae, 4, 10 : *magister* (*sapientiae*).
Terence, *Andria*, l. 54 : *magister* (*praeceptor*).
Varro, *Apud Nonium Marcellum*, p. 448 : *magister* (*ludi* or *artium liberalium*).
Vegetius, *Epitoma rei militaris*, 3, *pr.*, and 3, *magister armorum*.
Virgil, *Aeneis*, 8, 515 : *magister* (*praeceptor*).
5, 669, and 9, 172 : *magistri* (*praeceptores*).
Georgica, 4, 283 : *magister* (*rei rusticae*).

Magister Navis

Ausonius, *Mosella*, 204.
Corpus Glossariorum Latinorum, II, 126, 11 ; 356, 20, and 419, 21 ;
IV, 363, 8 and 9 ;
V, 114, 58.
C.I.L. XIV, 2028, Ostia.
Digesta, XIV, 1, 1, pr., 2, 3, 4, 5, 10, 12, 13, 17, 18, 19, 20, 23, 24 ;
XIV, 1, 4, 1, 3, and XIV, 1, 5 pr., 1 ; also XIV, 1, 7, and XIV, 2, 2 pr., 6, 7 ;
XIX, 2, 13, 2 ;
XXXIX, 4, 11, 2.
Gaius, *Institutiones*, 4, 71.
Horace, *Carmina*, 3, 6, 31.
Juvenal, *Satirae*, 4, 45 ; 12, 79.
Livy, *Ab Urbe Condita*, 29, 25, 7.
Lucan, *Pharsalia*, 2, 696.
Martial, *Epigrammata*, 10, 104, 16.
Silius Italicus, *Punica*, 4, 717.
Valerius Flaccus, *Argonautica*, 1, 18, and 382 ; 2, 391 ; 3, 109 : 4, 269 ; 8, 202.
Vegetius, *Epitoma Rei Militaris*, 4, 43.
Virgil, *Aeneis*, 1, 115 ; 5, 176, 224, and 867 ; 6, 353.

Magister Operum

Columella, *De re rustica*, 1, 8, 17 and 18 ; 1, 9, 1 and 2.
Styled *magistri singulorum officiorum*, 1, 8, 11, and 11, 1, 27.

Magister Pecoris

Ausonius, *Epigrammata*, 58, 5.
Cicero, *In Verrem*, 5, 7.
Columella, *De re rustica*, 7, 6, 9.
Livy, *Ab Urbe Condita*, 1, 4, 6.
Servius, *In Vergilii Aeneida*, 7, 485.
Varro, *De re rustica*, 1, 2, 14 ; 2, 1, 23 ; 2, 2, 20 ; 2, 3, 8 ; 2, 10, 2 and 5, also 10.

Virgil, *Aeneis*, 12, 717.
Eclogae, 3, 101.
Georgica, 2, 529; 3, 445.

Here follow references to other *magistri*, intrusted with the care and training of animals.

Apuleius, *Florida*, 12.
Metamorphoses, 7, 27; 10, 17, also 23 and 35.
Boethius, *De consolatione philosophiae*, 3, 2, 10.
Horace, *Epistulae*, 1, 2, 64.
Juvenal, *Satirae*, 14, 246.
Martial, *De spectaculis*, 10, 1 and 17, 3, and 18, 1 and 22, 1.
Epigrammata, 14, 80, 1.
Prudentius, *Peristephanon*, 11, 91.
Silvius Italicus, *Punica*, 4, 614.
Vegetius, *Epitoma rei militaris*, 3, 24.
Virgil, *Georgica*, 3, 118 and 185.

Magister Societatis

Cicero, *Ad Atticum*, 5, 15, and 11, 10 (*promagister*).
Ad Familiares, 13, 9, 2, and 65, 1 (*promagister*).
In Verrem, 2, 70, 169 (*promagister*), 71, 173, and 74, 182; also 3, 71, 167 and 168.
Paulus Diaconus, *Epitome Festi*, 126 M.

Magister Tabernae

Digesta, XIX, 2, 13, 4.
Paulus, *Sententiae*, 2, 8, 3.

Magister Pagi

Bulletin archéologique du Comité des Travaux historiques, 1894, p. 344, pagus Thigillavensium (Hadrian); 1909, p. 78, Announa.
Calpurnius, *Ecloga*, 4, 125.
Corpus Glossariorum Latinorum, II, 126, 9.
C.I.L. I, 801, 802, 804; XIV, 2105; VI, 32, 455 (Rome). All these inscriptions are from the close of the first century B.C.
III, 7484, Ainan Chisi (Moesia Inferior); III, 7847, Micia (Dacia).
V, 4148, *pagus Farracticanensis.*
VIII, 5683, 5705, 19, 135, Sigus; 5884 (*magistratus*), 19,199, Sila; 6267–71, 6273–97, Phua; 6339, Azelis; 7070, uncertain *pagus* near Cirta; 17257 (= 10,833), 198 A.D., and 17,258, after 201 A.D., Zattara; 18,896, 18,900, Thibilis.
IX, 726, Larinum; 3046 (?), *pagus Interprominus;* 3137 (= I, 1280), 3138 (= I, 1279), Lavernae; 3440, Petuinum; 3521, Furfo; 4206, 4208, Septaquae; 5814, Montefano.
X, 814, 853, 1042, 1074 c, 924 (*ministri*), Pompeii; 3772 (= I, 571), 94 B.C., *pagus Herculaneus.*
XI, 1947, 1948, Perusia; 3040, 4–3 B.C., *pagus Stellatinus;* 3196 (*et magister*), Nepete.

XII, 5370, *inter Narbonem et Tolosam.*

XIII, 5, Consoranni; 412, *civitas Trebellorum;* 604, Burdegala; 1670, *pagus Condate;* 2507, Ambarri.

Ephemeris Epigraphica, 8, 474, *conventus Capuae.*

Notizie degli Scavi, 1899, p. 474 (*magistra*), Liguria.

Paulus Diaconus, *Epitome Festi*, 126 and 371 M.

Recueil de la Société archéologique de Constantine, 1901, p. 162, Phua.

Siculus Flaccus, *De condicionibus agrorum*, pp. 146, 164.

Mittheilungen des deutschen archaeologischen Instituts, Römische Abtheilung, 1914, p. 130, Laira.

Magister Vici

Asconius, *In Pisonianam*, 6.

Bulletin de la Société archéologique bulgare, I, 1910, p. 116.

Bullettino Communale di Roma, 1888, p. 328, Rome.

Bullettino dell' Instituto di Diritto Romano, 1906, p. 115 (*ministri*), 2 B.C., Rome.

Cicero, *In Pisonem*, 4, 8.

Corpus Glossariorum Latinorum, III, 298, 49 and 50; 525, 4.

C.I.L. I, 1237, Puteoli.

IV, 60, Pompeii.

V, 1890, Concordia; 8211, Aquileia.

VI, 1324, 23 B.C.; 2221 (I, 804), before 12 B.C.; 33, 2 B.C.; 34, 3 B.C.; 35, 45–46 A.D.; 128, 6 B.C.; 282, 4 A.D.; 283, 7–6 B.C.; 445, 446, 447 (*ministri*); 448, 4 B.C.; 449, 450, 451, 452, 453, 454, 760, 761, 763, 764, 765, 767, 801, 802, 2222, 150 A.D.; 975, 135 A.D., 2223, 2224, 2225, 2225 *a*, 2226, 2227, 2228: Rome.

IX, 4120, Aequiculi; 3435 (*aediles*), *Peltuinum.*

XI, 851, Mutina; 3585, Castrum Novum; 4798, 4815, 4821, Spoletum; 6013, Sentinum; 6237, Fanum Fortunum; 6359, 6362, 6367, Pisaurum.

XII, 5370, *ad Narbonem.*

XIII, 4310, *vicus Bodatius;* 4316, *ad Mogontiacum.*

XIV, 2263, *ager Albanus.*

Curiosum Urbis Regionum, XIV. *Passim.* After 357 A.D.

Ephemeris Epigraphica, IV, 746, 747, Rome.

VII, 12–77, Rome.

IX, 470, Castia; 685, *ager Tusculanus.*

Martial, Epigrammata, 10, 79.

Livy, *Ab urbe condita*, 34, 7, 2.

Notizie degli Scavi di Antichità, 1914, p. 362, 70 A.D., Rome.

Notitia Regionum Urbis XIV. Passim. 334–337 A.D.

Paulus Diaconus, *Epitome Festi*, 126 and 371 M.

Urbs Constantinopolitana Nova Roma. Passim. 408–450 A.D.

Magister Vici Canabensium

Archaeologische Epigraphische Mittheilungen aus Oesterreich-Ungarn, 8, p. 32, Küstendje.

C.I.L. III, 1008, Apulum; 6162, 6166, 6167, Troesmis; 14,409, 14,412, *vicus Trullensium;* 14,214, 26, *vicus Ulmetus.*
VII, 12, Regni; 333, Aurula; 346 (?), Old Carlisle.

MAGISTER CONVENTUS VICANI

C.I.L. II, 2636, Asturica; 2782, Clemia; 3408, Carthago Nova; 5007, *ager Olisiponensis.*
III, 1533, Jonic; 1820, Narona; 3776, 3777, Nauportus; 7536, near Toni.
V, 1829, 1830, Julium Caricum.

MAGISTER MUNICIPII

C.I.L. XI, 863, Mutina.

MAGISTER CASTELLI

C.I.L. VIII, 6272, 6297, 6299, Phua; 6044, Arsacal; 9317, *ad Tipasam.*

MAGISTER CURIAE

C.I.L. VIII, 11,008, Hr Zian; 14,683, 185 A.D., Smitthus.
Plautus, *Aulularia,* 1, 2, 29, and 2, 2, 3.
(Pseudo-) Asconius, *In Verrem,* 1, 8, 22.

MAGISTER FANI

(*a*) In *pagi* of the *ager Campanus*

C.I.L. X, 3772 (= I, 571), 94 B.C.; 3774 (= I, 564), 112–111 B.C.; 3775, 110 B.C.; 3776–3777 (= I, 565), 108 B.C.; 3778 (= I, 567), 106 B.C.; 3779 (= I, 566), 106 B.C.; 3780 (= I, 568), 104 B.C.; 3781 (= I, 569); 3782 (= I, 572), before 71 B.C.; 3783 (= I, 573), 71 B.C.; 3784 (= I, 575); 3785 (= I, 574); 3786, 15 A.D.; 3787.
Ephemeris Epigraphica, VIII, 473, 474.
Notizie degli Scavi, 1893, p. 164.

(*b*) In *conventus vicani*

C.I.L. II, 3433, 3434, Carthago Nova.
III, 1769, 1770, 1792, 1798, 1799, 1801, 1802, 1827 (?), Narona.
V, 1830, Julium Caricum.
XII, 5388, Tolosa.

(*c*) In the Roman *conventus* at Delos

Bulletin de Correspondance Hellénique, I, p. 87, no. 36, *ca.* 100 B.C.
IV, p. 190, 97 B.C.
XXVI, p. 536, 112–111 B.C.
XXXI, p. 439, no. 30, 97 B.C., and p. 442, no. 33.
XXXIII, p. 493, no. 15, 113 B.C., and p. 496, no. 16, *ca.* 100 B.C.; also p. 501, no. 17, and p. 503, no. 18, 57–56 B.C.
XXXIV, p. 402, no. 53, 150–125 B.C., and p. 404, no. 54, *ca.* 100 B.C.
C.I.L. III, 7212 (= *BCH.* VIII, p. 118); 7217 (= *BCH.* VIII, p. 97), *ca.* 150 B.C.; 7218 (= *BCH.* I, p. 285), before 150 B.C.; 7225 (= *BCH.* VIII, p. 145); 7226 (= *BCH.* VIII, p. 186); 14,203[4] (= *BCH.* XXIII, p. 56).

(*d*) In municipalities

C.I.L. I, 1345, Cosmum Puerinum.
II, 5349, 128, *lex Coloniae Genetivae Juliae*, Urso.
V, 8251, 8258, Aquileia.
VI, 335, *magister Herculis;* 30,888, *magistri Herculis*, Rome.
IX, 1456, *magistri Bellonae*, Ligures Baebiani; 1534, Beneventum; 2362, 2363, 2365, *magistri sacrorum Iunonis Augustae*, Allifae.
X, 3918, 3924, Capua; 4620, Culbuteria; 5388, Aquinum; 6073, *magistri Iovis Optimi Maximi*, Formiae.
XI, 6108, *magistri Apollinis*, Forum Sempronii; 2360, Cosa.
XII, 4525, Narbo.
XIV, 2982, Praeneste.

MAGISTRAE FANI

C.I.L. V, 5026, Tridentum; 8253, Aquileia.
X, 39, *magistrae Proserpinae*, Vibo, and 6511, *Magistrae Matris Matutae*, Cora.
XI, 2630, Cosa; 3246, *magistrae Minervae*, Sutrium.
XIV, 2997, 3006, *magistrae Matris Matutae*, Praeneste.

MINISTRI FANI

C.I.L. III, 1967, 1968, 8690: *ministri ad Tritones*, Salonae.
V, 3101, Vicita; 5026, Tridentum; 8253, Aquileia.
VIII, 6961, *ministri dei Saturni*, Cirta.
X, 824–827, 3 to 58 A.D., *ministri Fortunae Augustae*, Pompeii; 884–893, *ministri Augusti*, Pompeii. Of the inscriptions recording *ministri Augusti* the following are datable: 884, 25 B.C.; 885–6, 14 B.C.; 890, 2 B.C.; 891, 1 B.C.; 892, 3 A.D.; 895, 23 A.D.; 898, 31 A.D.; 899, 32 A.D.; 901–2, 34 A.D.
XIV, 2982, Praeneste.
Notizie degli Scavi, 1902, p. 470, Corfinium.

MAGISTER LARUM AND MAGISTER LARUM AUGUSTI

C.I.L. II, 2013, Singila; 2181, Adamuz; 2233, Corduba; 3563, Lucentum; 3113, Cabeza del Griego; 4293, 4297, 4304, 4306, 4307, 4309, 6106, Tarraco.
V, 792, Aquileia; 3257, 3258 (?), 1 B.C., Verona.
IX, 2825, Histonium; 423, Venusia; 3424, Peltuinum; 3657, Marsi Maruvium; 6293, Caudium.
X, 773, Stabiae; 1582, 1 A.D., Puteoli; 5761, 6 B.C; 5762, 2 B.C., Casinum; 6556, 6557, Veletriae; 7514, Sardinia.
XI, 804, Bonnonia; 2998, Viterbo.
XII, 406, 18–19 A.D., Massilia.

MINISTRI LARUM AND LARUM AUGUSTI

C.I.L. V, 3257, Verona.
IX, 3657, Marsi Maruvium.
X, 137, Potentia; 205, Grumentum; 1269, Nola; 3789 (= I, 570), 94 B.C. and 3790, 26 B.C., Capua; 7953, Sardinia.
XIV, 3562, Tibur.

Competaliasti at Delos

Bulletin de Correspondance Hellénique, XXIII, pp. 62, 63, 64, 99–98 B.C.; 67, 94 B.C.; 70, 93 B.C.
VII, p. 13, 97–96 B.C.
XXXI, p. 441, 98–94 B.C.
XXXIII, p. 505.

Magister Fundi

C.I.L. VIII, 11,217, *fundus Iubaltianensis*, 295–305 A.D.

Magister Saltus

C.I.L. VIII, 10,570, *saltus Burunitanus*, 180–183 A.D.

Magister Fratrum Arvalium

Bullettino Communale, 1911, p. 129 ff., 239 A.D.
C.I.L. VI, 970; 2023–2119, 14, 241 A.D.; 32,379, 32,340, 32,344, 32,352, 32,374.
Cf. Henzen, *Acta Fratrum Arvalium*, and Gatti, *Arvales* in De Ruggiero's *Dizionario Epigrafico*, vol. I, pp. 682 ff. The latter has a list of the Masters and Vice-Masters.

Magister Haruspicum

C.I.L. VI, 2161, Rome.
XI, 4194, Interamna.
XIV, 164, Ostia.

Magister Collegi Lupercorum

C.I.L. X, 6488, Ulubrae.
XIV, 2105 (= I, 805), Lanuvium.
Notizie degli Scavi, 1898, p. 406.

Magister Pontificum

C.I.L. VI, 1422, after 212 A.D.; 1700; 2120, 155 A.D.; 2158, after 382 A.D., *promagistri*, Rome.
X, 1125, after Constantine I, *promagister*, Abellinum.
VIII, 7115, and 7123, *magistri*, Cirta.

Magister XVvirum Sacris Faciundis

C.I.L. I², part 1, p. 29.
VI, 32,323, 29 and 57, 17 B.C.; 32,326, 6; 32,328, 15; 32,332, 2, 203–204 A.D.
X, 3698, 289 A.D., and 6422, 213 A.D., *promagistri*.
Monumentum Ancyranum, 4, 36–37.
Pliny, *Naturalis Historia*, 28, 2.
Tacitus, *Annales*, 6, 12.

Magister Saliorum

C.I.L. II, 3864, 3865, Saguntum.
VI, 2170, Alba.
Historia Augusta, *Vita Aureliani*, 4, 4.
Valerius Maximus, *Facta et Dicta Memorabilia*, 1, 1, 9.

Magister Sodalium Augustalium Claudialium

C.I.L. VI, 1985, 1986, and 1987, 213–2, 14 A.D. (= XIV, 2388–91).

Magister Augustales

C.I.L. III, 862, and 912, Napoca.
V, 6775 and 6784, Alba Pompeia; 7646 *ager Salusensis.*
IX, 20, Lupiae; 423, Venusia; 1048, *ager Compsimus;* 5020, Hadria.
X, 1209, Abella; 1404 (?), Herculaneum; 1055, Pompeii; 6114, Formiae; 7552 and 7601 (?), Carales.
XI, 1026, *a*, and 1029, Brixellum; 1061, Parma; 1604, 1606, 1611, and 1614, *a*, Florentia; 2631, Cosa; 3083, and 3135, Falerii; 3200, 12 B.C., Nepete; 4581, Carsulae.
XIV, 2974, Praeneste.

Magister Capitolinorum

C.I.L. VI, 2105, Rome
X, 6488, Ulubrae

Magister Cerialium

C.I.L. IX, 2835 and 2857, Histonium.
Bulletin Archaéologique du Comité des Travaux Historiques, 1909, procès-verbaux, pp. *xvii*, *xviii*, Trinesia.
Comptes Rendus de l'Academie des Inscriptions et Belles-Lettres, 1910, p. 135 (near Carthage).

Magister Martinus

Cicero, *Pro Cluentio*, 15, 43 (*ministri Martis*).
C.I.L. IX, 4068, *a*, and 4070, Carsioli.

Magister Mercurialis

C.I.L. III, 1769, 1770, 1775, 1792, 1799, 1801, 1802, and 1827, *IIIIIII viri magistri Mercuriales*, Narona.
IX, 54, *et Augustalis*, Brundisium.
X, 1152, Arbellinum, 1272, *Augustalis*, Nola; 3773 (?), Capua; 4589 and 4591, *Augustalis*, Caratia.
XI, 1417, Pisa.
Notizie degli Scavi, 1901, p. 26, *Augustalis*, Viggiano in Bruttium.

Magister Herculaneus

C.I.L. XIV, 3658, 3665, and 3681, *et Augustalis*, Tibur.
Notizie degli Scavi, 1910, p. 298, Sora.

Magister Collegii Minervae

Suetonius, *Vita Domitiani*, 4, 4.

Magistri of Unofficial Religious and Funerary Colleges

Apollo and the Genius Augusti

C.I.L. IX, 804, Bonnonia.

Bacchus

C.I.L. X, 104 (= I, 196), *Senatus Consultum de Bacchanalibus*, 186 B.C., *Ager Teuranus*.

Livy, *Ab urbe condita*, 39, 18, 9.

Bona Dea

C.I.L. V, 759 (cf. 757, 8), and 762, *magistrae*, Aquileia.
V, 5026, 2, Tridentum.
VI, 2239, Rome.
XI, 3866 and 3869, Capua.
XIV, 3437, Civitella.

Diana and Antinous

C.I.L. X, 2112, col. 1, *magister collegii;* col. 2, 8, and 14, *magistri cenarum*, 133–136, 6 A.D., Lanuvium.

Genius of Pannonia Superior

C.I.L. III, 4168, 228 A.D., Savaria.

Hercules

C.I.L. III, 1339, Veczel.
IX, 3424, Peltuinum.
IX, 3907 (= I, 1172) (?), Alba Fucens.
IX, 3857, Supinum.

Juppiter Cernenus

C.I.L. III, p. 295 f., Alburnum Maius.

Juno

C.I.L. X, 202, *magistra*, Grumentum.

Mars Ficanus Augustus

C.I.L. XIV, 309, Ostia.

Mater Deum and Navis Salvia

C.I.L. VI, 494, Rome.

Mens Bona

C.I.L. I, 1237, Naples.
X, 472, Paestum.
X, 1550, Puteoli.
X, 5512, 6513, and 6514, Cora.
XIV, 3564, Tibur.

Mithras

C.I.L. V, 5511, Lacus Verbanus.
VI, 47, 556, 717, 734, 1675, and 2151, Rome.

Minerva Medica (?)

Orelli, *Inscriptionum Latinarum Selectarum Collectio*, 2634, *magister odariarius*, Rome.

Obsequens Dea

C.I.L. V, 814, *magistra*, Aquileia.

Silvanus

C.I.L. X, 444, *vallis Silari superioris.*

Silvanus Martius

Mittheilungen des archaeologischen Instituts, Römische Abtheilung, 1908, p. 37, 39 B.C., Cervetri.

Venus

C.I.L. III, 1963, 1969, and 1971, *magistrae*, Salonae.

Uncertain Colleges

C.I.L. III, 4150, Savaria.
V, 1890, Concordia.
V, 8750, *magister primus de numero erolorum seniorum*, Concordia.
VI, 813, Rome.
VI, 10,301, 10,303, 10,305, 10,306, 10,308, 10,310, 10,311, 10,312, 10,313, 10,314, 10,315, 10,316, 10,317, 10,318, 10,319, and 10,320, Rome.
IX, 1948, Perusia.
IX, 3359, Piuna.
X, 4847, 32 A.D., Venafrum.
XI, 715, *magistralis*, Bonnonia.
XI, 1417 (*Mercuriales?*), Pisa.
XI, 2132, Elusium.
XIV, 2847, 2870, 2883, 2894, and 3027, Praeneste.
Notizie degli Scavi, 1909, p. 312, no. 17, Rome.

MAGISTRI IN COLLEGIA DOMESTICA

C.I.L. II, 2229, Corduba.
VI, 188, 236, 4051, *magisterium*, 6214, 6316, 6376, 8512, and 9409, Rome.
VI, 10,395, *fasti* of a college in the *familia Augusta*, 4 B.C.–1 A.D., Rome.
VI, 8639, *fasti officialium domus Augustae*, 48–50, and 65–69 A.D., *magistri* and *magistrae*, Rome.
X, 3942, Capua.
X, 6638 (= I, p. 327), *fasti collegii vernarum*, 38–51 A.D., Antium.
X, 6679, Antium.
XII, 3356 and 3637, Nemausus.
XIII, 1550, Putaeni.
XIV, 3015, Praeneste.
Notizie degli Scavi, 1901, p. 99, and 1902, p. 56, Rome.

MAGISTRI IN COLLEGES OF ARTIZANS AND TRADESMEN

Aeditui

C.I.L. XIV, 2637, Tusculum.

Aerarii

Bullettino Communale di Roma, 1904, p. 49, Rome.

Apparitores

C.I.L. VI, 9861, 9862, and 9863, *magistri quinquennales*, Rome.

Aromatorii

C.I.L. VI, 384, *magistri quinquennales*, Rome.

Artifices

C.I.L. VI, 9927, Rome.

Centonarii

C.I.L. III, 4496, *a*, 243 A.D., Carnutum.
V, 3411, and 3439, Verona.
VI, 7861, and 7862, *magistri quinquennales*, Rome.
XI, 970, Rhegium.
XI, 1354, 255 A.D., Luna.
XII, 2754, *ager Volcarus*.

Cisiarii

C.I.L. XIV, 2874, Praeneste.

Coques atrienses

C.I.L. XIV, 2875, Praeneste.

Coques Falisci

C.I.L. XI, 3078, Second century B.C., Sardinia.

Dendrophori

C.I.L. V, 7904, Nicia.
XIV, 309, Ostia.

Fabri and Fabri tignuarii

C.I.L. III, 3580, 201 A.D., Acquincum.
III, 1016, 1097 (?), Apulum.
III, 8086, Ratiaria, time of Severus and Caracalla.
III, 8819 and 14,243, Salonae.
V, 4489, Brixia.
V, 5310, *magister officiorum collegii fabrum*, and 5272, Comum.
VI, 148 and 321, *magistri quinquennales*, Ostia.
VI, 996, 7, and 9406, Rome.
VIII, 2690, Lambaesis.
IX, 5450, Falerii.
IX, 5754, Ricina.
XI, 126, Ravenna.
XI, 970, *magistri fabrum et centonariorum*, 190 A.D., Regium Lepidum.
XI, 5816, *magistri quinquennales*, Iguvium.
XII, 68, Salinae.
XII, 719 and 738, Arelate.
XII, 1191, Vienna.
XIV, 5, 128, 160, 299, 370, 371, 374, 407, 418, 430, and 2630: *magistri quinquennales*, Ostia.
XIV, 3009, *magistri quinquennales*, Praeneste.
Klio, 1910, p. 496, Sarmizegetusa.
Notizie degli Scavi, 1903, p. 217, Novara.

Farmacopuli

C.I.L. V, 4489, Brixia.

Fullones, Fontani, Magistri Fontis, Collegia Aquae

C.I.L. VI, 154, 123 A.D.; 155, 69 A.D.; 156, 105 A.D.; 157, 131 A.D.; 158, 131, 40 A.D.; 159, 140 A.D.; 160, 160 *a*, 161, 162, 160 A.D.; 163, 165, 268, 57 A.D.; 10,298, 1 *b*, 2, 5, 8, 9, 15, and 17, Rome.
IX, 5450, Falerii.
XI, 4771 (I, 1406), *magistri quinquennales*, Spoletum.
XIII, 8345, Colonia Agrippensium.

Glutinarii et Topiarii

Bullettino Communale di Roma, 1902, p. 99, Tusculum.

Hastiferi

C.I.L. XII, 1814, Vienna.

Horrearii

C.I.L. VI, 108 and 246, Rome.

Incolae et Opifices

C.I.L. XI, 6211, Sena Gallica.

Lani

C.I.L. VI, 167 and 168, Rome.
XIV, 2877, Praeneste.

Lintiones

C.I.L. XI, 3209, Nepete.

Mercatores pecuarii

C.I.L. XIV, 2878, Praeneste.

Mimiarii

C.I.L. III, 3980, Siscia.

Navales

American Journal of Archaeology, 1908, p. 39, Praeneste.

Piscatores et Urinatores

C.I.L. VI, 29,700, 29,701, and 29,702, Rome.

Synhod magna Psaltum

Bullettino Communale di Roma, 1888, p. 408, Rome.

Retiarii

C.I.L. X, 1589, Puteoli.

Sartores

C.I.L. VIII, 7158, Cirta.

Scaenici Latini

C.I.L. XIV, 2299, Albanum.

Tibicines

C.I.L. VI, 3696 and 3877, *magistri quinquennales*, Rome.

Utricularii

C.I.L. XII, 719, Arelate.
XII, 3351, Nemausus.

Viatores

C.I.L. VI, 1933, *magister trium decuriarum*, and 1942 (= 7446), Rome.

Omnia Collegia

C.I.L. V, 4449, *qui magisterio eorum functi sunt*, Brixia.

Magistri Iuventutis, or Iuvenum

C.I.L. III, 4272, Brigetio.
V, 8211, Aquileia.
IX, 4457 and 4520, *ager Amiternius.*
IX, 4545 and 4549, Nursia.
IX, 4691 and 4696, Reate.
IX, 4753 and 4754, *vallis Canera.*
IX, 4883, 4885, 4888, 4889, Trebula Mutuesca.
XI, 3938, Lucus Feroniae.
XI, 3215, Nepete.
Musée Belge, 1899, pp. 191–192, nos. 32–36, leaden *tesserae* of uncertain provenance. No. 34 dates from the time of Nero.

Magistri Collegii Veteranorum

Archaeologische Epigraphische Mittheilungen aus Oesterreich-Ungarn, 1884, p. 76, Carnutum.
C.I.L. III, 4496, *a*, Carnutum.
IX, 3907 (= I, 1172), Alba Fucens.

Ministri in Religious and Funerary Colleges

College of Mens Bona

C.I.L. X, 4636, Cales.

College of Mithras

C.I.L. XI, 5737, *menesterium*, Sentinum.

College of Saturnus

C.I.L. VIII, 6961, Cirta.

College of Venus

C.I.L. VI. 32,468, Rome.

Collegium funeraticum

C.I.L. VI, 10,311, Rome.

Uncertain Colleges

C.I.L. V, 762, *ministrae*, Aquileia.
XIV, 2982, Praeneste.

Ministri in Colleges of Artizans and Tradesmen

Aerarii

Bullettino Communale di Roma, 1904, p. 49, Rome.

Cisiarii

C.I.L. XIV, 2874, Praeneste.

Fullones or Fontani

C.I.L. VI, 154, 155, 156, 157, 158, 159, 163, and 165, Rome.

Magister XX Hereditatium

Wilmann, *Inscriptiones*, 1293, Lugdunum.

Promagister XX Hereditatium

C.I.L. VI, 1620, Rome.
VIII, 20,684, Saldae.
IX, 5835, Auximum.
XI, 1326, Luna.

Promagister Hereditatium

C.I.L. XIII, 1810, Lugdunum.

Promagister Frumenti Mancipalis, Promagister Portuum

C.I.L. III, 14,195, 4–13, Ephesus.

Magister Privatae

Note. — The principal literary references to this and to the following Masters may be found in *Roman Magistri in the Civil and Military Service of the Empire*, published in *Harvard Studies in Classical Philology*, vol. XXVI (1915), pp. 73 ff.
C.I.L. III, 12,043 and 12,044 (= 13,059), 314 A.D., Crete.
VI, 1630, Rome.
VIII, 822, Turca.

Magister Privatae Egypti et Libyae

C.I.L. III, 18, Alexandria.

Magister Summarum Rationum

C.I.L. VI, 1618, Rome.
VIII, 822, Turca.

Magister Memoriae

C.I.L. VI, 510, 376 A.D.; 1764 and 8621, Rome.
XII, 1524, *ager Vocontiorum.*

Magister Epistularum

C.I.L. VI, 510, 376 A.D., Rome.
Ephemeris Epigraphica, VII, 262, Thubursicum Bure.

Magister Libellorum

C.I.L. VI, 510, 376 A.D., Rome.
X, 4721, *ager Falerinus.*
XII, 1254, *ager Vocontiorum.*

Magister Sacrarum Cognitionum

C.I.L. V, 8972, Aquileia.
VI, 510, 376 A.D., Rome.

Magister Studiorum

C.I.L. VI, 1608, 1704, and 8638, Rome.
X, 4721, *ager Falerinus*.

Magister Admissionum

C.I.L. XIV, 3457, Sublaqueum.

Magister Officiorum

C.I.L. VI, 1721 (= Dessau, *Inscriptiones Latinae Selectae*, no. 1244), 355–360 A.D., Rome.
VIII, 989, Missua.
Dessau, *Inscriptiones Latinae Selectae*, 9043.

Magister Ballistarius

C.I.L. V, 6632, *ager Novariensis*.

Magister Cohortis

C.I.L. III, 10,307, Intercisa.

Magister Equitum

C.I.L. V, 8278, Aquileia.

Magister Kampi

C.I.L. VIII, 2562, Lambaesis, time of Alexander Severus.

Magister Numeri

C.I.L. VIII, 21,568, Ala Milaria.

Magister Castrorum

C.I.L. VII, 268, Isurium, Fifth century, A.D.
VIII, 4354, 578–582, Ain Ksar.

Magister Militum

C.I.L. II, 4320, 598–590 A.D., Carthago Nova.
III, 88, 371 A.D., Arabia Petra; 3653, 371 A.D., Salva; 4668, 4669, and 4670, Carnutum; 5670, *a*, 370 A.D., Fafina; 6399, Salonae; 10,596, 365–367 A.D., Salva; 11,376, Carnutum (cf. Hirschfeld, *Kleine Schriften*, p. 651, n. 3).
V, 8120, 3, Cremona; 8120, 4, about 525 A.D., Milan.
VI, 1188, 1189, 1190, 1731, 1732, 1733, 1734 (nos. 1731–1734 from 405–408 A.D.), 31,914, and 32,050, 589 A.D., Rome.
VIII, 101, time of Justinian, Capsa; 259, time of Justinian, Sufes; 1863, time of Justinian, Themeste; 4354, 578–582 A.D., Ain Ksar; 4677, Madaura, and 4799, Gardianfala, time of Justinian.
IX, 4051, 398–408 A.D., Carseoli.
Dessau, *Inscriptiones Latinae Selectae*, no. 9217 *a* and *b*, Rusguniae, Mauretania.

APPENDIX B

I. MASTERS OF THE OFFICES TO 700 A.D.

A.D.			
321	Heraclianus	(*Occ.*),	*Codex Theodosianus*, XVI, 10, 1.
323	Proculianus	(*Occ.*),	*Codex Theod.*, XI, 9, 1.
324	Martinianus	(*Or.*),	Aurelius Victor, *Epitome*, XLI, 6; Lydus, *De Mag.*, 2, 25; Zosimus, 2, 25.
324	Palladius		Lydus, *De Mag.*, 2, 25.
346	Eugenius	(*Occ.*),	Athanasius, *Apologia ad Constantinum*, 3; cf. *C.I.L.* VI, 1721.
350–51	Marcellinus	(*Occ.*),	Zosimus, 2, 43, 4; 46, 3; 47, 2.
350–54	Palladius	(*sub Gallo Caesare*),	Ammianus, 22, 3, 3.
355	Florentius (*agens pro magistro officiorum*),	(*Or.*),	Ammianus, 22, 5, 12.
359–360	Florentius	(*Or.*),	Ammianus, 20, 2, 2; 22, 3, 6.
360	Pentadius	(*sub Juliano Caesare*),	Ammianus, 20, 8, 19.
360	Felix	(*Occ.*),	Ammianus, 20, 9, 5.
360	Anatolius	(*Occ.*),	Ammianus, 20, 9, 8; Zosimus, 3, 29, 3; 30, 4.
362	id.		*Codex Theod.*, XI, 39, 5.
363	id.		Magnus Carrhenus, *Fragmenta Historicorum Graecorum*, vol. IV, p. 5.
365	Ursatius	(*Occ.*),	Ammianus, 26, 5, 7.
365	Euphrasius	(*Or.*),	Ammianus, 26, 7, 4.
366	id.		Ammianus, 26, 10, 8.
Before 368	Ampelius	(*Occ.*),	Ammianus, 28, 4, 3.
368	Leo	(*Occ.*),	Ammianus, 28, 1, 12.
368	Remigius	(*Occ.*),	Ammianus, 27, 9, 2; *Codex Theod.*, VII, 8, 2 (?).
370	id.		Ammianus, 28, 6, 8, and 30.
373	id.		Ammianus, 29, 5, 2.
374	Leo	(*Occ.*),	Ammianus, 30, 2, 10.
375	id.		Ammianus, 30, 5, 10.
376 to 379	Siburius	(*Occ.*),	*Monumenta Germaniae Historiae, Auctores Antiquissimi*, VI, p. *cxxxi*.
379	Syagrius	(*Occ.*),	*Codex Theod.*, I, 15, 10; VII, 12, 2.
380	Florus	(*Or.*),	*Codex Theod.*, VI, 27, 3; VIII, 15, 6.
381	id.		*Codex Theod.*, VI, 29, 6.

381	Palladius	(*Or.*),	*Codex Theod.*, X, 24, 3.
382	id.		*Codex Theod.*, VI, 27, 4.
384	id.		*Codex Theod.*, VII, 8, 3.
382	Macedonius	(*Occ.*),	Severus, *Sacra Historia*, 2, 48.
386	Principius	(*Occ.*),	*Codex Theod.*, I, 9, 2.
389	Caesarius	(*Or.*),	*Codex Theod.*, VIII, 5, 49.
390	Rufinus	(*Or.*),	*Codex Theod.*, X, 22, 3; Lydus, *De Mag.*, 2, 10; 3, 40.
393	Theodotus	(*Or.*),	*Codex Theod.*, VII, 8, 4.
394	id.		*Codex Theod.*, VII, 1, 14.
395	Marcellus	(*Or.*),	*Codex Theod.*, VI, 29, 8; XVI, 5, 29; *De Medicamentis*, *tit.*
395 (?)	Hosius	(*Or.*),	*Codex Theod.*, VI, 27, 7.
396	id.		*Codex Theod.*, VI, 26, 6; 27, 8; 27, 9.
398			*Codex Theod.*, VII, 8, 5; X, 22, 4.
397	Hadrianus	(*Occ.*),	*Codex Theod.*, VI, 26, 11.
399	id.		*Codex Theod.*, VI, 27, 11.
404	Anthemius	(*Or.*),	*Codex Theod.*, XVI, 4, 4; VI, 27, 14; X, 22, 5.
405	Aemilianus		*Codex Theod.*, I, 9, 3; VI, 34, 1.
			400 A.D. (?) *Codex Theod.*, VII, 8, 8.
408	Naemorius	(*Occ.*),	Zosimus, 5, 32, 26.
408	Olympius	(*Occ.*),	*Codex Theod.*, XVI, 5, 42; Zosimus, 5, 35.
409	Johannes	(*Occ.*),	Sozomenus, IX, 8.
410	Gaiso	(*Occ.*),	*Codex Theod.*, IX, 38, 11.
412	Namatius	(*Occ.*),	*Codex Theod.*, VI, 27, 15.
414	Helio	(*Or.*),	*Codex Theod.*, XIII, 3, 17.
415	id.		*Codex Theod.*, I, 8, 1; VI, 27, 17.
416	id.		*Codex Theod.*, VI, 27, 18; 26, 17; 33, 1.
417	id.		*Codex Theod.*, VI, 27, 19.
424	id.		Olympiodorus, *Fragmenta Historicorum Graecorum*, vol. IV, p. 68, ch. 46.
424	id.		*Codex Theod.*, I, 8, 3.
425	id.		Olympiodorus, *F.H.G.*, vol. IV, p. 68, ch. 46.
426	id.		*Codex Theod.*, VI, 27, 30.
427	id.		*Codex Theod.*, VII, 8, 14; XIII, 3, 18.
430	Johannes	(*Or.*),	*Codex Theod.*, VII, 8, 15.
430	Paulinus	(*Or.*),	*Codex Theod.*, VI, 27, 3; *Chronicon Paschale*, wrongly, 421 and 444.
435	Valerius	(*Or.*),	*Codex Theod.*, VI, 28, 8; VII, 8, 16.
441	Flegetius	(*Or.*),	*Novellae Theodosii*, 21. (*Codex Just.*, I, 31, 3 Phlegetius.)
443	Nomus	(*Or.*),	*Novellae Theod.*, 24.
444	id.		*Novellae Theod.*, 25; *Codex Just.*, I, 24, 4. Undated: *Codex Just.*, XII, 19, 7 and 8; 21, 6; 26, 2.
			449 (?) Priscus, *F.H.G.*, vol. IV, p. 97, fg. 13.

448	Martialius	(*Or.*),	Priscus, *F.H.G.*, vol. IV, p. 77, fg. 7.
449	Opilio	(*Occ.*),	*Novellae Valentiniani*, 28.
450	id.		*Novellae Val.*, 30.
451	Vincomalus	(*Or.*),	Mansi, vol. V, pp. 97, 185 ff., 497, 500, 505.
452	id.		*Codex Justinianus*, I, 3, 23 (Calch.); cf. XII, 40, 10.
456	Euphemius	(*Or.*),	Priscus, *F.H.G.*, vol. IV, p. 102.
457	Martialius	(*Or.*),	*De Caer.*, 1, 91.
Between 457 and 470	Patricius	(*Or.*),	*Codex Just.*, XII, 19, 9; 20, 3 and 5; 50, 22.
id.	Euphemius	(*Or.*),	*Codex Just.*, XI, 10, 6, and 7.
id.	Johannes	(*Or.*),	*Codex Just.*, XII, 5, 3; 25, 3; 59, 8.
470	Hilarianus	(*Or.*),	*Codex Just.*, I, 23, 6; XII, 19, 10; 59, 9.
474	id.		*Codex Just.*, XII, 25, 4. Undated: *Codex Just.*, XII, 7, 2; 40, 11.
474	Eusebius	(*Or.*),	*Codex Just.*, XII, 29, 2. *De Caer.*, 1, 94.
475–477 (?)	Patricius	(*Or.*),	Candidus, pp. 474, 475, Bonn.
Between 474 and 491 (Zeno)	Illyrianus	(*Or.*),	*Codex Just.*, XII, 40, 11.
	Longinus	(*Or.*),	*Codex Just.*, XII, 29, 3.
478 to 484	Illus	(*Or.*),	Theophanes, pp. 196, 197, 198. Marcellinus Comes, *Chronicon*, A. C., 484.
484	Johannes	(*Or.*),	*Codex Just.*, XII, 21, 8.
485	Pamprepius	(*Or.*),	Theophanes, p. 201.
492	Eusebius	(*Or.*),	*Codex Just.*, I, 30, 3.
497	id.		*Codex Just.*, II, 7, 20. Undated: *Codex Just.*, XII, 1, 18; 5, 5; 10, 2; 19, 11.
507–511	Eugenes	(*Regni Gothici*),	Cassiodorus, *Variae*, 1, 12, and 13.
504–518	Celer	(*Or.*),	*Codex Just.*, IV, 29, 21. Marcellinus Comes, *Chronicon*, A. C., 504. Procopius, *De bello Gothico*, 1, 8. *De Caer.*, 1, 93. Undated: *Codex Just.*, XII, 19, 12.
520	Tatianus	(*Or.*),	*Codex Just.*, XII, 19, 14.
522	Hermogenes	(*Or.*),	Theophanes, p. 276, Bonn.
522–523	Boethius	(*Regni Gothici*),	*Anonymus Valesianus*, 14, 85.
524	Licinius	(*Or.*),	*Codex Just.*, XII, 33, 5.
523–527	Cassiodorus	(*Regni Gothici*),	*Variae*; cf. *M.G.H.*, XII, pp. *x–xi*.
527	Tatianus	(*Or.*),	*Codex Just.*, I, 31, 5; XII, 19, 15. *De Caer.*, 1, 95. Undated: *Codex Just.*, XII, 19, 14.
After 527	Cyprianus	(*Regni Gothici*),	*Anonymus Valesianus*, 14, 85.
id.	Petronius	(*Regni Gothici*),	*Praescriptio libelli Cassiodorani de stirpe sua.*
528 (?)	Theophilus	(*Or.*),	*Codex Just.*, 1 *de Justiniani codice confirmando*, 529 A.D., *ex magister.*
530	Hermogenes	(*Or.*),	Procopius, *De bello Persico*, 1, 13.

532	Hermogenes (*Or.*),	*Codex Just.*, V, 17, 11.
533	id.	*Chronicon Paschale; Codex Just.*, I, 3, 53; V, 17, 11; VII, 24, 1; IX, 13, 1; XI, 48, 24.
533	Trebonianus (*Or.*),	*Codex Just.*, 1, 17, 2 pr.
534	id. (*Or.*),	*Codex Just.*, I, *de emendatione Codicis Justiniani;* I, *de novo codice*, 528 A.D.: *magisteria dignitate inter agentes decoratus.*
535	Hermogenes (*Or.*),	*Novellae Just.*, 2; 10; 138.
536	Trebonianus (*Or.*),	*Novellae Just.*, 23.
539	Basilides (*Or.*),	*Novellae Just.*, 85; *Chronicon Paschale*, *anno*, 532, ποιῶν τὸν τόπον τοῦ μαγίστρου Ἑρμογένους ἐν Κωνσταντίνου πόλει.
539 to 565	Petrus (*Or.*),	Procopius, *Historia Arcana*, 16; *De bello Gothico*, 4, 11; *De Caer.*, I, 84, rubric; *Novellae Just.*, 123, 546 A.D.; 137, 565 A.D.
565	Anastasius (*Or.*),	Corippus, *Panegyr. in laudem Justini*, II, *pr.* 30.
579	Theodorus (*Or.*),	Theophylactus, 3, 25. Menander Protector, *F.H.G.*, vol. IV, p. 257, fr. 55.
588	id. (*Or.*),	*Historiens des Gaules et de la France* (Boquet), vol. IV, p. 85.
596 to 603	Domentziolus (*Or.*),	Theophanes, pp. 451, 460.
626	Bonus (*Or.*),	*Chronicon Paschale.*
VI–VII Century	Isaac (*Or.*),	Schlumberger, *Sigillographie de l'Empire byzantin*, p. 563.

II. MASTERS OF THE OFFICES IN THE BYZANTINE EMPIRE

Leo III (717–740),	
Nicetas Xylinites, Master,	Theophanes, p. 400; Mansi, vol. XI, col. 742, (680 A.D.).
Constantine V (740–775),	
Theophanes,	Theophanes, p. 415.
Petros,	Theophanes, p. 442.
Leo IV (775–779),	
Petros,	Theophanes, p. 456.
Constantine VI (779–797),	
Petros,	Theophanes, p. 464.
Michael Lachanodrakon,	Theophanes, p. 468.
VIII–IX Centuries,	
Johannes,	Schlumberger, *Sigillographie*, p. 563.
Nicephorus I (802–811),	
Theoktistos,	Theodore of Studion, *Epistulae*, 1, 24.
Stauricius (811),	
Theoktistos,	Theophanes, p. 492.

Michael I (811–813),	
Theoktistos,	Theophanes, p. 500.
Michael II (820–829),	
Christophoros,	Genesius, p. 35.
Stephanos,	Theodore of Studion, *Epist.*, 2, 76.
Irenaios,	Ps. Simeon, 622.
Theophilus (829–842),	
Alexios Musele,	Theophanes Continuatus, p. 108.
Manuel Armenios,	Genesius, p. 73; Theophanes Cont., p. 148.
Theophilus-Michael III (842–867),	
Arsaber, Stephanos, Bardas,	Theophanes Cont., p. 175.
Manuel Armenios,	Genesius, p. 83.
Basil,	Theophanes Cont., p. 238; Genesius, p. 111.
Petronas,	Genesius, p. 97.
Theodatakes,	Nicetas, *Vita Ignatii*, in Mansi, vol. XVI, p. 237.
Basil I (867–886),	
Manuel,	Theophanes Cont., p. 307.
Theodoros,	Mansi, vol. XVI, p. 309.
Christophoros,	Mansi, vol. XVI, pp. 44, 54, etc.
Leo VI (886–912),	
Stephanos,	Theophanes Cont., p. 354.
Stylianos,	Theophanes Cont., p. 354.
Katakalon,	Theophanes Cont., p. 359; *De Administrando Imperio*, ch. 45, p. 199.
Theodatakes,	Theophanes Cont., p. 361.
Stylianos,	*Vita Euthymii*, 3 (De Boor). *Novellae Leonis VI*, 1 and 18. Schlumberger, *Sigillographie*, p. 553.
Erikorikios,	*De Administrando Imperio*, ch. 43, p. 185.
Aspasakios,	*De Administrando Imperio*, ch. 44, pp. 191, 193.
Genesius,	*Correspondence of Leon*, Δελτίον τῆς Ἱστορικῆς καὶ ἐθνολογικῆς Ἑταρείας τῆς Ἑλλάδος, vol. I, p. 377 f.
Leon,	*Vita Euthymii*, p. 189 (De Boor).
Constantine VII (912–958),	
Stephanos, Johannes Eladas, Leo Phokas,	Theophanes Cont., pp. 380, 381, 385, 388, 390.
Nicetas,	Theophanes Cont., pp. 413, 417.
Bardas Phokas,	Theophanes Cont., pp. 436, 459.
Johannes Kurkuas,	Theophanes Cont., p. 443; *De Administrando Imperio*, ch. 45, pp. 200, 204.
Kosmas, Romanos Saronites, Romanos Mousele,	Theophanes Cont., p. 443.

Pankratios,	*De Administrando Imperio*, ch. 45, p. 204.
Kurkenios,	*De Administrando Imperio*, ch. 46, pp. 206–208, 210–213.
Pankratios II,	*De Administrando Imperio*, ch. 46, p. 207.
Adranse,	*De Administrando Imperio*, ch. 46, p. 207.
Georgios,	*De Administrando Imperio*, ch. 46, p. 206.
David,	*De Administrando Imperio*, ch. 46, pp. 212, 213.
Simeon,	*Chronicle*, cited on title page only.
Basil II (963–1025),	
Nicephoros Uranos,	Cedrenus, II, p. 454.
Prusianos,	Cedrenus, II, p. 468, 469, 483.
Gregorios,	Cedrenus, II, p. 478.
Michael,	Cedrenus, II, p. 481.
Boris,	Leo Diaconus, p. 159.
Romanus III (1028–1034),	
Prusianos,	Cedrenus, II, p. 487.
Romanos Skleros,	Cedrenus, II, p. 487.
Michael,	Cedrenus, II, p. 488.
Basiliskos,	Cedrenus, II, pp. 501, 502.
Demetrios,	Cedrenus, II, p. 503.
Michael IV (1034–1042),	
Apolaphar,	Cedrenus, II, p. 514.
Georgios Maniakes,	Cedrenus, II, pp. 541, 545; Michael Attaliota, p. 11.
Skleros,	Cedrenus, II, p. 547.
Constantinos,	Psellus, p. 73.
Constantine IX (1042–1055),	
Basileios Theodoreanos,	Cedrenus, II, p. 553; Michael Attaliota, p. 21.
Jobanesices,	Cedrenus, II, p. 557.
Karikios,	Cedrenus, II, p. 559.
Michael,	Cedrenus, II, p. 565.
Constantinos Arianites,	Cedrenus, II, pp. 596, 597, 601; Michael Attaliota, p. 34.
Isaac Komnenos,	Cedrenus, II, p. 615.
Katakalon Kekaumenos,	Cedrenus, II, p. 615.
Theodora (1055–1057),	
Isaac Komnenos,	Cedrenus, II, p. 620.
Aaron Ducas,	Cedrenus, II, p. 628.
Michael,	Cedrenus, II, p. 634.
Constantine X (1059–1067),	
Basileios Apolaphos,	Joannes Scylitzes, p. 654.
Nicephoros Botaniates,	Joannes Scylitzes, p. 654; Michael Attaliota, pp. 56, 83, 97.
Basilias Apokapes,	Michael Attaliota, p. 83.
Michael VII (1067–1078),	
Nicephoros Bryennios,	Joannes Scylitzes, pp. 693, 694; Michael Attaliota, p. 154.
Eustathios,	Joannes Scylitzes, p. 701.

Diogenes,	Michael Attaliota, p. 99.
Petros Libellios,	Michael Attaliota, p. 111.
Josephus Trachaniota,	Michael Attaliota, p. 149.
Basilakes,	Michael Attaliota, p. 155.
Phokas,	Michael Attaliota, p. 224.
Nicephoros III (1078–1081),	
Michael Attaliota,	Michael Attaliota, *Historia*, cited on title page only.
Alexios I (1081–1118),	
Unnamed Magistros,	Anna Comnena, p. 95.
XI–XII Centuries,	
Christophoros,	Schlumberger, *Sigillographie*, p. 463, no. 1.
Maria (*magistrissa*),	Schlumberger, *Sigillographie*, p. 532, nos. 8 and 9.

INDEX

PART II

THE OFFICE OF THE GRAND CHAMBERLAIN IN THE LATER ROMAN AND BYZANTINE EMPIRES

The Index to Part II
will be found on pages 315–324

PREFATORY NOTE

IN the following pages an attempt has been made to present a comprehensive account of the Office of the Grand Chamberlain under the Later Roman and Byzantine Empires. For the better understanding of the nature and traditions of this office, a brief consideration of the activities and the position of Chamberlains of an earlier day seemed essential, and an introductory chapter was prepared dealing with the Chamberlains of the Republic and the Principate. In the last chapter the careers of several of the most prominent Grand Chamberlains have been sketched, in order to present concrete examples of the important extra-legal activities of the incumbents of this office.

The present study is an elaboration of a doctoral thesis bearing the same title, during the preparation of which the writer received the guidance and encouragement of Professors Arthur E. R. Boak and Henry A. Sanders, of the University of Michigan, of whose assistance he here makes grateful acknowledgment.

JAMES E. DUNLAP

UNIVERSITY OF MICHIGAN
August, 1923

CONTENTS

CHAPTER I

CHAMBERLAINS OF THE REPUBLIC AND PRINCIPATE

The rapid expansion of Roman territory and the great increase in the number of slaves during the period of the Republic were factors of great importance in shaping the social institutions of Rome. These two changes made possible a wealthy landed aristocracy, out of which there developed in the city a leisure class, whose interests lay successively in politics, business, and display. A growing desire for comfort and ease introduced slaves into the life of the city, and the love of display multiplied their number out of all reason. This development was the more rapid because the rough and uncultured Romans, brought by wider conquests into close touch with the luxurious refinement of the Greeks, the Carthaginians, and the peoples of the Orient, sought to add to their own rugged simplicity the graces of older and alien cultures. As might have been expected, they failed to grasp the essence of the superior refinement which they coveted, but in the obvious externals they soon ceased to borrow from their neighbors, whom they rivalled or even surpassed in ostentatious luxury.

The first city slaves at Rome probably performed necessary menial tasks about the house. After them, in all likelihood, came the educated slaves, who would be of great assistance to their masters in the capacity of secretaries and general body-servants. A very busy man would find need of runners, announcers, and the like, and his importance could be judged, to a certain extent, from the number of his servitors. An indolent but jealous and wealthy neighbor would be unable to brook the thought of being outdone by another, and would set slaves at useless tasks, solely for the sake of appearing important.

But service which was at first a luxury soon became a necessity, and new luxuries were then devised. In Rome, one result of these tendencies was an extensive and exact subdivision and classification of personal and household service, and the assignment of each distinguishable class of duties to a single servant or to a corps of them. At some time in the course of this development there was created a class of servants known as chamberlains (*cubicularii*), to whom was intrusted the most intimate and private attendance upon their masters.

I. Chamberlains of the Republic

In assigning duties about the bedchamber to special servants, it is probable that the Romans were merely adopting an oriental custom. Certainly it is a well-attested fact that from early times oriental princes had intrusted the protection of their wives and the guarding of their couches to servants whom the Greeks designated as 'eunuchs' (εὐνοῦχοι). This word, of uncertain origin, was sometimes applied to virile servants in high and confidential positions; generally, however, it implied that such servants had been subjected to *castratio*,[1] a practice which was first employed, according to tradition, by the fabulous Semiramis.[2]

That eunuch chamberlains were to be found among the Persians at the court of Darius the Great (522–485 B.C.) is hardly to be doubted.[3] They were present also at the court of Xerxes (485–465 B.C.), for it was through the connivance of Mithridates, the king's chamberlain, that Artabanes succeeded in assassinating the great Persian.[4] Satibarzanes was chamberlain of Xerxes' son, Artaxerxes (465–425 B.C.),[5] and Bagoas, the Egyptian eunuch of Artaxerxes III, Ochus (359–338 B.C.), entirely dominated his master and finally poisoned him, only to be poisoned himself when caught in a similar attempt on the life of Darius III, Codomannus (336–330 B.C.).[6] The successor of Bagoas may have been Tireus, one of the chamberlains who were captured along with the wife and daughters of Darius by Alexander,[7] who escaped and announced to his master, shortly before the battle of Arbela, the death of his queen. About a century later there was

[1] See Hastings, *Encyclopaedia of Religion and Ethics*, vol. V, p. 579, s.v. *eunuch*, for the meaning of the word and similar words in oriental languages.

[2] Ammianus Marcellinus, XIV, 6, 17; Claudian, *In Eutropium*, I, 339 ff.

[3] Xenophon, *Cyropaedia*, VII, 5, 65: τοὺς περὶ τὸ ἑαυτοῦ σῶμα θεραπευτῆρας ἐποιήσατο εὐνούχους. Cf. also VI, 1, 33; VI, 4, 11; Herodotus, III, 130; VIII, 105: παρὰ τοῖσι βαρβάροισι τιμιώτεροί εἰσι οἱ εὐνοῦχοι, πίστιος εἵνεκα τῆς πάσης τῶν ἐνορχέων.

[4] Diodorus, XI, 69, 1: ἀνακοινωσάμενος δὲ τὴν ἐπιβουλὴν πρὸς Μιθριδάτην τὸν εὐνοῦχον, ὃς ἦν κατακοιμιστὴς τοῦ βασιλέως καὶ τὴν κυριωτάτην ἔχων πίστιν.

[5] Plutarch, *Moralia*, 173 E.

[6] Diodorus, XVI, 47, 4 to XVII, 5, 6.

[7] Plutarch, *Alexander*, 30: τῶν δὲ θαλαμηπόλων τις εὐνούχων, οἳ συνεαλώκεισαν ταῖς γυναιξί.

a chamberlain in attendance, apparently, upon Cleopatra, the wife of the Seleucid monarch, Antiochus the Great (223–187 B.C.).[1]

It has been intimated that in the East a man who was not *castratus* might still be a 'eunuch' or chamberlain. This was true at Rome also. No chamberlains of the Republican period and only a few of those of the Early Empire are specifically described as eunuchs in the commonly accepted sense. During the first two centuries of the Empire, at least, the great majority of Roman chamberlains, it may be inferred, were not so mutilated.

The first chamberlains at Rome to whom ancient literature makes reference were attendants of Julius Caesar. Suetonius relates that when Caesar was on his way to Asia in the year 75–74 B.C., "he was captured by pirates in the neighborhood of the island of Pharmacussa, and remained among them, not without the greatest indignation, for almost forty days, in the company of one physician and two chamberlains."[2] Apparently as early as the time of this strange episode a young Roman of wealth and station might be attended by chamberlains, not only when at home, but also when he went abroad.

Some four years later (70 B.C.) Cicero, assailing the friends of Verres, declared that even their doorkeepers and their chamberlains courted his (Verres's) favor, and that their freedmen, their slaves and their handmaids loved him.[3] At this time chamberlains seem to have been regular members of families of the wealthier class at Rome, some of whose representatives Cicero was attacking. It is scarcely possible to estimate how long this part of the household service had been recognized as distinct from the rest, but the context of the passage cited suggests that a chamberlain was thought to hold a position of more dignity than that of the common servants.

Furthermore, since the chamberlain is mentioned together with the doorkeeper, it seems quite probable that he served his master in the capacity of an announcer or introducer of callers. This supposition is substantiated by another passage, in which Cicero, writing from

[1] *Bulletin de Correspondance Hellénique*, vol. IV (1880), pp. 217 f.: Κράτερον Κρατέρου Ἀντιοχέα, τὸν τροφέα Ἀντιόχου Φιλοπάτορος . . . καὶ ἐπὶ τοῦ κοιτῶνος τῆς βασιλίσσης.

[2] Suetonius, *Julius*, 4: *circa Pharmacussam insulam a praedonibus captus est, mansitque apud eos, non sine summa indignatione, prope quadraginta dies cum uno medico et cubicularis duobus.* Cf. Plutarch, *Caesar*, 2. 1: μεθ' ἑνὸς φίλου καὶ δυοῖν ἀκολούθοιν. Suetonius and Plutarch evidently employed the same source in relating this story, but at this point Suetonius seems to have followed it more closely than Plutarch, who was probably translating from a Latin author: cf. Velleius Paterculus, II, 41, 3 to II, 43.

[3] Cicero, *In Verrem Actio II*, III, 4, 8: *Hunc vestri ianitores, hunc cubicularii diligunt; hunc liberti vestri, hunc servi ancillaeque amant.*

Cilicia in the year 50 B.C., tells his friend that he eschews the pomp and ceremony upon which it was the custom of provincial governors to insist; that the provincials have easy access to him directly, and not through chamberlains.[1] Here the inference is quite plain that even at the time when Cicero was writing, the chamberlain of the governor was usually a kind of Cerberus set to guard his master's ease by turning aside all but the most important petitioners. His interference must have been vexatious to the provincials, and it is doubtful whether many of those who came empty-handed succeeded in gaining an audience with their governor.

A passage quoted from Alfenus Varus (*fl. circa* 38 B.C.) emphasizes the personal nature of the chamberlains' service, listing them among those who had the care of their master's person and appearance.[2]

In considering the foregoing passages, which are all that can be identified with certainty as referring to the time of the Republic, it must be borne in mind that the chamberlains of this period were simply body-servants of Roman citizens and that in no case did they have any official position. The chamberlains who have been mentioned as guarding the approach to provincial governors were in no sense members of their official staffs, but were personal attendants enjoying a temporary importance borrowed from their masters.

II. Chamberlains of the Principate

Not until the time of Augustus was there an official household at Rome of such importance as to make the development of a highly organized service possible. But with the establishment of the Principate and a permanent court, there gradually arose many institutions which would have been not only intolerable, but quite impossible under the old Republican system. It was, indeed, very slowly and with extreme caution that Augustus, posing as a modest private citizen, introduced imperial institutions, whether of a public or private nature.[3] Among the latter was the new organization of the palace service, including the chamberlains. It would be unprofitable to attempt to trace here, for the nature of the sources does not permit it, the various steps in the development of the powers and privileges of the imperial

[1] Cic., *Ad Atticum*, VI, 2, 5: *aditus autem ad me minime provinciales; nihil per cubicularium.*

[2] *Digesta*, L, 16, 203: *qui ad eius corpus tuendum atque ipsius cultum praepositi destinatique essent, quo in genere iunctores (unctores ?), cubicularii, coci, ministratores . . . numerarentur.*

[3] Cf. Fairon, *L'Organisation du Palais Impérial à Rome, Musée Belge*, vol. IV (1900), p. 6.

chamberlains of the Principate. A composite view of the period will, however, be helpful.[1]

The corps of the chamberlains was composed of:

1. the *a cubiculo*,
2. the *supra cubicularios*,
3. the *decurio cubiculariorum*,
4. the *cubicularii* and *cubiculariae.*

Of the last named class certain members were distinguished by the fact that they had special duties to perform. Such were:

a. the *ab aegris cubiculariorum*,
b. the *a frumento cubiculariorum*,
c. the *a veste cubiculariorum*,
d. the *a locis cubiculariorum*,
e. the *scriba cubiculariorum.*

The man who bore the title of *a cubiculo* was the chief of all the chamberlains. This view, which is that of both Rostowzew and Cesano, has been assailed by Michiels,[2] but without sufficient reason. Apparently Michiels has felt that the person described as *supra cubicularios* could be no other than the chief of the entire corps of chamberlains, and has therefore been compelled to assign the *a cubiculo* to a lower station. He seems, indeed, to understand the words *a cubiculo* to mean nothing more than "attached to the cubiculum" — an equivalent expression for *cubicularius.* Challenging the statements of Rostowzew in support of the view that the *a cubiculo* was the chief of the corps of chamberlains, he adduces three arguments against them:

First: that although all persons mentioned as *a cubiculo* in inscriptions are freedmen, while the great majority of *cubicularii*, at least during the first century of the Principate, are slaves, there is no warrant in this fact for the conclusion that the *a cubiculo* was the chief of the corps; for in actual numbers we know of more *cubicularii* of free station than men of like condition bearing the title of *a cubiculo.* This point is well made, but it neither proves nor disproves anything. Michiels goes on to remark, however, that the decurion of chamberlains in the *Corpus Inscriptionum Latinarum*, VI, 5747, *C Iulius divi Aug(usti) l(ibertus) Felix Ivatianus decurio cubicularius*, is described only by the title *cubicularius*, meaning, presumably, that he is not an *a cubiculo.* This remark seems to be quite without point, for if he

[1] For a more complete treatment, see Cesano, in De Ruggiero, *Dizionario epigrafico*, s.v. *cubiculum;* Rostowzew, in Pauly-Wissowa, *Real-Encyclopädie*, s.v. *cubicularius;* Michiels, *Les cubicularii des Empereurs Romains*, *Musée Belge*, vol. VI (1902), pp. 364–387.

[2] *Musée Belge*, vol. VI (1902), pp. 384–386.

was a decurion in the imperial service, it is hardly to be supposed that he would be an *a cubiculo* also; and if, as is not improbable, he was a decurion in a *collegium*, there is nothing remarkable in his being simply *cubicularius* in the actual chamber service.

Second: that even if all the famous chamberlains are called *a cubiculo* in inscriptions, they are never so designated by the authors of the time. There may be many reasons for this fact, but it is scarcely necessary to seek them, for the phenomenon can be illustrated by many instances from a later period. Thus, in the Late Empire, after the establishment of the office of *praepositus sacri cubiculi*, it is comparatively seldom that this official title is met outside of the constitutions of the Emperors. Such periphrases were employed as *spado*, *eunuchus*, *cubicularius*.[1]

Third: that although an *a cubiculo* is named earlier than a *cubicularius* among the persons mentioned in *C.I.L.*, VI, 5197, we cannot assume, as does Rostowzew, that the former ranked above the latter, for we do not know that the persons whose names are here recorded are mentioned in order of rank — indeed, two *pedisequi*, two *coci*, two *ab argento* are mentioned in different places without a hint that the one was superior to the other. The remark is true and pertinent. There is, however, another point to be noted here; viz., that there are no variants in the titles of the *pedisequi*, *coci* and *ab argento*, and that the only variant is to be found in the case of the chamberlains mentioned above. It seems improbable that two different titles referring to the same position should have been used on the same stone. That such was the case, however, is the implication of Michiels's argument, in which it is assumed that *cubicularius* and *a cubiculo* are synonymous expressions.

The criticisms of Michiels are salutary, but hardly constructive, for he has neither proved his own contention, that the *supra cubicularios* was the chief of all the chamberlains, nor disproved that of Rostowzew and Cesano; viz., that the *a cubiculo* held this position. It seems probable that the term *a cubiculo* was applied on the analogy of *a memoria*, *a libellis* and similar expressions, and it is generally agreed that these terms refer not only to the various bureaus, but also in a large number of cases, to the officials in charge of these bureaus.[2]

The *a cubiculo*, as the chief of the chamberlains, was probably responsible, for the conduct of his subordinates, directly to the Emperor, except at such times as the latter might choose to deal personally with

[1] See Appendix B. [2] Cf. Karlowa. *Römische Rechtsgeschichte*, vol. I, pp. 544–545.

the individuals of the service. He was almost constantly in the presence of his master, and there was probably nothing unusual in the relations between the Emperor Gaius and his chamberlain, Helicon, who "played ball and exercised and bathed and dined with Gaius, and was with him when he went to retire, having been appointed to the post of chamberlain and chief of the palace body-guard, a post such as no other held, and such as to afford him at his convenience and leisure the hearing of the Emperor." [1]

Thus the chamberlain naturally became the close confidant of the Emperor, to whose whims, whether good or ill, he obsequiously ministered, and whose confidence he found it advantageous to cultivate. Since, on the one hand, he was privy to many of the Emperor's thoughts and plans, and, on the other, could gain his ear as could no other, perhaps, at the court, he was sought out by courtiers and those desirous of obtaining office, and in this and other ways exercised an influence which extended far beyond the palace walls. In more than one instance an *a cubiculo* succeeded in so dominating the will of the Emperor that he became the virtual master of the Empire.

It must be borne in mind that, in spite of the exceptional powers wielded by the *a cubiculo*, his position was by no means a public one.[2] He was merely one of the Emperor's most trusted servants, whose peculiar position gave him temporarily an unusual amount of importance. As with other servants, the Emperor might discharge him at pleasure and put in his place whomever he might choose. A new Emperor, upon his accession, sometimes retained the chamberlains of the former ruler,[3] but more often the slave or freedman who had served him in that capacity as a private citizen must have been retained as *a cubiculo* by the new Emperor.

In only two cases is it recorded that an *a cubiculo* was in the service of a woman; both of these men served in the imperial household, the one under Domitia, the wife of Domitian,[4] and the other under Acte, the freedwoman and concubine of Nero.[5]

Of the second chamberlain in rank, the *supra cubicularios*,[6] we

[1] Philo, *Legatio ad Gaium*, 27: συνεσφαίριζε καὶ συνεγυμνάζετο καὶ συνελούετο καὶ συνηρίστα καὶ μέλλοντι κοιμᾶσθαι παρῆν Γαίῳ, τὴν τοῦ κατακοιμιστοῦ καὶ κατ' οἰκίαν ἀρχισωματοφύλακος τεταγμένος τάξιν, ὅση μηδενὶ προσῆν ἄλλῳ, ὡς μόνος ἔχειν εὐκαιρούσας καὶ σχολαζούσας ἀκοὰς αὐτοκράτορος, κτλ.

[2] This was also true of the early officials *ab epistolis*, etc. Cf. Hirschfeld, *Die Kaiserlichen Verwaltungsbeamten bis auf Diocletian*, p. 318.

[3] Cf. *Corpus Inscriptionum Latinarum*, VI, 8765: *a cubiculo augustorum.*

[4] *C.I.L.*, VI, 8570: *Hermae Augusti liberto a cubiculo Domitiae Augustae. . . .* Cf. VI, 8979.

[5] *C.I.L.*,VI, 8760: *Dis manibus Helio Actes Aug(usti) l(ibertae) liberto a cubiculo.*

[6] Michiels makes this officer the chief of the imperial chamberlain service. *Musée Belge*, vol. VI (1902), pp. 384 f. See pp. 169 f.

know but little. Our information is drawn entirely from epigraphic sources and is not conclusive. An examination of such evidence as we have, however, reveals the fact that the *supra cubicularios* was, in almost every known instance, in the service of a woman.[1]

The one *supra cubicularios* of whom this cannot be said definitely was, according to the editors of the *Corpus Inscriptionum Latinarum*, a freedman of Lucius Statilius Taurus,[2] but there is nothing impossible in the supposition that he served as the *supra cubicularios* of the wife of Taurus. It may not be too daring to suggest that while the *a cubiculo* was the chief of the chamberlains of the household and a constant attendant upon the master of the house, the chamberlains of the women's apartments may have been under the direction of the *supra cubicularios*, whose position was inferior to that of the *a cubiculo*, but not necessarily dependent upon it in the sense that he received his orders from that official.

It is not altogether certain that the decurion of chamberlains (*decurio cubiculariorum*) should be included in the organization of the palace service. It is quite possible that he was merely an official in one of the corporations (*collegia*) of the freedmen and slaves of the imperial household.[3] There are two reasons, however, for supposing that the decurion was a member of the palace staff.

The first reason is that Suetonius applies this title to the famous chamberlain Sigerius (though he erroneously calls him Saturius),[4] and it seems scarcely probable that he would have used the title of an official of a corporation to describe the semi-public position (as it might be termed) of Sigerius. It is to be concluded, therefore, that *decurio cubiculariorum* was the actual title of an official in the imperial service, unless indeed we assume that Suetonius employed the word *decurio* carelessly as an equivalent for some other title.

A second reason for including this official is that it is quite likely that the organization of the corporations of the imperial household

[1] Of Livia, wife of Augustus, *C.I.L.*, VI, 3954 (*Mon. Liv.*): *Myrtilus supra cubicu(l . . .)*, etc.; 3955 (*Mon. Liv.*): *Paschus Amaranti supra cubicular(ios)*; 8766: *M. Livius Augustae l(ibertus) supra cubicularios.*

Of Marcella Agrippa, *C.I.L.*, VI, 4439 (*Mon. Marc.*): *Heros Marcel(lae) supra cubic(ularios).*

Of an unknown woman, *C.I.L.* VI, 33842: *Alexae Eburnaes ser(vo) supra cubicul(arios).*

[2] *C.I.L.*, VI, 6645: *T. St[atili] Taur[i l(ibertus)] supra c(ubicularios)*, etc. The stone is so broken that the initial *c*, which is thought to stand for the word *cubicularios*, is little better than a conjecture.

[3] Cf. Mommsen, *C.I.L.*, X, p. 213 n.: . . . *nam in collegiis certe domus imperatoriae et decuriones frequentissime inveniuntur. . . .*

[4] *Domitianus*, 17: (*Domitianum*) *saucium et repugnantem adorti Clodianus cornicularius, et Maximus Partheni libertus, et Saturius decurio cubiculariorum. . . .*

was based upon that of the various branches of the imperial service from which their members were recruited.[1] If this were established as a fact, there would be presumptive evidence in any reference to a decurion of chamberlains that such an official was to be found among the ranks of the palace service.

We know almost nothing of the position or duties of the decurion of chamberlains. Of the four known occupants of the office,[2] the greatest fame was enjoyed by Sigerius, chamberlain of Domitian and fellow conspirator with Parthenius against the life of the Emperor. He was undoubtedly subordinate to Parthenius, who was *a cubiculo* to the Emperor,[3] but any further statements regarding his position or duties must be conjectural. His title makes it possible that he was in charge of a division of ten chamberlains.

It is clear that the corps of chamberlains was large and that it was subdivided in some manner, but there is nothing to indicate that the decurion was in any way connected with these subdivisions. It should be noted that he is an officer not found outside the imperial household, so far as is known, and that he served in the women's apartments as well as in those of the men.[4]

The chamberlains, properly so called, among whom women as well as men are to be numbered,[5] performed the actual service of the corps. This concerned the minutest details of the most intimate attendance upon their master or mistress. The corps seems to have been divided into two or more groups, called *stationes*, since inscriptions bear testimony to a *statio prima*,[6] and a *statio secunda*,[7] but there is no indication of the basis or the purpose of this division. Friedlaender put forth the hypothesis that the first station served in the immediate presence of the Emperor, and that the second station was less closely attached to his person.[8] It has been pointed out by Michiels, however, that this would have constituted an honorary division and, consequently, would have received more frequent mention than is actually the case.[9] The latter writer is in practical

[1] Cf. Waltzing, *Corporations Professionelles*, vol. I, p. 360, n. 1.

[2] Sigerius, Dio Cassius, 67, 15; Nicodemus Sponsianus, *C.I.L.*, VI, 3959; C. Iulius Felix Ivatianus, *C.I.L.*, VI, 5747; Helladius, *C.I.L.*, VI, 8773.

[3] *C.I.L.*, VI, 8761.

[4] Cf. *C.I.L.*, VI, 3959 a (*Mon. Liv.*): *Nicodemus Sponsian(us) dec(urio) cubiculario(rum)*.

[5] Cf. *C.I.L.*, VI, 9315: *Hic requiescit cubicularia dom(i)n(ae)*.

[6] *C.I.L.*, VI, 8532: . . . *Alexander Marcellianus et Encolphius Domitianus cubiculari stationis primae*, etc.; 8774: . . . *Glauco cubiculario stationis primae*. . . . Cf. also, 8518; 8775; 8776.

[7] *C.I.L.*, VI, 5195: *D. m. Crescenti vernae Caesaris n(ostri) cubiculario stationis II*. . . .

[8] *Darstellungen aus der Sittengeschichte Roms* (ed. 7), vol. I, p. 54.

[9] *Musée Belge*, vol. VI (1902), p. 382.

agreement with Marquardt, who holds to a division on the basis of service during the day and night.[1]

There are suggestions that each station had a more or less complete organization of its own. Thus inscriptions contain the record of one freedman who was "superintendent of the grain supply of the imperial chamberlains of the first station,"[2] and of another who was "chamberlain and *a locis* of the chamberlains of the first station."[3] These two inscriptions seem to indicate that the superintendent of the grain supply and the *a locis* performed their respective duties with reference to the chamberlains of the first station only, which would imply that that division, and we may safely assume the second station also, had a special organization.

The fact that there were separate organizations for the two stations, and especially the fact that each had its own superintendent of the grain supply, would seem to indicate that the two divisions served in different places. It does not seem probable, either on Friedlaender's hypothesis that both stations served the Emperor, the one in greater and the other in less proximity to his person, or on that of Marquardt and of Michiels that the one served the Emperor by day and the other by night, that the stations would have required two superintendents of the grain supply. Indeed these facts can be satisfactorily explained only by assuming that the two stations had practically identical duties, but were so far separated, whether by distance or otherwise, that a common organization was impracticable. Precisely these conditions would obtain if the first station served the Emperor and the second station the Empress. This seems to be the most natural interpretation of the evidence,[4] and is in keeping with the suggestion already made, that in the time of the Principate the chamberlains of the Empress were directed by a special officer, the *supra cubicularios*.[5]

Attached to the service of the imperial chamber, and probably numbered among the chamberlains, were several functionaries who were distinguished from the rest by their specific duties. The chamberlains' physician (*ab aegris cubiculariorum*) was one of these.[6] He possessed a fair degree of medical skill, no doubt, and was the regular attendant upon those of the chamberlains who might need the care of a physician. The superintendent of the chamberlains' grain supply

[1] *Privatleben der Römer* (2d ed.), vol. I, p. 144, n. 5.

[2] *C.I.L.*, VI, 8518: . . . *a frumento cub(iculariorum) Caesar(is) n(ostri) sta(tionis) I*. . . .

[3] *C.I.L.*, VI, 8775: . . . *cubicul(ario) et a locis cubicul(ariorum) stat(ionis) I*. . . .

[4] *C.I.L.*, VI, 5195, quoted on page 173 need not preclude this interpretation.

[5] See p. 172.

[6] Cf. *C.I.L.*, VI, 8771; 33749.

(*a frumento cubiculariorum*) [1] was charged with the task of providing the food supply of the chamberlains. The superintendent of the chamberlains' wardrobe (*a veste cubiculariorum*) [2] probably had the oversight of the clothing of the chamberlains. It would be his duty to see that there was an adequate supply of garments for all occasions, and the whims of some of the Emperors and their love of display must have made his task rather exacting. He may have had a corps of tailors, fullers, and other artisans under his orders. The *a locis cubiculariorum*,[3] whom we know from but a single inscription,[4] performed duties which we cannot now determine. It is, perhaps, not impossible that his title referred to his position in one of the funerary associations, and that his duties were in some way connected with the allotment of *loci*, or burial niches, in the association's *columbarium* for the members of the society.

There was, finally, a secretary of chamberlains (*scriba cubiculariorum*),[5] who may have had actual duties about the palace, such as the keeping of records of the chamberlains and their equipment, and the performing of other clerical tasks which might be required for the proper ordering of the corps. It is far more probable, however, that he was a secretary in one of the corporations which have already been mentioned.[6]

The question now arises as to the place occupied by the numerous barbers, anointers, perfumers, and other attendants,[7] in the organization of the palace service. It is possible that these servants were chamberlains whose duties were rather sharply defined, making it possible to refer to them by a more specific title than could be done in the case of the other members of the corps, so that it became customary to omit the word chamberlain in speaking of them. There is not, however, sufficient evidence for such identification, and it seems better to assume that some servants who were possessed of special skill fell

[1] *C.I.L.*, VI, 8518; 8771; 8772; 33769. [2] *C.I.L.*, VI, 33771.

[3] Michiels, *Musée Belge*, vol. VI (1902), pp. 382; 383, n. 4, gives as the title of this functionary *a locis cubiculi*, but there is sufficient evidence to show that the form here given is preferable. Cf. *C.I.L.*, VI, 8767 a: *scr(iba) cubiculariorum;* 8770 = 33749: *ab aegris cubiculario r(um);* 8772: *a frumento cubiculariorum;* 8773: *decurioni cubiculariorum.* Apparently there is not a single clear example of the form *cubiculi* in titles of this kind. Reading *C.I.L.*, VI, 8775, *a locis cubiculi stationis primae*, Michiels concluded that the *stationes* were assigned definite posts about the *cubiculum.* This hypothesis rests on no firmer basis than his unsupported reading *cubiculi.* [4] *C.I.L.*, VI, 8775 (quoted above, p. 174, n. 3).

[5] *C.I.L.*, VI, 8767 a; 8768; 8769; 33770.

[6] Cf. Waltzing, *Corporations Professionelles*, vol. I, p. 415; vol. IV, p. 428.

[7] Cf. Marquardt, *Privatleben* (2d ed.), vol. I, pp. 144 ff. Fairon, *L'Organisation du Palais Impérial à Rome, Musée Belge*, vol. IV (1900), pp. 5–25.

slightly outside the regular categories of servants. It is not necessary to suppose that the organization of the palace was complete.

As to the political and social status of the chamberlains, it is worth noting that those who bear the title *a cubiculo* in the inscriptions which have been preserved were universally freedmen, and that, in general, the same was true of the rest of the chamberlains after the first century.[1] In the matter of offices, not only did some of the chamberlains hold more than one position in the service of the imperial household, being intrusted with such duties, also, as those of the official *a memoria*,[2] or taster (*praegustator*)[3] or *a locis*,[4] but there are recorded some cases of extreme interest, giving evidence that the office of *a cubiculo* to the Emperor did not unfit its occupant for important public positions. For example, Lucius Aurelius Nicomedes, who had been the *a cubiculo* of Lucius Aurelius Verus, held two priesthoods, three civil posts, and one military office, was the recipient of a public horse and three military decorations.[5]

Most striking, and in some ways most significant, is the fact that several of the imperial chamberlains, especially those of high rank, came to exercise exceptional powers, to the extent, in some instances, that they even rivalled the Emperors themselves in the control of the administration. Such were Helicon, who was the favorite of Gaius;[6] Parthenius, who was granted insignia of high power by Domitian,[7] but who was later a member of the conspiracy which compassed his death and the accession of Nerva;[8] Cleander[9] and Eclectus,[10] the notorious chamberlains of Commodus.

The records of the imperial chamberlains extend down to the reign of Elagabalus, but in his reign they are abruptly broken off, and we know nothing further regarding this part of the imperial service until

[1] Cf. Cesano, in De Ruggiero, *Dizionario Epigrafico*, s.v. *cubiculum*, p. 1282.

[2] *C.I.L.*, VI, 8618: . . . *a memoria et cubiculo Aug(usti) ser(vi)*.

[3] *C.I.L.*, X, 6324: . . . *praegustator et a cubiculo Neronis*. . . .

[4] *C.I.L.*, VI, 8775 (quoted above, p. 174, n. 3). The *a locis* may have been an officer in a corporation. See p. 175.

[5] *C.I.L.*, VI, 1598: [*L. Aurelius L. Caesaris l(ibertus) Nicomedes, qui et*] *Ceionius et Aelius vocitatus est, L. Caesaris fuit a cubiculo et divi Veri imp(eratoris) nutr*[*itor, a divo Antonino Pio equo publico et sac*]*erdotio Carniniensi, item pontif(icatu) min(ore) exornatus, ab eodem proc(urator) ad silic(es) et praef(ectus) vehicul(orum) factus et ab imp(eratore) Antonino* [*Aug(usto) et divo Vero cura copiarum exercit*]*us ei iniunct*[*a?*], *hasta pura et vexillo et corona murali donatus, proc(urator) summarum rat(ionum) cum Ceionia Laena uxore hic situs* [*est*]. *Cf.* VI, 8498: . . . *a cubiculo Aug(usti) proc(uratori) thesaurum*, etc.; X, 6573: *a cubiculo proc(urator)* [. . . . .] *a frum(ento) accensus patro* [. . . . .], etc.

[6] Philo, *Legatio ad Gaium*, 27.

[7] Dio Cass., 67, 15.

[8] Suet., *Dom.*, 16 ff.; Eutropius, 8, 1; Zonaras, 11, 19.

[9] Herodian, 1, 12 ff.; Dio Cass., 72, 9 ff.; Lampridius, *Commodus Antoninus*, 6, 3 ff.

[10] Herodian, 1, 17 ff.; Dio Cass., 72, 4 ff.; Zon., 12, 6.

after the reforms of Diocletian, with the single exception of a reference to the grief of the chamberlains at the death of Carus.[1] This lacuna is probably to be explained by the disturbed condition of the Roman world during this period, and the unfortunate lack of contemporary historical writings which this condition produced. Inscriptional evidence also fails during the third century, and it is perhaps not surprising that in the meagre records which remain there is no mention of chamberlains.

While the foregoing discussion has dealt largely with the chamberlains of the Emperors, it is not to be supposed that it applies solely to them. The Princeps was indeed but the "First Citizen," and his household, at the outset, differed in no important detail from those of other citizens of Rome. It is true that it acquired greater splendor and magnificence than private citizens could afford to maintain, and Roman gentlemen probably considered that the appointments of their houses were complete though they had but two or three chamberlains. Men of great wealth, however, doubtless took pride in their expensive and elaborate establishments, and an occasional Croesus might even boast a corps of chamberlains comparable in size and in organization to that of the Princeps.

In the more modest houses of Roman gentlemen of the Principate the chamberlains seem still to have stood between their masters and those who wished to see him, as they did in the time of Cicero,[2] and at times to have acted very disagreeably toward callers. Seneca, the great moralist of Nero's day, said: "Some take it to heart that they are pushed about by the hairdresser, and they talk about the abusiveness of the doorkeeper, the haughtiness of the announcer, the disdain of the chamberlain." [3]

It was not at Rome alone that chamberlains were known during the period of the Principate. The New Testament mentions a certain Blastus, chamberlain of Herod, the governor of Palestine,[4] and a eunuch of Candace, queen of the Ethiopians of Meroe or Abyssinia, who may have been her chamberlain, though he is described merely as being in charge of all her treasure.[5]

[1] Vopiscus, *Carus*, 8, 7. It is easy to believe that chamberlains were among the eunuchs ousted from the palace by Gordian III. Julius Capitolinus, *Gordiani Tres*, 23, 7–25, 4.

[2] See p. 167 f.

[3] *Dialogorum Liber*, II, 14, 1; *Quidam se a cinerario impulsos moleste ferunt et contumeliam vocant ostiarii, nomenclatoris superbiam, cubicularii supercilium.*

[4] *Acts* xii. 12, 20: Βλάστον τὸν ἐπὶ τοῦ κοιτῶνος τοῦ βασιλέως.

[5] *Acts* viii. 27: ἀνὴρ Αἴθιοψ εὐνοῦχος δυνάστης Κανδάκης βασιλίσσης Αἰθιόπων, ὃς ἦν ἐπὶ πάσης τῆς γάζης αὐτῆς.

CHAPTER II

FROM DIOCLETIAN TO JUSTINIAN

By the close of the third century the old Republican form of Roman government had been replaced by an undisguised absolutism, which was maintained by force of arms, and justified, if justification were necessary, by the Emperor's assumption of divinity. Earlier monarchs had not hesitated to demand from the provincials the honors due to deity, but it remained for Diocletian to carry the principle to its logical completion and to declare himself unequivocally a god. Roman and barbarian, peasant and prince, all alike were compelled to acknowledge, and humble themselves before, his godhead. With Constantine's acceptance of Christianity this position became impossible, and the rulers of the Roman Empire no longer professed to be deities, but mortals ruling by divine sanction, the representatives of God upon earth. Thus the principle of the "divine right of kings" was substituted for that of the inherent rights of divinity without sacrificing the monarch's claim to absolute control of his subjects.

To provide a fitting capital for the divinely appointed ruler of the Roman Empire, Constantine the Great built, between the Bosphorus and the Golden Horn, a "New Rome," "guarded of God," and known from that day as Constantinople, in honor of its founder. Here he placed the seat of his government, in a very city within the city, for the imperial residence was surrounded by other edifices, audience halls, churches, barracks, banquet halls and baths, a huge hippodrome, the senate house, a great public forum and extensive pleasure gardens, among which moved not only the richly costumed grandees and their ladies, but a huge throng of less important personages — ecclesiastics, palace guards, attendants, clerks, lackeys, artisans and menials of every kind.

I. The Imperial Court of the Fourth and Fifth Centuries

Walled about on all sides by ministers and retainers, the Emperor lived in the midst of this throng, but aloof, as befitted a superior being;

for only the most trusted of his personal servants had free access to his presence. Elaborate ceremonies marked his every public act. His appearance at the church, the races, state banquets or imperial audiences was the occasion for a splendid ritual. The court officials in graded ranks and garbed in gorgeous ceremonial robes followed him in a long and stately procession, or, in an impressive silence, made obeisance before him as they were ushered, each in his turn, into his presence. No detail was omitted which would render these ceremonies more imposing, or which would emphasize the exalted position of the monarch.

Most conspicuous among the officials of the court were the great ministers of state. The reorganization of the imperial administration by Diocletian and Constantine had given complete expression to the bureaucratic system, placing the control of the various branches of the government in the hands of a few departmental chiefs, who directed the activities of their bureaus while residing at the court.

Among these heads of administrative departments the Pretorian Prefect (*praefectus praetorio*), the head of the civil administration of the provinces, was of the highest rank. The Masters of the Soldiers (*magistri militum*), who were the chief military officials of the Empire, stood next to him.

More intimately connected with the life of the court were the holders of the *dignitates palatinae*, those offices whose duties did not call their incumbents away from the capital. Two of these, the Count of the Sacred Largesses (*comes sacrarum largitionum*) and the Count of the Privy Purse (*comes rerum privatarum*), were important treasury officials, under whose direction was a large corps of assistants known as *palatini*. The Master of the Offices (*magister officiorum*) was director of the corps of *agentes in rebus*, which constituted the imperial secret service. He supervised the extensive secretarial bureaus, controlled the palace guards, and had charge of the corps which arranged the court ceremonies. Furthermore, almost all of the *officia* of the palace were under his jurisdiction.

The Quaestor (*quaestor sacri palatii*), the Emperor's chief legal adviser, was entrusted with the framing and publishing of imperial edicts, and exercised important appellate jurisdiction. These palace officials were known as Counts of the Consistory (*comites consistoriani*) and were members of the Emperor's deliberative and advisory council, at the meetings of which the Quaestor presided. To this number might be added the Counts of the Body Guard (*comes domesticorum equitum*, *comes domesticorum peditum*) and a number of important but subordinate dignitaries. There were also about the court many distinguished persons who did not hold offices, but were given high rank by the conferring of the honorary titles of Count or Patrician.

Numbered among the *dignitates palatinae*, and prominent in all the activities of the court was the Grand Chamberlain (*praepositus sacri cubiculi*), the history and nature of whose office will be set forth in the following pages. It will be sufficient to state here that he was the Emperor's chief attendant, and supervised most of the branches of the palace service. He was powerful, not because of the importance of his duties, but because his position made it possible for him so to ingratiate himself with the Emperor as to wield very great influence. Consequently all other officials stood in dread of him. But they also despised and hated him, for he was a eunuch, a social outcast, with whom they would normally have held no relations. Furthermore he was, after all, but the Emperor's body-servant, not a minister of the Empire, and officials of high position can hardly have regarded him otherwise than as an interloper in their ranks.

II. The History of the Office of Grand Chamberlain

The development of the Grand Chamberlain's office in the period before Diocletian has already been set forth in its salient points. In the course of three centuries a body-servant of the Emperor had succeeded in rising to a position of influence second to none in the Empire, save, possibly, that of the Emperor himself.

The history of this office in the period after Diocletian is at once a repetition and a continuation of its history under the Principate. Out of the period of reorganization the Grand Chamberlain emerged as a minor government official, invested with certain authority and honors, and enjoying a place in the official hierarchy of the court; for Diocletian's enthusiasm for the bureaucratic system had led him to organize under it everything capable of such organization.

From the very nature of his duties, however, the Grand Chamberlain still had the Emperor's ear, and by skilful flattery and shrewd insinuation he succeeded in repeating, under new conditions, the success he had attained under the Principate. He was rapidly promoted to one of the most honorable ranks in the Empire, and his extra-legal power, still based upon his intimacy with the Emperor, was often far greater than that of his supposed superiors. Indeed, it was often the Grand Chamberlain who actually administered the Empire, and Ammianus Marcellinus ironically remarks that the Emperor Constantius "had considerable influence, if the truth be told, with Eusebius, his Grand Chamberlain." [1]

The exact time of the establishment of the office of *praepositus sacri cubiculi* is not known, and peculiar difficulties present themselves in any attempt to arrive at a definite date, chiefly as a result of the fact that the duties of this official differed but slightly from those of the *a cubiculo* of the preceding centuries. The change of title was not so noteworthy an event as to be chronicled in any of the accounts of this period which still survive, and the paucity of imperial constitutions dating from the early years of the governmental reform renders the best source for the study of official titles almost valueless for this period.

The first Grand Chamberlains of whom there is record were Urbicius and Olybrius, who held this position under Constantine the Great at the time of the foundation of the new city of Constantinople,[2] about the year 326.[3] Codinus makes the statement that Euphrates, the Chief Eunuch of the Bedchamber, Urbicius and Olybrius, the Grand Chamberlains, and others gave Constantine "their assistance and approval in such building of the God-guarded city," [4] and cites his authorities for this statement, including "Eutropius the Sophist, who was with Julian the Apostate in Persia" (the author, therefore, of the *Breviarium Historiae Romanae*),[5] and others, "all of whom, being eye-witnesses of the things done at that time, have described them accurately." [6]

If the Grand Chamberlains were called upon to give their "assistance and approval" in the matter of the new capital, it may fairly be assumed that they enjoyed the Emperor's esteem and were officials of some importance at the court. This would seem to imply that their office had been in existence for some time, but how long can only be conjectured. The mention of Euphrates, the Superintendent of

[1] Amm. Marc., XVIII, 4, 3.

[2] See Lambeck on Codinus, *De Originibus Constantinopolitanis*, 9 A, ταῦτα ἐπράχθη (ed. Bonn, p. 225).

[3] Gibbon-Bury, *Decline and Fall of the Roman Empire*, vol. II, chap. xvii, *init.* The dedication occurred in 330.

[4] *De Originibus Constantinopolitanis*, 18, 1 ff.: συμπραττόντων αὐτῷ καὶ συνευδοκούντων εἰς τὴν τοιαύτην οἰκοδομὴν τῆς θεοφρουρήτου πόλεως Εὐφράτου παρακοιμωμένου, Οὐρβικίου καὶ Ὀλυβρίου τῶν πραιποσίτων, κτλ. For further details as to the part played by Euphrates, cf. Cedrenus, *Compendium Historiarum*, 496, 7 ff.

[5] Cf. Eutrop., *Breviarium*, 10, 16.

[6] Codinus, *loc. cit.*: οὗτοι πάντες αὐτόπται γενόμενοι τῶν τηνικαῦτα πραχθέντων ἀκριβῶς ταυτὶ συνεγράψαντο.

Chamberlains,[1] appears to indicate that an organization of the chamberlains had already, in 326, been effected along lines somewhat similar to those suggested in the Theodosian Code and elsewhere toward the end of the fourth century, when the Superintendent of Chamberlains was undoubtedly a subordinate of the Grand Chamberlain.[2]

This same Euphrates, furthermore, is credited with the conversion of Constantine to Christianity,[3] a very plausible statement, for the intimate relations between the Superintendent of Chamberlains and the Emperor would have offered an excellent opportunity for Euphrates to plead the cause of the new faith.[4]

The date of Constantine's conversion is commonly given as 312, when, according to the ecclesiastical historians, he beheld in the heavens the sign of the Cross. If Euphrates held the position of Superintendent of Chamberlains at that time, it is probable that the organization of the chamberlain service is to be referred to Diocletian, for Constantine was engaged in successive wars until 324, and gave little attention to organization until after that date. This conclusion is not surprising, for it is known that Diocletian reorganized the palace service very extensively, and it seems hardly probable that so prominent a corps as that of the chamberlains should not have been included in this reform.

The official position and duties of the Grand Chamberlain during the first three quarters of a century after the reforms of Diocletian are not precisely known. Conjectures based on the prominence of such men as Eusebius, the Grand Chamberlain of Constantius II,[5] are likely to be far from the truth, as will readily be understood when one considers the great discrepancy which existed in the period before Diocletian between the power and influence of the *a cubiculo* and his essentially lowly position. The single fact upon which reliance can be placed is that the Grand Chamberlain of the later period was unquestionably the successor of the *a cubiculo* of the Principate, holding

[1] Codinus describes Euphrates as παρακοιμώμενος, a term which came into use at a later period to describe a Byzantine official. He can hardly have been other than the *primicerius sacri cubiculi*, a large portion of whose duties were later assigned to the παρακοιμώμενος. These offices will be considered at another point.

[2] See p. 203.

[3] Codinus, *op. cit.*, 21, 8 f.: Εὐφράτῃ τῷ παρακοιμωμένῳ αὐτοῦ, ὅστις καὶ ἐποίησε τὸν μέγαν Κωνσταντῖνον Χριστιανόν, κτλ.

[4] The fact that this sane and sober tradition of Constantine's conversion persisted for more than a thousand years in the presence of the seemingly authentic account of the miraculous conversion which is given by Eusebius (*De vita Constantini*, 1, 28) and others, and in an age of miraclemongers, makes it worthy of more consideration than it seems to have received.

[5] See pp. 260–270.

the same supervision over the chamberlains, and enjoying similar intimacy with the Emperor.

Whatever may have been the Grand Chamberlain's official position in the early years of the Later Empire, it seems probable that he had become director of the majority of the palace servants by about the middle of the fourth century. In speaking of the circumstances leading to the death, in 369,[1] of Rhodanus, the rapacious Grand Chamberlain of Valentinian, John Malalas describes him as "very powerful and wealthy and the manager of the palace, being chief eunuch and in high honor."[2] It is possible, of course, that Malalas refers to an unauthorized control of the palace, due to his influence with the Emperor, but the word *διοικοῦντα*, which he employs, suggests a legitimate control.

It is obvious from a constitution of Valentinian II, dated 384, that under Valentinian I a law or laws were enacted prescribing the order of precedence and the remuneration of government officials,[3] and it may safely be assumed that matters of official rank and title were also prescribed at the same time. These enactments probably occurred about the year 372, for there is a constitution of that date, relating to the rank of the City and Pretorian Prefects and the Master of Horse and Foot.[4] It was possibly in the course of this legislation that official recognizance was given to the hitherto informal[5] title of *illustris*, and that the new title *spectabilis* was created.

To precisely what officials these titles were first granted is not clear, but a constitution dated September 16, 384, at Constantinople, and therefore presumably emanating from Theodosius I, makes mention of the ex-Grand Chamberlains, with the statement that their "exceeding and continuous care of our divine person has placed them among the highest dignitaries."[6] This can mean only that the Grand Chamberlain had been elevated to the rank of an *illustris*, probably during the reign of Theodosius, or after January 19, 379,[7] for the words *nostri numinis* seem to refer to the author of the law.

[1] *Chronicon Paschale*, p. 557.

[2] *Chronographia*, 339, 22 f.: *τὸν δὲ πραιπόσιτον τοῦ παλατίου αὐτοῦ ὀνόματι Ῥοδανόν, ἄνδρα δυνατώτατον καὶ εὔπορον καὶ διοικοῦντα τὸ παλάτιον, ὡς πρῶτον ὄντα ἀρχιευνοῦχον καὶ ἐν μεγάλῃ τιμῇ ὄντα, ζῶντα ἔκαυσεν, κτλ.*

[3] *Codex Theodosianus*, VI, 5, 2: *Caelestis recordationis Valentinianus genitor numinis nostri singulis quibusque dignitatibus certum locum meritumque praescribit*, etc.

[4] *Codex Theodosianus*, VI, 7, 1.

[5] Cf. Jullian, in Daremberg et Saglio, *Dictionnaire des Antiquités*, s.v. *illustris*.

[6] *Codex Theodosianus*, VII, 8, 3: . . . *ex praepositis quoque sacri cubiculi, quos tanta et tam adsidua nostri numinis cura inter primas posuit dignitates*, etc.

[7] Cf. Clinton, *Fasti Romani*, *anno* 379.

Now the only reasonable explanation of this mention of the Grand Chamberlain's elevation is that his title had not heretofore appeared among the *illustres* (except, of course, in the constitution sanctioning that elevation), and that some explanation of the fact that it was included among them in this law was thought necessary, — or that it was to remind the Master of the Offices, to whom it was addressed, that the Grand Chamberlain was now an *illustris* and not to be overlooked in the enforcement of the law. In either case it would seem to be indicated that the date of the Grand Chamberlain's elevation was shortly before that of the law in which it is mentioned, that is, before September 16, 384.

Two other laws support this inference. The first was enacted in 380 and provided that the four Counts of the Consistory, who were specifically designated by title, should be accorded the same respect and honors which the Prefects received. The Grand Chamberlain was not mentioned in this law.[1] This is not conclusive evidence that he was not yet an *illustris*, for he might have been a member of that order and still not have been entitled to the same honors as the Counts of the Consistory. This seems improbable, however, for the fact that the Counts last mentioned were accorded the same public recognition as the Prefects makes it clear that the division of the *illustres* into distinct classes, so well attested half a century later, had not yet been accomplished, and therefore, if the Grand Chamberlain had been a member of this high order, we should expect to find him mentioned in this law as enjoying equal privileges with the Counts of the Consistory.

More convincing evidence is to be found in the second of the two laws. It was enacted on December 9, 382, and provided that "the highest dignitaries [*i.e.*, the Prefects and Masters of the Soldiers], also the Counts of the Consistory, likewise our Notaries and all Chamberlains and ex-Chamberlains" should be exempt from *munera sordida*.[2] Here the Notaries and Chamberlains seem to form a group apart from the Counts of the Consistory, and the Grand Chamberlain seems to have ranked below the Chief of the Notaries. Since the latter had not risen above the rank of a *spectabilis* in 425,[3] the Grand Chamberlain also was in all probability only a *spectabilis* at the close of the year 382.

[1] *Codex Theodosianus*, VI, 9, 2.

[2] *Codex Theodosianus*, XI, 16, 15: *Maximarum culmina dignitatum, consistoriani quoque comites, notarii etiam nostri et cubicularii omnes atque ex cubiculariis ab omnibus sordidis muneribus vindicentur.*

[3] Cf. *Notitia Dignitatum orientis*, XVIII; *occidentis*, XVI.

It is safe to conclude, therefore, that the Grand Chamberlain was elevated to the rank of an *illustris* between December 9, 382, and September 16, 384.

Hirschfeld entertains the opinion that the Grand Chamberlain became an *illustris* under Arcadius and Honorius through the powerful influence of the eunuch Eutropius, who occupied that office.[1] This opinion seems to be in direct contradiction to the evidence of the constitutions just cited. Furthermore, it is probable that if Eutropius had been the first eunuch to hold the rank of an *illustris*, as he was to hold the Consulship and Patriciate, Claudian, in his tirade against the fallen minister,[2] would have made mention of that fact; but although he describes the Consulship and Patriciate as defiled because of their tenure by Eutropius, he does not mention the defilement of the rank of *illustris* — presumably because other eunuchs had already held that honor.

In the constitution of 384, in which the Grand Chamberlain is first described as an *illustris*, the Counts of the Consistory, that is, the Count of the Sacred Largesses, the Count of the Privy Purse, the Master of the Offices, and the Quaestor, precede him in order of mention. It is therefore necessary to conclude that they, too, were *illustres* in that year. There is no improbability in this conclusion, for the Counts of the Consistory are known to have been of that grade of honor in the year 385.[3]

In a law of 409 (or 412) promulgated at Ravenna, the order of the titles is reversed, and the Grand Chamberlain is mentioned before the Counts of the Consistory.[4] At that time, therefore, he took official precedence over them in the Western Empire. It is not unlikely that the same order obtained in the Eastern Empire also. Seeck has stated that in the East the Grand Chamberlain ranked last among the *illustres* in 414, and possibly was not elevated above that position before 422.[5] This statement is based on the fact that in a subscript to a law of 414 the Grand Chamberlain is mentioned after the Count of the Sacred Largesses.[6]

[1] *Rangtitel der römischen Kaiserzeit, Sitzungsberichte d. k-Preuss. Akad. d. Wissensch.*, 1901, p. 599.
[2] *In Eutropium.*
[3] Cf. Boak, *The Master of the Offices*, p. 45.

[4] *Codex Theodosianus*, XI, 18, 1: . . . *non praepositum sacri cubiculi . . . non magistrum officiorum, quaestorem vel comites sacri ac privati aerarii inlustres*, etc. For date see Mommsen's edition, *ad loc.*

[5] *Quaestiones de Notitia Dignitatum*, p. 13: *Praepositus sacri cubiculi Theodosii magni temporibus omnibus illustribus dignitatibus postponebatur, qui ordo in Orientis partibus certe ad annum 414 servabatur, fortasse anno 422 demum sublatus est.*

[6] *Codex Theodosianus*, XI, 28, 9, *subscript.: De eadem re scribtum edictum ad populum: ad Marcianum comitem sacrarum largitionum: Musellio praeposito sacri cubiculi de titulis ad domum sacram pertinentibus. . . .*

The subscript of the Second Novel of Marcian would be equally good evidence that the same order existed in 450,[1] but Seeck surely would not contend that at that late date the Grand Chamberlain held so inferior a position. The explanation of this order of mention lies, in both cases, in the fact that these laws directly concerned the treasury officials, and that the Grand Chamberlain, as chief of the treasury of the Crown Lands, held a far more limited and less important position than did the chiefs of the other treasuries, and that the heads of the treasuries are mentioned in these subscripts in the order of importance of their charges. Seeck's statement is therefore baseless, and in the absence of evidence to the contrary, it seems best to assume that in 409 the order of rank in the East was similar to that in the West.

It is to be noted that although the City and Pretorian Prefects, the Masters of the Soldiers, the Grand Chamberlain, and the four Counts of the Consistory were all alike *illustres* in 384, and presumably enjoyed the same privileges, they did not continue on exact parity. At some time about the beginning of the fifth century ceremonial distinctions were made between the first and second classes of *illustres*. It would appear that prior to 422 the Grand Chamberlain had belonged to the second or lower class, together with the Counts of the Consistory, for in that year he was advanced to the first class, where he was given equal rank with the City and Pretorian Prefects and the Masters of the Soldiers.[2] This final promotion, it is expressly stated, was given in recognition of the exceptional merit of the Grand Chamberlain Macrobius.[3]

It is not known whence came the funds for the maintenance of the chamberlains during the first century and a quarter of their organization. That the Steward of the Household had some supervision of the disbursements, at least, of the corps is suggested by the fact that his staff included accountants, but no deduction can be drawn from such frail evidence. There is, in fact, no indication that there

[1] *Scripta Palladio viro inlustri praefecto praetorio Orientis; Hermogeni viro inlustri comiti sacrarum largitionum; Genethlio viro inlustri comiti rerum privatarum; Maximino viro inlustri comiti et praeposito sacri cubiculi. . . .*

[2] *Codex Theodosianus*, VI, 8, 1: *Qui sacri cubiculi nostri fuere praepositi vel nunc esse coeperunt vel quos postea sors ad adscendendi huius gradum fastigii devocarit, ea dignitate fungantur, qua sunt praediti, qui eminentissimam praetorianam vel urbanam meruerint praefecturam aut certe militarem magisteriam potestatem, ita ut sit inter eos post depositas administrationes nulla discretio. . . .*

[3] *Ibid.: . . . nos ad hanc promulgationem Macrobi viri inlustris merita provocarunt.* It is useless to attempt to connect this Macrobius with the author of the Satires. Cf. Smith, *Dictionary of Greek and Roman Biography and Mythology*, vol. II, p. 888.

was a special source of revenues to meet the requirements of the palace service, or that there were any financial officials connected with the *cubiculum*, before the year 414. By that time certain imperial estates in Cappadocia (*domus divina per Cappadociam*) which had been under the control of the Count of the Crown Lands (*comes domorum per Cappadociam*) since as early as the year 379,[1] were assigned to the Grand Chamberlain, and the Count of the Crown Lands became one of his subordinates.

This is clear from a constitution of that year, 414, concerning the remission of unpaid revenues which were due the several treasuries, including that of the Crown Lands. This is addressed to Anthemius, the Pretorian Prefect, and is followed by a subscript to the effect that "in regard to this same matter there had been written a proclamation to the people; to Marcianus, Count of the Sacred Largesses; to Musellius, the Grand Chamberlain, so far as relates to the sections pertaining to the Crown Lands," and to certain other officials.[2]

The reason for placing the Crown Lands of Cappadocia under the control of the Grand Chamberlain is not known. Other portions of the imperial domains seem to have remained under the supervision of the Count of the Privy Purse,[3] even though their revenues went to the maintenance of other branches of the palace service.[4] The intention can hardly have been to limit the expenditures of the Grand Chamberlain by setting aside for his use the income from these estates, for, on the one hand, the steady increase of his influence would suggest an extension rather than a restriction of his liberties and, on the other, extravagance about the court seems to have been encouraged rather than restrained. When Mark the Deacon was in Constantinople in attendance upon Porphyrius of Gaza, he beheld the ceremonial procession at the baptism of Theodosius II, the splendor of which so dazzled him that he professed his inability to describe it, and Porphyrius could only exclaim that if earthly glory could be so great, what must be the glory of heaven.[5]

Only a short time before, Synesius of Cyrene, a petitioner at the court of Arcadius, had publicly censured the extravagance of the imperial court. He had seen the Emperor clad in purple and in gold, his tunic, his girdle, his shoes studded with gems brought from distant

[1] *Codex Theodosianus*, VI, 30, 2.

[2] *Codex Theodosianus*, XI, 28, 9, *subscript.* (quoted above, p. 185, n. 6).

[3] Cf. *Notitia Dignitatum or.*, XIV, 3.

[4] His, *Domänen der römischen Kaiserzeit*, p. 28.

[5] Marcus Diaconus, *Vita Porphyrii*, 47.

mountains and barbarous seas, and he had seen the pavement of the palace strewn with gold dust, the transportation of which from its distant source required the service of a whole staff of carriers by land and sea.[1] Chrysostom had been astounded by the wanton extravagance of the court, and indignantly preached the vanity of riches,[2] and Claudian was not silent regarding the luxury of the capital of the East.[3] Eutropius, the Grand Chamberlain, was in full control of the court under Arcadius, and if wealth flowed as water, it was in compliance with his wish. Such waste, however, made necessary an almost inexhaustible source of revenue. The regular treasury could ill support this heavy drain, and for this reason, perhaps, the Grand Chamberlain was given control of the Crown Lands of Cappadocia, by the exploitation of which he might add to the appropriations from the treasury a sum sufficient to support his extravagance.

If the Crown Lands came into the control of the Grand Chamberlain during the incumbency of Eutropius — and no other period offers so plausible an explanation for this innovation — the transfer can be dated within narrow bounds, for it must have occurred after the murder of Rufinus, in 395, left Eutropius the most powerful person about the court, and before the overthrow of the eunuch in the course of the year 399.

To insure the collection of the revenues from the Crown Lands, it was customary, at least at the end of the fifth century, for the Grand Chamberlain to send specially authorized agents, known as *canonicarii*,[4] to assist the regular tax-gatherers in forcing the payment of taxes.[5]

For three-quarters of a century following the acquisition of the control of the Crown Lands in Cappadocia, there seems to have been little change in the office of the Grand Chamberlain. In the year 422 mention is made of the Grand Chamberlain's jurisdiction over certain of the humblest tillers of the Crown Lands,[6] but it seems not unlikely that he had held this right since the time when he was made chief administrator of these domains. By 485, however, his relative rank in the official hierarchy had undergone a change. In a constitution of

[1] *De Regno*, 2.

[2] Cf. *De Eutropio Capto*, etc.

[3] *In Eutropium*, 1, 191 ff.; 2, 63 ff.; 326 ff.

[4] *Novellae Justiniani*, XXX, 7, 1: τῶν κατὰ καιρὸν ἐκπεμπομένων κανονικαρίων παρὰ τοῦ ἐνδοξοτάτου πραιποσίτου, κτλ.

[5] Cf. Seeck, in Pauly-Wissowa, *Real-Encyclopädie*, s.v. *canonicarius*.

[6] *Codex Justinianus*, III, 26, 11.

that year he is mentioned after the Master of the Offices and the Quaestor.[1] This was probably not the result of any degradation of the Grand Chamberlain or his office, but is evidence of the fact that his influence was increasing less rapidly in this period than was that of the Master and Quaestor, who were therefore elevated above him.

III. The Grand Chamberlain and His Office

1. *The Grand Chamberlain's Official Designation*

The title *praepositus* is unique among the designations of the great ministers of the Empire.[2] There were several Prefects of high rank, not a few Masters, and many Counts, but none of these titles was chosen to describe the office of the Grand Chamberlain. Instead, he was given a designation which was commonly applied to army officials of inferior rank, and to heads of unimportant divisions of the palace service. Since Diocletian reorganized his court on a military basis and transformed it into a moving camp, the term *praepositus*, as applied to the Grand Chamberlain, was possibly a relic from a time when he was known as *praepositus castrorum*, the title usually given to the chief administrators of strictly military camps. There is no instance, however, in which the Grand Chamberlain is described by this title.

It is possible that the Grand Chamberlain's official title was of more humble origin. Inscriptions of the period of the Principate record the presence at the court of *praepositi* who directed small corps of the servants about the palace. There were the chief cooks, known as *praepositi cocorum*,[3] chief carvers, styled *praepositi structorum*,[4] chief cellarers, called *praepositi cellariorum* [5] or *praepositi cellaris*,[6] chief custodians of the plate, to whom was applied the title *praepositus argenti* [7] or *praepositus auri*.[8] Mention is made of chief bakers, known as *praepositi pistorum*,[9] and of a chief artisan of the palace, called *praepositus opificibus domus Augustae*.[10]

None of these titles is to be found in the *Notitia Dignitatum*, and it is difficult, in the absence of inscriptions, to point to their use else-

[1] *Codex Justinianus*, III, 24, 3: . . . *qui magistri officiorum vel quaestoris officio functus aut sacri nostrae pietatis cubiculi praepositus post depositam administrationem senatorio ordini sociatus est*, etc.

[2] The title *praepositus largitionum* is used once, in *Codex Theodosianus*, VIII, 5, 18, for the regular title, *comes sacrarum largitionum*.

[3] *C.I.L.*, VI, 8752.

[4] *C.I.L.*, VI, 9045.

[5] *C.I.L.*, VI, 8746–7.

[6] *C.I.L.*, VI, 8745.

[7] *C.I.L.*, VI, 8729.

[8] *C.I.L.*, VI, 8732–3.

[9] Marini, *Papiri diplomatici*, CXXI, 40; 64.

[10] *C.I.L.*, VI, 8646.

where in the sources for the Later Empire. This is not strange, however, for circumstances would but seldom give to men of such humble rank sufficient prominence to occasion mention by historians.

These titles are, in a way, comparable to that of *praepositus sacri cubiculi*, or Grand Chamberlain, and by analogy it might be supposed that the latter was merely the chief of the chamberlains, an official of lowly station, at least in theory, whose duties were limited to the control of the servants of the Emperor's bedchamber.

There seems to be nothing to indicate which, if either, of the two sources which have just been suggested is the true origin of the title *praepositus sacri cubiculi.*

2. *The Number of Grand Chamberlains*

Since, as has been shown, the chamberlain was a member of the ordinary household of the better class in Republican times, and under the Principate families of wealth maintained a chamber service not incomparable to that of the Princeps, it is not surprising to find that in the Later Empire there were chamberlains of high rank serving others than the Emperor. In the middle of the fourth century there was a complete chamberlain service under the direction of a *praepositus* at the court of each of the Caesars.

While this may have been in imitation of the imperial court of that period, or merely a continuation of a custom long observed by the leading Roman families, it is much more probable that it represents the practice which obtained during the period of the divided Empire under Diocletian and Constantine. The head of the chamberlains of the Caesar probably never bore the title of *praepositus sacri cubiculi* so long as his master remained satisfied with the title of Caesar, for the attribute of divinity was reserved for the imperial court and person. There is no evidence that the Caesars were served by *praepositi* of their own except in those cases in which they maintained their own courts and exercised independent administrative powers.

Of these chamberlains of the Caesars, mention may be made of Gorgonius, chief of the chamberlains of the ill-fated Gallus,[1] who was brought to trial for complicity in the acts of the Caesar and, though admitting his guilt, was saved by the intrigues of his fellow eunuchs in the service of Constantius.[2]

Eutherius was the Grand Chamberlain of Julian when the latter

[1] Ammianus Marcellinus, XV, 2, 10: *Gorgonius, cui erat thalami Caesariani cura commissa.*
[2] *Ibid.*

was Caesar in Gaul,[1] and ably defended him before Constantius against the charges of a calumniator. It is possible that he later became the Grand Chamberlain of Julian as Emperor, for, having retired as the chamberlain of the Caesar, he was later called to the palace.[2]

Although there are no extant records of Grand Chamberlains during the time of Diocletian or the earlier part of the reign of Constantine, it seems altogether probable that they were to be found at the court of each of the Emperors. When the Empire was again divided, at the death of Theodosius I, a Grand Chamberlain was appointed to serve at the court of Honorius, in the West,[3] and, though the records are very incomplete, this office was probably maintained until the fall of the Western Empire, for Theodoric, who continued the Western organization, was served by Grand Chamberlains.[4]

There was commonly a second Grand Chamberlain to be found at the imperial court. It will be remembered that the first mention of these officials associated the names of two men, Urbicius and Olybrius.[5] So also in an inscription there appear together the names of Antiochus and Parthenius, ex-Grand Chamberlains.[6]

In cases of this kind it is probably to be understood that one of these officials served in the *cubiculum* of the Emperor, and the other in that of the Empress. As early as the time of Constantius there is definite reference to a corps of chamberlains who attended the wife of the Emperor.[7] Under Arcadius the eunuch Amantius served the Empress Eudoxia,[8] and in the time of Leo and Anthemius (467–472) mention is made of the chamberlains both of the Emperor and of the Empress.[9] Less than a quarter of a century later, at the election of the Silentiary Anastasius to succeed the Emperor Zeno, two Grand Chamberlains are mentioned,[10] and the same Anastasius, as Emperor,

[1] *Op. cit.*, XVI, 7, 2: *Eutherius praepositus cubiculi.*

[2] *Op. cit.*, XVI, 7, 6: *digressus ad otium, adscitus postea in palatium.*

[3] See Appendix A.

[4] See p. 223.

[5] Codinus, *De Originibus Constantinopolitanis*, 18, 1 ff. Cf. p. 181, n. 4.

[6] *C.I.L.*, XV, 7131 (= VI, 31946): *(De) massa pontis Veri Antiochi et Parteni v(irorum) c(larissimorum) ex p(rae)p(ositi) s(acri) c(ubiculi).*

[7] Socrates Scholasticus, *Historia Ecclesiastica*, 2, 2: τῇ τε τοῦ βασιλέως γαμετῇ καὶ τοῖς εὐνούχοις αὐτῆς.

[8] Marcus Diaconus, *Vita Porphyrii* (ed. Haupt, *Abhandlungen d. kgl. Akademie d. Wissensch. zu Berlin*, 1874, pp. 171–215), 188, 22: Ἀμαντίῳ τῷ κουβικουλαρίῳ τῆς δεσποσύνης; 189, 12: τὸν εὐνοῦχον Ἀμάντιον, καστρήσιον ὄντα τῆς βασιλίσσης.

[9] *Codex Justinianus*, XII, 5, 3: *cubicularios tam sacri cubiculi mei quam venerabilis Augustae.*

[10] Constantine Porphyrogenitus, *De Caerimoniis Aulae Byzantinae*, 418, 8: καὶ συνεισῆλθον αὐτῇ οἱ δύο πραιπόσιτοι, κτλ.

made reference to Grand Chamberlains both in his own apartments and in those of the Empress Ariadne.[1]

From this evidence it is a fair assumption that the twofold organization of the chamberlains dated from the early years of the reform of Diocletian and Constantine, especially in view of the fact that the Steward of the Household had in his staff, presumably from the time of the reorganization of the palace service, an accountant for the *cubiculum* of the Emperor and another for the Empress.[2]

It need hardly be pointed out that the Grand Chamberlain of the Emperor held a far more important and influential position than did the Grand Chamberlain of the Empress. When reference is found to one of these officials and no statement is made as to the *cubiculum* in which he served, it is always to be understood that he was the Emperor's chamberlain.

3. *The Grand Chamberlain's Tenure of Office*

It is one of the essentials of autocratic government that the great ministers to whom are intrusted the various branches of that government should be under the control of the autocrat — appointed by him and subject to removal from office at his hands. There can be little question that this principle was observed at the court of the Late Roman Empire, and that it applied to the Grand Chamberlain as to the other ministers. Some officials, it is true, were appointed or reappointed annually by the Emperor, as was the Master of the Offices,[3] and, of course, the Consuls, the traditions of whose office, extending back for centuries, could not be lightly broken.

The Grand Chamberlain's office, however, had no tradition of annual or regular appointment under the Principate, and no trace of such appointment is to be found in the practice of the Later Empire. Like the Counts of the Sacred Largesses and the Privy Purse, the Grand Chamberlain was not a magistrate, but a 'minister,' and as such did not, at least in the period before Justinian, receive the formal appointment which was accorded to magistrates, but was selected and appointed without formality, at the Emperor's desire.[4] There was, of

[1] *Codex Justinianus*, XII, 5, 5: . . . *duobus viris illustribus praepositis utriusque sacri cubiculi tam nostrae pietatis quam nostrae serenissimae coniugis*, etc.

[2] *Notitia Dignitatum or.*, XVII, 7 and 8; *occ.*, XV, 8 and 9.

[3] Cf. Boak, p. 148 ff. of this volume.

[4] John Lydus, *De Magistratibus*, 2, 27 (191, 13 ff.): κόμητα γὰρ λαργιτιώνων . . . καὶ κόμητα πριβάτων . . . οὐκ ἄν τις ἐν ἀρχόντων ἀριθμήσειέ ποτε καταλόγῳ, θεραπόντων δέ· [οὐδὲ γὰρ] προαγωγῆς ἄρχουσι πρεπούσης ἀξιοῦνται, κατὰ δὲ τὸ δοκοῦν τῇ βασιλείᾳ πρόσφατον ἔχουσι καὶ λανθάνουσαν τὴν γένεσιν. Fuss inserts the words οὐδὲ γάρ, which the sense of the passage seems to demand.

course, no automatic advancement to these high offices from lower positions, as was the case among the lesser subordinates of the various bureaus.

The term of the Grand Chamberlain's office was likewise subject to the Emperor's pleasure. Some incumbents saw years of service, while others soon gave place to new appointees. Thus, Eusebius, Grand Chamberlain to Constantius, held this position from 335 until after 361, but at least five men held the same office during the forty-two year reign of Theodosius II. No doubt the service of some Grand Chamberlains was terminated by natural death. Others probably won the displeasure of their sovereign and were forced to retire from duty, and more than one lost his life by the order of the Emperor or at the hands of an enraged mob. There were not wanting, however, those who retired with honor and distinction and the favor of their masters. Such, at least, seems to be the implication of certain laws bestowing high favors upon ex-Grand Chamberlains. For example, when Macrobius retired from this office in 422, in recognition of his merits a law was enacted bestowing upon all Grand Chamberlains and ex-Grand Chamberlains absolute equality with the highest officials of the Empire.[1]

4. *The Honors, Titles, and Privileges of the Grand Chamberlain*

When the office of Grand Chamberlain became a public one and was given a place in the official hierarchy, it was natural that its occupants should receive titles of honor as did those of other offices. In the early years of the post-Diocletian Empire the only title for officials of high station was *vir clarissimus*, which was indicative of senatorial rank.[2]

Almost all of the important offices of the Empire admitted their occupants to this rank, and gave them and their descendants the right to the senatorial title. This was not true, however, of the office of Grand Chamberlain. A law of the Emperor Zeno clearly indicates that it was only after they had retired from office that the Grand Chamberlains could be admitted to the senatorial rank,[3] and the fact that they had held one of the highest dignities in the Empire did not entitle them to such admittance, as is proved by a law of Anastasius which makes the ex-Grand Chamberlains' enjoyment of certain

[1] *Codex Theodosianus*, VI, 8, 1. Cf. also VII, 8, 3; VII, 8, 16.

[2] Hirschfeld, *Rangtitel der römischen Kaiserzeit*, p. 593.

[3] *Codex Justinianus*, III, 24, 3: *qui . . . sacri nostrae pietatis cubiculi praepositus post depositam administrationem senatorio ordini sociatus est*, etc.

privileges contingent upon their enrolment in the senatorial order.[1] It seems probable that there was some objection to admitting eunuchs to this aristocratic body, which still retained some of its Republican traditions.

Nearly a century after the reorganization of the Empire by Diocletian, the Emperor Valentinian, about the year 372, instituted two new orders of rank, the *spectabiles* and the *illustres*.[2] It is probably true that most persons chosen to the offices which conferred the right to these higher titles were already of senatorial rank, and in this sense the *spectabiles* and *illustres* may be said to have formed small circles of high officials within the class known as *clarissimi*,[3] but, as has already been shown in the case of the Grand Chamberlain, lack of senatorial status did not debar officials from the use of the higher titles.

All officials of any prominence in the Empire were classed in these three ranks. Only a few of the most important heads of administrative bureaus bore the rank of *illustris;* a larger but still comparatively small number, composed chiefly of intermediate administrative officers, were known as *spectabiles;* and the remainder were generally *clarissimi*.

The Grand Chamberlain probably never belonged to this lowest class of officials, but it seems quite likely that he was ranked among the *spectabiles* for a short time. It has already been shown that he was raised to the rank of an *illustris* some time between 382 and 384, and that this honor was likewise conferred upon the Counts of the Consistory at about the same time.[4]

It may be added that these officials seem to have enjoyed equal rank and honors for the next quarter of a century, and this fact gives some probability to the assumption that their advancement was contemporary for several years prior to the time when it comes under observation. Since there is conclusive evidence that one of the Counts of the Consistory, the Master of the Offices, was a *vir spectabilis* in the year 378,[5] the inference may therefore be drawn that previous to 379 the Grand Chamberlain was also of this rank.

The evidence for the Grand Chamberlain's advance to the *illustres*, under Theodosius I, has already been given.[6] At first, his place in the official order of precedence was the last of the *illustres*, following the Counts of the Consistory, but by 409 (or 412) he had been given

[1] *Codex Justinianus*, XII, 5, 5: *Iubemus duobus viris illustribus praepositis utriusque sacri cubiculi . . . post finitam militiam si senatorio fuerint consortio sociati. . . .*

[2] See p. 183.

[3] Cf. Boak, p. 20 of this volume.

[4] See p. 184 f.

[5] *Codex Theodosianus*, VIII, 5, 35: *spectabilis viri officiorum magistri.*

[6] See p. 183 f.

further advancement, and in that year ranked before the Counts of the Consistory.[1] He seems to have made no further advance in the official hierarchy before the year 422, when he was promoted from the lower, or second, class of the *illustres*, in which he had been associated with the Counts of the Consistory, to the first class, where he was ranked with the Pretorian and City Prefects and the Masters of the Soldiers.[2]

This division of the *illustres* into classes was based on the order of ceremonial precedence, and seems trivial; but it was not so regarded at the court, where the endless and intricate ceremonial observances emphasized every minute distinction of rank, and gave ample opportunity for the indulgence of official pride. After the year 422, the Pretorian Prefect, City Prefect, Master of the Soldiers, and Grand Chamberlain took precedence, while in office, in the order named, but after retiring from office they were all alike *illustres* of the first class, and their order of precedence was determined solely by the date of their induction into office. A similar rule was observed by the Counts of the Consistory, who constituted the second class of *illustres*, but no conditions of service or priority of appointment could give them precedence over the most recent recruit to the first class.[3]

It is not known how long the Grand Chamberlain held the fourth place in the official hierarchy, but by the year 485 a promotion of the Master of the Offices and the Quaestor to positions immediately following the Masters of the Soldiers had resulted in the effectual reduction of the Grand Chamberlain to the sixth place.[4]

In addition to these grades of honor, to which the incumbents in the various offices of the Empire were entitled, there were certain personal honorary distinctions which the Emperor might bestow at will upon those about the court. Most common of these were the titles of Count and Patrician. In but one instance is the Grand Chamberlain spoken of as a Count, in a law of Marcian, dating from the year 450.[5] The singularity of this use of the title challenges an explanation.

Long before 450 some even of the Grand Chamberlain's own subordinates were known as Counts. There was the Count of the Imperial Wardrobe (*comes sacrae vestis*), so known as early as 412,[6] and the Count of the Crown Lands, who came under the Grand Chamberlain's direction before 414.[7] The Steward of the Household also

[1] See p. 185. [2] *Codex Theodosianus*, VI, 8, 1 (quoted above, p. 186, n. 2).

[3] Cf. Gothofredus, *ad Codicem Theodosianum*, VII, 8, 16.

[4] *Codex Justinianus*, III, 24, 3 (quoted above, p. 189, n. 1).

[5] *Novellæ Marciani*, II, *subscript.: Maximino viro inlustri comiti et praepositi sacri cubiculi.*

[6] *Codex Theodosianus*, XI, 18, 1. [7] See p. 187.

was a Count in 390,[1] and a law of 413 makes it known that before that date the *cura palatii*, a dependent of the Steward, might be honored with the title of Count of the First Rank.[2] It seems highly improbable that these dependents of the Grand Chamberlain should have enjoyed the use of a title to which he could lay no claim. Indeed, in a court where title and order of precedence were formally regarded as the principal emoluments of office, such a situation would be well nigh impossible. It seems probable, therefore, that the Grand Chamberlain also was a Count and that his full title was *vir illustris comes et praepositus sacri cubiculi.*

The rank of Count must have been conferred upon the Grand Chamberlain during the second quarter of the fourth century, for within this period it was granted to many of the officials of the palace,[3] but the absence of constitutions of these years addressed to him makes it impossible to substantiate this supposition. It is noteworthy, however, that during the latter half of the century there is no reference to the Grand Chamberlain as a Count, although the general literature of that period is especially rich in notices concerning him. The avoidance of the title may be explained in the case of the Grand Chamberlain as it has been in that of the Master of the Offices.[4] The word *Comes* was a personal distinction and not an essential part of his title. Furthermore, as all Grand Chamberlains were Counts, it was felt unnecessary to designate them as such, and this distinction came to be ignored, even in official address.

The Patriciate was the highest honor which the Emperor could bestow. The first Grand Chamberlain to receive it was Eutropius,[5] who held this office under Arcadius until 399. His dishonorable fall in that year was the occasion for a law abrogating all the honors which had been conferred upon him, including, of course, the Patriciate.[6] It might be supposed that after this disgrace no more Grand Chamberlains would be elevated to patrician rank, but Lausus, who also held this office under Arcadius, was a Patrician,[7] as was Antiochus,[8] Grand Chamberlain under both Arcadius and Theodosius II. Antiochus be-

[1] *Codex Theodosianus*, VI, 30, 12.

[2] *Op. cit.*, VI, 13, 1.

[3] Cf. Boak, pp. 29, 31 of this volume.

[4] Boak, p. 44 of this volume.

[5] Sozomen, *Historia Ecclesiastica*, 8, 7: Οὗτος γὰρ . . . μόνος καὶ πρῶτος ὧν ἴσμεν ἢ ἀκηκόαμεν, ὑπάτου καὶ πατρὸς βασιλέως ἀξίᾳ ἐτιμήθη. Claudian, *In Eutropium*, 1, 109; 2, 68 f.; 2, *Praefatio*, 2.

[6] *Codex Theodosianus*, IX, 40, 17.

[7] Codinus, *De Signis Constantinopolis*, 37, 16 ff.: τὰ δὲ Λαύσου οἶκος ἦν Λαύσου πατρικίου καὶ πραιποσίτου, ὅστις ἀρχὰς πολλὰς καὶ δόξας διήνυσεν ἐν τοῖς χρόνοις Ἀρκαδίου τοῦ υἱοῦ Θεοδοσίου τοῦ μεγάλου.

[8] Theophanes, *Chronographia*, 148, 13: Ἀντίοχον τὸν πραιπόσιτον καὶ πατρίκιον.

came involved in a dangerous palace intrigue, whereupon Theodosius compelled him to take priestly orders, and then, further to weaken him, debarred all ex-Grand Chamberlains from both patrician and senatorial rank.[1]

The Emperor Zeno placed further restrictions upon the use of the title of Patrician, allowing it to be conferred only upon such as were of consular or prefectorian rank, and thus more surely excluding the Grand Chamberlain. This restriction was later removed by Justinian, who made it possible for any who bore the title of *illustris* to receive the Patriciate.[2] In the interval between these two Emperors there are no recorded instances of a Grand Chamberlain's being accorded the honor of the Patriciate.

Eutropius was also Consul,[3] but this was an exceptional honor, granted to no eunuch before Eutropius and apparently to none after him.

Among other marks of honor may be mentioned the formal modes of referring to the higher officials of the Late Empire. Numerous expressions similar to "Your Honor" and "Your Excellency" were employed in accordance with a more or less definite scheme to indicate various ranks of dignitaries.[4] Only once is such a distinction applied to the Grand Chamberlain, when he, or his office, is mentioned as *tui culminis*.[5]

Such privileges as were conferred upon the Grand Chamberlain appear not to have been exceptional, but similar to those which were granted to others of the *illustres*. In 382 all chamberlains and ex-chamberlains (Grand Chamberlains were undoubtedly included) were exempted from the obligations of *munera sordida*.[6] In 384 the ex-

[1] Malalas, 361, 1 ff.: Ὁ δὲ αὐτὸς Θεοδόσιος βασιλεὺς ἐποίησε κακῶς Ἀντιόχῳ τῷ πραιποσίτῳ καὶ πατρικίῳ, δυναμένῳ ἐν τῷ παλατίῳ καὶ κρατήσαντι τῶν πραγμάτων. ἦν γὰρ καὶ ἀναθρεψάμενος τὸν αὐτὸν Θεοδόσιον ἐν τῇ ζωῇ τοῦ αὐτοῦ πατρὸς, ὡς κουβικουλάριος καὶ διοικῶν ἀπὸ τοῦ αὐτοῦ πατρὸς Ἀρκαδίου τὴν πολιτείαν Ῥωμαίων. καὶ ἔμεινε μετὰ τὸ πληρῶσαι αὐτόν, ὡς πατρίκιος καταυθεντῶν τοῦ αὐτοῦ Θεοδοσίου. καὶ ἀγανακτήσας κατ' αὐτοῦ ἐδήμευσεν αὐτὸν καὶ κουρεύσας ἐποίησε παπᾶν τῆς μεγάλης ἐκκλησίας Κωνσταντινουπόλεως, ποιήσας διάταξιν μὴ εἰσέρχεσθαι εἰς ἀξίας συγκλητικῶν ἢ πατρικίων τοὺς εὐνούχους κουβικουλαρίους μετὰ τὸ πλήρωμα τῆς αὐτῶν στρατείας, τοῦτ' ἐστὶ τοὺς ἀπὸ πραιποσίτων παλατίου. καὶ ἐτελεύτα ὁ αὐτὸς Ἀντίοχος, ὢν πρεσβύτερος.

Theophanes, *Chronographia*, 148, 12 ff.: Θεοδόσιος ὁ βασιλεὺς Ἀντίοχον τὸν πραιπόσιτον καὶ πατρίκιον τὸν καὶ βαΐουλον αὐτοῦ ἐποίησε παππᾶν, δημεύσας καὶ τὸν οἶκον αὐτοῦ, ὡς κατεπαιρόμενον τῶν βασιλέων καὶ καταφρονοῦντα αὐτοῦ· διὸ καὶ νόμον ἔθετο μὴ εἰσέρχεσθαι εἰς πατρικίου ἀξίαν εὐνοῦχον.

[2] *Novellae Justiniani* LXII, 2, 5: *Si qui autem illustri dignitate decorati sunt, liceat eis patriciatus codicillos accipere, etsi non consulares existant, quod constitutio divae memoriae Zenonis irrite postulabat.*

[3] Claudian, *In Eutrop.*, 1, 286; 2, *praef.* 9; Soz., *Hist. Eccles.*, 8, 7. Cf. p. 196, n. 5.

[4] Cf. Boak, p. 114 of this volume.

[5] *Codex Justinianus*, III, 26, 11.

[6] *Codex Theodosianus*, XI, 16, 15.

Grand Chamberlains, together with other high officials of the court, were given the privilege of having one private house free from the demands of *hospitium*.[1] In 435 this exemption was extended to one half of the second house; one third of the remaining half was subject to requisition.[2] In 409 (or 412) Grand Chamberlains and ex-Grand Chamberlains were excused from the necessity of furnishing recruits and horses.[3]

The Emperor Zeno conferred upon the ex-Grand Chamberlains and other high officials the privilege of being tried in no other court than that of the Emperor himself, or before such judges as he might appoint for this specific purpose, providing, further, that any penalties which these judges might impose should be subject to imperial sanction and revision.[4]

The Emperor Anastasius granted to the ex-Grand Chamberlains the privilege of using the *cingulum*, or belt of office, as often as they wished to inspect their estates or to travel for any other reason. This gave them the right to the use of the state post-service and all the accommodations along the route which were customarily granted to those travelling on official business.[5]

No information has been preserved regarding the privileges which the Grand Chamberlain enjoyed in the matter of the issuance of passes (*evectiones*) for the use of the state post. The Pretorian Prefects and the Master of the Offices might issue, apparently in their own names, an unlimited number of passes, but other officials were presented annually with a limited number of blank passes, to be used by their subordinates when travelling on official business.[6] Böcking has suggested that the Grand Chamberlain may have had fifteen of these blank passes, the ordinary number allowed to the Masters of the Soldiers.[7]

The need of the Grand Chamberlain for these passes was not limited, however, as Böcking seems to suggest, to those used in administering the Crown Lands in Cappadocia, for he must have found frequent occasion to despatch messengers over the state roads on private errands at the Emperor's desire. It seems probable, therefore, that the Grand Chamberlain, although not issuing passes in his own name, was permitted to use as many blank passes as necessity might require — a privilege which the two treasury officials also enjoyed.

[1] *Op. cit.*, VII, 8, 3.

[2] *Op. cit.*, VII, 8, 16.

[3] *Op. cit.*, XI, 18, 1.

[4] *Codex Justinianus*, III, 24, 3.

[5] *Op. cit.*, XII, 5, 5.

[6] Seeck, in Pauly-Wissowa, *Real-Encyc.*, s.v., *cursus publicus*.

[7] *Notitia Dignitatum*, I, 234.

5. *The Duties of the Grand Chamberlain*

a. His Administrative Competence

Available sources give no definite indication of the duties of the Grand Chamberlain during the Later Empire. He exercised a broad administrative supervision, embracing not only the activities of the chamberlains, properly so called, but also of the keepers and attendants of the imperial wardrobe, the cooks, waiters, pages, janitors, and many others. It is not to be supposed, however, that he concerned himself with the petty details of the palace service, but that he left such matters to the Superintendent of Chamberlains, the Steward of the Household, and other subordinates. A consideration of the activities of these subordinate administrative heads, and of the organization of their various corps, is perhaps the best means to an appreciation of the extent of the Grand Chamberlain's control. As the subject can, however, be most conveniently treated by itself, it has been reserved for an ensuing section.

b. His Juridical Competence

The juridical competence of the Grand Chamberlain seems to have been much more limited than was that of other bureau heads. After Diocletian's reorganization the City Prefects exercised civil and criminal jurisdiction in Rome and Constantinople, and to a distance of one hundred miles from these cities, but an exception was made in the case of members of the various governmental bureaus. It was a recognized principle of the Late Empire that the great ministers who stood at the heads of the respective bureaus had jurisdiction over all those who were subject to their administrative control, and that from their decision there was no appeal.[1] Thus, the Masters of the Soldiers at one time exercised jurisdiction over the military forces along the frontiers of the Empire;[2] the Master of the Offices heard, in his own court, cases involving his dependents, the *agentes in rebus*, the *admissionales*, the *cancellarii*, the *decani*, and others,[3] and the Counts of the Sacred Largesses and the Privy Purse had courts in which their subordinates appeared.[4]

That there was a court of the Grand Chamberlain in the middle of the fifth century is made clear by a law regarding the cultivators of the Crown Lands in Cappadocia. Cases to which slaves or the renters

[1] Bethmann-Hollweg, *Der römische Civilprozess*, vol. III, p. 139 f.

[2] Boak, *Roman Magistri*, *Harvard Studies in Classical Philology*, vol. XXVI (1915), p. 148.

[3] Boak, pp. 66 ff. of this volume.

[4] *Codex Justinianus*, XII, 23, 12.

of land (*coloni*) or of houses (*inquilini*) were parties, were placed under the sole jurisdiction of the Count of the Crown Lands and the Grand Chamberlain.[1]

It does not seem probable that men in such unfortunate circumstances as slaves and *coloni* would have carried their cases to Constantinople, nor is there any indication that the Grand Chamberlain made judicial trips into Cappadocia. It seems more likely that he merely reviewed cases which had already been heard by the Count of the Crown Lands.

It may be observed that there is in the law just cited nothing which could suggest the creation of a new court. The Grand Chamberlain, it must be inferred, had previously exercised jurisdiction of some kind, but there is no evidence that it extended to others than the tillers of the Crown Lands, and these persons were not, in the narrow sense, subordinates of the Grand Chamberlain. There seems to be no evidence whatever to justify the assumption that the Grand Chamberlain ever had jurisdiction over those who were under his administrative control.

Other considerations give support to this conclusion. During the fifth century many of the subordinates of the Grand Chamberlain were placed under the sole jurisdiction of the Master of the Offices, as the chamberlains,[2] the corps charged with the care of the imperial wardrobe (*schola sacrae vestis*),[3] the *ministeriani*,[4] and the Silentiaries (*silentiarii*).[5]

The law placing the last named corps under the sole jurisdiction of the Master of the Offices states that this was done so that they might not be kept from the performance of their duties by being haled into different courts. From this statement the conclusion has been drawn that the Grand Chamberlain did not have jurisdiction over his subordinates, else they would have stood trial in his court.[6] This deduction is supported by a similar law with a similar purpose concerning the chamberlains.[7]

c. His Personal and Ceremonial Duties and Activities

The personal duties of the Grand Chamberlain in relation to the Emperor are no more specifically indicated than are his administrative

[1] *Codex Justinianus*, III, 26, 11: *Artaxi praeposito sacri cubiculi. Hac lege sancimus, ut, sive agat domorum nostrarum colonus aut inquilinus aut servus seu pulsetur ab aliquo super criminali vel civili negotio, non alibi quam tui culminis ac viri spectabilis comitis domorum petatur examen . . . Anno* 442.

[2] *Codex Justinianus*, XII, 5, 3. [3] *Op. cit.*, XII, 25, 3. [4] *Op. cit.*, XII, 25, 4.

[5] *Op. cit.*, XII, 16, 4. [6] Boak, p. 41 of this volume. [7] *Codex Justinianus*, XII, 5, 3.

and juridical duties. He seems to have been in almost continual attendance upon the Emperor, as had been his predecessor in the times of the Principate. Thus Eusebius was present and even took part in a conference between Constantius and the bishops Liberius and Epictetus,[1] and Eutropius stood at the side of the Emperor Arcadius when the latter sat as judge at the trial of Timasius, who had incurred the Grand Chamberlain's disfavor.[2]

In the time of Justinian the Grand Chamberlain sat in the imperial box at the races,[3] and at the palace had the right to enter the Emperor's presence unannounced.[4] This seat in the imperial box, and the right to enter unannounced into the Emperor's presence might well be classed as privileges, but their origin, especially in the latter case, must have been in the frequent demands of the Emperor for the services of his chief body-servant.

The ceremonial duties of the Grand Chamberlain in the secular observances of the period before Justinian are occasionally mentioned in the portions of the work of Peter the Patrician which have been incorporated in the *De Caerimoniis* of Constantinus Porphyrogenitus. In 457, Leo I, at the ceremony by which he was proclaimed Emperor, came to the vestry (*mutatorium*) of the church of St. John Baptist, removed his crown and handed it to the Grand Chamberlain, who carried it on his hands (ὑποκάτω βαστάζει) to the holy table (τράπεζα). Here he handed it to the Emperor, who placed it upon the table and, probably after a dedicatory prayer, took it again and handed it to the Grand Chamberlain. The latter bore it back to the vestry, where the Emperor once more placed it upon his head.[5] The ceremony was repeated in all its essential details at "the church" (τὴν ἐκκλησίαν), that is, at St. Sophia, except that the bishop here placed the crown on the Emperor's head.[6] At the banquet in the palace, following the ceremony, both Grand Chamberlains (τοὺς πραιποσίτους) dined at the Emperor's table.[7]

After the death of the Emperor Zeno, the Empress Ariadne appeared before the people in company with many of her nobles, among them the two Grand Chamberlains (οἱ δύο πραιπόσιτοι), and

[1] Cassiodorus, *Historia Tripartita*, 5, 17.

[2] Zosimus, 5, 9: καὶ ὁ μὲν βασιλεὺς προυκάθετο δικαστής, Εὐτρόπιος δὲ παρεστώς.

[3] Petrus Patricius in Const. Porph., *De Caer.*, 418, 8 ff.: οἱ δύο πραιπόσιτοι . . . καὶ οἱ ἄλλοι πάντες, ὅσοι ἔθος ἔχουσιν συνθεωρεῖν τῷ βασιλεῖ ἐν ταῖς ἱπποδρομίαις.

[4] *Op. cit.*, 442, 20 ff.: καὶ πρὸς τὸν βασιλέα εἰσερχόμενος, ὥσπερ τὸ παλαιὸν ὁ πραιπόσιτος, ἀμέσως εἰσέρχεται.

[5] *Op. cit.*, 413, 12 ff.

[6] *Op. cit.*, 414, 20 ff.

[7] *Op. cit.*, 416, 11 ff.

addressed the throng.[1] Later, as the nobles were discussing the choice of a new Emperor, the Grand Chamberlain Urbicius made the thoughtful suggestion, which met with approval, that the Empress herself should choose her future consort.[2] When her choice had fallen on Anastasius, in the course of the coronation ceremonies which followed, the crown was again placed on the holy table, as described above, and the Grand Chamberlain assisted in the observance as before.[3] This was done also at the choice of Justin I.[4]

In 474, when Leo I proclaimed his son, Leo II, Emperor, the Grand Chamberlain handed the crown to the former, who placed it upon the head of the new Emperor,[5] and a like ceremony was observed when Justin made Justinian Augustus.[6]

The Grand Chamberlain introduced to the Emperor's presence a Silentiary designate, to receive his staff of office,[7] and was himself intrusted with the investiture of a *referendarius*, which, however, consisted merely in conveying to him, without important ceremony, the insignia of office.[8] He also welcomed with a kiss, in the palace of the Emperor, ambassadors from other courts.[9]

It is possible that in those ceremonies described above, in which the Grand Chamberlain was intrusted with the crown, he was acting as the formal head of the department of the Imperial Wardrobe, which had the supervision of the imperial robes and ceremonial regalia. It is interesting to note, in this connection, that during a battle with the Alemanni Valentinian removed his helmet, adorned with gold and precious stones, and placed it in the custody of his chamberlain.[10]

IV. The Subordinates of the Grand Chamberlain: Their Organization, Duties, and Privileges

The scope of the Grand Chamberlain's supervision can best be appreciated by a consideration of the duties of his subordinates. The unfortunate loss of those chapters of the *Notitia Dignitatum* which dealt with the Grand Chamberlain and the organization of his staff, renders the treatment of this part of the palace service very difficult, for no other source supplies the definite and detailed information which this work must once have offered. It is clear, however, that in the

[1] *Op. cit.*, 418, 8 ff. [2] *Op. cit.*, 421, 20 ff. [3] *Op. cit.*, 425, 15 ff.
[4] *Op. cit.*, 430, 20 ff.: καὶ τὰ λοιπὰ ἀκολούθως γέγονεν κατὰ τὸ σχῆμα Ἀναστασίου.
[5] *Op. cit.*, 432, 9 ff. [6] *Op. cit.*, 433, 8 ff.: καὶ πάντα κατὰ τὸ ὅμοιον σχῆμα ἐγένετο.
[7] *Op. cit.*, 389, 4. [8] *Op. cit.*, 390, 4 ff.
[9] *Op. cit.*, 394, 13: δέχονται ἀπὸ τοῦ πραιποσίτου ἀσπαζόμενοι αὐτόν.
[10] Ammianus Marcellinus, XXVII, 10, 11.

fifth century, after his position among the great ministers at the court had been established, the Grand Chamberlain's administrative control embraced:

1. The Superintendent of the Chamberlains
   (*primicerius sacri cubiculi*),
2. The Steward of the Household
   (*castrensis sacri palatii*),
3. The Count of the Crown Lands of Cappadocia
   (*comes domorum per Cappadociam*),
4. The Count of the Imperial Wardrobe
   (*comes sacrae vestis*),
5. The Decurions and Silentiaries
   (*decuriones, silentiarii*),
6. The Private Imperial Treasurer
   (*sacellarius*).

1. *The Superintendent of the Chamberlains* (*primicerius sacri cubiculi*)

The first Superintendent of Chamberlains mentioned in the extant accounts of the reorganized Empire was Euphrates, who held this position under Constantine the Great in the year 326, and possibly as early as 312.[1] From the time of its establishment this office was subject to the control of the Grand Chamberlain. This is clear from the title of its incumbent, *primicerius sacri cubiculi*, for the word *primicerius* was used in the titles of none but those who occupied subordinate administrative positions,[2] and the words *sacri cubiculi* leave no doubt regarding the corps to which he belonged. Further evidence that he was attached to the chamberlain service is to be found, moreover, in the fact that he is mentioned among the subordinates of the Grand Chamberlain in a constitution issued by Honorius and Theodosius.[3]

[1] See pp. 181 f.

[2] Cf. *Notitia Dignitatum, passim.* The one exception seems to be the Chief of the Notaries (*primicerius notariorum*), *op. cit.*, *or.*, XVIII; *occ.*, XVI.

[3] *Codex Theodosianus*, XI, 18, 1: *Tirones . . . praebere noluimus inlustres viros praefectos . . . non magistros militum vel comites domesticorum simile munus adstringat, neque enim tirones de facultatibus eorum poscendi sunt, quorum virtus triumphis nostris subiugat de hoste captivos; non praepositum vel primicerium sacri cubiculi, non castrensem, non comitem sacrae vestis, non ceteros cubicularios*, etc. C. Jullian, in Daremberg et Saglio, *Dictionnaire des Antiquités*, vol. III, Part I, p. 386, n. 7, questions the reliability of this law (*j'avoue qu'on ne peut trop se fier à cette loi*), apparently because the Count of the Domestics is mentioned directly after the Masters of the Soldiers, as if he ranked next to them. The reason which he suggests for the unusual order in which the officials are here mentioned is hardly acceptable. Instead of the usual order according to rank or precedence in the official hierarchy, the titles of subordinate officials are mentioned in

That the position of the Superintendent of the Chamberlains was of some importance is shown by the fact that he was among those who assisted Constantine in the building of his new capital.[1] In the year 425 he ranked first among the *spectabiles*,[2] the second order of rank in the Empire at that time.

The Superintendent of the Chamberlains probably did not gain his position by the regular order of promotion by which other holders of primiceriates were elevated to that rank. It was customary for new members of the various bureaus to be enrolled in the lowest rank, and to receive regular advancement from one rank to another until they arrived at the head of their respective corps, when they were very commonly known as *primicerii*.

That such a rule applied to the Notaries,[3] the Palatines of the Count of the Sacred Largesses,[4] the *agentes in rebus*,[5] the *castrensiani*,[6] the *decani*,[7] and others,[8] is well attested. It might be inferred that, by analogy with other *primicerii*, the Superintendent of Chamberlains had risen through successive grades of his office until, being the oldest in point of years of service, he had attained the highest rank, but there is no evidence that this was the case. Furthermore, it should be remembered that he was a rather important official, ranking high in the hierarchy of the court, and that it is, therefore, dangerous to suppose that what was true of the very lowly *primicerii* of other divisions of the court service was true of him also. The rules for advancement which were applied to the lower officials were probably not followed, at least with any regularity, in the case of such an important member of the court as the Superintendent of the Chamberlains. Such positions must have served as rewards in the Emperor's hands.

It is quite conceivable that in the first years of Diocletian's reorganization, when the Grand Chamberlain held a less prominent place among the court officials, the position of the Superintendent of the Chamberlains was comparable to that of other *primicerii*, and that as his superior gained recognition and influence, he, too, received advancement; but whatever his station may once have been, it may be

this law immediately after those of their respective superiors. This order is not systematically followed with the less important officials, but such groups as are given are instructive. This is not the only instance in which the regular order of mention is violated. Cf. p. 186.

[1] Codinus, *De Originibus Constantinopolitanis*, 18, 1 ff.

[2] *Notitia Dignitatum or.*, I, 17; *occ.*, I, 15.

[3] Cassiodorus, *Variae*, VII, 16, 3.

[4] *Codex Theodosianus*, VI, 30, 5; 14; 22.

[5] *Op. cit.*, VI, 27, 4; 9.

[6] *Op. cit.*, VI, 32, 1.

[7] *Op. cit.*, VI, 33, 1.

[8] *Op. cit.*, VIII, 7, 1.

accepted as certain that at the time of the composition of the *Notitia Dignitatum* it was not regarded as equal to that of others bearing a similar title, for in that work a whole chapter was given to him and to his staff,[1] whereas none of the other *primicerii* were given such prominence.

Because of the *lacunae* in the *Notitia Dignitatum*, the duties of the Superintendent of the Chamberlains are not readily to be determined. He may have slept in close proximity to the Emperor, for the Greek title, παρακοιμώμενος, which is sometimes applied to him seems to indicate such a practice. He probably had immediate oversight of the chamberlains, for the Grand Chamberlain's attendance upon the Emperor must have made it impossible for him to exercise personally the close supervision which would have been required.

So far as can be determined, the only honorary distinction to which the Superintendent of the Chamberlains could lay claim was that of ranking first among the *spectabiles*, as indicated above.

He is specifically mentioned but once in the Codes. This occurs in a law by which he and other chamberlains were granted exemption from the necessity of furnishing recruits and horses,[2] but he was probably included with the other chamberlains as a recipient of immunity from the *munera sordida* and *hospitium*, and the demands of the post and courier service.[3]

The ordinary chamberlains who performed the various duties about the *cubiculum* of the Emperor, as was the case with those who attended the Empress, were generally eunuchs. Some women also were attached to the corps,[4] and though nothing is said of their duties, it may be assumed that they attended the Empress. The number of these attendants, men and women, is unknown, but the implication of many passages is that it was rather large.[5] As a rule the chamberlains must once have been slaves, for only on this supposition can their mutilation be satisfactorily explained, and many of them probably were presented as gifts to the Emperor.[6]

The large number of chamberlains and the variety of tasks which they must have performed would naturally give rise to some kind of differentiated organization. The eunuchs who prepared the Emperor's couch, those who attended him at the bath, his barbers, anointers, and others who performed similar personal services, all of whom were

[1] *Or.*, I, 17; *occ.*, I, 15.
[2] *Codex Theodosianus*, XI, 18, 1.
[3] *Op. cit.*, XI, 16, 15.
[4] *Codex Justinianus*, XII, 5, 4.
[5] Cf. Zosimus, 205, 19 ff.: τοῦ πλήθους τῶν περὶ τὴν βασιλικὴν θεραπείαν εὐνούχων, κτλ.
[6] *Codex Justinianus*, XII, 5, 4.

probably included among the chamberlains of the later period, must have had their respective chiefs, known perhaps as *primicerii*,[1] who were subordinates to the Superintendent of the Chamberlains. These *primicerii* were probably ordinary chamberlains whose years of service had brought them by a program of regular advancement to their positions of prestige. Such at least was the customary manner of advancement in other corps.[2]

There are two passages which may refer to these subordinate *primicerii*. In 396 there was granted to the chamberlains of the first rank (*primus locus*) the privilege of nominating members to the corps of the *agentes in rebus*.[3] It seems impossible definitely to determine who were included among these chamberlains of the first rank, but it may be assumed that their station was comparable to that of the Counts of the second rank, with whom they are mentioned, and to whom the same privilege was granted. The *proximi scriniorum* were Counts of the second rank[4] and their administrative position was not unlike that of a *primicerius* of one of the divisions of the corps of chamberlains.

The second passage is from a law of 428, stating that all chamberlains who went out from the *cubiculum* before attaining first rank, with the exception of the Steward of the Household and the Count of the Crown Lands, were to enjoy certain privileges.[5] There is evidence here that continued service as a chamberlain led to advancement to the first rank, but it is by no means apparent precisely what officials were included in this category. If the Steward and the Count of the Crown Lands had not yet arrived at the first rank, it is clear that the first rank, in this law, cannot be that of the subordinate *primicerii*, whose position has just been discussed. Neither can it be that of the Superintendent of the Chamberlains, as will presently be shown.[6]

The chamberlains were the recipients of several privileges. In

[1] This title was given to the chiefs of other branches of the palace service, as the *decani* (*Codex Theodosianus*, VI, 12; *Codex Justinianus*, XII, 27, 1 and 2; XII, 59, 10, sec. 2), the *lampadarii* (*Novellae Valentiniani*, XXXVI), the *protectores* (Ammianus Marcellinus, XVIII, 3, 5; *Codex Justinianus*, XII, 17, 4 and 5).

[2] See p. 204.

[3] *Codex Theodosianus*, VI, 27, 8: *In numero agentum in rebus crescant quos comitum secundi ordinis vel cubiculariorum nostrorum primi dumtaxat loci vel tribunorum urbaniciorum petitio fecerit militare. . . .*

[4] *Op. cit.*, VI, 26, 17; date, 416.

[5] *Codex Justinianus*, XII, 5, 2: *Hac nostrae mansuetudinis aeterna lege sancimus, ut omnes cubicularii, qui de nostro cubiculo exeunt, antequam primum locum obtineant, excepto castrensi et comiti domorum, his privilegiis perfruantur. . . .*

[6] See pp. 209 f.

382 all chamberlains and ex-chamberlains were granted exemption from *munera sordida*.[1] In 428 this exemption seems to have been reaffirmed or, possibly, extended and made to include those who had been enrolled in the ranks of the chamberlains, but who had retired before the full term of service had been completed.[2]

In the time of the Emperor Leo it was provided that all chamberlains should be subject to the sole jurisdiction of the Master of the Offices.[3] At about the same time a law was enacted granting to all those who had come or should come into the service of the *cubiculum* as gifts to the Emperor the status and legal capacities of free men and providing that if any had been enrolled in the corps without their masters' consent or knowledge they could be reclaimed only by legal action, and within five years. This law applied to both men and women.[4]

2. *The Steward of the Household* (*castrensis sacri palatii*)

The early history of the office of the Steward of the Household is as little known as is that of the Grand Chamberlain. The office developed out of that of the *procurator castrensis* of the Principate,[5] to which had been assigned, from about the time of Claudius, the financial administration of the palace service,[6] and as a consequence of this a somewhat extensive control of the palace personnel and its organization.[7]

After the reorganization by Diocletian and Constantine, the Steward of the Household seems still to have retained a certain amount of financial control over the chamberlains, for there were in his staff an accountant (*tabularius*) for the Emperor and another for the Empress.[8] It is even possible that in the early years of the Late Empire the Steward was not under the administrative direction of the Grand Chamberlain, and that his control of the palace finances served as a partial check upon the latter's extravagance. It could not have been a very effective check, however, for no palace official would dare to oppose with much vigor the Grand Chamberlain, who was the Emperor's most intimate servant; any of his demands might be based upon an imperial order.

[1] *Codex Theodosianus*, XI, 16, 15.
[2] *Codex Justinianus*, XII, 5, 2.
[3] *Op. cit.*, XII, 5, 3.
[4] *Op. cit.*, XII, 5, 4.
[5] Hirschfeld, *Die kaiserliche Verwaltungsbeamten bis auf Diocletian*, p. 317.
[6] *Op. cit.*, p. 312.
[7] Fairon, *La Ratio Castrensis*, *Musée Belge*, vol. II (1898), p. 241.
[8] *Notitia Dignitatum or.*, XVII; *occ.*, XV.

Some doubt that the Steward was ever a subordinate of the Grand Chamberlain has been expressed by Karlowa,[1] by Schiller,[2] and by Reid,[3] and there are several other writers who make no mention of the relation.[4] There is no occasion for such meticulous restraint. That the Steward was one of the Grand Chamberlain's subordinates is apparent from a law of Honorius and Theodosius in which he is mentioned among the chamberlains, that is, among the dependents of the Grand Chamberlain.[5]

Another law, of Theodosius and Valentinian, by which certain privileges or exemptions were granted to "all the chamberlains," makes a special exception of the Steward of the Household and the Count of the Crown Lands.[6] There would certainly be no need of making such an exception if these men were not chamberlains. Finally, it is to be noted that Amantius, a eunuch in the service of the Empress Eudoxia, wife of Arcadius, is twice referred to by a contemporary as Steward,[7] and no fewer than six times as a chamberlain.[8] Such contemporary evidence of both official and general character can scarcely be impugned, and is abundant justification for the categorical assertion that the Steward of the Household was a subordinate of the Grand Chamberlain.

The Steward of the Household, as a not inconspicuous member of the palace organization, received certain honorary distinctions at the hands of the Emperor. Before 390 he had received the title of Count, as he was addressed as *comes et castrensis* in a law of that year.[9] It is probable that he was a *vir clarissimus* at that time, unless indeed the fact that he was generally a eunuch debarred him from that order.[10] Not much later he was raised to the second grade of honor, and in 416 was described as a *vir spectabilis comes et castrensis sacri palatii*.[11] The

[1] *Römische Rechtsgeschichte*, vol. I, p. 847: *In Abhängigkeit vom* praepositus sacri cubiculi *mag auch der* castrensis sacri palatii *gestanden haben.*

[2] *Geschichte der römischen Kaiserzeit*, vol. 2, p. 106: *Noch weniger lässt sich das Verhaltniss der letzteren* (praepositus sacri cubiculi) *zum Castrensis Sacri Palatii angeben.*

[3] *Cambridge Medieval History*, vol. I, p. 29: "Whether the *castrensis sacri palatii* was independent or subordinate, cannot be determined."

[4] De Sanctis, in De Ruggiero, *Dizionario Epigrafico;* De Villafosse, in Daremberg et Saglio, *Dictionnaire des Antiquités;* Seeck, in Pauly-Wissowa, *Real-Encyc.;* in each instance, s.v. *castrensis.*

[5] *Codex Theodosianus*, XI, 18, 1: *non praepositum vel primicerium sacri cubiculi, non castrensem non comitem sacrae vestis, non ceteros cubicularios. . . .* Cf. p. 203, n. 3.

[6] *Codex Justinianus*, XII, 5, 2; quoted, p. 206, n. 5.

[7] Marcus Diaconus, *Vita Porphyrii*, 37; 40 (ed. Haupt, 189, 12; 190, 14).

[8] *Op. cit.*, 36; 38 *bis;* 39; 41; 43 (ed. Haupt, 188, 22; 189, 16; 189, 22; 190, 1; 191, 8; 191, 31).

[9] *Codex Theodosianus*, VI, 30, 12.

[10] Cf. p. 194.

[11] *Codex Theodosianus*, VI, 32, 1.

same mode of address was used in a law of 422,[1] and in the *Notitia Dignitatum* also he is described as *spectabilis*, though the word *comes* has here been omitted from his title.[2]

The relation of the Steward of the Household to the chamberlains of the first rank[3] presents a difficult question. A law of Theodosius and Valentinian, dated 428, states that all chamberlains who went forth from the *cubiculum* before attaining first rank (*antequam primum locum obtineant*), with the exception of the Steward of the Household and the Count of the Crown Lands, were to enjoy certain privileges.[4]

This obviously implies that the two officials who were excepted had not yet reached first rank — for otherwise the exception would be meaningless — and the significance of the temporal conjunction *antequam* can only be that by longer service they might expect to do so. What, then, was this first rank which they might attain? Certainly it was not that of the Grand Chamberlain, and it is almost as certain that it could not have been that of the Superintendent of the Chamberlains, for there is no evidence of a regular order of advancement to this post. It has already been indicated that the chamberlains of the first rank were probably the *primicerii* of the various groups of chamberlains.[5]

Clearly this explanation cannot be applied to the law which has just been quoted, for although the Steward and the Count of the Crown Lands were certainly of higher rank than the *primicerii*, they had not yet reached the first rank, in the sense in which that expression is used in this law. Moreover, it would appear that the chamberlains of the first rank, that is, the *primicerii*, were more or less numerous, constituting a group similar to that of the Counts of the second rank and the city tribunes, with whom they are mentioned; but in the law now under consideration, since the Steward and the Count of the Crown Lands had not yet attained first rank, and since the only chamberlains superior to them were the Grand Chamberlain and the Superintendent of the Chamberlains, it is obvious that the first rank could not have comprised a group of officials, but only one or two persons, at the most.

No reason is given for the exclusion of the Steward of the Household and the Count of the Crown Lands from the benefits of this law, which were such as all chamberlains might be expected to enjoy, and

[1] *Op. cit.*, VI, 32, 2. [2] *Or.*, XVII; *occ.*, XV. [3] See p. 206.
[4] *Codex Justinianus*, XII, 5, 2; quoted above, p. 206, n. 5. [5] See p. 206.

which the Steward certainly did enjoy in the Western Empire.[1] If it could be assumed that the exception did not originally appear in the law, but is a later interpolation, the difficulty would at once disappear, and the explanation that the *primicerii* constituted the first rank of chamberlains could be applied to this law also. However, to make an unwarranted assumption that the text has been contaminated, in order to evade the difficulty which it presents, would be scarcely better than to disregard the difficulty entirely, as Seeck,[2] De Sanctis,[3] De Villafosse,[4] and others have done. For the present, at least, the problem seems to permit of no solution.

Freedom from *munera sordida* and the obligation of *hospitium* was granted to the Stewards and the ex-Stewards of the Household, together with many other high officials of the palace, in 382.[5] Exemption from the necessity of furnishing recruits and horses was bestowed on the Steward by a law of 409.[6]

The duties of the Steward of the Household are nowhere specifically defined. The control of the funds for the maintenance of the palace service, which he may have inherited from the *procurator castrensis*, probably passed from his hands at an early date, and the only suggestion that he ever exercised this control is to be found in the fact that accountants for the *cubiculum* of the Emperor and for that of the Empress were included in his *officium*.[7]

It seems reasonably certain that the Steward supervised all the appointments and attendants of the palace, with the exception of the chamberlains, who were directly under the supervision of the Superintendent of the Chamberlains, and the palace guards, the corps of ushers, and a few others, who were directed by the Master of the Offices.[8] This supervision he exercised under the general oversight of the Grand Chamberlain. The sphere of his activities is fairly well defined by the *Notitia Dignitatum*, in the one remaining chapter dealing with the palace servants, as follows:

Sub dispositione viri spectabilis castrensis: Paedagogia, Ministeriales dominici, Curae palatiorum.

Officium autem suprascripti viri spectabilis castrensis habet: Tabularium dominicum, Tabularium dominarum Augustarum, Adiutorem, Chartularium et scrinium ipsius et ceteros palatinos officii suprascripti.[9]

[1] *Codex Theodosianus*, XI, 18, 1. [2] Pauly-Wissowa, *Real-Encyc.*, s.v. *castrensis.*
[3] De Ruggiero, *Dizionario Epigrafico*, s.v. *castrensis.*
[4] Daremberg et Saglio, *Dict. des Ant.*, s.v. *castrenses.*
[5] *Codex Theodosianus*, XI, 16, 15. [6] *Op. cit.*, XI, 18, 1.
[7] See p. 207. [8] Cf. Boak, p. 28 of this volume. [9] *Or.*, XVII. Cf. *occ.*, XV.

The terms *paedagogiani* and *ministeriales* are rarely found in the accounts of the system after Diocletian, except in the codes, which give no indication of the duties and privileges of such unimportant servants. It seems quite apparent, moreover, that the ordinary writer made no attempt to distinguish between the two kinds of service, but spoke indifferently of *ministri*,[1] *pueri*,[2] *παιδάρια*,[3] and so on. Ammianus Marcellinus offers one illuminating remark when he says that Procopius, because of the lack of imperial robes, on his assumption of imperial rank, wore a "tunic spangled with gold, as would a *regius minister*, and was clad from heel to waist after the fashion of a *paedagogianus puer*." [4]

This seems to be the sole passage in general literature in which these two corps of servants are clearly distinguished. For further information it is permissible to draw upon the period of the Principate, for while the duties and ranks of higher officials may have varied greatly under the organizations of different times, the actual tasks to be performed must have been much the same whether the chief potentate was Princeps or Emperor, and the pages and ministers of the time after Diocletian were probably employed in much the same way as were those of the earlier centuries.

a. The Pages (*paedagogiani*)

Under the Principate and no later, probably, than the reign of Hadrian, there was established at Rome, near the palace, a school for the training of pages.[5] Young boys of handsome appearance were here taught the arts and graces of court service. They were delicately nurtured and pampered, and were as careful of their complexions and appearance as was the most frivolous and fastidious lady of the court.[6] They were richly and fantastically clad,[7] and were grouped according to size, color of hair, and other characteristics.[8]

In groups or singly they attended the Emperor at home and abroad,[9]

[1] Corippus, *In Laudem Justini*, 2, 86.

[2] *C.I.L.*, VI, 8977.

[3] Julian, *Misopogon*, 350 D.

[4] XXVI, 6, 15: *tunica auro distincta ut regius minister, indutus a calce in pubem in paedagogiani pueri speciem. . . .*

[5] Cf. Gatti, *Del Caput Africae nella Seconda Regione di Roma, Annali dell' Instituto Archeolog. di Roma*, 1882, pp. 191–220.

[6] Seneca, *Epistulae Morales*, 123, 7.

[7] Seneca, *De Vita Beata*, 17, 2; *De Tranquilitate Animi*, 1, 8; Pliny, *Naturalis Historia*, 33, 12 and 54; Amm. Marc., XXVI, 6, 15; cf. *C.I.L.*, VI, 8977.

[8] Seneca, *Epist. Mor.*, 95, 24; Martial, III, 58, 30.

[9] Julian, *Misopogon*, 350 D.

at the table,[1] the bath,[2] and on the chase.[3] That they ministered to the basest lusts of the Emperor and, possibly, of his favorites, is only too well attested.[4] The pages had a special apartment, barracks or dormitory, which was known as the *paedagogium*, and here they slept, apparently in a common room.[5]

The pages entered the service of the Steward of the Household when quite young, certainly before puberty,[6] and their term of service might be as long as fifteen years.[7] It seems probable from the extreme youth of some of these pages, from the gorgeousness of their costumes, and from the times and occasions when they served, that their purpose was rather to lend splendor to the court, to divert the eye and pique the fancy than to perform any serious tasks.

b. The Servants of Special Function (*ministeriales*)

The *ministeriales*, known also as *ministeriani*, were, as their name suggests, groups of servants, to each of which was assigned a specific type of duty (*ministerium*). The supervision of the Steward of the Household seems to have extended only to the *ministri* who were connected with the apartments of the Emperor, for they are described as *dominici*, a term which is used in another connection in the same chapter of the *Notitia* to distinguish the accountant of the Emperor's *cubiculum* from that of the *cubiculum* of the Empress.[8] The conclusion is natural that the *ministri* who were in the service of the Empress were under the direction of the *castrensis* of her own apartments; of this official there is a contemporary record from the time of Arcadius.[9]

There is no specific description of the duties of the *ministeriales*. If it may be assumed that the pages had no important duties about the palace other than to lend color and charm to an already gorgeous scene; if it may be assumed also that the functions of the *curae palatii* [10] concerned the material condition of the imperial palace, it may safely be inferred that all, or almost all, other tasks connected with the maintenance of the palace fell to the lot of the *ministeriales*, for there is no trace of any other corps to which these duties were assigned. Toward the close of the Principate "fullers and tailors and bakers and butlers"

[1] Ulpian, *Dig.*, XXXIII, 7, 12, 32.

[2] Pliny, *Naturalis Historia*, 33, 12.

[3] Ammianus Marcellinus, XXIX, 3, 3.

[4] Seneca, *Epist. Mor.*, 47, 7; 95, 24.

[5] This was true of Pliny's house, at least. Cf. Pliny, *Epist.*, VII, 27, 13.

[6] Amm. Marc., XXIX, 3, 3: *adultus quidam ex his quos paedagogianos appellant*, etc. Cf. Seneca, *Epist. Mor.*, 95, 24.

[7] *Codex Theodosianus*, VIII, 7, 5.

[8] See p. 210.

[9] Marcus Diaconus, *Vita Porphyrii* (ed. Haupt), 189, 12: τὸν εὐνοῦχον 'Αμάντιον, καστρήσιον ὄντα τῆς βασιλίσσης.

[10] See pp. 214 f.

were included among the *ministri*,[1] and there are epigraphic references to corps of cooks,[2] bakers,[3] cellarers,[4] and the purveyors of luxuries for the Emperor's table.[5] There were also the carvers,[6] the waiters,[7] the cup-bearers,[8] the tasters,[9] the superintendent of the banquet hall,[10] the decorators of the banquet hall,[11] and a host of others.

The *ministri* were divided into two classes, and known accordingly as *statuti* or *supernumerarii*, the former being members of the regular corps and in active service, and the latter being additional members, who enjoyed many of the privileges which were accorded to the *statuti*, and awaited promotion to their ranks to fill the vacancies made by the annual retirement of the members longest in service. The supernumeraries were appointed in some instances, if not always, by the Emperor himself. Each of these two classes was subdivided into first, second, and third forms (*formae*). There seems to have been a regular order of advancement among the *ministri*, from the third to the second, and from the second to the first form, depending upon the length of their service.

After the year 422 vacancies among the *statuti* of the first form were filled by promotion alternately from the first or second form of the supernumeraries and the second or third form of the *statuti*. The third form of the supernumeraries was thus the lowest of all. A supernumerary, of whatever form, if transferred to the *statuti* for any reason other than to fill a vacancy in the first form was ranked as last, that is, as youngest in the service, of the third form.[12] Why such disabilities should be placed upon a man transferred from even the highest rank of the supernumeraries does not appear. It may be that there were so many supernumeraries that the chance of being chosen for promotion from the first form of that class to the first form of the *statuti* was very small, and that the smaller number of *statuti* of the second form, from which appointments to the first form were made, rendered pro-

[1] Lampridius, *Alexander Severus*, 41: *fullones et vestitores et pistores et pincernae, omnes castrenses ministri.* Salmasius inserted *et* before *omnes.*

[2] *C.I.L.*, VI, 6246–9; 8750–5.

[3] *C.I.L.*, VI, 4010–2.

[4] *C.I.L.*, VI, 7281; 8745–6; cf. Ulpian, *Dig.*, XXXIII, 7, 12, 9.

[5] *C.I.L.*, VI, 5353; 6619; 8945–6; cf. Sen., *Epist. Mor.*, 47, 8.

[6] *C.I.L.*, VI, 8795; 9045–8.

[7] *C.I.L.*, VI, 4351; 5200; 5351; 5751; 5858; 5873; Seneca, *Epist. Mor.*, 95, 24; Corippus, *In Laudem Justini*, 2, 86.

[8] *C.I.L.*, VI, 1884; 8815–7; 8866.

[9] *C.I.L.*, VI, 602; 1956; 5355; 9003–5.

[10] *C.I.L.*, III, 536; VI, 1884; 9083; XI, 3612.

[11] *C.I.L.*, VI, 5187; 5196; 8643–5; 8666; 8818.

[12] *Codex Theodosianus*, VI, 32, 2.

motion by that route more rapid, in consequence of which it might be a real advance to pass from the first form of the supernumeraries to the last of the *statuti*.

c. The Caretakers of the Palace (*curae palatii*)

The caretakers of the palace were known by the odd title *curae palatii*, for which Mommsen was unable to find a parallel.[1] The duties of these officials seem to have been concerned with the material condition of the palace and, possibly, of its furnishings.[2] Such duties can most easily and abundantly be exemplified from the time of the Principate. Of those years there is mention of the custodian of the furniture (*a supellectile*) of the several imperial residences,[3] the *atriensis*, who had charge of the valuable articles displayed in the *atrium*,[4] and who was assisted by a custodian of the paintings (*a tabulis*),[5] a custodian of the picture galleries (*a pinacothecis*),[6] a custodian of the ancestral masks (*ad imagines*),[7] and a custodian of the statues (*a statuis*).[8]

There was also the custodian of the valuables (*procurator thesaurorum*),[9] who had the care of the valuable plate, jewels, and other imperial treasures. His supervision was exercised through the two departments, *ab auro*[10] and *ab argento*. In the former served the custodian of the golden eating vessels (*praepositus auri escari*),[11] the custodian of the golden goblets (*praepositus auri potori*),[12] and the custodian of the jewelled gold (*praepositus auro gemmato*).[13] In the department *ab argento* were to be found the custodian of the silver goblets (*praepositus argenti potori*),[14] and the custodian of the stage (?) silver (*ab argento scaenico*).[15] The department *a Corinthis* was charged with the care of the costly Corinthian bronzes,[16] and the department *ab ornamentis* cared for the wealth of jewels which belonged to the crown.[17]

Bury's recent statement that the *decani* were subordinates of the

[1] *Ostgothische Studien*, *Neues Archiv*, vol. XIV, p. 513, n. 1: *Verwendung des Wortes in gliecher Bedeutung kann ich sonst nicht nachweisen.*

[2] Cf. Cassiodorus, *Variae*, 7, 5.

[3] *C.I.L.*, VI, 8525: *a supellectile castrensis; C.I.L.*, VI, 8654: . . . *de domu Tiberiana; C.I.L.*, VI, 3719: . . . *domus auriae;* cf. also *C.I.L.*, VI, 4035–6; 4357; 5358 b; 8973; 9049.

[4] *C.I.L.*, VI, 3942; 6040; 8639 b; 8738–40; X, 713. Cf. Phaedrus, *Fabulae*, II, 5, 11–13: *ex alticinctis unus atriensibus cui tunica ab umeris linteo Pelusio erat destricta, cirris dependentibus.*

[5] *C.I.L.*, VI, 3970.

[6] *C.I.L.*, VI, 10234.

[7] *C.I.L.*, VI, 3972.

[8] *C.I.L.*, VI, 4032.

[9] *C.I.L.*, VI, 8498.

[10] *C.I.L.*, VI, 8737.

[11] *C.I.L.*, VI, 8732.

[12] *C.I.L.*, VI, 8733; 8969.

[13] *C.I.L.*, VI, 8734–5.

[14] *C.I.L.*, VI, 8729.

[15] *C.I.L.*, VI, 8731.

[16] *C.I.L.*, VI, 5847; X, 692; cf. Pliny, *N. H.*, 34, 6–8.

[17] *C.I.L.*, VI, 3991–2.

Steward of the Household[1] is apparently based solely on Böcking's conjectures,[2] and cannot be sustained. It seems certain that they served under the Master of the the Offices.[3]

d. The Staff of the Steward of the Household

As for the staff (*officium*) of the Steward of the Household, the accountants (*tabularii*) of the Emperor and Empress and their significance in the consideration of the palace organization have already been mentioned.[4] The secretary (*chartularius*) and his staff (*scrinium*) were intrusted with the records and rolls of the palace service. A law of 416 contains evidence that at that time the length of service in any given capacity in the staff of the Steward was limited to two years. This law is an apparent attempt to correct abuses of a similar regulation of earlier date, for it specifically states that the incumbents must vacate their offices at the expiration of their two-year term, and that the vacancies thus caused must be filled by advancing from the lower ranks of the same *officium* those whose previous service had shown them worthy.[5]

e. The Privileges of the Steward's Subordinates

Several privileges were granted to all the *castrensiani*, as those were called who served under the Steward of the Household. By a law of rather uncertain date it was provided that, when a *castrensianus* died intestate and without heirs (*nec superstites dereliquerit successores*), his property should go to his fellow-servants.[6] In the first half of the fourth century the subordinates of the Steward were granted exemption from the excessive financial burdens which were imposed upon the leading citizens of the municipalities.

This privilege was highly valued and many men sought admission to the corps for the sole purpose of obtaining this exemption. Such an abuse demanded correction, and for this purpose it was provided by a law of 346 that an investigation be made, and such members of the palace corps as were found to have curial obligations be returned to their civic duties.[7] In 352 it was enacted that none of the subordinates of the Steward of the Household nor their sons or grandsons should be held to curial or other similar obligations; that they should

[1] *Imperial Administration*, p. 98.
[2] *Notitia Dignitatum*, II, Part I, pp. 299 f.
[3] Cf. *Codex Theodosianus*, VI, 33, and Gothofredus *ad loc.* Also Seeck, in Pauly-Wissowa, *Real-Encyc.*, s.v.
[4] See pp. 207, 210.
[5] *Codex Justinianus*, XII, 25, 1.
[6] *Codex Theodosianus*, X, 14, 1; date, 315, or in the time of Constantius. Cf. Mommsen's note *ad loc.*
[7] *Codex Theodosianus*, XII, 1, 38.

not be called upon to assist in the collection of taxes or the recruiting and transportation of new soldiers.[1] In 409 (or 412) all subordinates of the Grand Chamberlain, including, probably, the *castrensiani*, were exempted from the necessity of furnishing recruits and horses.[2] Possibly the Steward of the Household became careless about enrolling in his service those who merely sought by this means to escape duties elsewhere, for in 390 a law was addressed to him, providing that no one be admitted to service in his corps without the recommendation of the Emperor.[3]

In addition to these general privileges, special privileges were granted to various of the Steward's subordinates. Mention may be made of a law of 353, providing that after fifteen years' service the pages and *ministeriales* should be held free from all curial obligations.[4] Some time before 474 the *ministeriales* (*sacro ministerio nostro deputati*) were placed under the sole jurisdiction of the Master of the Offices. A law of that date reaffirmed this provision, and assured the *ministeriales*, their mothers, wives, husbands and sons of special consideration if summoned into court, and placed restraints upon those who wished to prefer charges against them on trivial grounds.[5]

This law was originally followed by a "brief" (*brevis*) containing the names of the various staffs of the *ministeriales*,[6] but this has unfortunately disappeared. That this list was appended to the law at the end may be taken to indicate that it was of considerable length, so that it could not be incorporated in the body of the law.

The *cura palatii* was exempted from the necessity of furnishing recruits or horses by a law of 409 (or 412).[7] In addition to those further privileges and honors which he enjoyed in common with other dependents of the Steward of the Household, as set forth above, he was ranked with the ex-Counts of the Dioceses of Egypt and Pontica upon the completion of his term of service, provided that he had previously been made a Count of the First Rank. If he had not been so honored while in service, he was ranked among the ex-Dukes of the Provinces. These honors were bestowed upon him in 413. For many years previous to that date (*antiquitus*) he had been privileged to attend imperial banquets, and to adore the Emperor.[8]

[1] *Op. cit.*, VI, 35, 3; for the date, cf. Mommsen's note *ad loc.*

[2] *Op. cit.*, XI, 18, 1.

[3] *Codex Theodosianus*, VI, 30, 12.

[4] *Op. cit.*, VIII, 7, 5.

[5] *Codex Justinianus*, XII, 25, 4.

[6] *Codex Justinianus*, XII, 25, 4: *sacro ministerio nostro deputatos, quorum officia singillatim brevis subter adnexus continet.*

[7] *Codex Theodosianus*, XI, 18, 1.

[8] *Codex Theodosianus*, VI, 13, 1.

3. *The Count of the Crown Lands* (*Comes domorum per Cappadociam*)

The Count of the Crown Lands supervised certain estates in Cappadocia, known as the Crown Lands in Cappadocia (*domus divina per Cappadociam*).[1] These estates came into existence either through the confiscation of the lands of pagan temples by Constantine and his sons,[2] or as the crown lands of conquered kings,[3] and consisted of vast holdings in various parts of the province, comprising possibly as much as one half of the total acreage.[4] These estates may at first have been a part of the *res privata*, but they seem to have been definitely set apart from it a number of years prior to 379, for previous to that year two different organizations of the Count's *officium* had been tried and found unsatisfactory.[5]

The revenues from the estates in Cappadocia almost certainly belonged to the Privy Purse in 379, for in that year it was enacted that the Count of the Privy Purse should send a man from among his subordinates to serve as head of the *officium* of the Count of the Crown Lands, so that the latter, through fear of his superior, might be made to refrain from abuses.[6] By the year 414, however, the Crown Lands in Cappadocia were definitely under the direction of the Grand Chamberlain,[7] and the revenue from these domains flowed thereafter into his treasury. An attempt has been made above to divine the reason for the transfer of the Crown Lands to the Grand Chamberlain.[8]

As early as 442 the Count of the Crown Lands had jurisdiction over the slaves, renters of land (*coloni*) and of houses (*inquilini*), within the borders of the domains.[9] His decisions seem to have been subject to review by the Grand Chamberlain.[10] Probably the court of the Count of the Crown Lands was not of great importance, for in 536 it is stated that few cases were heard there, and that appeals from it were very rare.[11]

1 In the sixth century known also as *tamiaca praedia*, *ἡ ταμειακὴ κτῆσις* or *τὰ ταμειακὰ χωρία*, even officially. Cf. *Novellae Justiniani*, XXX, *passim*.

2 Seeck, in Pauly-Wissowa, *Real-Encyc.*, vol. IV, 652, s.v. *comites;* His, *Domänen der römische Kaiserzeit*, pp. 36 ff.

3 Pelham, *Imperial Domains and the Colonate, Essays on Roman History*, p. 278; His, *op. cit.*, p. 29.

4 Pelham, *loc. cit.*, note 3.

5 *Codex Theodosianus*, VI, 30, 2: *Prisco iam ordine revocato de palatino potius officio ad gerendum principatum officii comitis domorum per Cappadociam mittantur, quales comes etiam domorum, si secus se gesserit, vereatur. Idoneos itaque singulis annis e numero mittendariorum ad hoc eligere debebis et mittere.*

6 *Ibid.*

7 *Codex Theodosianus*, XI, 28, 9, *subscript;* quoted above, p. 185, n. 6.

8 See pp. 187 f.

9 *Codex Justinianus*, III, 26, 11.

10 See pp. 199 f.

11 *Novellae Justiniani*, XX, 2: *ἀλλ' οὖν οὔτε πρότερον πολλαί τινες ἐκινοῦντο δίκαι παρ' αὐτῷ οὔτε ἐκ τοῦ δικαστηρίου τοῦ κατ' αὐτὸν ἐφέρετό τις σχεδὸν ἔφεσις ἐνταῦθα.*

It has been indicated that the Count of the Crown Lands was assisted by a staff in 379, when he was a subordinate of the Count of the Privy Purse. There can be no doubt that the same was true after he was made subject to the orders of the Grand Chamberlain. His duties in connection with the administration of the Crown Lands must have demanded the assistance of a comparatively large corps, but there is scant information regarding it. There is reference to these assistants in one of Justinian's Novels, and specifically to certain *summarii*, who may be supposed to have existed before the time of Justinian.[1] The codicils (*probatoriae*) of those employed in the staff of the Count of the Crown Lands were prepared by the *scrinium sacrarum epistularum*.[2]

Nothing is known regarding the honors which were granted to the Count of the Crown Lands, nor is it clear what privileges he enjoyed. None of those granted to the chamberlains prior to 414, the date when he is first found as a member of the *cubiculum*, can be assumed to have pertained to him, though it is not improbable that when he became a subordinate of the Grand Chamberlain these privileges were conferred on him. He was specifically excluded from the benefits of the law of 428 which excused from the burdens of the post and courier service other chamberlains who had retired before completing their terms of office.[3]

4. *The Count of the Imperial Wardrobe* (*Comes sacrae vestis*)

The Count of the Imperial Wardrobe is mentioned but once in the codes.[4] He was a subordinate of the Grand Chamberlain, as is indicated by the fact that his name appears among those of officials known to be dependent on him. Grossi-Gondi cannot be right in saying that the Count of the Imperial Wardrobe ranked above the Counts of the Sacred Largesses and the Privy Purse.[5] His statement is based on the fact that the former is mentioned before the latter officials in the one law in which his title is to be found; but in that law the general principle that officials be mentioned in the order of their precedence most certainly has been violated.[6]

[1] XXX, 1, 1.

[2] *Codex Justinianus*, XII, 59, 10, 4.

[3] *Codex Justinianus*, XII, 5, 2. See pp. 206 f.

[4] *Codex Theodosianus*, XI, 18, 1; quoted, p. 203.

[5] Cf. De Ruggiero, *Dizionario Epigrafico*, vol. II, Part I, p. 487, s.v., *comes*. The Protovestiarius of the eleventh century and later did hold a very exalted position. See p. 231.

[6] See p. 263, n. 3.

There is very little known about the Count of the Imperial Wardrobe at any period, but this is particularly true of the first two centuries of the reorganized Empire. There is almost no guidance here save the title of the official and the knowledge that one of the features of the court of the Orient was the great attention paid to the matter of official robes and vestments. At the end of the fifth century, however, there is mention of certain *vestitores* (βεστήτορες),[1] and *vestisacrani* (βεστοσακράνοι),[2] who were doubtless subordinates of the Count of the Imperial Wardrobe. To them was intrusted the care of the imperial robes and ceremonial regalia, and perhaps their manufacture.

It is not improbable that there was a treasury of some importance connected with the Imperial Wardrobe, for gifts brought to the Emperor by envoys were despatched to this bureau in order that their value might be determined.[3] Perhaps it may be inferred from this custom that the gifts which envoys brought were customarily rich articles of wearing apparel. *Vestitores* held a cross at the side of the Emperor Leo I, at a certain point in the inaugural ceremony.[4] The *vestisacrani* seem to have assisted in the preparation of the body of the Emperor Zeno for burial.[5]

There was a Chartulary in the staff of the Count of the Imperial Wardrobe, whose duties were probably connected with the records of the corps. He prepared applications (*petitoria*) for those seeking admission to the corps, and when these were countersigned by the Emperor the applicant was admitted to the service.[6]

The members of the corps of the Imperial Wardrobe (*schola vestis sacrae*), their mothers and wives were placed under the jurisdiction of the Master of the Offices by Leo and Anthemius.[7]

An interesting account is preserved of the part played by the attendants of the Imperial Wardrobe in the inauguration of the Emperor Justin I. The fact that they are spoken of merely as chamberlains in this passage does not conceal their identity. The officials of the palace had nominated Justinian as the successor to the throne left vacant by the death of Anastasius, and, pounding on the ivory doors of the private apartments, demanded of the chamberlains the imperial robes and insignia. The chamberlains refused to comply. At last,

[1] Petr. Patr. (Const. Porph.), *De Caer.*, 414, 7.
[2] *Op. cit.*, 407, 10; 422, 9.
[3] *Op. cit.*, 407, 7 ff.
[4] *Op. cit.*, 414, 5 ff.
[5] *Op. cit.*, 422, 8 ff.
[6] *Op. cit.*, 390, 15 ff.
[7] *Codex Justinianus*, XII, 25, 3.

however, when all factions had unanimously agreed upon Justin, they at once produced the desired regalia.[1]

In the one constitution in which the Count of the Imperial Wardrobe is specifically mentioned it is stated that he should not be compelled to furnish recruits and horses.[2] It is probable that he enjoyed freedom also from *munera sordida* and *hospitium*, and the burdens of the post and courier service, as did other subordinates of the Grand Chamberlain.[3]

5. *The Decurions and Silentiaries* (*Decuriones, silentiarii*)

That the Silentiaries were subordinates of the Grand Chamberlain is shown by two laws, one dating from the beginning of the fifth century, and the other from its close, both of which deal with the Silentiaries and are addressed to the Grand Chamberlain.[4] Another law of the middle of the fourth century makes mention of the Silentiaries and their officers, the Decurions, in close connection with the pages and *ministeriales*.[5] This would appear to indicate that the two groups of officials were associated in service in some manner or other. As the pages and *ministeriales* undoubtedly belonged to the Grand Chamberlain's organization at the time when this law was written, the same was probably true of the Silentiaries. There is, however, no definite information regarding their place in this organization. They did not belong to the corps of the Steward of the Household, at least in the earlier part of the fifth century, for they are not mentioned as his subordinates in the *Notitia Dignitatum*. They must, therefore, have been dependent, in the persons of the Decurions, directly upon the Grand Chamberlain, or they were under the direction of the Superintendent of the Chamberlains.[6]

As it was a part of the duty of the Silentiaries to maintain order and silence at the meetings of the Consistory, and their part in the court ceremonial, of later days at least, was not inconspicuous, it seems better to suppose that they were not connected with the limited service of the bedchamber, but were directly dependent on the Grand Chamberlain, the varied character of whose duties would find expression in the varied service of his own corps of subordinates.

[1] Petr. Patr. (Const. Porph.), *De Caer.*, 428, 7 ff.

[2] *Codex Theodosianus*, XI, 18, 1.

[3] See p. 206; *Codex Theodosianus*, XI, 16, 15.

[4] *Codex Theodosianus*, VI, 2, 26; date, 428; *Codex Justinianus*, V, 62, 25; date, 499.

[5] *Codex Theodosianus*, VIII, 7, 5: . . . *ii dumtaxat qui ministeriales et paedagogiani et silentiarii et decuriones exsistunt*, etc.; date, 354.

[6] Cf. Böcking, *Notitia Dignitatum*, II, Part I, p. 299.

Originally the Silentiaries seem to have numbered thirty, in the charge of three Decurions, but supernumeraries were later attached to the corps, for in the time of Theodosius II certain privileges were limited to this number as constituting the whole corps of earlier times.[1] It is hardly to be supposed that any distinction was made between the regular members of the corps of Silentiaries by this law, but that those who were excluded from its benefits were, as stated, supernumeraries.

The duty of the Silentiaries seems to have been to guard the person of the Emperor,[2] and to maintain silence and order about the imperial apartments and the Consistory.[3] So characteristic was this silence that the meetings of the Consistory were described as 'Silences' (*silentia*).[4] The Silentiaries were often intrusted with special missions to the provinces.[5]

In 499 the Silentiaries enjoyed the honorary designation of *viri clarissimi*,[6] and within the next thirty years they were advanced to the rank of the *spectabiles*.[7]

Numerous privileges were granted to the Decurions and Silentiaries. They were freed from all curial obligations at the end of fifteen years' service, by Constantius.[8] In 409 (or 412) the Decurions were exempted from the obligation of furnishing recruits,[9] and in 415 Honorius and Theodosius provided that after completing their term of service the Decurions should be ranked among the ex-Dukes, and should enjoy equal honors with them; that they be enrolled in the Senate, and be freed from the senatorial distributions and from the payment of taxes upon land (*descriptio glebalis*).[10]

In 423 the ex-Decurions and ex-Silentiaries, whether they had retired from active service or had entered the service of some more ele-

[1] *Codex Theodosianus*, VI, 23, 4: . . . *ut triginta* (*sc. silentiarii*) *tantummodo numero haec privilegia consequantur, decuriones quoque tres, quos numquam plures fieri inveterata consuetudo permisit.*

[2] *Codex Theodosianus*, VI, 23, 4: . . . *cum* . . . *exculpatas excubias peregerint*, etc.; *Codex Justinianus*, V, 62, 25: . . . *circa latus nostrum militantes.*

[3] Procopius, *De Bello Persico*, 243, 11 ff.: Ἀδόλιον . . . βασιλεῖ μὲν ἀεὶ ἐν παλατίῳ τὰ ἐς τὴν ἡσυχίαν ὑπηρετοῦντα (σιλεντιαρίους Ῥωμαῖοι καλοῦσιν οἷς ἡ τιμὴ αὕτη ἐπίκειται), κτλ. Agathias, *Historiae*, 297, 1 ff.: Παύλῳ . . . ὃς δὴ ταπρῶτα τελῶν ἐν τοῖς ἀμφὶ τὸν βασιλέα σιγῆς ἐπιστάταις, κτλ. Lydus, *De Mensibus*, 11, 23 ff.: σιγῆς δὲ τοῖς πολλοῖς βουλευομένοις δεῖ· διὰ τοῦτο ἐκ τῆς περὶ τὴν σιγὴν σπουδῆς (σιλέντιον δ' αὐτὴν πατρίως καλοῦσιν) σιλεντιαρίους ἔκριναν ὀνομάζειν αὐτούς.

[4] *Novellae Justiniani*, LXII, 1, 2.

[5] Athanasius, *Apologia*, 2; Amm. Marc., 20, 4; Symmachus, *Epist.*, 24.

[6] *Codex Justinianus*, V, 62, 25.

[7] *Op. cit.*, III, 28, 30, sec. 3; date, 528.

[8] *Codex Theodosianus*, VIII, 7, 5; date, 353 or 354.

[9] *Op. cit.*, XI, 18, 1.

[10] *Op. cit.*, VI, 23, 1.

vated corps, were granted immunity from the demand for recruits and horses, and from certain other burdens to which officials were generally subject.[1] To these privileges were added, in 432, freedom from payment for the maintenance of the post and courier service, from *munera sordida*, and the like.[2] Five years later these privileges were confirmed and slightly extended, and exemption from the obligation of *hospitium* was added, with the restriction that all these privileges should apply to but thirty Silentiaries and three Decurions, and should be acquired only after thirteen years' service.[3]

During the last quarter of the fifth century the Emperor Zeno granted to the Silentiaries and their wives the privilege of being tried only in the court of the Master of the Offices.[4] At the close of the century Anastasius authorized a constitution which provided that any wealth which came into the hands of a Silentiary through the opportunities which his position offered be regarded as *peculium castrense*, that is, as freed from the control of the *pater familias*. The Silentiaries were also excused from acting as guardians or trustees, and their children from filling the office of praetor.[5]

It has already been shown that the Empress had a well-organized chamberlain service of her own. In this organization were to be found four Silentiaries, who were men of good report and had been chosen by the Empress from among the Silentiaries of the Emperor.[6] This was certainly true in the time of Justinian, and there can be little doubt that the same custom prevailed in earlier days.

The ceremony of the investiture of a Silentiary is preserved in the writings of Peter the Patrician. The candidate, clad in the *tunica atrabatica*, was introduced into the presence of the Emperor by the Grand Chamberlain. Here he received from the hands of the Emperor the golden staff which was the symbol of his office.[7]

Pancirolus in his commentary on the *Notitia Dignitatum* pointed out that the office of Silentiary was bought and sold,[8] a fact which seems to be clearly indicated in the law of Anastasius concerning the members of this corps.[9] A direct reference to this sale of the office

[1] *Op. cit.*, VI, 23, 2.

[2] *Op. cit.*, VI, 23, 3.

[3] *Op. cit.*, VI, 23, 4. This law and that cited in the preceding note have been combined in *Codex Justinianus*, XII, 16, 3, under the date 432.

[4] *Codex Justinianus*, XII, 16, 4.

[5] *Codex Justinianus*, XII, 16, 5; date, 497–499, probably 498. Cf. V, 62, 25.

[6] Petr. Patr. (Const. Porph.), *De Caer.*, 389, 18 ff.

[7] *Op. cit.*, 389, 1 ff.

[8] *Fol.* 40, *verso*.

[9] *Codex Justinianus*, XII, 16, 5: . . . *nec ipsam militiam vel suffragium, quodcumque pro ea vel ab isdem viris devotis silentiariis vel a parentibus eorum . . . datum est.*

is to be found in the chapters by Peter the Patrician to whom reference has been made. The details of the transaction are, however, not clear.[1]

6. *The Private Imperial Treasurer* (*Sacellarius*)

It is not at all improbable that there was a special treasurer under the direction of the Grand Chamberlain. Bury says: "Now the Emperors, manifestly, must always have had a private purse (apart from the treasuries of the *res privata* and *sacrae largitiones*), and an official in charge of it. Such an official, if he were mentioned in the *Notitia Dignitatum* at all, would have appeared in the officium of the Praepositus — where there is an unfortunate lacuna in our texts."[2] There is absolutely no evidence for such an official, and only the reasonableness of Bury's statement can be offered as justification for including this mention of a hypothetical subordinate.

It will be understood that there is no support for the title Sacellarius (σακελλάριος) in this period, but such an official was prominent in the Byzantine organization, and Bury identifies him as early as the time of Justinian.[3] As the word Sacellarius is indubitably Latin in origin, it is not unlikely that the title was in use at a still earlier date.

V. The Grand Chamberlain at the Ostrogothic Court

It is evident from the writings of Cassiodorus and others that the organization of the Ostrogothic court of Theodoric was very similar to that of the Western Roman Emperors to whose power he succeeded. There is record of an intriguing Grand Chamberlain, Triwanis, described as *praepositus cubiculi*, in the year 519,[4] and in 541 a certain Seda, eunuch and chamberlain of King Theodoric, was buried. That he was a man of some prominence is probable, for he is described as a *vir spectabilis* (?).[5] He also may have been a Grand Chamberlain, though this is doubtful.

During this period, as in the time of the Principate, there were Grand Chamberlains, or officials with similar duties, at the Persian court. Specific mention is made of one Usthazanes.[6]

1 Petr. Patr. (Const. Porph.), *De Caer.*, 389, 11 ff.: ἔξωθεν δὲ ποιοῦσιν προσσυμβόλαια πρὸς ἀλλήλους μετὰ τοῦ πιπράσκοντος ὁ ἀγοράζων.

2 *The Imperial Administrative System in the Ninth Century*, pp. 80 f.

3 *Op. cit.*, p. 85.

4 Anonymus Valesianus, 82. Cf. also 76.

5 *C.I.L.*, XI, 310: *Hic requiescit in pace vir spectabilis* (VIR SBL) *Seda ignucus et cubicularius regis Theodorici*, etc.

6 Sozomen, *Hist. Eccl.*, 2, 9: Οὐσθαζάνης πρεσβύτης εὐνοῦχος, τροφεὺς Σαβώρου, καὶ μείζων τῆς βασιλέως οἰκίας, κτλ.

CHAPTER III

FROM JUSTINIAN TO NICEPHORUS BRYENNIUS

I. The Development of the Byzantine Court

The long reign of Justinian saw both the culmination of the system of administration which had been inaugurated by Diocletian and Constantine and the beginning of a series of changes which at length resulted in the substitution of the Byzantine for the Late Roman type of organization. It has already been stated that one of the most marked characteristics of the organization of Diocletian and Constantine was the successive subordination of government officials, one to another, in a rather extensive system of grades, with the whole administrative machinery finally dependent upon a small circle of ministers of state, who were responsible solely to the Emperor.

In the sixth century this strict subordination began to give way to a more loosely knit organization, in which many of the previously dependent officials were placed on an equal footing with their former superiors. Provincial governors became directly responsible to the Emperor, and the offices of Vicar and Pretorian Prefect were abolished. The military was united with the civil administration, and the Masters of the Soldiers disappeared. The old ministries of the Master of the Offices, the Count of the Sacred Largesses and the Count of the Privy Purse, whose competences had embraced a variety of distinct departments, were broken up and assigned to several independent officials. Thus the small circle of ministers of state which had existed under the system of Diocletian and Constantine was widely expanded by the substitution of the principle of coördination for that of subordination.

Besides the Emperor, the Pretorian Prefect, the Masters of the Soldiers, the Grand Chamberlain, the Master of the Offices, and the Counts of the Sacred Largesses and the Privy Purse had been the most imposing figures at the court during the fourth and fifth centuries, and had contributed greatly to that impressive splendor and ceremony which had evoked the admiration and awe of barbarian and Byzantine alike. It would be natural, therefore, to suppose that the disappearance of some of these ministers and the diminution of the powers of the others would somewhat dim the glory of this imperial Olympus, but such was not the case. Pomp and ceremony had become a tradition so deeply rooted in the life of the court as to be self-perpetuating, and not dependent, as at first, upon the presence and participation of the mighty.

For some time after the reörganization by Diocletian, office and honor had gone hand in hand, but before long it became customary for the Emperor to confer honorary positions upon those to whose merits he wished to give recognition. Thus, in addition to the earlier honorary offices of Count and Patrician, there were honorary Consuls besides the active Consuls, honorary Prefects besides the active Prefects, and honorary Masters of the Soldiers besides the active officials of the same name. Gradually this practice was extended to almost all of the offices in the hierarchy, and as honorary officials came to outnumber those in actual service, the title by which both were known began to indicate courtly rank rather than official position.

The predominating importance in the Byzantine court of ceremony over actual duties of administration seems to be indicated by the fact that, though the influence of the old offices declined and their administrative significance, in some cases, entirely disappeared, still, in the ceremony of the court, the old titles remained, possessed of much the same honor which had attached to them in early days, and only to a limited extent were new grades of honor introduced to correspond to new offices. Thus the hierarchy of office had become a hierarchy of rank, and the life of the court, which had formerly depended largely upon the presence of important administrative officials, was now dependent almost entirely upon the activities of a host of ceremonial functionaries of little significance in the administration of the Empire.

Their most important duties were to wear the various kinds of tunics and shoes which were deemed proper on specific state occasions, to march in long lines before or behind the Emperor when duty called him from the seclusion of his private apartments, or to stand silently in solemn ranks about the audience chamber while some petitioner for imperial favor made humble obeisance before the august ruler of the Eastern world.

Justinian gave impulse to this increased emphasis upon ceremony by reasserting the divine right of rulers, by multiplying titles of honor, and by rebuilding in marvellous splendor the imperial quarter of Constantinople. The conflagration which occurred during the riot of 532 made necessary much rebuilding, and the Emperor spared no expense or endeavor in his desire to make his capital the most gorgeous and the most magnificent which the world had seen.

Upon this stage the Grand Chamberlain still continued to play an important rôle. His administrative competence was considerably diminished during the first century of the period, but ceremonially his prominence was increased. More important, however, is the fact that in the time of Justinian and until far into the Byzantine period he continued to exercise the same influence and to enjoy the same prestige, as a result of his close association with the Emperor, that had been characteristic of his position in the preceding centuries.

II. Modifications in the Office of the Grand Chamberlain

It seems almost impossible to trace the steps in the history of the Grand Chamberlain's office in the period which is about to be considered. There is a disappointing paucity of legal constitutions after the time of Justinian, and the gloom which settled over Europe in the seventh and eighth centuries has obliterated the memory of many events, not only of those but also of preceding years. It is characteristic of the period that much of our information concerning it has been preserved through the interest of antiquaries and writers on court etiquette; and sources of such unusual character, although supplying much descriptive detail, are peculiarly unsatisfactory on the side of historical information.

In the case of the Grand Chamberlain, data of a historical nature concerning the period following Justinian are exceptionally scanty. Dates are almost entirely wanting, and while some of the changes in his office can be dated within half a century, there are others of which it can only be said that they occurred between the fifth and the tenth centuries. Since a satisfactory historical account of the Grand Chamberlain's office during this period is so manifestly impossible, only a brief summary of the changes which it suffered will be presented.

At the beginning of Justinian's reign the Grand Chamberlain was an important official in the imperial court. He had very extensive control of the palace organization, with a large number of subordinate officials under his direction, was invested with the important financial and administrative duties relative to the Crown Lands, and probably sat in the Emperor's Council or Consistory. Furthermore, his close relations to the Emperor made it possible for him to exercise an unusual influence, which was felt in all branches of the administration and which extended far beyond the palace walls.

In the course of the sixth and seventh centuries many of the Grand Chamberlain's administrative duties were transferred to other officials, or those who were immediately responsible for them were made independent of his control. The administration of the Crown Lands and of the revenues derived from them passed to other hands during the reign of Justinian, the Silentiaries seem to have become subordinates of the Master of the Offices not much later, the Imperial Wardrobe was transferred to an independent official, and the multifarious duties which had been under the supervision of the Steward of the Household were distributed among several new officials, none of whom was under the direction of the Grand Chamberlain. Even the corps of eunuchs who served in the imperial sleeping apartments was given an independent organization, and by the close of the ninth century all that was left to the Grand Chamberlain of the important administrative competence of the fifth century was the supervision of the corps of chamberlains which attended the Emperor in the less private portions of the palace.

Meanwhile another change was taking place. The important ministry of the Master of the Offices was gradually weakened in a manner very similar to that by which the competence of the Grand Chamberlain was reduced. The ceremonial duties which he had performed in the sixth century had passed almost entirely from his control by the end of the ninth century, and no small portion of them had fallen to the Grand Chamberlain's lot. Moreover, the attention to court formalities had increased, and in the numerous descriptions of the ceremonies of the ninth and tenth centuries the Grand Chamberlain is easily the most prominent figure.

This prominence was given a very concrete expression on the occasions when the Emperor was absent from the capital, for at such times the Grand Chamberlain acted as vice-regent, and presided at all the functions of the court. On other occasions he frequently acted as the representative of the Emperor, who held himself aloof from his subjects and often addressed them, when need arose, through the mouth of his *praepositus*.

The culmination of the Grand Chamberlain's influence seems to have been reached during the first half of the tenth century. Prior to that time the history of the office was one of growing prestige, marked by advancement in rank and preferment in ceremonial activities, and by the incumbency of such powerful men as John, Bahanes, and Joseph Bringas, who were conspicuous during the reigns of Michael III, Basil I, and Constantine VII, respectively; but shortly afterward that prestige was on the wane, and the office of Grand Chamberlain soon suffered eclipse by the growing importance of the Parakoimomenos, or Chief Eunuch of the Bedchamber. The same Grand Chamberlain, Joseph Bringas, who must have been the proud leader of many of the court ceremonies described by Constantine Porphyrogenitus, was promoted (for his change of title cannot be considered in any other light) from his former office to that of Chief Eunuch of the Bedchamber by Romanus II,[1] the son and successor of Constantine.

While the Grand Chamberlain may still have occupied a conspicuous place in the palace ceremonies, in the period after Romanus II, his name appears with much less frequency in the chronicles of significant events, and finally, in the middle of the eleventh century, gives place entirely to the titles of the Chief Eunuch of the Bedchamber and the Protovestiarius or Chief of the Wardrobe.

The reason for this development is not hard to discover. The Grand Chamberlain's duties had originally kept him in the closest intimacy with the Emperor, and had helped him to acquire a very extensive control of affairs lying far outside the limits of his original competence. His activities as an official of the court were indeed more conspicuous than the personal service rendered the Emperor. When his competence was felt to be too extensive to be in harmony with the spirit of the Byzantine organization, the less important portion of his duties was assigned to a newly created official, the Chief Eunuch. But it was precisely the apparently minor duties of personal attendance upon the Emperor which had made possible the development of the Grand Chamberlain's power, and which would henceforth, inevitably, exalt the position of the Chief Eunuch.

The eventual disappearance of the Grand Chamberlain's office was a natural consequence. Its incumbent had became no more than a figurehead, the nominal director of the Chamberlains of the Cubiculum, whose actual control was left almost entirely to the Superintendent of the Chamberlains. As the Grand Chamberlain's administrative control of the Chamberlains passed ever more completely into the hands

[1] Theophanes Continuatus, 469, 17 ff.

of their Superintendent, and as his personal influence with the Emperor declined, the vacuity of his office became continually more apparent. At length the office was discontinued, probably by the failure to appoint successors to those who died during their incumbency, and the discontinuance seems to have caused little remark; there is, at least, no record of it. The last Grand Chamberlain of whom mention is made was Constantinus, who held this position under Michael IV, the Paphlagonian (1034–1042).[1]

It seems impossible to determine with precision the date of the disappearance of the Grand Chamberlain's office. It is known, however, that innovations in the matter of official honors were made by the Emperors of the latter half of the eleventh century. Thus, at the time of his accession, Constantine X, Ducas (1059–1067), is said to have created new honors[2] and to have bestowed official distinctions upon many persons. Nicephorus III, Botaniates (1078–1081), also was lavish in the bestowal of honors,[3] and may well have created new titles, but there is no explicit statement to this effect. Of Alexius I, Comnenus (1081–1118), it is said that he created new honors and modified some already in use.[4] By the end of the reign of Alexius the catalogue of official dignities had been extensively modified, and it is reasonable to assume that the office of Grand Chamberlain was abolished before the close of the eleventh century.

The new honors established by Constantine X are not named, nor is there any suggestion of the discontinuance of the Grand Chamberlain's office during his reign, or any definite indication that the newly created honors in any way encroached upon the province of the Grand Chamberlain. Nevertheless, the possibility that they did so cannot be denied.

It is indeed possible that to Constantine should be attributed the invention of the new title, Great Domestic (ὁ μέγας δομέστικος), which appears once[5] in connection with an incident in the reign of his successor, Michael VII, Ducas (1067–1078). While the use of the new title in this case may be anticipatory, it seems clear that not later than the beginning of the reign of Nicephorus Botaniates the official title of the Domestic contained the adjective μέγας, for Alexius Comnenus, who was at that time put in charge of the expeditions against Ni-

[1] Michael Attaliota, *Historia*, 33, 22. [2] Michael Attaliota, *op. cit.*, 71, 11 ff.

[3] *Op. cit.*, 275, 9 ff. Nicephorus Bryennius, *Commentarii*, 129, 5 ff.

[4] Anna Comnena, *Alexias*, vol. I, 148, 11 ff. (Read 147, 9 to 149, 9.); Codinus, *De Officiis Constantinopolis*, 7, 1 ff.; 16 ff.

[5] Nicephorus Bryennius, *Comment.*, 66, 21, *circa* 1072.

cephorus Bryennius, among a variety of other designations, is twice described by contemporary historians as Great Domestic.[1] The sudden frequency with which this new title is met in the accounts of the reign of Botaniates would leave little doubt that it had been devised by him, were it not for the single instance in which it appears before the time of his accession.

The information concerning the changes in titles made by Alexius I is a trifle more satisfactory. Such terms as σεβαστοκράτωρ[2] πανυπερσέβαστος,[3] πρωτοσέβαστος,[4] and στρατοπεδάρχης[5] appear for the first time in his reign, and there is also mention of the Great Primicerius (ὁ μέγας πριμικήριος).[6] The former titles were unquestionably devised by Alexius, but the latter was perhaps introduced by the same Emperor who originated the title of the Great Domestic and, possibly, the other titles also of which the adjective μέγας forms a part, several of which are mentioned by Codinus.[7]

The excessively laudatory titles seem to have been purely honorary distinctions, and to have imposed no duties. This was not true of either the Great Primicerius or the Great Domestic. The former, when first mentioned, seems to have been in active command of troops,[8] and he had certain duties in the field at a much later date.[9] The principal duties of the Great Domestic were likewise of a military nature.[10]

In the later days of the Byzantine Empire, however, these officials had special duties in the court ceremonial, and seem at that time to have performed many acts similar in nature to those of the Grand Chamberlain in the ceremonial of the tenth century. Thus, it was the duty of the Great Primicerius to present to the Emperor his sceptre.[11]

[1] Stages in the development of the new title from the former δομέστικος τῶν σχολῶν (ἄρχοντα τῶν τῆς δύσεως στρατευμάτων . . ., ὃν πάλαι δομέστικον τῶν σχολῶν ἐκάλουν, νυνὶ δὲ μέγαν καλοῦσι δομέστικον, Niceph. Bryen., *Comment.*, 19, 21 ff.) are suggested by the different designations the historians apply to this official, as δομέστικον τῶν σχολῶν τῆς δύσεως, Niceph. Bryen., 130, 8; δομέστικος τῆς δύσεως, Michael Attal., 250, 20; τοῦ μεγάλου δομεστίκου τῆς δύσεως, Anna Comnena, vol. I, 332, 20; μεγάλου δομεστίκου τῶν δυτικῶν τε καὶ ἀνατολικῶν στρατευμάτων, Anna Comn., vol. I, 335, 21; τὸν μέγαν δομέστικον, Niceph. Bryen., 66, 21; Scylitzes, 736, 11. The form ὁ μέγας δομέστικος was finally adopted, and persisted to the last days of the Empire. Cf. Codinus, *De Officialibus Constantinopolis*, 7, 15.

[2] Codinus, *De Off.*, 7, 1.

[3] *Op. cit.*, 7, 16.

[4] *Op. cit.*, 9, 10 (See commentary on this line by Gretzer and Goar, in the Bonn edition.); Anna Comn., vol. I, 148, 7.

[5] Codinus, *De Off.*, 12, 3; Anna Comn. vol. II, 139, 12.

[6] Anna Comn., vol. I, 199, 3, *anno* 1082.

[7] *De Off.*, chap. 2, pp. 9–12.

[8] Anna Comn., vol. I, 199, 3 ff.

[9] Codinus, *De Off.*, 33, 14 ff.

[10] Anna Comn., vol. I, 332, 20; vol. I, 335, 20; Michael Attal., 289, 1 ff.; Niceph. Bryen., 130, 8 ff.; Codinus, *De Off.*, 83, 6 ff.

[11] Codinus, *De Off.*, 33, 4 ff.; cf. 45, 13 ff.

Of the Great Domestic it is stated that it was his duty to attend the Emperor, and to serve him in any way which might be required,[1] a commission which in breadth is singularly like that of the Grand Chamberlain. More particularly, he seems to have carried the Emperor's sword on those occasions when he was present at court ceremonies;[2] he led the first rank of the nobles;[3] he stood next to the Emperor at table, and placed before him the viands which had been prepared and presented by the staff of the Domestic of the Table (ὁ τῆς τραπέζης δομέστικος).[4] On Christmas Day he took charge of the distribution of the Emperor's largesses,[5] and he himself received his portion directly from the Emperor's hand.[6]

Of all the new offices, the one which seems most like that of the former Grand Chamberlain is that of the Protovestiarius (ὁ πρωτοβεστιάριος). When Nicephorus III, Botaniates, at his accession, bestowed a multitude of honors upon his courtiers, it was the Protovestiarius who received the newly appointed officials and presented them to the people.[7] The Grand Chamberlain had once performed a similar task.[8] In later years the Protovestiarius also handed to the Emperor his crown,[9] as the Grand Chamberlain had done before,[10] and if he chanced to see a speck or a ζωΰφιον or anything of a similar nature on the Emperor's garment or headdress, he alone was privileged to remove it,[11] an honor which none could have enjoyed in an earlier day save the Grand Chamberlain.

In the closing days of the Empire, therefore, when the *De Officialibus* attributed to Codinus was written, many of the duties which the Grand Chamberlain had performed in the tenth century had been transferred to the Great Domestic, the Great Primicerius, and the Protovestiarius. It is not stated at what time these changes were made, but the office of the Great Domestic is known to have come into existence as early as the year 1078; that of the Great Primicerius, as has been intimated, may well have been originated at the same time, and by that year the Protovestiarius had replaced the Grand Chamberlain in certain characteristic ceremonies. It is, perhaps, permissible to suppose that the

[1] *Op. cit.*, 33, 1.

[2] *Op. cit.*, 29, f.; 44, 17, ff.; 44, 22 ff.

[3] *Op. cit.*, 57, 18.

[4] *Op. cit.*, 59, 18 ff.

[5] *Op. cit.*, 60, 15 ff.; 61, 3 ff.; 62, 2; 62, 6.

[6] *Op. cit.*, 62, 14 f.

[7] Michael Attal., 275, 15 ff.

[8] See pp. 252, 254.

[9] Codinus, *op. cit.*, 49, 20 ff.

[10] See pp. 201 f., 250.

[11] Codinus, *op. cit.*, 50, 3 ff.: Ἔχει δὲ καὶ τοῦτο ἴδιον καὶ ἐξαίρετον, ὅτι ἐάν τι ζωΰφιον ἴδῃ ἢ πηλὸν ἢ ἄλλο τι περὶ τὸ ῥοῦχον τοῦ βασιλέως, τὸ σκιάδιον ἐκβάλλων τὴν χεῖρα ἐκτείνας ἐπαίρει ἢ καθαίρει τοῦτο ἀνερωτήτως, μηδενὸς τῶν ἄλλων ἁπάντων ἀρχόντων ἄδειαν ἔχοντος τοῦτο ποιῆσαι, εἰ μὴ τούτου καὶ μόνου.

office of Grand Chamberlain, of which nothing is heard after the reign of Michael IV, the Paphlagonian (which ended in 1042), was discontinued not later than the accession of Botaniates in 1078, and its remaining competence transferred to different officials, of whom the Protovestiarius was one, and the Great Domestic and Great Primicerius seem to have been others.

1. *The Number of the Grand Chamberlains*

In the period before Justinian, as has been shown, there were regularly two Grand Chamberlains at the imperial court, one of whom served the Emperor, the other the Empress. In the later period there was a third, who served the Patriarch of Constantinople as early as the time of Heraclius (610–642).[1] By a ruling of that Emperor the Grand Chamberlain of the Patriarch, in case he was a deacon, was second in rank after the Grand Chamberlain of the Emperor, therefore probably following immediately after the Grand Chamberlain of the Empress; but if he was a presbyter, he ranked next to the Emperor's Grand Chamberlain.[2]

The office of Grand Chamberlain of the Patriarch had ceased to exist before the tenth century, for Constantine Porphyrogenitus describes it as obsolete in his time.[3] The mention of it in the chapter describing the promotion of the Prohedros of the Senate, which cannot have been earlier than the time of Nicephorus Phocas (963–969),[4] is in a sentence which apparently is not a part of the original composition [5] and which is probably to be considered an antiquarian's gloss. As the Grand Chamberlain of the Patriarch seems to have taken almost no part in the ceremonies of the court, and since his office, being ecclesiastical rather than imperial, does not fall within the scope of the present investigation, he may be omitted from further consideration.

There are clear indications that in the Byzantine period the number of the Grand Chamberlains at the imperial court was quite small. Thus, to one of the Christmas feasts of the ninth century, described by Philotheos, there were invited "the chiefs of the organization of the mystic chamber, to wit: Grand Chamberlains, eunuch Proto-

[1] Const. Porph., *De Caer.*, II, 39. [2] *Op. cit.*, 637, 8 ff.

[3] *Op. cit.*, 637, 3 f.: Ἰστέον, ὅτι καὶ ὁ πατριάρχης τὸ παλαιὸν ἴδιον εἶχεν πραιπόσιτον. The chapter is identified as the composition of Constantine by the introductory Ἰστέον, ὅτι. See Bury, *The Treatise De Administrando Imperio*, sec. 6; *Byzantinische Zeitschrift*, vol. XV (1906).

[4] Bury, *English Historical Review*, vol. XXII (1907), p. 212.

[5] Const. Porph., *De Caer.*, 442, 16 ff.

spathars, Primicerii and Ostiarii, in number, eight." [1] Later, in enumerating the officials to be invited to banquet with the Emperor at the time of Pentecost, Philotheos speaks of "the Grand Chamberlains, with the eunuch Protospathars and Primicerii, in number, six." [2] It is evident that even if it be considered that there are but two classes of officials referred to in this passage, namely, the Grand Chamberlains and the Primicerii of Protospathar rank, the number of Grand Chamberlains could not have exceeded four, and that if in this and the preceding passage the eunuch Protospathars and the Primicerii be regarded as separate classes of officials, the number of Grand Chamberlains is limited to two.

Other passages in the *Kletorologion* strongly suggest the existence of but two Grand Chamberlains. In his catalogue of the different grades of honor Philotheos mentions "the Patrician Grand Chamberlain,"[3] and "the non-Patrician Grand Chamberlain."[4] In the chapter on the imperial largesses he speaks of "the Grand Chamberlain," [5] and of "the Grand Chamberlains who are Protospathars." [6] As there seems to be no warrant for the use of the plural number in the latter passage, Bury is of the opinion that the singular should be substituted for it.[7] It is evident, therefore, that in the time of Philotheos there could not have been more than four Grand Chamberlains, but it seems probable that there were only two. This inference is further strengthened almost to the point of certainty by corroborative testimony of both earlier and later date.

It is related that shortly before his murder, in 866, the Caesar, Bardas, had a prophetic dream in which he beheld Saint Peter sitting on a high throne and listening to the complaints of the former Patriarch, Ignatius, who had been deposed by the Emperor and the Caesar. Finally the Saint promised retribution, and forthwith he gave "to one of two who stood by him like Grand Chamberlains in robes of gold" [8]

[1] *Op. cit.*, 750, 15 ff.: τοὺς προὔχοντας τῆς τάξεως τοῦ μυστικοῦ κουβουκλείου, οἷον πραιποσίτους, πρωτοσπαθαρίους εὐνούχους, πριμικηρίους, ὀστιαρίους, τὸν ἀριθμὸν η′. Perhaps the comma after εὐνούχους should be omitted, thus making πρωτοσπαθαρίους εὐνούχους πριμικηρίους a single class. Cf. 731, 6 f.: πριμικήριοι εὐνοῦχοι τοῦ κουβουκλείου (εἰ δὲ καὶ πρωτοσπαθάριοί εἰσιν, κτλ.), and the following note.

[2] *Op. cit.*, 778, 15 ff.: καὶ συνεστιῶνται τῷ βασιλεῖ οἱ πραιπόσιτοι σὺν τοῖς εὐνούχοις πρωτοσπαθαρίοις καὶ πριμικηρίοις, τὸν ἀριθμὸν ἕξ. Note the omission of the article before πριμικηρίοις.

[3] *De Caer.*, 730, 12: ὁ πατρίκιος καὶ πραιπόσιτος.

[4] *Op. cit.*, 730, 17: ὁ πραιπόσιτος μὴ ὢν πατρίκιος.

[5] *Op. cit.*, 784, 4: τὸν πραιπόσιτον.

[6] *Op. cit.*, 784, 10: τοὺς πρωτοσπαθαρίους καὶ πραιποσίτους.

[7] *Imperial Administrative System*, p. 124.

[8] Genesius, *Reges*, 104, 13 ff.: ἑνὶ δύο τινῶν παρ' αὐτῷ ἱσταμένων ὡσεὶ πραιποσίτων χρυσοενδύτων, κτλ. On golden robes, cf. *Acta Sanctorum*, 27 June, *Vita S. Sampson*, chap. 1, sec. 6.

a short sword, and bade him put to death an Emperor, who was standing on the right hand, and then a Caesar, who stood at the left. It is true that these two golden-robed persons were seen in a dream, but it is not likely that in such details as this the dream, or the account of it, differed from actual custom.

Porphyrogenitus, writing within half a century of the time of the composition of the *Kletorologion*, speaks in at least two instances as if there were but two Grand Chamberlains. In the ceremony of the promotion of a Master the candidate was led into the audience chamber by a Grand Chamberlain, and the insignia of office with which he was to be presented were handed to the Emperor by "the other Grand Chamberlain."[1] When a Grand Chamberlain was to be invested with his office, he was led into the Emperor's presence by "the other Grand Chamberlain" or the Superintendent of the Chamberlains.[2] The implication of both of these passages is that there were but two Grand Chamberlains.

There is conclusive evidence, therefore, that in the ninth and tenth centuries the number of Grand Chamberlains was two. Of these two, the more important was still, as in the period before Justinian, a close attendant upon the person of the Emperor, and because of his preeminence was frequently styled simply "the Grand Chamberlain," though he is occasionally spoken of as "the First Grand Chamberlain" (ὁ πρωτοπραιπόσιτος).[3]

The specific duties of the second Grand Chamberlain are so vaguely indicated that it is impossible to determine whether or not he served the Empress as in the earlier period, but his presence in a large number of ceremonies in which the Empress seems not to have participated, leads to the conjecture that he was not closely attached to her *cubiculum*. This is further supported by the fact that it was "the Grand Chamberlain," that is, the Emperor's Grand Chamberlain, who took the leading part in the Empress's reception of her court.[4]

2. *The Grand Chamberlain's Title, Rank, and Honors*

The official designation of the Grand Chamberlain had been changed, at the time of Diocletian's reorganization, from the rather unassuming form, *a cubiculo*, to *praepositus sacri cubiculi*, which was

[1] *De Caer.*, 233, 1: ὁ ἕτερος πραιπόσιτος.

[2] *Op. cit.*, 261, 21 f.: καὶ νεύουσιν οἱ δεσπόται, κἂν τε πραιπόσιτος ἕτερός ἐστι, κἂν πριμικήριος, καὶ ἐπαίρει τὸν . . . πραιπόσιτον, καὶ εἰσάγει αὐτόν.

[3] *Op. cit.*, 527, 6; 623, 18; 624, 2; 625, 20.

[4] *Op. cit.*, 67, 13 ff.; 595, 22 ff.

more in accord with the supermundane character of the new imperial government. This official title remained unchanged as late as the year 536, for it appears in an imperial constitution of that date.[1] It seems probable, however, that it was modified shortly thereafter, for an inscription of the year 565 describes Narses as *ex-praepositus sacri palatii*,[2] and in the legend carved in the base of the column of Phocas in the Roman forum Smaragdus is similarly described.[3]

It is true that this title had been employed before,[4] but not, so far as is known, in official documents. Its appearance in the works of the historians and chronographers of the time is scarcely surprising or significant, in view of the variety of circumlocutions which they employed.[5]

The evidence of these inscriptions, however, is nearly as reliable as would be that of imperial constitutions, and points quite clearly to a change in the Grand Chamberlain's title. Such a change in title would probably be occasioned by some change in duties or official position, and it is not impossible that the modification of the Grand Chamberlain's competence, which relieved him to such an extent of the charge of the bedchamber and made him the master of the palace ceremonies and the Emperor's deputy, was effected even during Justinian's time.

References to the Grand Chamberlain are exceedingly scarce from the beginning of the seventh to the latter part of the ninth centuries, and as they exhibit the lack of uniformity in the use of titles which has already been noted as characteristic of the general literature of the period, they are worthless as evidence regarding the official designation of the Grand Chamberlain. After the middle of the ninth century, however, the references become much more numerous, and, since they appear in records of quasi-official nature, and in compilations on court etiquette, constitute reliable evidence. The Grand Chamberlain is no longer described as *praepositus sacri palatii*, but simply as *praepositus* (ὁ πραιπόσιτος), a title by which he continued to be known for at least two centuries,[6] and probably until the discontinuance of the office.

Before the time of the accession of Justinian, as has already been shown, the Grand Chamberlain had risen to a position of high rank

[1] *Novellae Justiniani*, XXX. [2] *C.I.L.*, VI, 1199. [3] *C.I.L.*, VI, 1200.

[4] Cf. Du Cange, *Glossarium Mediae et Infimae Latinitatis*, s.v. *praepositus palatii.*

[5] See Appendix B.

[6] Cf. Const. Porph., *De Caer.*, *passim;* Constantinus was *praepositus* under Michael IV. Cf. Michael Attaliota, 33, 22.

in the official hierarchy, and was included with the Prefects, the Master of the Soldiers, the Master of the Offices, and the Quaestor in the first class of the *illustres*. In the sixth century there was created a new grade of honor, higher than that of the *illustres*,[1] to which all of the *illustres* of the first rank were soon raised. Henceforth they were spoken of as *gloriosissimi* or, in Greek, as ἐνδοξόταποι. This title appears as early as 435,[2] and occasionally thereafter [3] until the year 530, but from that time on its appearance is so frequent as to indicate that it had become an official title of address.[4]

In 536 the Grand Chamberlain was officially described as *gloriosissimus*,[5] and for the next two centuries probably enjoyed this form of address.[6] *Gloriosissimus*, as a title of rank, appears frequently in the *Acta* of the third Council of Constantinople, held in 680, but after the establishment of the new grades of honor in the seventh or eighth centuries it seems slowly to have passed out of use. Philotheos employs it but once in his book on banquet ceremonials, written at the very close of the ninth century. He speaks then of the "rank of the most glorious Masters,"[7] but this instance is so exceptional as to appear to be but a relic of the former official use of the title.

It will be remembered that the Patriciate was closed to eunuchs by a constitution of Theodosius II, and that further restrictions were placed upon the use of the title by the Emperor Zeno.[8] These were all swept away by Justinian, who made all officials of the rank of the *illustres* eligible.[9] This included, of course, the Grand Chamberlain, and not long afterward Narses, who held that position under Justinian, was admitted to the Patriciate.[10] Smaragdus, the Grand Chamberlain of the Emperor Phocas, was also honored with the Patriciate.[11]

[1] *Codex Justinianus*, VII, 62, 38, (date, 529): . . . *sive illustri dignitate decoratur sive etiam maiore*, etc.; IV, 32, 26 (date, 528): . . . *illustribus quidem personis sive eas praecedentibus*, etc.

[2] *Codex Theodosianus*, I, 1, 6, sec. 2: *Antiochus amplissimus adque gloriosissimus praefectorius ac consularis*.

[3] Petr. Patr. (Const. Porph.), *De Caer.*, 419, 8; 421, 2.

[4] *Codex Justinianus*, V, 70, 7, sec. 6, of the City Prefect (date, 530); *Novellae Justiniani* XIV, end, of the Master of the Offices (date, 535); XX, 1 and 2, of the Quaestor (date, 536).

[5] *Novellae Justiniani*, XXX, 6, 2; 7, 1. Calopodius seems to have received the office of Grand Chamberlain prior to 536, and is described by Theophanes (360, 13) as ἐνδοξότατος. No date can be assigned to the designation, however.

[6] It is to be noted, however, that in the subscript to the *Constitutio Pragmatica* (*Appendix Constitutionum Dispersarum*, VII, 27) of the year 554 Narses is not mentioned as *gloriosissimus*, but merely as *illustris*.

[7] Const. Porph., *De Caer.* (Philoth., *Kletorologion*), 710, 19: ἡ τῶν ἐνδοξοτάτων μαγίστρων ἀξία.

[8] See p. 197.

[9] *Novellae*, LXII, 2.

[10] Codinus, *De Aedificiis Constantinopolis*, 86, 12; *C.I.L.*, VI, 1199.

[11] *C.I.L.*, VI, 1200.

An almost total absence of references to the Grand Chamberlain during the ensuing two and a half centuries is followed by repeated mention of Bahanes, the Grand Chamberlain of Basil I, as *patricius et praepositus*,[1] and the same words (ὁ πατρίκιος καὶ πραιπόσιτος) were used by Philotheos in 899,[2] with an implied suggestion of generalization, as if it were customary for the Grand Chamberlain, that is, the Emperor's, or First, Grand Chamberlain, to be a Patrician. It is not unlikely that the same custom began to be observed with regard to the second Grand Chamberlain about the end of the ninth century.

Besides his colleague of patrician rank, Philotheos also mentions a non-patrician Grand Chamberlain,[3] whom it is very natural to identify with the Grand Chamberlain and Protospathar to whom reference is made in another passage of the same work.[4]

Some evidence that this identification is correct is to be found in the fact that the non-patrician Grand Chamberlain immediately preceded the Protospathars in the ceremonial order,[5] precisely as the patrician Grand Chamberlain preceded the eunuch Patricians.[6] Any lingering doubt is removed when it is observed that the *Taktikon* discovered and edited by Uspenski substitutes for the words ὁ πραιπόσιτος μὴ ὢν πατρίκιος, of the *Kletorologion*, the more exact description, ὁ πραιπόσιτος καὶ πρωτοσπαθάριος.[7]

Narses is the first Grand Chamberlain mentioned as Protospathar,[8] but it seems probable that he had not, at the time to which the passage refers, been made Grand Chamberlain, for the Protospathars of the time of Justinian had active duties as commanders of the corps of Spathars, whose office had not developed, as yet, into a grade of rank, and these would have been likely to embarrass him had he been advanced to the higher station.

The next instance is of a much later date, being that of Theophilus, Protospathar and Grand Chamberlain in the year 869.[9] Since

[1] Cf. citations of Mansi, p. 239, notes 2–5 (date, 869); Const. Porph. *De Caer.*, 503, 9 (date, 871).

[2] Const. Porph., *De Caer.* (*Kletorologion*), 730, 12.

[3] *Op. cit.*, 730, 17: ὁ πραιπόσιτος μὴ ὢν πατρίκιος. Note that the negative particle is μή not οὐ.

[4] 784, 10: τοὺς πρωτοσπαθαρίους καὶ πραιποσίτους. The singular number should probably be substituted for the plural here. Cf. p. 233.

[5] Const. Porph., *De Caer.* (*Klet.*), 730, 17.

[6] *Op. cit.*, 730, 12.

[7] *Izviestiia russkago arkheologicheskago instituta v Konstantinopolie*, vol. III (1898), p. 118. The date of the *Taktikon* is 842–856 A.D. Cf. Bury, *Imp. Adm. Syst.*, p. 12 ff.

[8] Theoph., 367, 9.

[9] Mansi, *Sacrorum Conciliorum Nova Collectio*, vol. XVI, 84 C: *Theophilus laudabilissimus protospatharius et praepositus.*

Bahanes was the patrician Grand Chamberlain in the same year,[1] there is an actual historical example of the contemporary existence of Grand Chamberlains of different rank, to accord with the generalized description given by Philotheos. In describing banquet ceremonials Philotheos commonly mentions the Masters, the Grand Chamberlains (plural), and the Proconsular Patricians (sometimes simply "Patricians") in this order.[2]

From the fact that both Grand Chamberlains are so frequently mentioned before the ranks of the Patricians, it is natural to suppose that they enjoyed equal rank, and that they were both Patricians; and since there seem to be no references to Grand Chamberlains of Protospathar rank after the time of Philotheos, there can be little doubt that this conclusion is sound.

This elevation of the second Grand Chamberlain to the Patriciate must have occurred after the year 869, when Theophilus was a Protospathar, and before the composition of the *Kletorologion*, in 899. If it be assumed that it took place shortly before the latter date, the slight inconsistency in the work of Philotheos is most easily explained. In preparing his descriptions of ceremonies he designated both Grand Chamberlains as Patricians, in accordance with the current practice, but when, in correcting an earlier list of dignities, to be included in his handbook, he met with the title of the Grand Chamberlain and Protospathar, he felt that there was not, as yet, sufficient precedent to justify him in eliminating all mention of this grade of rank, and accordingly he merely changed the entry to indicate that this was the place of "the non-patrician Grand Chamberlain, if there be one" (ὁ πραιπόσιτος μὴ ὢν πατρίκιος).

During the fifth century there had come into use certain complimentary appellations which were used in addressing the higher officials, but which were apparently not indicative of degrees of rank.[3] There is no positive evidence that the Grand Chamberlain was personally described by any of these new designations before the ninth century, though he seems to have been included by Justinian among the officials referred to as *viri magnifici illustres*.[4]

[1] Mansi, *op. cit.*, vol. XVI, 80 D.

[2] Const. Porph., *De Caer.* (*Klet.*), 741, 17; 760, 8; 761, 21; 763, 18; 764, 4; 765, 1; 769, 5; 773, 13; 776, 3; 776, 19; 777, 12; 779, 22; 780, 1; 781, 2; 787, 4. Occasionally the Proconsular Patricians are named before the Grand Chamberlains (753, 20; 759, 11), and in one passage this is true of the Patricians (758, 18).

[3] Cf. Boak, p. 46 of this volume; Koch, *Die Byzantinischen Beamtentitel*, pp. 43, 51.

[4] *Novellae*, LXII, 2, sec. 2; date 537.

It is quite possible, also, that certain brick stamps found in Italy and Sicily, and bearing the name of a certain Christian, Narses (Narsis), who was a *vir excellentissimus*, may refer to the great Grand Chamberlain of Justinian.[1] In the *Acta* of the Fourth Council of Constantinople (869), however, Bahanes (Βαάνης), the Grand Chamberlain of Basil I, is referred to indifferently as *magnificentissimus*,[2] as *famosissimus*,[3] and as *laudabilissimus*,[4] for the last of which the Greek account gives πανεύφημος.[5] In the work of Philotheos the Grand Chamberlain is described as λαμπρότατος, that is, *illustris*.[6]

The process of reorganization which resulted in the perfection of the Byzantine administrative system, affected the relative rank of the Grand Chamberlain. The offices of the Pretorian Prefect and of the Master of the Soldiers passed out of existence, that of the Quaestor suffered a severe reduction in rank, and that of the City Prefect, though still important, had met a similar fate. Of all the *illustres* who in the time of Justinian ranked above the Grand Chamberlain, only the Master of the Offices, now known simply as "the Master" (ὁ μάγιστρος), still held that position at the end of the ninth century.

Philotheos presents two lists of dignities which bear upon the question of the Grand Chamberlain's rank.[7] In the first, after the title of the Patriarch of Constantinople, and other titles which were reserved for the royal family, there are mentioned in the following order, the Masters, the Rector (ὁ ῥαίκτωρ), the Synkellos (ὁ σύγκελλος) of Rome, the Synkellos of Constantinople, other Synkelloi, if present, the Archbishop of Bulgaria, the patrician eunuchs.[8]

Since the Grand Chamberlain, if a Patrician, commonly preceded other Patricians, it might be supposed that he followed the Archbishop of Bulgaria in the ceremonies in which this list was employed. When this is compared with the second list given in the *Kletorologion*, it at once becomes apparent that it is the more complete, in that it gives the titles of the royal family and a number of ecclesiastical titles which are not mentioned in the second list. However, inasmuch as the titles which appear in the descriptions of ceremonies in the latter part of the *Kletorologion* are more in accord with those of the second

1 *C.I.L.*, X, 8045, 14.
2 Mansi, *op. cit.*, vol. XVI, 54 B; 55 A; 56 D; 97 C; 97 E; etc.
3 *Op. cit.*, vol. XVI, 18 D; 19 D; 19 E; 27 C; 30 C; 36 C; 97 E; etc.
4 *Op. cit.*, vol. XVI, 18 B; 80 B; 80 E.
5 *Op. cit.*, vol. XVI, 309 E; 316 D; 327 E; etc.
6 Const. Porph., *De Caer.* (*Klet.*), 722, 10.
7 *Op. cit.*, 726, 19 ff.; 730, 11 ff.
8 *Op. cit.*, 727, 3 ff.

list, it is not unreasonable to suppose that the latter represents the common ceremonial order, and that the fuller list was employed at those times alone when the observance of some especially religious festival demanded the presence of the ecclesiastics.

In the second of the two lists the Master, the Rector, the Synkellos, and the patrician Grand Chamberlain are mentioned in this order.[1] This does not seem, however, to represent the relative prominence of the officials. The Synkellos was an ecclesiastical dignitary,[2] who appears but seldom in the ceremonial descriptions. The office of the Rector was not established until the latter part of the ninth century,[3] and in the tenth century ceremonies in which he participated he always sat with the Grand Chamberlains.[4]

The manner in which this is stated, as if the Rector had no place of his own, gives some indication of the relative importance of the Rector and the Grand Chamberlains, and contains the suggestion that the former was considered as inferior to the latter. It has already been observed that in the lengthy accounts of the ceremonies of the court which comprise the latter half of the *Kletorologion*, the Grand Chamberlain is almost invariably mentioned directly after the Master,[5] and this may be accepted as the place commonly accorded him in the hierarchy of the ninth and tenth centuries, for, in a court such as was maintained by the Byzantine Emperors, prominence in the court ceremonial is, after all, the best criterion of rank.

In the list of the grades of dignity which were open to eunuchs, Philotheos names the Patricians first, followed by the Grand Chamberlains and the Protospathars.[6] This, and the fact that the non-patrician Grand Chamberlain ranked only as the foremost of the Protospathars, may be taken to indicate that the patrician Grand Chamberlain occupied his high rank in the hierarchy by virtue of the Patriciate, and not by virtue of his office. Still, if the office of the Emperor's Grand Chamberlain always bore with it the rank of Patrician, as it doubtless did in the Byzantine period, it is somewhat idle to discuss whether it was office or grade of honor which placed the Grand Chamberlain in such a prominent position in the ceremonial order.

The relative position of the non-patrician Grand Chamberlain has already been described as immediately preceding the other Proto-

[1] *Op. cit.*, 730, 11 ff. [2] Bury, *Imp. Adm. Syst.*, p. 116. [3] *Op. cit.*, p. 115.

[4] Const. Porph., *De Caer.*, 530, 4 ff.: ἰστέον ὅτι ἀεὶ ὁ ῥαίκτωρ τοῖς πραιποσίτοις συγκαθέζεται . . . ἐν ταῖς . . . προελεύσεσι.

[5] See p. 238. [6] Const. Porph., *De Caer.* (*Klet.*), 722, 3 ff.

spathars, to which honorary grade he also belonged. Between him and his fellow Chamberlain of the patrician rank there intervened four grades, in the following ascending order: the patrician Strategoi, the proconsular Patricians, those who were styled proconsular Patricians and Strategoi, and the patrician eunuchs.[1]

Mention has already been made of the fact that before the time of Justinian ex-Grand Chamberlains might be enrolled in the senatorial order.[2] It would appear that during Justinian's reign the Grand Chamberlains were admitted to that body while they were in active service also, for this privilege was granted to Patricians, men of consular or prefectorial rank, to the Masters of the Soldiers, and to the *viri magnifici illustres*,[3] a designation which probably included those officials who directly followed in the regular order of precedence the Masters of the Soldiers, that is, the Master of the Offices, the Quaestor, the Grand Chamberlain, and the two Counts of the treasury.

In the middle of the ninth century, Bahanes, the Grand Chamberlain of Basil I, is mentioned as one of the members of the Senate at the time of the Fourth Council of Constantinople, in the year 869.[4] Philotheos also mentions the Grand Chamberlain as a member of the imperial Senate,[5] and he still belonged to that order in the time of Nicephorus Phocas (963–969).[6] Frequent reference is made in the *Kletorologion* to officials who were **ὑπὸ καμπάγιον**, that is, according to Bury, "those who wear the kampagion, some kind of footgear." [7] The Grand Chamberlain's name appears in the list of such favored officials.[8] Certain dignitaries are described by Philotheos as "Nobles of the Lausiakon," which was a section of the imperial palace. The Grand Chamberlain belonged to this group also.[9] The significance of the last two classifications is not apparent: doubtless they are to be explained as ceremonial distinctions.

[1] *Op. cit.*, 730, 13 ff. [2] See p. 193.

[3] *Novellae Justiniani*, LXII, 2, 2: *cetero omni post patricios consortio tam consularium quam praefectoriae dignitatis, quibus etiam magistros militum connumeramus nec non viros magnificos illustres, secundum suae dignitatis tempora in magnam curiam tam convenientibus quam considentibus et sententiam ferre habentibus licentiam.*

[4] Mansi, *op. cit.*, vol. XVI, 37 C: *praesente quoque sacro senatu, videlicet . . . Bahane magnificentissimo patricio et praeposito*, etc. Cf. also 143 E; 158 A.

[5] Const. Porph., *De Caer.* (*Klet.*), 741, 16 f.: μεγιστάνας ἐκ τῆς βασιλικῆς συγκλήτου, τὸν ἀριθμὸν ιβʹ, οἷον μαγίστρους, πραιποσίτους, κτλ.

[6] *Op. cit.*, 442, 15: τοῦ πραιποσίτου καὶ τοῦ ἑταιρειάρχου καὶ λοιπῶν συγκλητικῶν.

[7] *Imp. Adm. Syst.*, p. 38.

[8] Const. Porph., *De Caer.* (*Klet.*), 759, 9 f.: φίλους ἐκ τῶν συγκλητικῶν, τοὺς ὑπὸ καμπάγιον πάντας, οἷον μαγίστρους, ἀνθυπάτους, πραιποσίτους, κτλ.

[9] *Op. cit.*, 787, 3 ff.: τοὺς ἄρχοντας τοῦ λαυσιακοῦ, οἷον . . . μαγίστρους, πραιποσίτους, κτλ.

3. *The Grand Chamberlain's Administrative Competence*

It has already been stated that the administrative competence of the Grand Chamberlain suffered a rather severe restriction in the period following the reign of Justinian. Few of the details of the process which resulted in this modification are known. In the following pages an attempt has been made to present all the facts which can be ascertained regarding the Grand Chamberlain's loss of supervision over those who were under his direction in the fifth century.

a. The Superintendent of the Chamberlains

The office of Superintendent of Chamberlains continued to exist through the period which followed Justinian, and is met in the ninth and tenth centuries,[1] but its competence was no longer that of the earlier days. The Chamberlains had been divided into two corps, of which one served in the sleeping apartments, and was known as the Chamberlains of the Bedchamber,[2] and the second group, serving in the other private apartments of the palace was known as the Chamberlains of the *Cubiculum.*[3] This second group remained under the direction of the Superintendent of the Chamberlains, and the latter was still dependent upon the Grand Chamberlain. In the tenth century ceremonies of the promotion of a *cubicularia* of the Empress,[4] and the *cubicularius* of the Emperor,[5] it is specifically stated that the Superintendent of Chamberlains must assist.[6] This was because he was director of the Chamberlains, apparently of both *cubicula.* Furthermore, when the Grand Chamberlain was giving the Chamberlain his charge, he bade him honor all dignitaries, and "especially his Grand Chamberlains." [7] This clearly indicates that the Chamberlains were in direct control of the Superintendent, and that he, in turn, was under the Grand Chamberlain.

The control of the Chamberlains of the Bedchamber was no longer in the hands of the Superintendent of the Chamberlains, but had been transferred to a new official, the Chief Eunuch of the Bedchamber, known as the Parakoimomenos (παρακοιμώμενος).[8] This new official

[1] *Op. cit.*, 721, 21: τῷ πριμικηρίῳ τοῦ κουβουκλείου; Const. Porph., *De Caer.*, 623, 3 ff. Perhaps the πριμμικήριος τῆς αὐλῆς of the 14th century (Codinus., *De Off.*, 10, 13 *et alibi*) was the same official under a new title.

[2] Const. Porph., *De Caer.* (*Klet.*), 734, 21: οἱ κουβικουλάριοι τοῦ βασιλικοῦ κοιτῶνος, often mentioned as κοιτωνῖται. Cf. 710, 8; 711, 9.

[3] *Op. cit.*, 734, 22: οἱ κουβικουλάριοι τοῦ κουβουκλείου.

[4] Const. Porph., *De Caer.*, II, 24. [5] *Op. cit.*, II, 25. [6] *Op. cit.*, 623, 3 ff.; 625, 5 ff.

[7] *Op. cit.*, 626, 3 f.: μάλιστα δὲ τοὺς αὐτοῦ πραιποσίτους.

[8] Const. Porph., *De Caer.* (*Klet.*), 784, 5.

was independent of the Grand Chamberlain, and the attendants of the Bedchamber were thus removed from the supervision of the official who had originally been their chief.

The early history of the office of the Chief Eunuch is difficult to trace. There is reference to it as early as the time of Constantine, but this, it seems, can only be an anachronism on the part of Codinus.[1] The same author applies this title to Chrysaphius,[2] and to Amantius,[3] in the time of Theodosius II. In his chronicle of the events of the year 594, Theophanes mentions repeatedly the Chief Eunuch of Mauricius,[4] and under the year 772 speaks of a certain Theophanes who bore this title.[5] It was not until the reign of Theophilus (829–842), however, that this servant became a regular member of the palace organization,[6] and even then his position was only semi-official, and his appointment devoid of any ceremony whatever,[7] being, in this respect, much like the appointment of any private servant. His influence steadily increased, however, until he outranked and finally, in part, supplanted the Grand Chamberlain.[8]

Although the Chief Eunuch must have wielded considerable influence in the tenth century, it appears that he played a very inconspicuous part in the ceremonies of the court, for he is mentioned but once in the *De Caerimoniis*,[9] except in the account of the opposition to the newly proclaimed Emperor, Nicephorus Phocas, which was led by the Chief Eunuch Joseph.[10]

b. The Steward of the Household

Bury, following Mommsen, states that the office of the Steward of the Household seems to have disappeared during the sixth century.[11] This is somewhat surprising, for it appears to have been of no small importance in the first part of the fifth century, at the time of the composition of the *Notitia Dignitatum*. There is no trace of a Steward at the Ostrogothic court, but there was an important official of the rank of the *spectabiles*, known as *curapalates*, whose duties were similar to those of the *curae palati* at Constantinople.[12]

It appears therefore that at Ravenna the office of the Steward of the Household had lapsed, and that the competence of the office had

[1] See pp. 181 f.
[2] *De Signis Constantinopolis*, 47, 12 f.
[3] *De Aedificiis Constantinopolis*, 105, 2.
[4] 440, 11, 14, 17; 441, 6.
[5] 701, 11.
[6] Const. Porph., *De Administrando Imperio*, chap. 50, end.
[7] Const. Porph., *De Caer.* (*Klet.*), 725, 14.
[8] See p. 228.
[9] See above, note 7.
[10] Const. Porph., *De Caer.*, I, 96.
[11] *Imp. Adm. Syst.*, p. 120.
[12] Cassiodorus, *Variae*, 7, 5.

been divided between two or more dignitaries. In Constantinople, however, there was a certain *ex-cura palati* (ἀπὸ κουροπαλατῶν) described as a Patrician[1] in the reign of Justin I. As the Patriciate was conferred only on the highest officials of the Empire, it can scarcely be supposed that this *ex-cura palati* had been one of the very inferior *curae palati* mentioned among the subordinates of the Steward in the *Notitia Dignitatum.* Furthermore, Justinian indicated his nephew Justin as successor to the throne by conferring on him this title.[2] From these facts Bury concludes that as early as the time of Anastasius a new *cura palati*, entirely distinct from the subordinates of the Steward, had been created.[3]

It seems hardly probable, however, that if such a new office had been created — one which ranked high in the official hierarchy — it would have been given the same name as that of a subordinate and rather humble office, whether or not that office was still in existence. Moreover, it is known that by the year 413 it was possible for the *cura palati* who was a subordinate of the Steward to become a Count of the First Rank, and that for some time he had been privileged to attend the imperial banquets and to adore the Emperor.[4] Might it not, then, be more reasonable to suppose that the process of disintegration which has been noted in the West was repeated in the East, and that the patrician *cura palati* of the time of Justin I was none other than the former subordinate of the Steward, now made an independent official and raised to a high rank? Such a supposition would help to explain the waning influence of the Steward of the Household.

The Steward, however, did not disappear in the sixth century, for in the ninth century there was an official who bore the same title and performed certain of the duties of the *castrensis* of the fifth century.[5] The fact that the duties of this official still concerned the imperial table is not without significance, but his title is of the highest importance. Had this Latin title, anomalous as it was, once passed out of use, it would most certainly not have been revived in a Greek court. It can only be concluded that office and title both persisted, whatever changes they may have undergone.

[1] *Chronicon Paschale*, 613, 17; Theoph., 168, 21; John Malalas, 413, 11.

[2] Corippus, *In Laudem Justini*, 1, 134 ff. Cf. Bury, *Imp. Adm. Syst.*, p. 34.

[3] *Imp. Adm. Syst.*, pp. 33 f.

[4] *Codex Theodosianus*, VI, 13, 1.

[5] Const. Porph., *De Caer.* (*Klet.*), 742, 11: τοῦ καστρησίου τῆς βασιλικῆς τραπέζης. See also 744, 6; 9; 15; 748, 3; 750, 22; 755, 3. Bury himself mentions this official, *Imp. Adm. Syst.*, p. 126.

It is not improbable that at the close of the ninth century the title of *castrensis* was passing out of use. Philotheos employs it seven times,[1] but in the later parts of the *De Caerimoniis* the *castrensis* is mentioned but once, and in this case seems to have been not a palace official, but a servant of the Patriarch.[2]

c. The Count of the Crown Lands

The administration of the Crown Lands in Cappadocia remained in the hands of the Grand Chamberlain throughout the fifth and well into the sixth century. In 536, when Justinian united Cappadocia Prima and Cappadocia Secunda, some minor changes were made in the administration of the Crown Lands. The personnel of the retinue of the Count of the Crown Lands had hitherto included thirteen officials known as First and Second Masters (*μαγίστερες πρῶτοι καὶ δεύτεροι*), each of whom apparently administered one of the thirteen estates of which the Crown Lands were composed. There were now added thirteen more officials, each supervising the collection of the revenues of one of these estates.[3] The control of the Crown Lands in Cappadocia was still left, however, in the hands of the Grand Chamberlain.[4]

The subsequent changes in this department have been treated by Bury.[5] About the time of the revision of the Cappadocian administration, mention is made of the Crown Lands in Arabia,[6] and Phoenicia Libanensis,[7] in such a way as to make it clear that they were no longer under the control of the Count of the Privy Purse, as they had been a little more than a century earlier.[8] It seems probable that they had been joined to the Crown Lands in Cappadocia, and that all these estates together comprised a single administration.

By the year 566 a Curator of the Crown Lands, with the honorary appellation of *magnificentissimus* (*μεγαλοπρεπέστατος κουράτωρ τῶν οἰκιῶν*), had taken the place of the Count of the Crown Lands, whose rank, as already stated, had been that of a *spectabilis*.[9] The law in which this Curator is mentioned enumerates all officials who had financial charges, but the Grand Chamberlain is not included in their number. The inference is that all the Crown Lands, including those in Cappadocia, had been transferred from the control of the Grand Chamberlain to that of the new Curator. This may have oc-

[1] Cf. preceding note.
[2] 28, 4.
[3] *Novellae Justiniani*, XXX, 2.
[4] *Op. cit.*, XXX, 6.
[5] *Imp. Adm. Syst.*, pp. 79, 100.
[6] *Novellae Justiniani*, CII, 1; date, 536.
[7] *Justiniani Edicta*, IV, 2; undated.
[8] *Notitia Dignitatum or.*, XIV, 3.
[9] Justin II, *Novellae*, I, 4.

curred as early as 557, for a Curator of that date administered "the estates and property" (οἴκων τε καὶ κτημάτων) of the Emperor.[1]

d. The Count of the Imperial Wardrobe

The Imperial Wardrobe, which had been a part of the Grand Chamberlain's administration during the fifth century, passed from his control after the time of Justinian. The title of the official directly in charge of this department was changed, as were many others, in the time of Justinian or shortly thereafter, and in the ninth century he appears not as Count of the Imperial Wardrobe, but as Protovestiarius (ὁ πρωτοβεστιάριος),[2] and the department which was under his superintendence came to be known as "the Private Imperial Wardrobe" (τὸ οἰκειακὸν βασιλικὸν βεστιάριον).[3] As the Protovestiarius and his fellow Vestitores were, however, under the direction of the Deuteros of the Palace in the ninth century,[4] they do not call for further consideration here. That the Protovestiarius eventually supplanted the Grand Chamberlain in certain of his activities is stated elsewhere.[5]

e. The Silentiaries

By the time of Philotheos the Silentiaries also had passed from the control of the Grand Chamberlain, and were under the direction of the Master of the Ceremonies (ὁ ἐπὶ καταστάσεως),[6] with whom they very often appear in the ceremonies of the tenth century.[7]

It seems quite probable that the Grand Chamberlain lost control of the Silentiaries during the reign of Justinian, for, according to a statement of John Lydus, the chief of the court ushers (ὁ ἀμισσιωνάλιος) was, in the sixth century, "the first of the Silentiaries,"[8] and the corps of ushers (*admissionales*) had long been dependent upon the Master of the Offices.[9] Since the Silentiaries must have had rather conspicuous ceremonial duties, it was quite natural that they should be placed under the control of the Master of the Offices, who was the director of the court ceremonial during the sixth century.[10] In the process of disintegration of the Master's competence, many of

[1] Agathias, *Historiae*, 284, 16 f.
[2] Const. Porph., *De Caer.* (*Klet.*), 784, 13; 786, 15.
[3] Const. Porph., *De Caer.*, 465, 14; 17; 478, 9.
[4] Const. Porph., *De Caer.* (*Klet.*), 724, 14.
[5] See pp. 228, 231.
[6] Const. Porph., *De Caer.* (*Klet.*), 720, 16 ff.
[7] Const. Porph., *De Caer.*, 69, 11; 81, 15; 89, 9 f.; 99, 22; 100, 18; 103, 14; etc.
[8] 183, 5 f.: τοῦ πρώτου τῶν λεγομένων σιλεντιαρίων (ἀμισσιωνάλιος καλεῖται), κτλ.
[9] *Notitia Dignitatum or.*, XI, 17.
[10] Boak, p. 92 ff. of this volume.

his ceremonial duties were taken over by the Master of the Ceremonies (ὁ ἐπὶ καταστάσεως), whose office developed out of that of the chief of the court ushers.[1]

f. The Grand Chamberlain's *Legatarius*

The work of Philotheos contains reference to a Legatarius of the Grand Chamberlain (τὸν λεγατάριον τοῦ πραιποσίτου).[2] There seems to be no way of determining what the duties of this official were, but he must have served in the *officium* of the Grand Chamberlain. Officials bearing similar titles were members of the *officia* of the Logothete of the Military Treasury (ὁ λογοθέτης τοῦ στρατιωτικοῦ),[3] and of the Chartulary of the Vestiarium.[4]

g. The Private Imperial Treasurer, *Sacellarius*

It has been suggested above[5] that prior to the time of Justinian there may have been a private imperial treasurer, known as the Sacellarius. There is mention in later times of such an official, as, for example, of Theodore, the Imperial Sacellarius.[6]

There seems to have been another treasury, presided over by an official with the simple title, Sacellarius,[7] as distinguished from the Imperial Sacellarius, and corresponding probably to the *res privata* of an earlier day. This treasurer belonged to the Imperial Council (σέκρετα),[8] and had under his control a chartulary,[9] notaries[10] with the rank of Spathars,[11] and a πρωτοκαγκελλάριος.[12] He had oversight, in the days of Philotheos, of all *officia*,[13] a duty once belonging to the Master of the Offices.[14]

In some instances chamberlains held the office of Sacellarius, but it seems almost impossible to determine whether they were the private imperial treasurers, or had charge of the *res privata*. There is the case of Stephanus, Grand Chamberlain and Sacellarius under Justinian II,[15] and that of Bahanes, another Grand Chamberlain who was also Sacellarius.[16]

[1] *Op. cit.*, p. 51.
[2] Const. Porph., *De Caer.* (*Klet.*), 750 8.
[3] *Op. cit.*, 718, 15.
[4] *Op. cit.*, 719, 16.
[5] See p. 223.
[6] Theoph., 517, 4: Θεόδωρον σακελλάριον; 517, 19: τὸν βασιλικὸν σακελλάριον; *anno* 625.
[7] Const. Porph., *De Caer.* (*Klet.*), 713, 20; 715, 15; 717, 12; etc.
[8] *Op. cit.*, 715, 14 ff.
[9] *Op. cit.*, 714, 2; 715, 17; 721, 23; etc.
[10] *Op. cit.*, 752, 5.
[11] *Op. cit.*, 735, 21.
[12] *Op. cit.*, 738, 9.
[13] *Op. cit.*, 717, 12.
[14] Boak, pp. 63 ff. of this volume.
[15] Theoph., 562, 2 f.: σακελλάριον . . . καὶ πρωτοευνοῦχον.
[16] Const. Porph., *De Caer.*, 503, 9.

The Grand Chamberlain's Ceremonial Activities

The ceremonies of the Emperor's court had been under the supervision of the Master of the Offices in the sixth century, but by the close of the ninth century had passed into the hands of the Grand Chamberlain and the Master of Ceremonies (ὁ ἐπὶ καταστάσεως).[1] This transfer of duties, which was the result of a gradual change, had been largely effected by the end of the eighth century, and after the lapse of another hundred years, the Master (of the Offices) is no longer mentioned in a ceremonial capacity. The division of the ceremonial duties between the Grand Chamberlain and the Master of the Ceremonies seems to have left the elaborate preparations in the hands of the latter,[2] while the former was in charge of the progress of the ceremony itself. It is probable, however, that neither of them had authority to depart widely from the precedent which had been established for such observances.

The ceremonies described in the work of Constantine Porphyrogenitus are so numerous, so long and so varied, that they cannot be set forth separately in these pages. They include ceremonies and processions for all the important church festivals, and for secular observances such as the promotion of greater and lesser dignitaries of the court, the coronation of an Emperor, his marriage, birthday, or funeral; the reception of foreign envoys, the races, banquets, even the Emperor's bath. In all these ceremonies the Grand Chamberlain participated, generally in a very conspicuous manner. It may be said that he acted on all occasions as the Emperor's assistant, but the precise nature of his rôle varied with the type of the ceremony, or of the particular ceremonial act in which he was engaged.

In religious ceremonies the Emperor sought to give evidence of his adherence to the Christian faith, and of his support of the church. He was a suppliant, who prostrated himself in humility — albeit imperial humility — before God. He was himself the chief actor in these ceremonies, but was personally assisted, whenever such assistance was permissible, by the Grand Chamberlain. Similar assistance was given him at certain points in secular ceremonies, also, as when the conferring of some high dignity required that the Emperor participate actively in the observance. When the Byzantine fondness for pomp made a ceremonial occasion of such personal matters as the Emperor's bath, the distinction between ceremonial activities and

[1] Cf. Boak, pp. 98 ff. of this volume.

[2] Const. Porph., *De Caer.*, 183, 2.

personal service almost disappeared, but as there is no indication that the Grand Chamberlain served the Emperor in a private personal capacity, it may be assumed that in all these cases he was performing a ceremonial act.

The chief purpose of many of the court functions seems to have been to emphasize the exalted position of the Emperor. At such times the Emperor took almost no active part. He sat in state while his subjects paid him honor in a variety of ways. Inconspicuous as were the Emperor's activities on such occasions, he seems, nevertheless, to have been regarded formally as the director of the ceremonies. This function he performed through the assistance of the Grand Chamberlain, to whom he gave signs at proper times and who thereupon, either personally or through an assistant, directed the next detail of the ceremony. Thus the Grand Chamberlain was practically the master of the ceremonies. In many of these ceremonies the Grand Chamberlain seems to have acted in a double character, as the Emperor's assistant, and also as one of his courtiers, for he had his own place among the *vela*, or honorary classes of court officials, which paid their respects to the Emperor on such occasions.

There were, finally, occasions when the Grand Chamberlain acted as the Emperor's deputy, *ex persona imperatoris*, and himself conferred minor dignities, or otherwise represented the Emperor.

Some of the ceremonies described by Constantine Porphyrogenitus belonged entirely to one or another of the types which have been mentioned, but more of them present a mixture of types. Thus the religious observances at the church were generally preceded and followed by observances of a secular nature, and the public ceremonies attending an imperial audience were usually preceded by a semi-private observance when the Emperor laid aside his ordinary cloak to be clad, by the Grand Chamberlain and his assistants, in his ceremonial robes.

Ceremonial acts show a tendency to become conventional or stereotyped, and an involved ceremony will be found to consist of a series of conventional acts, all or nearly all of which are to be found in other ceremonies, sometimes without any very important variations in their sequence. Therefore, while it is impossible to describe in detail the ceremonies of the Byzantine court, the more important ceremonial acts may be mentioned.

One of the most common of these ceremonial acts, occurring with especial frequency in the religious ceremonies, was the giving of candles by the Grand Chamberlain to the Emperor when he was about to pray,[1] or the receiving of candles from his hand when the prayer had been completed.[2] This ceremonial act was used as early as the year 768, in the ceremonies attending the elevation of the sons of Constantine V to the rank of Caesars.[3]

Very frequently nothing is said as to the manner in which the Grand Chamberlain disposed of the candles which were returned to him, but he seems to have handed them at times to a chamberlain,[4] or, more frequently, to the Master of the Ceremonies.[5] In one ceremony the Grand Chamberlain is said to have given the candles to the priests,[6] and in another to have placed a candle on the *solea* (σωλαία), the elevated portion of the floor in front of the inner sanctuary of the church.[7] In one passage the Grand Chamberlain handed to the Emperor not a candle (κηρίον) but a lamp (λαμπάς).[8]

It has already been suggested that in the period before Justinian the care of the Emperor's crown may have been intrusted to the Grand Chamberlain.[9] It seems to have been the privilege of the Grand Chamberlains in the later period also, to assist the Emperors by placing their crowns or tiaras upon their heads,[10] or by removing them when the occasion required.[11] On some occasions, however, the crown was placed on the Emperor's head by the Patriarch.[12] Especially interesting in this connection is the statement that in the funeral ceremony of an Emperor or Empress, it was the Grand Chamberlain who removed the crown from the former monarch's head when the body had been brought to the place of burial.[13]

A somewhat similar duty of the Grand Chamberlains, mentioned a few times in the *De Caerimoniis*, was that of assisting the Emperor

[1] Const. Porph., *De Caer.*, 7, 23; 29, 20; 64, 12; 65, 15; 74, 8; 75, 9; 76, 1; 112, 2; 116, 20; 117, 7 and 17; 118, 8; 120, 11 and 20; 121, 10; etc. If Leich's emendation of 8, 1 be adopted, it appears that in the ceremony here described the candles were handed to the Grand Chamberlain by an ordinary chamberlain. This fact is not elsewhere mentioned, but may fairly be assumed to have been customary.

[2] *Op. cit.*, 64, 15 and 21; 65, 18; 73, 23; 74, 5 and 20; 75, 2 and 10; 76, 14; 102, 18; 103, 1; 112, 5 and 18; 126, 8; 132, 21; 133, 20; etc.

[3] *Op. cit.*, 224, 1.

[4] *Op. cit.*, 8, 11.

[5] *Op. cit.*, 64, 15; 75, 2 and 11; 76, 15; 112, 5; 126, 8; 132, 22; 145, 8; 165, 5 and 13; etc.

[6] *Op. cit.*, 141, 12.

[7] *Op. cit.*, 133, 21.

[8] *Op. cit.*, 16, 21. Cf., however, 65, 12 f.: τὸ κηρίον, ἤγουν ἡ λαμπάς.

[9] See pp. 201 f.

[10] Const. Porph., *De Caer.*, 9, 10; 25, 19 f.; 62, 14; 68, 20; 80, 14; 99, 9; 104, 22; 109, 3; 129, 14; etc.

[11] *Op. cit.*, 14, 15 f.; 32, 22; 64, 5; 69, 23; 84, 21; 107, 20; 109, 24; 132, 16; 136, 14; 145, 3; 146, 8; 169, 3; etc.

[12] *Op. cit.*, 31, 18; 135, 13. In the latter passage the Grand Chamberlain is said to hand the crown to the Patriarch, who then places it upon the head of the Emperor.

[13] *Op. cit.*, 276, 18.

to don his ceremonial robes,[1] though this task was usually performed by *vestitores*, probably at the Grand Chamberlain's direction.[2] The Grand Chamberlains also put on the Emperor's girdle.[3]

On those occasions when the Emperor intended to make a gift to the church, the Grand Chamberlain usually carried the purse,[4] and when the Emperor bestowed largesses upon the attendants at the church, it was the Grand Chamberlain who took the purses from the Cashier (ὁ ἄργυρος) and gave them to the Emperor who in turn presented them to their recipients.[5] On many other occasions the Grand Chamberlain rendered personal assistance to the Emperor. On Easter, when the Patriarch bestowed the loaf of bread marked with a cross upon the Emperor, the latter passed it to the Grand Chamberlain to be borne back to the palace.[6] During the Christmas ceremonies, if a guardsman or a Count was to be appointed, the Grand Chamberlain handed to the Emperor a guardsman's truncheon,[7] or a Count's 'commission' (ὡρατίωνα),[8] and the Emperor presented it to the chosen attendant, thus confirming his appointment.

Somewhat similarly, at the promotion of a Patrician, the Grand Chamberlain took from the Deuteros the tablets which were the insignia of the Patrician rank, and handed them to the Emperor,[9] who bestowed them upon the candidate. The same ceremonial act occurred in the advancement of a candidate for proconsular rank.[10]

There were instances when the Grand Chamberlain's ceremonial acts were even more in the nature of personal service than any which have been mentioned. Thus, in the course of the amusing ceremony of the Emperor's bath,[11] the Grand Chamberlain handed to the Emperor the 'holy soap.'[12]

The activities of the Grand Chamberlain most conspicuous in the secular ceremonies of the court are those of a master, or director, of ceremonies. As such he ushered into the presence of the Emperor, one by one, the various *vela*, or ranks of court officials, who made obeisance to their sovereign and then took appointed places about the

[1] *Op. cit.*, 16, 12; 137, 5. Cf. Geo. Monachus, *De Michaele et Theodora*, 832, 22 ff.

[2] Const. Porph., *De Caer.*, 9, 8 ff.; 149, 1; 543, 9; etc.

[3] Codinus, *De Aedificiis Constantinopolis*, 125, 3 ff.

[4] Const. Porph., *De Caer.*, 65, 5; 68, 24; 76, 22; 133, 4; 135, 15; 142, 1; 145, 15 and 23; 166, 14; 182, 8 and 12; etc.

[5] *Op. cit.*, 18, 13 f.; 68, 13 f.; 135, 8 ff.; etc.

[6] *Op. cit.*, 18, 24.

[7] *Op. cit.*, 131, 2.

[8] *Op. cit.*, 131, 12.

[9] *Op. cit.*, 248, 6 f.

[10] *Op. cit.*, 256, 12 f.

[11] *Op. cit.*, 2, 12.

[12] *Op. cit.*, 555, 11 f.: τὴν ἁγίαν στακτήν.

audience chamber.[1] At an ordinary audience (δοχῇ) the *vela* were sometimes ushered in by the *ostiarius* or some other less important official, at the order of the Grand Chamberlain.[2] It was the Grand Chamberlain who ushered into the presence of the Empress the different ranks of the court ladies.[3]

Those who were designated for high honors at the court were generally escorted into the Emperor's presence by the Grand Chamberlain. He brought in the new Empress at the time of her coronation and wedding,[4] and with the Master conducted Caesars who were to be crowned before the throne.[5] He participated in a like manner in the advancement of a *nobilissimus*,[6] and without the assistance of the Master led forward a *curopalates*.[7] He also introduced a Master designate,[8] or a *patricia zoste* designate,[9] or a *rector*,[10] or a *prohedros* of the Senate.[11] It was perhaps natural that the Grand Chamberlain should escort into the Emperor's presence, as members of his own corps, those men and women who were to be appointed Chamberlains (κουβικουλάριοι, κουβικουλαραίαι) to the Emperor or Empress.[12] Before doing so, it was customary that he give them instructions as to the duties they should perform, and a charge.[13]

In the case of less elevated personages the Grand Chamberlain might pass an order to another official, who thereupon escorted the candidate to the throne.[14] When, however, a Domestic of the Guard (δομέστικος τῆς σχολῆς), a Drungarius of the Fleet, certain treasury officials, or others were to be appointed, the Logothete was called upon to introduce them.[15] The Grand Chamberlains waited outside until the newly appointed officials had been led from the audience chamber. They then escorted them into the presence of the assembled ranks of courtiers, and formally presented them. The duty of summoning or admitting the Patriarch especially seems to have fallen to the Grand Chamberlain,[16] though in the time of Constantine Porphyrogenitus the Referendarius of the Patriarch performed this duty at times.[17]

[1] *Op. cit.*, 23, 9 to 25, 6; 61, 5 to 62, 4; 234, 21 to 235, 5; 246, 20 to 247, 11; etc. The last passage cited gives the most detailed account.

[2] *Op. cit.*, 9, 22, and scholium.

[3] *Op. cit.*, 67, 13 ff.; 595, 22 ff.

[4] *Op. cit.*, 208, 12 ff.

[5] *Op. cit.*, 219, 8 ff.; 220, 4 ff.

[6] *Op. cit.*, 227, 5 ff.; 227, 17 ff.

[7] *Op. cit.*, 229, 18 f.

[8] *Op. cit.*, 232, 18 ff.; 233, 9 ff.; 235, 5 ff.

[9] *Op. cit.*, 257, 21 ff.; 259, 3 ff.

[10] *Op. cit.*, 528, 5 ff.

[11] *Op. cit.*, 441, 2.

[12] *Op. cit.*, II, 24; 25.

[13] *Op. cit.*, 623, 19 ff.; 625, 20 ff.

[14] *Op. cit.*, 238, 1 ff.

[15] *Op. cit.*, 525, 20 f.

[16] *Op. cit.*, 68, 7; 79, 10; 91, 6 and 15; 92, 3 ff.; 112, 25; 113, 12; 125, 18; 135, 5; 140, 8; 146, 14; 151, 23; 160, 11 ff.; etc. Cf. scholium on 116, 8.

[17] *Op. cit.*, 616, 2; 621, 5 f.

The duty of welcoming foreign ambassadors to the court and of presenting them to the Emperor, which the Grand Chamberlain claimed in the period before Justinian,[1] seems, at a later time, to have been shared with the Logothete of the Course.[2] When Luitprand was at the court of Nicephorus Phocas, in 968, his conversations were first with the *curopalati* and the Logothete,[3] and it was to them that he addressed a plea for the hearing of his petition.[4]

On occasions the Grand Chamberlain assisted candidates in removing their ordinary robes and donning those of the new order to which they were to be elevated,[5] but whether he did this personally, or through the aid of the *vestitores*, is not clear, for where he is said to have done this it may be that it was done by his assistants at his order.[6]

One of the most common features of the Byzantine ceremonies was the acclamations of the officials of the bedchamber, of the court, and of the factions. When the proper moment in a ceremony arrived, some official gave them the word of command, and they shouted in return, "Long live the Emperor," or words of similar purport (εἰς πολλοὺς χρόνους, εἰς πολλοὺς καὶ ἀγαθοὺς χρόνους, εἰς πολλοὺς καὶ ἀγαθοὺς χρόνους ὁ Θεὸς ἀγάγοι τὴν βασιλείαν ὑμῶν). When the acclamations were given by the Chamberlains, it was but natural that the Grand Chamberlain should lead them. The signal which he used in such cases was to pronounce the supposedly Latin word, Βιτ, which the translator has rendered *Fit*. Thereupon the Herald (φονοβόλος) of the Cubiculum said in a loud and harmonious voice, καλῶς, and the Chamberlains, in a barbarous mixture of Greek and Latin, cried, καλῶς ἤλθετε οἱ μουλτουσάνοι or ἄνω φιλλικήσιμε.[7]

In many other instances, especially when the felicitations were to be shouted by the higher ranks of officials, it was the Grand Chamberlain who gave the signal, by shouting the word, κελεύσατε.[8] When lower grades of officials expressed their good will, it was commonly in response to a signal given by the Master of the Ceremonies,[9] or, if

[1] See p. 202.

[2] Cf. Const. Porph., *De Caer.*, 588, 2 ff.; 593, 12 ff.; 595, 2.

[3] *Legatio*, 344 C.

[4] *Op. cit.*, 349 E. The Logothete's encroachment upon the Grand Chamberlain's competence is mentioned by Bieliaev, *Byzantina: ocherki, materialy i zamietki po vizantiiskim drevnostiam*, vol. II (1893), p. 17. This work is inaccessible to the author.

[5] Const. Porph., *De Caer.*, 233, 6 ff.; 235, 13 ff.; 263, 13 f.; 441, 1 f.; 529, 11 f.; etc.

[6] Cf. *op. cit.*, 624, 4 ff.; 625, 16 ff.

[7] *Op. cit.*, 21, 18 ff.; 69, 17 ff.; 136, 10 ff.

[8] *Op. cit.*, 129, 21; 149, 7; 154, 12; 193, 18; 203, 5; 204, 3; 209, 17; 226, 15; 228, 14; 230, 13; 232, 8; etc.

[9] *Op. cit.*, 10, 9 ff.

the dignitaries were of still humbler grade, by a Silentiary.[1] In either case, however, the Grand Chamberlain first gave a sign to the leader of the acclamations.[2]

During the ceremonies, information intended for the Emperor was regularly imparted to him by the Grand Chamberlain.[3]

In ceremonial matters as in administrative affairs the Grand Chamberlain sometimes acted *in loco imperatoris*. This was most notable in the ceremonies attending the appointment, in the tenth century, of certain officials of the court. Thus, when the Emperor wished to appoint a City Prefect, he summoned both the Grand Chamberlain and the man chosen for advancement into his presence, and then commanded the former, "Go and present him as Prefect of the City."[4] The Grand Chamberlain thereupon took the candidate in charge, invested him with his official robes and, with brief ceremony, presented him to the assembled throng of courtiers.[5] Even less formality seems to have been observed in the case of the promotion of a Quaestor.[6]

A Demarch also was presented to his faction by the Grand Chamberlain,[7] and a man designated by the Emperor as ὁ δευτερεύων of a faction was publicly presented to the Demarch by the Grand Chamberlain or, if the Demarch was sick, the appointee was delivered by the Grand Chamberlain to certain members of the court who escorted him to the house of the Demarch, and there presented him.[8] A very similar practice obtained in the promotion of an Assessor (σύμπονος) to the City Prefect or a Logothete of the Praetorium,[9] and in the appointment of an ἀντιγραφεύς.[10] At the times when the Emperor made his donations to the factions, he intrusted the duty to the Grand Chamberlain, who presented the money to the Demarch.[11]

It is clear that the Grand Chamberlain was closely connected with the activities of the race-course. When preparations were being made for the races, the Grand Chamberlain was instructed by the Emperor to give directions for the contest. Attended by all the mem-

[1] *Op. cit.*, 10, 18 ff.

[2] The scholium on, *De Caer.*, 87, 4, indicates that in the absence of a Grand Chamberlain the sign was given by the Primicerius of the *cubiculum* (Ἰστέον ὅτι, πραιποσίτου μὴ ὄντος, νεύει τῷ σιλεντιαρίῳ ὁ πριμικήριος τοῦ κουβουκλείου). This scholium may date from a time when the office of Grand Chamberlain no longer existed.

[3] Const. Porph., *De Caer.*, 16, 12 f.; 65, 26 f.; 66, 21 f.; 79, 8 f.; 90, 18 f.; 92, 1 f.; 129, 9 ff.; 269, 20 f.; 543, 1 ff.; 621, 3 ff.; 633, 17 f.; etc.

[4] *Op. cit.*, 263, 12: Ἄπελθε καὶ παράδος αὐτὸν ὕπαρχον πόλεως.

[5] *Op. cit.*, I, 52.

[6] *Op. cit.*, I, 54.

[7] *Op. cit.*, I, 55.

[8] *Op. cit.*, I, 56.

[9] *Op. cit.*, I, 57.

[10] *Op. cit.*, I, 58.

[11] *Op. cit.*, 300, 14 to 20.

bers of the Cubiculum, and by the Master of the Ceremonies with all the Silentiaries, he proceeded to a point where all the racers and their Decani awaited him. Through the midst of these the Demarchs and the Actuarius approached the Grand Chamberlain and made obeisance to him.[1] The retinue which attended the Grand Chamberlain on this occasion, and the respect with which he was saluted are marks of his importance in regard to the celebrations in the hippodrome. During the ceremonies preceding and following the races, the Grand Chamberlain seems to have been directly in attendance upon the Emperor.[2] When the racing was about to begin, however, he left the Emperor's side, and took his place upon an elevated platform (ἐπάνω τῶν βάθρων), whence he ordered the Patricians to approach and salute the Emperor, and again to take their seats.[3] Apparently he also directed the races from this point.

When the urn was shaken to determine the order of the racers, a Silentiary stood close by, representing the Grand Chamberlain (ἐκ προσώπου τοῦ πραιποσίτου).[4] On the morning of the races, apparently, the Grand Chamberlain exercised a summary jurisdiction in disputes between the Demarchs,[5] which presumably concerned the races.

It was his duty also to issue orders to all the officials of the race-course regarding the careful performance of their duties.[6]

From the mutilated chapter which closes the *De Caerimoniis* (II, 56), it appears that the various ranks of officials made certain donations in the hippodrome which were used for the maintenance of the attendants. It was provided that these donations be made to the Grand Chamberlains and that they make disbursements therefrom to the various attendants of the hippodrome who were enrolled on their register, according to the recommendations of the Chartularies. The Grand Chamberlains seem not to have been sufficiently jealous of these prerogatives, and through their neglect the handling of the donations, and even the appointment of the attendants, and the regulation and payment of their wages, had fallen into the control of the Military Treasury and the Chartularies and Notaries. The abuse was corrected by the imperial constitution of which *De Caerimoniis*, II, 56, is a fragment, about the time of Constantine Porphyrogenitus.[7]

[1] *Op. cit.*, 304, 2 to 13. [2] *Op. cit.*, 305–306. [3] *Op. cit.*, 307, 8 to 18.
[4] *Op. cit.*, 312, 20 f. [5] *Op. cit.*, 313, 20 f. [6] *Op. cit.*, 363, 3 ff.
[7] See Bury's discussion in *English Historical Review*, vol. XXII (1907), pp. 219–221.

The duties of the Grand Chamberlain were not limited to the ceremonies. An interesting suggestion as to the variety of his activities is to be found in the account of the proceedings of the Fourth Council of Constantinople, which was held in the year 869. Bahanes, the Grand Chamberlain of the Emperor Basil I, was present at many of the meetings of the Council, and often took a prominent part in their deliberations. He frequently is said to have spoken for the Senate,[1] but he also spoke for the Emperor.[2]

The clearest indication of the Grand Chamberlain's importance is the fact that when the Emperor was absent from the capital, it was he who temporarily administered the Empire as vice-regent. Porphyrogenitus states that of old it was the custom of Emperors, when departing on a military expedition, to intrust their own powers to the Grand Chamberlain, and to the Master and Prefect (of the city) the supervision of the city's administration and of the common welfare.[3]

When thus administering the government in the Emperor's stead, the Grand Chamberlain was known as ὁ διέπων[4] or ὁ ἀπομονεύς.[5] Porphyrogenitus' statement that this custom was observed 'of old' suggests a more remote period than his own century. It may indeed refer to an occasion as early as the time of Justinian. It is stated that when that Emperor[6] was called from the city, the *tribunus praesentalis* was left behind to guard it.[7] He was assisted by the City Prefect, apparently, who also welcomed the Emperor on his return.[8] Perhaps the Master (*i.e.*, of the Offices) also remained in the city, for if the Emperor did not enter through the Golden Gate the Count of the Admittances (ὁ ἀδμισσιωνάλιος) welcomed him at the palace gate, "for the Master had so ordered him." [9]

There is no mention here of the Grand Chamberlain's exercising supervision of the city. Indeed, the participle ἀπομείνας, applied to

[1] Mansi, *op. cit.*, vol. XVI, 30 D: *Bahanes ex persona sacri senatus*, etc. Cf. 34 A; 144 E; 152 A; 317 D.

[2] *Op. cit.*, vol. XVI, 99 D: *Bahanes . . . iussus ab imperatore dixit*, etc. Cf. 100 B; 135 B; 159 D.

[3] Περὶ ταξειδίων (*De Caer. I, Appendix*), 503, 10 ff.: τὸ παλαιὸν ἐκράτει τοῖς βασιλεῦσιν ἔθος, ἐξερχομένου τοῦ βασιλέως ἐπὶ φοσσάτου τὸν πραιπόσιτον παρεᾷν τὴν ἑαυτοῦ ἀρχῆς ἐπικράτειαν, καὶ τῷ μαγίστρῳ καὶ τῷ ἐπάρχῳ τὴν τῆς πολιτείας καὶ τοῦ κοινοῦ τὴν διοίκησιν.

[4] *Op. cit.*, 506, 2.

[5] *Op. cit.*, 501, 13.

[6] Bury, *Eng. Hist. Rev.*, vol. XXII (1907), p. 439, n. 57, dates the section on pages 495–498 in the time of Justinian.

[7] Περὶ ταξειδίων, p. 495, 6: ἀλλ' ὁ μὲν τριβοῦνος πραισεντάλιος ὁ ἀπομείνας εἰς παραφυλακὴν τῆς πόλεως, κτλ.

[8] *Op. cit.*, 497, 12 f.: δέχεται κατὰ τὸ ἔθος τὸν ἔπαρχον τῆς πόλεως καὶ τὸν ἀπομονέα, κτλ.

[9] *Op. cit.*, 498, 9 f.: οὕτω γὰρ συνεῖδεν γενέσθαι ὁ μάγιστρος, κτλ.

the *tribunus praesentalis,* seems strongly to suggest that he was the ἀπομονεύς. Nevertheless, as the same participle is applied within the space of two lines to other high officials,[1] too much importance must not be attached to this fact.

It seems quite possible that even though he is not specifically mentioned by title the Grand Chamberlain may have been ὁ ἀπομονεύς under Justinian. Certainly he held this distinction at a later time, and it does not appear likely that Porphyrogenitus would consciously have employed the same term in the compass of a few pages to designate two different officials without mentioning the fact. It would seem even a little inconsistent for him to describe an old ceremony in which the Grand Chamberlain was not the Emperor's vice-regent, and then to state that 'of old' or 'in former times' the Emperor was so represented by the Grand Chamberlain.

The Grand Chamberlain was appointed to act thus in the capacity of vice-regent by the Emperor Theophilus (829–842),[2] by Basil I (867–886),[3] and by Nicephorus Phocas in 968.[4]

When Theophilus returned he was welcomed by the Grand Chamberlain and other important officials,[5] and on his formal entry into the city, the three who had administered the government in his absence presented him with a golden crown, set with gems.[6] The Grand Chamberlains then preceded him on his triumphal march.[7] When Basil entered the city, the Grand Chamberlain, as vice-regent, and the Prefect prostrated themselves before him, and then presented him with a golden crown and a victor's laurel wreath. For these they were handsomely rewarded.[8] The Grand Chamberlain then accompanied the Emperor to the church of the Holy Virgin, where he handed him tapers to be burned at the altar.[9]

It appears that at times the Grand Chamberlain himself might bc represented by another.[10]

The investiture of the Grand Chamberlain was the occasion of an elaborate ceremony in the Golden Banquet Hall (χρυσοτρίκλινος), in which the Emperor presented the candidate with the insignia of his office, ivory tablets, — similar, no doubt, to the familiar consular diptychs, — which resembled those of the Patricians, except that they

[1] *Op. cit.*, 495, 5: οἱ ἀπομείναντες ἄρχοντες.

[2] *Op. cit.*, 503, 21 ff.

[3] *Op. cit.*, 503, 6 ff.

[4] Luitprand, *Legatio*, pp. 362, 364.

[5] Περὶ ταξειδίων, 504, 4 ff.

[6] *Op. cit.*, 506, 1 ff.

[7] *Op. cit.*, 506, 13 ff.

[8] *Op. cit.*, 501, 12 ff.

[9] *Op. cit.*, 502, 5.

[10] Zonaras, vol., III, p. 47, 9: ὁ εὐνοῦχος . . . τὴν τοῦ πραιποσίτου διέπων ἀρχήν.

were not inscribed.[1] If the candidate was made a Protospathar at the same time, he received the further insigne of a golden collar, set with pearls and precious stones, such as officials of that rank were entitled to wear.[2] If, however, it was the patrician rank that was conferred upon him, he received, in addition to the insignia of a Grand Chamberlain, those of the patrician order, namely, inscribed ivory tablets.[3]

In pursuance of an ancient custom, it was necessary for newly appointed officials to make certain donations to those who participated in one way or another in the conferring of the honor. The Grand Chamberlain, if he was made a Protospathar at the same time, made a donation of a pound of gold to some unmentioned beneficiary, and to the Deuteros of the Palace, who prepared the ivory tablets, twenty-four milaresia.[4] If he was made a Patrician his donation was the same as others of that rank made,[5] two pounds of gold to the eunuchs of the Cubiculum, and eight pounds of gold distributed among the other eunuchs.[6] The fact that the Grand Chamberlain always received the rank either of Protospathar or Patrician explains why Philotheos does not indicate the amount of the donations to be made by the Grand Chamberlain as such.

The Atriklines (ὁ ἀτρικλίνης), who was in charge of the imperial invitation lists, was also the recipient of donations from newly appointed officials. In the case of the Grand Chamberlains, this amounted to twelve milaresia.[7]

In a similar manner the Grand Chamberlains received donations upon the elevation of many dignitaries; the amount of these gratuities varied somewhat according to the importance of the offices to which they were promoted.[8] The Officialioi, or members of various staffs, were required to give him twenty-four milaresia each, because he had announced their promotion on behalf of the Emperor (ἐκ προσώπου τοῦ βασιλέως).[9] In the time of Constantine Porphyrogenitus,[10] Patricians, when promoted to that rank, gave certain sums of money as donations to the Grand Chamberlains, who then divided them according to a fixed schedule among a large number of minor officials and servants.[11] The amount distributed by him does not equal

[1] Const. Porph., *De Caer.* (*Klet.*), 722, 10 ff.
[2] *Op. cit.*, 722, 4.
[3] *Op. cit.*, 722, 16.
[4] Const. Porph., *De Caer.* (*Klet.*), 722, 13 ff.
[5] *Op. cit.*, 722, 15 f.
[6] *Op. cit.*, 710, 8 ff.
[7] *Op. cit.*, 788, 15 ff.
[8] *Op. cit.*, 708, 10 ff.; 721, 8 ff.
[9] *Op. cit.*, 723, 2 ff.
[10] Bury, *Eng. Hist. Rev.*, vol. XXII (1907), p. 226, assigns *De Caerimoniis*, II, 55 to him.
[11] Const. Porph., *De Caer.*, II, 55.

the amount he received, and it is possible that the small remainder fell to him.[1]

When a new Emperor was proclaimed, he advanced the Grand Chamberlains to a higher rank, if they were not already Patricians, and gave them the privilege of nominating for honorary distinctions such of their relatives and dependents as they might choose.[2]

Regular largesses were given by the Emperor at the Brumalia, and on the anniversaries of his coronation and of the founding of the Empire. On these occasions the Grand Chamberlain received the largest amount paid to any one official, twenty milaresia.[3]

[1] Suggested by the Latin translator, p. 806.
[2] Const. Porph., *De Caer.* (*Klet.*), 712, 9 ff.
[3] *Op. cit.*, 785, 5.

CHAPTER IV

THE CAREERS OF PROMINENT GRAND CHAMBERLAINS

In the preceding pages an attempt has been made to present all the facts which can be ascertained relative to the official position, duties, and emoluments of the Grand Chamberlain, and his relation to the other members of the court. It has been repeatedly stated, however, that much of the importance attaching to his office was due, not to his official status or to his legal powers, but to his close association with the Emperor, and the influence, resulting from this association, which he was able to exercise upon the Emperor, and so also upon the other members of the court circles. With the purpose of setting forth the nature and variety of these extra-legal activities of the Grand Chamberlain, accounts of the lives of three prominent incumbents of that office, together with a brief eulogy of a fourth, are presented in the following pages.

Eusebius, Eutherius, Eutropius, and Narses were doubtless exceptional characters, and the life of no one of them could be regarded as typical of the lives of Grand Chamberlains in general, but their combined activities may be taken as fairly representing the range of possible action of any holder of that office. It is doubtful whether complete knowledge of the acts of all Grand Chamberlains would greatly broaden this range, but it would probably furnish still other examples of rapid rise to power, of devices for subjecting the Emperor's will to the wishes of his attendants, of brilliant careers of intrigue, extortion, and assassination, of final disgrace and violent death; examples also of nobility of character and of that unswerving loyalty which begets criticism rather than flattery, and of undoubted ability.

I. The Grand Chamberlain Eusebius

The first Grand Chamberlain of the Later Roman Empire whose career can be traced in any detail was Eusebius, who held this position throughout the reign of Constantius II. Of his antecedents and early life nothing is known, and the earliest fact regarding him of which there is any record is that he was Grand Chamberlain at the time of the accession of Constantius, or soon after. It is quite probable that he had served the future Emperor in that capacity before the death of his father, Constantine the Great.

Constantius was not without good qualities, but these were largely obscured by his weakness and his vanity, his easy disposition, and his suspicious nature. He came to the throne, moreover, at the age of but twenty years, and his lack of experience, combined with the inherent faults of his character, made him an easy prey to the flatterers and informers by whom he was surrounded. The intimacy with the Emperor which Eusebius enjoyed as the result of his official position made him one of the most conspicuous of the intriguers.

Eusebius and the Arians

Intrigue had not been wanting in the later years of the reign of Constantine. The Arian faction had been overwhelmingly defeated at the Council of Nicaea, but many of the Arian party were unwilling to adhere to the strong position which the council had taken. In consequence, a marked reaction soon set in, and the defeated party, taking advantage of the changed tide of affairs, employed so well its influence with certain members of the court circles that their leader, Arius, was recalled from exile, and Constantine, on his death-bed, though still professing orthodoxy, received baptism at the hands of an Arian bishop.

It was but natural that the Arians should attempt to continue, under the new Emperor, the policies which had been so successful under his father. Very shortly after the death of Constantine (May 22, 337), hoping to retain favor at court, they sent to Constantius a certain presbyter of their sect who had access to some of the members of the imperial household. This presbyter bore to the Emperor a will, supposed to be that of the late Constantine, which made such disposition of the Empire as Constantius most desired.[1]

The initial advantage which the Arians obtained by thus gaining the Emperor's gratitude was not lost. The presbyter had found further favor in the eyes of the new Emperor, and was granted free access to the palace and to the members of the imperial family. He employed the opportunity to expound Arian doctrines to the Empress and to the court servants, and soon succeeded in bringing Eusebius, the Grand

[1] Socrates, *Hist. Eccl.*, 2, 2; Sozomen, *Hist. Eccl.*, 3, 1.

Chamberlain, to adopt them. This made it clear to the other eunuchs of the palace where their interests lay, and after the apostasy of their leader they were readily induced to accept the same doctrines. Eusebius then approached the Empress, and soon succeeded in persuading her to espouse the cause of the Arian party. Thus the Emperor was surrounded by persons of Arian sympathies, whose influence must have done much to confirm such Arian tendencies as he may already have shown.[1] Indeed, it is the obvious purpose of the church historians to place the responsibility for Constantius's desertion of the Nicene party upon the intriguing eunuchs of his retinue, and specifically upon Eusebius.[2]

Their statement of the case is, of course, incomplete, for there were other influences at work toward the same end, but it is enough to show that in the sectarian struggles of the next half century are to be seen the results of the machinations of the Grand Chamberlain and his associates.

The history of the reign of Constantius is full of the strife between Nicenes and anti-Nicenes, rendered more virulent by personal animosities and vile calumniations. The roads were filled with ecclesiastics posting to rival councils; bishops were seated and unseated, exiled and repatriated; Constantinople and Alexandria were at each other's throats; the Pope defied the Emperor and the Emperor placed the Pope under arrest. Arianism, with palace patronage, seemed in a fair way to overcome the orthodox faith.

Eusebius was doubtless a tireless supporter of the Arian faction, and on at least one occasion came into sharp conflict with the Nicenes. Liberius, the bishop of Rome, was one of the staunchest adherents to the Nicene faith, and so successfully frustrated the attempts of his enemies to secure a following in the West, that they finally enlisted the aid of the Emperor to secure his deposition. Constantius, thinking that the removal of the recalcitrant bishop would usher in a period of ecclesiastical harmony, despatched Eusebius with gifts and with letters, with which to bribe or threaten Liberius. But Liberius, moved by neither cupidity nor fear, employed the opportunity to reproach Eusebius and the Emperor for their heresy. Eusebius, "forgetting that he was in the presence of a bishop," departed with angry threats, and going to the martyry of St. Peter, deposited his bribe as a rich gift, hoping, probably, to produce a favorable impression

[1] Socrates, *Hist. Eccl.*, 1, 25; Sozomen, *Hist. Eccl.*, 3, 1.

[2] Zonaras, *Epitome*, XIII, 11, 14.

on the people of Rome. Liberius, discovering what the eunuch had done, ordered that the gift be rejected as unholy.[1]

The Grand Chamberlain was now highly incensed, and informed the Emperor that the bishop must be removed at any cost. He intimated to the other eunuchs that they should urge the same action, and this concerted endeavor could hardly meet with failure, for "most, nay, all of those about Constantius were eunuchs, and they possessed all power, since nothing was done except as they agreed to it."[2] The eunuchs, therefore, wove plots against Liberius, confident of their ultimate success, for they were "reckoned masters of the ecclesiastical courts," and with Constantius subject to their will "they directed the affairs of the church."[3]

Liberius was finally brought before the Emperor, where his fearless defiance won the admiration of all. Eusebius was present at this examination, and at one point viciously assailed the bishop, asking him if he intended to represent the Emperor as a Nebuchadnezzar. As a result of his uncompromising attitude, Liberius was exiled, but before he departed he further showed his independence by refusing gifts from the Emperor and the Empress, saying to Eusebius, who proffered them, "You have laid waste the churches of all the world, and do you presume to bring these gifts to me, as to a condemned man? Go, first, and learn to be a Christian."[4]

The original tenet of Arius, that the Father and Son were of entirely different essence (ἀνόμοιοι, ἑτεροούσιοι), had shocked the Council of Nicaea into a declaration that Father and Son were the same essence (ὁμοούσιοι). In their zeal to overthrow Arius a great number of bishops, especially those from the East, had subscribed to a statement of whose truth they were but half convinced, and there soon developed among them a strong body of conservative opinion, opposed both to strict Arianism and to the Nicene faith, and holding that Father and Son were neither the same essence nor of totally different essence, but of like essence (ὁμοιοούσιοι). From the standpoint of the strict Nicenes, this was Arianizing, and they turned their anathemas from the small and dwindling Arian party to the powerful and increasingly dangerous semi-Arians.

Toward the middle of the fourth century, however, Arianism was revived by Aëtius, who carried its logic even farther than had Arius himself. A number of bishops promptly joined this new and ultra-

[1] Athanasius, *Historia Arianorum*, 35–37. [2] *Op. cit.*, 37. [3] *Op. cit.*, 38.
[4] Theodoret, *Eccl. Hist.*, 2, 13; Cassiodorus, *Historia Tripartita*, 5, 17.

Arian sect, among them Eudoxius and Acacius, and Ursacius and Valens, all of them ecclesiastical intriguers. It was their desire that their tenets might be presented in some inoffensive guise to a church council, with the hope that they might be accepted.

In the year 358 arrangements were already being made for such a council of bishops from all parts of the Empire, but the uncompromising attitude of the Western bishops, who were staunch Nicenes, was well known, and the Aëtians felt that they would have far greater chance of success if they could present their creed to the more conformable semi-Arians of the East, sitting apart from their Western brothers. Eudoxius, therefore, sought the aid of his intimate associate, the Grand Chamberlain Eusebius, and through him succeeded in having the plans for the council changed so that the Western bishops would meet alone in Ariminum, while the Eastern bishops met in Seleucia. These two gatherings were held in the year 359, but the Aëtians, despite all their diplomacy, met with failure.[1]

It is obvious from the description of Eusebius's participation in these two episodes, that he played a significant, if not a conspicuous, part in the endless sectarian squabbles and intrigues of the reign of Constantius. It is not impossible that if the Arians had found him hostile, rather than favorable, to their hopes, Arianism, the strength of which always depended on court influence, might never have threatened the orthodox faith.[2]

Eusebius and Gallus

Political as well as ecclesiastical intrigues engaged the activities of Eusebius, and he played a conspicuous part in the downfall of Gallus. Constantius had been compelled by circumstances to recognize Gallus as Caesar, and had put him in control of the Eastern provinces. It was a dangerous expedient, for Gallus had sufficient cause for hatred toward the Emperor, and was not without friends. Constantius soon became suspicious of the Caesar, and his suspicions were so nursed by the eunuchs of the palace that he determined to weaken the power of his rival.

The most capable and the most powerful of the friends of Gallus was his uncle, Rufinus. At the beginning of the year 353 Rufinus was Prefect of the camp at Chalons-sur-Saône, where Constantius had ordered assembled a large force, preparatory to a campaign against the

[1] Sozomen, *Hist. Eccl.*, 4, 16, end.

[2] On the general subject see Gwatkin, *Studies of Arianism.*

Alemanni. Unfavorable weather made it impossible either to initiate the campaign or to bring in provisions, and the soldiers, chafing under their inactivity and the lack of sufficient food, showed mutinous tendencies.

The Emperor, then at Valencia, deliberately permitted matters to pass from bad to worse, hoping that the soldiers would murder Rufinus, and thus deprive Gallus of his principal ally. The Prefect, however, was skilful enough to maintain his authority over the soldiers, and when it was apparent that he was in no immediate danger, the Grand Chamberlain Eusebius was despatched by the Emperor with money, which he secretly distributed among the leaders of sedition, and thus restored the forces to their usual discipline.[1] That the eunuch was privy to the full treachery of this dealing is not to be doubted, and the fact that Constantius employed him for so delicate a mission is clear evidence that he placed the utmost confidence in him.

The next attack was aimed directly at Gallus, and was instigated by some of the unscrupulous schemers about the court, who sought to enhance their own prestige at his expense. Dynamius and Picentius seem to have been the leaders in this plot. They were men of mean station, who made a profitable business of blackmailing. Dynamius in particular was a thoroughgoing scoundrel, whose base devices brought him, for a short time, no little favor at court, together with an unsavory notoriety. Lampadius, the Pretorian Prefect, who suffered from excessive self-esteem, was also a member of the conspiracy. These men succeeded in attaching Eusebius to their coterie, and then began systematically to charge Gallus with designs against Constantius.[2]

Meanwhile Gallus had done much to bring discredit upon himself. He had wretchedly misgoverned the provinces intrusted to his charge, and had ruled with all the savagery of the worst oriental despot. An attempt upon his life roused his suspicions, and he entered upon a reign of terror.[3]

Constantius was no doubt moved by the reports coming from the East, and the interpretation put upon them by the little circle of conspirators must have made them even more disturbing. Finally, Gallus was summoned to appear before the Emperor in Milan. Reluctantly and with foreboding he set forth toward the West. In the middle of his journey he suddenly found himself in the hands of his enemies, under the direction of the powerful Grand Chamberlain. By the

[1] Ammianus Marcellinus, XIV, 10, 5. [2] Zosimus, 121, 5 ff. [3] Amm. Marc., XIV, 1–10.

latter he was subjected to a grilling inquiry, under which he admitted guilt in a large number of crimes. This information was despatched to the Emperor, who straightway sent servants to take the life of Gallus.[1] Very shortly after, however, he altered his decision and sent another deputation to prevent the execution of the sentence. This was met at its arrival by the enemies of Gallus, and was prevailed upon by the Grand Chamberlain Eusebius not to deliver the countermand until the Caesar had been killed.[2]

With Gallus out of the way, the violence of the Emperor was directed against the friends and partisans of the late Caesar, and it is significant that one of the first to be accused was Gorgonius, his Grand Chamberlain. This man not only admitted complicity in many of the undertakings of Gallus, but even confessed that he had been one of the chief instigators of them. It seemed that he would be condemned at once, but the eunuchs of the court, perceiving that one of their own class was in peril, rallied to his defence, and by skilfully contrived falsehoods succeeded in gaining his acquittal.[3]

Next to be charged with complicity in Gallus' schemes were troops of soldiers and members of his court. They were brought to Aquileia for trial, and to that place Arbetio, the Master of Horse, and Eusebius, the Grand Chamberlain, were sent by the Emperor to act as judges. They were arrogant and cruel men and could be counted on to deal severely with the offenders. The subsequent procedure was a mockery. Without troubling themselves to determine the truth of the accusations, these judges imposed sentences of stripes, or torture and exile, of service in the lowest ranks of the army, or death; and having "filled the sepulchres with dead bodies," returned to Milan with great pomp and ceremony, and reported their glorious exploits to the Emperor.[4]

In the course of the plots against Gallus, Eusebius and Arbetio succeeded in securing the recall of Ursicinus, the Master of Horse in the East. There seems to have been no valid reason for this action, save perhaps the jealousy of Arbetio, who was also a Master of Horse, serving at the court of the Emperor.[5]

The eunuchs were involved in this intrigue and roused suspicions that the sons of Ursicinus, young men of excellent qualities, were aiming at supreme power, and that Ursicinus was abetting them.[6] He was accordingly summoned to Milan on the pretext that the Em-

[1] *Op. cit.*, XIV, 11, 1–23.
[2] Zonaras, *Epitome*, vol. III, 47, 6 ff.
[3] Amm. Marc., XV, 2, 10.
[4] *Op. cit.*, XV, 3, 1–2.
[5] *Op. cit.*, XIV, 11, 2.
[6] *Op. cit.*, XIV, 11, 3.

peror desired his attendance at an important council.[1] There, after the death of Gallus, he was brought to trial on the charge of treason.[2] The conspirators roused the enmity of Constantius toward their victim by statements that the eastern provinces no longer looked to the Emperor for protection against the Persians, but sought the leadership of the Master of Horse.[3] Ursicinus resolutely stood his ground, but his denials bore little weight against the calumniations of the courtiers, and the Emperor finally yielded to the requests of Arbetio that the accused man be seized and put to death uncondemned.[4] Before this plan was put into effect, however, he repented of his decision, and Ursicinus was spared.[5]

The charges against Ursicinus seem to have been dropped, but he was still the object of enmity. In 355, when Silvanus, the Master of Foot in Gaul, was reported to have assumed the purple, Constantius hastily called a council to decide what action should be taken. None save Ursicinus, previously known as the "whirlpool of the East," was thought able to cope with the situation, and he was chosen for the task. But there was a secondary and sinister motive in the selection of Ursicinus for this difficult commission, for it was thought by his detractors that if he should fail, his desired ruin would be complete.[6] Ursicinus proved equal to the occasion, however, and his enemies were forced to await a better opportunity of compassing his fall.

Four years later, while Ursicinus was again in the East in command of Roman forces, and a Persian invasion was threatening, Eusebius renewed his attacks on him, holding him up "like a grim Gorgon's head" before the suspicious Emperor, and, "hammering on the same anvil day and night," continually repeated the charge that he was ambitious of greater power.[7] The officers of the court, as well as the chamberlains, knowing well the influence which Eusebius had, and desiring to win his favor, joined in his libellous attack. They proceeded warily, however, lest their plans miscarry, and awaited the slightest pretext to secure the execution of Ursicinus, which they seem to have had no doubts of their ability to accomplish.[8]

There were two causes for the Grand Chamberlain's bitter enmity toward the valiant old Master of Horse, according to Ammianus Marcellinus; one, that he alone did not require the aid of Eusebius as others did, and hence would not fawn upon him, and the other, that

[1] *Op. cit.*, XIV, 11, 4 and 5.
[2] *Op. cit.*, XV, 2, 1.
[3] *Op. cit.*, XV, 2, 2.
[4] *Op. cit.*, XV, 2, 4–5.
[5] *Op. cit.*, XV, 2, 6.
[6] *Op. cit.*, XV, 5, 18–19.
[7] *Op. cit.*, XVIII, 4, 2.
[8] *Op. cit.*, XVIII, 4, 6.

he would not surrender to Eusebius his house at Antioch, which the latter coveted.[1]

The attendants at the palace continued their attitude of malice, being urged on by the eunuchs who had contrived the plot, who looked for any means of increasing their wealth.[2] They branded Ursicinus as a greedy promoter of revolution, and soon secured his recall to the palace to succeed the murdered Barbatio as Master of Foot, thinking they could attack him more easily if he should be within their reach.[3] Sabinianus, a feeble old man, was sent to replace the veteran of many Persian campaigns, bearing letters from the Emperor requiring his predecessor's attendance at court, where he should receive higher dignities.[4] The provincials were dismayed at the thought of losing their protector, and not without reason, for the news of his recall was a signal to the Persians to make an incursion into Roman territory.[5]

Ursicinus obediently set out toward Italy, but had traversed but half the distance when he was met by messengers with letters from the Emperor ordering him to return at once to Mesopotamia, without either officers or a commission.[6] This was the result of another plot hatched at the palace by Eusebius and his crew, with a purpose similar to that which had resulted in sending Ursicinus into Gaul several years earlier. If the impending attack of the Persians should be repulsed, the success would be attributed to Sabinianus; but if it should not, Ursicinus would be charged with the failure.[7]

The expected Persian invasion came, and culminated in a seventy-three day siege of the fortified city of Amida, which Ursicinus defended with great valor and determination. In dire straits he despatched a messenger to Sabinianus, begging that he send to the city's relief a small force which he had in reserve, but the messenger was shown letters from the Emperor commanding that nothing should be done to endanger this force. This was but another feature of the plot to bring ruin and disgrace upon the greatest general the Empire possessed.[8] Advice indeed was given, and in abundance, but it was not advice of which Ursicinus had need, and Amida at last fell to the Persians.

Ursicinus in some manner escaped from the city when resistance was no longer possible, and returned to the court to take up his duties as Master of Foot. His enemies at once began spreading slander, and

[1] *Op. cit.*, XVIII, 4, 3.
[2] *Op. cit.*, XVIII, 5, 4.
[3] *Op. cit.*, XVIII, 5, 5.
[4] *Op. cit.*, XVIII, 6, 1.
[5] *Op. cit.*, XVIII, 6, 2–3.
[6] *Op. cit.*, XVIII, 6, 5.
[7] *Op. cit.*, XVIII, 6, 6.
[8] *Op. cit.*, XIX, 3, 2.

soon accused him openly of treasonable action at Amida.[1] The Emperor, who was always ready to listen to the most groundless charges, appointed Arbetio, who had earlier shown himself no friend of the general, and Florentius, the Master of the Offices, to investigate the matter. Proofs were offered showing that the town was lost because of Sabinianus's refusal of aid, but these were not accepted because the commission feared that Eusebius, the Grand Chamberlain, would be offended if Sabinianus were shown responsible.[2]

Ursicinus made a vigorous protest, but the only result was that his words were reported to the Emperor with a malignant interpretation, and the Emperor, thus inflamed, refusing to listen to any defence, deposed Ursicinus, and ordered him into retirement.[3] It would be a source of satisfaction to know that the general retired to his house in Antioch, and that the iniquitous Grand Chamberlain was thus balked of one of his desires.

Eusebius and Julian

It can scarcely be doubted that Eusebius was actively hostile to Julian throughout the reign of Constantius, but whether it was because of Julian's inoffensive mode of life in the years before he was created Caesar and his moderation in later days, or, perhaps, because of the fact that he had a friend at court in the person of the Empress Eusebia, the Grand Chamberlain seems to have been more circumspect and certainly less successful in his attempts against Julian than he had been in the cases of Gallus and Ursicinus.

Little is said of the plots against Julian. This may be attributed partly to the fact that Ammianus Marcellinus, from whose vivid narrative is drawn the information concerning most of the details of the court intrigues of the reign of Constantius, was a member of the staff of Ursicinus until the general's forced retirement, and was stationed in the neighborhood of Gallus's capital, so that he was able to observe the tactics employed against these men; thus he was far removed from Julian and knew of the intrigues against him only by report.

Julian himself is the only one to state that Eusebius was at any time hostile to him. While still a private citizen he had had one interview with Constantius and had been promised another, but the Grand Chamberlain did not permit this, for he dreaded lest Julian be taken into favor and be given a position of trust.[4] Ammianus speaks of

[1] *Op. cit.*, XX, 2, 1.
[2] *Op. cit.*, XX, 2, 2.
[3] *Op. cit.*, XX, 2, 3.
[4] Julian, *Ad Athenaios*, 274 A, B.

detractors of Julian at the court who had great influence with Constantius,[1] and it seems very probable that Eusebius was one of them, though he is not specifically mentioned.

When Julian became sole master of the Roman Empire, on the death of Constantius, he began at once to take action against the miserable plotters who had swarmed about the court, and Eusebius was sentenced to death as responsible for the murder of Gallus.[2]

He was a man, says Ammianus, full of ambition and cruelty, who had been elevated from the meanest rank to a position so high as almost to be lord of the Emperor, and so had become quite unbearable.[3] Yet, with all his influence and ambition, his love of wealth and his capacity for dishonesty, Eusebius was not the consummate rogue that Eutropius became a generation later. It is true that he succeeded by obsequious flattery and sly insinuation in turning many an occasion to his own ends, but he lacked the necessary audacity and strength of character to dominate the will of Constantius as Eutropius did that of Arcadius, and can be known, therefore, only as a contemptible schemer.

II. The Grand Chamberlain Eutherius

Mention has been made of Eutherius, the Grand Chamberlain of Julian at the time that the latter was Caesar in Gaul, and of the good service he performed for him when he was falsely accused before Constantius. He may not have influenced greatly the course of history, but his integrity and worth were in such contrast to the despicable qualities of Eusebius that it will be a relief to consider them shortly before taking up a still more dismal tale. All that is known of Eutherius is told by Ammianus Marcellinus, an austere writer, so grudging of praise that his admiration for the Grand Chamberlain must be considered well deserved. After recounting the acts of Eutherius, to which reference has just been made, he continues as follows:[4]

"The opportunity here reminds me to mention a few facts concerning this same Eutherius, which perhaps will hardly be believed; because if Numa Pompilius or Socrates were to say anything good of a eunuch, and were to confirm what they said with an oath, they would be accused of having departed from the truth. But roses grow up among thorns, and among wild beasts some are of a gentle disposition.

[1] XV, 2, 8; XVI, 12, 67; XVII, 11, 1; XX, 8, 4.
[2] Zonaras, XIII, 12, 26.
[3] XXII, 3, 12.
[4] XVI, 7, 4–8. Yonge's translation is given with but slight alteration.

And therefore I shall briefly mention a few of his most important acts which are well ascertained.

"He was born in Armenia of a respectable family, and having while a very little child been taken prisoner by the enemies on the border, he was castrated and sold to some Roman merchants, and by them conducted to the palace of Constantine, where, while growing up to manhood, he began to display good principles and good talents, becoming accomplished in literature to a degree quite sufficient for his fortune, displaying extraordinary acuteness in discovering matters of a doubtful and difficult complexion; being remarkable also for a marvellous memory, always eager to do good, and full of wise and honest counsel. A man, in short, who, if the Emperor Constans had listened to his advice, which, whether he gave it in youth or manhood, was always honorable and upright, would have prevented him from committing any errors, or at least any that were not pardonable.

"When he became Grand Chamberlain he sometimes also found fault with Julian, who, being tainted with Asiatic manners, was apt to be capricious. Finally, when he quitted office for private life, and again when he was recalled to court, he was always sober and consistent, cultivating those excellent virtues of good faith and constancy to such a degree that he never betrayed any secret, except for the purpose of securing another's safety; nor was he ever accused of covetous or grasping conduct, as the other courtiers were.

"From which it arose that, when at a late period he retired to Rome, and fixed there the abode of his old age, bearing with him the company of a good conscience, he was loved and respected by men of all ranks, though men of that class generally, after having amassed riches by iniquity, love to seek secret places of retirement, just as owls or moths, and avoid the sight of the multitude whom they have injured.

"Though I have often ransacked the accounts of antiquity, I do not find any ancient eunuch to whom I may compare him. There were indeed among the ancients some, though very few, faithful and economical, but still they were stained by some vice or other. Among the chief faults which they had either by nature or by habit, they were apt to be rapacious, or else boorish, and on that account contemptible; or else ill-natured and mischievous; or fawning too much upon the powerful; or too elated with power, and therefore arrogant. But of any one so universally accomplished and prudent, I confess I have neither ever read or heard. For the truth of this judgment I rely on the general testimony of the age."

III. The Grand Chamberlain Eutropius

The most rascally of all the Grand Chamberlains was Eutropius, the servant and master of Arcadius. For many of the details of his career the only source of information is the two books of the poem *In Eutropium*, written by Claudian. It is quite possible that in some of the minor details, especially of the earlier life of the eunuch, the evidence of this poem is not entirely reliable, for, since Claudian was attached to Stilicho, the enemy of Eutropius, he probably did not view events with impartial eyes. Furthermore, East and West alike were rejoicing over the deposition and disgrace of the Grand Chamberlain when Claudian wrote his poem, and derogatory statements would not only meet no denial, but would be popular wherever read. The villainy of Eutropius as Grand Chamberlain is too well established, however, to admit of question.

Eutropius was by birth an Asiatic, possibly an Armenian, and was made a eunuch in his earliest infancy that he might bring the higher price which was paid for such slaves.[1] As such treatment by parents of high rank is not very probable, there is reason to believe that he was born of low station, perhaps a slave. Later he was sold in one of the slave markets along the Euphrates, and afterwards, while still a boy, passed through the hands of many masters.[2] At length he became the favorite of a soldier by the name of Ptolemaeus, who, when he wearied of him, presented him to a certain Arintheus,[3] in whose employ he plied the arts of a panderer.[4] Arintheus gave him as a part of his daughter's dowry to his son-in-law, in whose house he served in the women's apartments.[5]

Growing old and uncomely and lacking strength for menial tasks, he was finally given his liberty because he was no longer considered of any value.[6] Presently he was enrolled among the lowest ranks of the palace service, to the great disgust even of the other eunuchs there employed,[7] and later, through the influence of Abundantius, who was consul under Theodosius in the year 393, was raised to the highest honors.[8]

Theodosius showed a special fondness for eunuchs,[9] and as Eutropius was not without ability, he soon succeeded in winning the confidence and favor of his master. In 394, before beginning war against the rebel Eugenius, the Emperor, being apprehensive of failure, de-

[1] Claudian, *In Eutrop.*, I, 44–49. [2] *Op. cit.*, I, 58 ff. [3] *Op. cit.*, I, 61–64.
[4] *Op. cit.*, I, 78. [5] *Op. cit.*, I, 104 ff. [6] *Op. cit.*, I, 110–132.
[7] *Op. cit.*, I, 145 ff. [8] *Op. cit.*, I, 154 ff. [9] Zosimus, 252.

spatched Eutropius, "one of the palace eunuchs, whom he trusted," to Thebais to consult a certain monk by the name of John, who was at that time in great repute as a seer. Victory was promised and, in the event, won.[1]

When Theodosius I died, in 395, the Empire fell to his two sons, Honorius ruling in the West, and Arcadius in the East. Honorius was but eleven years old, and the barbarian Stilicho was the virtual ruler at the Western court. Arcadius had attained the age of eighteen, and had he possessed any enterprise might have guided affairs in the East. He was "short, thin, and sallow, so inactive that he seldom spoke, and always looked as if he was about to fall asleep."[2] His appearance did not belie his character, for he was a puppet in the hands of Rufinus, and later, of Eutropius, who lorded it over him "as over a dumb brute."[3] East and West, therefore, were ruled and plundered, not by their rightful sovereigns, but by intriguing ministers.[4]

During the first year of Arcadius's reign, Rufinus, the Pretorian Prefect, because of the Emperor's miserable weakness, was in almost complete control of the administration of the East. Wishing to make this control more certain, and hoping, perhaps, to win imperial rank, he bent all his efforts toward accomplishing a marriage between his own daughter and the young Emperor. His plans met with such success that he was confident the nuptials would soon be solemnized, and, indeed, this expectation was a matter of general comment by the populace, who were none too well pleased that the Pretorian Prefect, who already enjoyed too much power, should thus fortify himself in its exercise.[5] At this juncture, however, matters of state called Rufinus from the capital, and during his absence his plans were brought to naught.

Eutropius had attained the station of Grand Chamberlain not later than the accession of Arcadius,[6] and in this position of eminence he began to be jealous of those whose influence was greater than his own. He sought, therefore, to employ his intimacy with the Emperor to his own advantage, or, since it amounted to the same thing, to the disadvantage of those above him.

It chanced that at this time there was an orphan daughter of the Frankish general Bauto, a young girl of exceptional beauty, living at Constantinople in the home of one of the aristocratic families.

[1] Sozomen, 7, 22. Cf. Claudian, *In Eutrop.*, 1, 312; Palladius, *Historia Lausiaca*, chaps. 43, 46.

[2] Oman, *Byzantine Empire*, p. 47, from Philostorgius, 11, 3.

[3] Zosimus, 261, 16. [4] *Op. cit.*, V, 1. [5] *Op. cit.*, 247, 12 ff. [6] See pp. 274 f.

Eutropius, described on this occasion as one of the eunuchs serving about the Emperor, found occasion to speak to Arcadius of her wonderful beauty, and to suggest that she was well suited to become his Empress.

Finding that his words were not unacceptable, the eunuch displayed a portrait of the girl, by which the Emperor's affections were so roused that he was easily persuaded to agree to a marriage. Eutropius then bade the people adorn the city and celebrate with merrymaking, as was their wont, the Emperor's nuptials. Then, setting forth with a crowd of attendants, he bore suitable wedding garments, not to the house of Rufinus, as the people and even his followers expected, but to the house where lived the beautiful Eudoxia.[1]

Rufinus, learning that his plans had been frustrated by Eutropius, attempted to compass his ruin, but did not accomplish his purpose, for he was murdered in the same year (395) by the Gothic captain Gainas, at the instigation of his enemy Stilicho, the Master of the Soldiers in Italy.[2] Since it was distinctly to the advantage of Eutropius that Rufinus be put out of the way, he lent his aid in this plot.[3] After his death he seized most of the wealth of the Prefect and sent his wife and daughter to Jerusalem where they spent the remainder of their lives.[4]

Up to this point in his career Eutropius is nowhere mentioned by ancient authorities as Grand Chamberlain, but there can be scarcely any doubt that he held that position when he undertook to bring about the union between Arcadius and Eudoxia. It does not seem likely that any of the lesser eunuchs would have dared to make such an attempt, and none but the Grand Chamberlain, surely, would have given orders to the people to make ready to celebrate the Emperor's marriage, or have taken fitting garments from the imperial wardrobe and led a pompous procession through the streets of the city to the home of the destined bride.

As these events occurred during the first year of the reign of Arcadius, it must be assumed that Eutropius was made Grand Chamberlain no later than the time of the young Emperor's accession. He may have been accorded this honor even before that date. When he made the journey to Thebais at the order of Theodosius he was described as "one of the Emperor's eunuchs who was trusted by him." [5] Now in the very nature of things the most trusted eunuch was the

[1] Zosimus, V, 3. [2] *Op. cit.*, 255, 10 ff. [3] *Op. cit.*, 256, 5 ff. [4] *Loc. cit.*

[5] Sozomen, VII, 22: ὃς πιστὸς ἦν αὐτῷ τῶν ἐν τοῖς βασιλείοις εὐνούχων.

Grand Chamberlain, and not infrequently it was that official who was sent on private missions by the Emperor. It is not impossible, therefore, that when Claudian states that Eutropius was raised, through the influence of Abundantius, to the highest honors [1] he is referring to the position of Grand Chamberlain.

When Eutropius had disposed of Rufinus in the manner just described, he himself became the chief minister of the Emperor and at once set about to rid the court, by whatever means possible, of those whose influence might curtail his own.[2] One of his first victims was Timasius, whom he himself had assisted to a position of prominence,[3] and who held the position of Master of the Soldiers. He made his attack with the assistance of a certain Bargus, who attached himself to Timasius for a short time and then accused him of aiming at imperial power. The offender was brought to trial; the Emperor himself proposed to sit as judge, with Eutropius, "who controlled the whole decision," sitting as assessor. A general protest was raised at the injustice of such a procedure and the trial was committed to others. Timasius was nevertheless condemned and sent into exile.[4] Bargus was rewarded with a military command, but was soon brought to trial by Eutropius and convicted on information given by his concubine.[5]

Eutropius was now seized with insatiable greed, and employed his energies to ruin wealthy men, that he might obtain their fortunes. He is even said to have had agents in all parts of the Empire, to search out and report to him those who were at all conspicuous for their riches.[6] One of the most flagrant cases of this kind was that of the same Abundantius who had been instrumental in raising the eunuch to power. Eutropius recommended to the Emperor that he be banished, and without formality he was sent to Phoenicia.[7]

The Grand Chamberlain now ruled with a high hand, for he "saw the laws beneath his feet," and the most eminent men of the Empire subject to his will. The prisons were filled with prominent men whose wealth the eunuch wished for his own, or whose opposition he wished to crush. Large numbers were exiled to lonely parts of Africa. The scourge was in constant use, and even his fellow eunuchs were a prey to the Grand Chamberlain's lust for gold.[8]

Imperial offices were bought and sold. The governorship of prov-

[1] *In Eutrop.*, 1, 156: *summos invasit honores.*
[2] Zosimus, 256, 16 ff.
[3] Eunapius of Sardis (*Fragmenta Historicorum Graecorum*), *frag.* 70.
[4] Zosimus, V, 9.
[5] *Op. cit.*, 259, 1–15. Cf. Eunapius of Sardis (*F. H. G.*), *frag.* 71.
[6] Zosimus, 259, 15–20.
[7] *Op. cit.*, 259, 20 ff. Claudian, *In Eutrop.*, 1, 167 ff. Eunapius of Sardis (*F. H. G.*), *frag.* 72.
[8] Claudian, *In Eutrop.*, 1, 173–191.

inces was given in exchange for a country seat, or an ancestral estate, and if the statements of Claudian may be accepted as accurate, a list of dignities and provinces, with the prices demanded for each, was publicly posted before the Grand Chamberlain's door.[1] When barbarian incursions reduced the number of such provinces at the disposal of the eunuch, he did not hesitate to divide those which remained in order that he might not suffer a decrease in his revenues.[2] To the same end he sat as judge and overrode the laws at will.[3]

From the statements of Claudian it appears that Eutropius even led an army into the field at one time. Bands of northern plunderers were overrunning Asia. Syria and Cappadocia were ravaged, herds and inhabitants driven off into captivity or slaughtered, fields wasted, walls destroyed and villages burned. The invaders held Eutropius and his force in contempt, and unhindered retired to their northern homes. The Grand Chamberlain had accomplished nothing, but returned to the capital like a victor exhausted by the hardships of a long campaign, and was enthusiastically received by his flatterers.[4]

There seems to be no other mention of this event in the historical writings of this period. It is possible that Claudian has somewhat magnified an insignificant incident which was discreditable to the Grand Chamberlain, but there is no very good reason to doubt the essential truth of the statements he has made.

The hostility between Eutropius and Stilicho was of some significance in the events of the closing years of the fourth century. It was but natural that jealousy should arise between the ministers who plundered the Eastern and the Western empires, and this jealousy was strong enough to render permanent the division of the Roman world which had been made by Theodosius. So great was the enmity between Eutropius and Stilicho that the eunuch, at least, considered national welfare a small matter if by sacrificing it he could gain an advantage over his rival.

In 396, when Alaric and his ruthless barbarians swept over Greece, there was no Eastern army to oppose them, and they left in their path such devastation that not even in the time of Zosimus had the country been rehabilitated.[5] Stilicho, fearing lest Alaric lead his bands into territory which was under his own control, and, possibly, with other motives not entirely altruistic, crossed the Adriatic and successfully opposed the barbarian, but he was not permitted to press his advan-

[1] *Op. cit.*, 1, 196–221. Cf. Zosimus, V, 1.
[2] *Op. cit.*, 2, 586.
[3] *Op. cit.*, 1, 229 ff.
[4] *Op. cit.*, 1, 236 ff.
[5] Zosimus, 252, 13 f.

tage. Far from being grateful to the Western commander for the relief he had brought to Greece, Eutropius was alarmed at the success of his rival, and informed him that Alaric had been appointed Master of the Soldiers by the Eastern Emperor, and was not to be hindered in the exercise of his powers. Stilicho could not continue his opposition to the raider without declaring open war upon the East, and so retired to Italy. This is the story given by Claudian.[1]

The version which Zosimus gives is somewhat different. According to his narrative, Stilicho failed to make the defeat of Alaric decisive, because he and his army had given themselves up to licentiousness and so allowed the trapped barbarian to escape.[2] Claudian may, perhaps, be suspected of suppressing unpleasant truths about Stilicho and of inventing a story which casts discredit upon the Eastern court. Zosimus, on the other hand, may be giving an account such as had gained currency about Constantinople, and may have been entirely ignorant of the Western version. Eunapius of Sardis states that many conflicting accounts of the incidents of this time were to be heard, and that people became so sceptical of the truth of these reports that they used to ask their informers, in sarcasm, "Where, pray, did Stilicho see you?" or, "You are not acquainted with the eunuch, are you?"[3] This much may be said in favor of the statements of Claudian: he was in a position to know the truth, and the fact that Alaric was made a Master of the Soldiers by the Eastern Emperor may be taken as circumstantial verification of his account.

After these events the hostility between Stilicho and Eutropius could no longer be dissimulated. Eutropius secured the passage of a decree by the Senate confiscating the property which Stilicho possessed in Constantinople,[4] and branding him as a public enemy, in order that he might be prevented from visiting Constantinople.[5] Apparently the eunuch stood in fear of revenge, and sought by this means to protect himself.[6]

It is not improbable that this fear was the reason for making more stringent the Cornelian law *De Sicariis*. By this new enactment very severe punishments were provided for any who should make common cause with any faction of soldiers or private citizens or barbarians for the purposing of compassing the death of an *illustris*.[7]

[1] *De Bello Getico*, 516 ff.

[2] Zosimus, 254, 18 ff.

[3] Eunapius of Sardis (*F. H. G.*), *frag.* 74.

[4] This seems to be the meaning of Claudian, *De Laudibus Stilichonis*, 1, 297 f.

[5] Zosimus, 260, 9 ff.

[6] Cf. Claudian, *In Eutrop.*, 2, 501 ff.

[7] *Codex Theodosianus*, IX, 14, 3.

In a second course of action Eutropius was only less reprehensible than in his treacherous dealings with Alaric. The district of Northern Africa, which was one of the territories administered by Stilicho for Honorius, was intrusted to the governorship of Gildo, a barbarian. Eutropius encouraged Gildo in a revolt against the Western Emperor, and induced him to associate himself with the administration of the East. Nothing but greed and his jealousy of Stilicho can have moved the Grand Chamberlain to this almost treasonable act. The measure met with some success at first, but Gildo's own brother, supplied with forces by Stilicho, soon defeated the rebel, and Africa was again firmly united to the West in 398.[1]

Ecclesiastical politics also occupied the attention of Eutropius. On the death of Nectarius, Bishop of Constantinople, in 397, a question arose as to who should be appointed to succeed him. Theophilus of Alexandria endeavored to seat a certain presbyter, named Isidore, who had done him good service, but Eutropius had a different purpose.

Some time before, he had visited Antioch on imperial business, and had there learned of John, a priest of that city [2] whose eloquence had won him the name of Chrysostom. It is possible that he thought to employ this marvellous gift of speech for his own purposes, for even an archbishop might be used, on occasion, to advantage. At any rate, when Chrysostom gave no heed to the request that he make the journey to Constantinople, and the people of Antioch became greatly excited at the thought of losing their beloved pastor, Eutropius resorted to strategy and force to gain his ends. He prevailed upon the Emperor to address a letter to the Count of the Orient, whose residence was in Antioch, asking him to devise some means whereby Chrysostom might be taken outside the city without rousing the naturally excitable population. This was accomplished on the pretext of a pious visit to one of the martyries outside the city walls. Here the unsuspecting priest was seized by a eunuch and the Master of the Offices, who had been sent from the capital for this purpose, and was hurried off to Constantinople.[3]

For some time Theophilus obstinately refused to ordain Chrysostom. Finally Eutropius confronted him with certain accusations which had been brought against him, and demanded that he either comply with his request or stand trial. Theophilus capitulated, and early in 398 John of Antioch was ordained bishop of Constantinople.[4]

[1] Zosimus, V, 11. Claudian, *De Bello Gildonico.*

[2] Palladius, *Vita Chrysostomi,* chap. 5.

[3] Palladius, *Dialogus,* chap. 5; Sozomen, 8, 2.

[4] Socrates, VI, 2.

If Eutropius hoped to find a complaisant courtier in Chrysostom he met with severe disappointment, for the utter venality of the Grand Chamberlain's administration escaped neither the eye nor the tongue of the Archbishop, and Eutropius lived to rue his part in the ordination.

Until the year 398 Eutropius was satisfied to control the administration of the East with no other title than that of Grand Chamberlain, but in that year he prevailed upon Arcadius to designate him as one of the eponymous consuls for 399, and to honor him with the rank of Patrician. This was an astounding occurrence. Never before had a eunuch been made a Patrician, and never before had the consulship, which still retained much of its Republican dignity, been so disgraced.[1]

News of the elevation was despatched to the court of Honorius, but was not at first given credence. "As well tell us," said the Romans, "of a white blackbird." [2] But the amazing report was confirmed, and immediately a strong public resentment manifested itself in the West. Claudian represents the personified city of Rome as appearing before Honorius and Stilicho, in Milan, and imploring that the eunuch be overthrown. In these words he may merely be giving form to the general sentiments of the people, but it is not impossible that a deputation from Rome actually presented this appeal. Certain it is that Rome never recognized the consulship of Eutropius, and the Western calendar gives the name of but a single consul for the year 399.[3]

If resentment was felt at Constantinople, it could not safely be expressed. When the Grand Chamberlain entered upon his office he took his seat in the audience-hall of the palace, clad in the consular *trabea*, to receive the congratulations of the people. The doors were thrown open, and the rabble and the senators, generals and magistrates pressed in, eager to fall at the knees, to touch the hand, or even to kiss the wrinkled visage of the eunuch. They hailed him as the bulwark of the laws and the "father of the Emperor," and set up statues of him through the streets, representing him as a judge, a consul, a general, mounted and on foot. They lauded him in inscriptions as sprung of noble stock, as a winner of enormous booty, as the third founder of the city.[4]

In return Eutropius gave lavish feasts, scattered gold among the crowds, and day after day provided entertainment in the theatre,

[1] Sozomen, VIII, 7.

[2] Claudian, *In Eutrop.*, 1, 348.

[3] Idatius, *Discriptio Consulum: Manlio et Theodoro v.c.*, that is, (Fl.) Mallius Theodorus.

[4] Claudian, *In Eutrop.*, 2, 62–83.

while his consort (*soror*) sought by means of extravagant banquets to win the favor of the matrons of the city.[1]

Trouble began for the eunuch almost with the beginning of his consulship. Gainas, the Gothic Master of the Soldiers of the East, resented the fact that he was not accorded the honors to which he deemed his long years of service entitled him, and was incensed, moreover, to see that all the riches derived from the sale of offices and the confiscation of estates were flowing into the already bulging coffers of Eutropius.[2]

Nursing his grievances, he awaited, therefore, the time when he could get revenge. He had not long to wait, for the Gothic tribune Tribigild, in command of the Gothic troops in Phrygia, presently requested higher honors for himself and better pay for his half-starved military colonists; but his suits were coldly dismissed by Eutropius.[3] Their common fate threw the two Goths together, and Tribigild, at the order of Gainas, began to plunder the fertile fields of Phrygia, and to sack the less protected towns.[4]

The country was thrown into a panic and asked protection from the capital. Arcadius, always incompetent, intrusted the whole situation to Eutropius,[5] who treated the revolt as an insignificant bit of brigandage to be quelled by legal enactments and judicial prosecution rather than by arms, and refused to consider it a menace to the Empire, "acting like the hunted ostrich, which, when its pursuers are close at hand, stands with closed eyes, and, turning its ridiculous head, thinks it is hidden because it does not see itself." [6]

Alarmed at last, he secretly tried to extinguish the conflagration by the promise of rich gifts, but to Tribigild the certainty of present rich spoil was preferable to the possibility of future bounty, and Eutropius was left no choice but to resort to arms.[7] Claudian draws a bold picture of the eunuch's unwarlike council of war which placed the fortunes of the Empire in the hands of a certain Leo,[8] who knew nothing of military matters, and was qualified for the task before him merely by his intimacy with Eutropius.[9]

Leo collected his army near the Hellespont, and for some time timidly avoided a conflict.[10] Meanwhile, with secret assistance from

[1] *Op. cit.*, 2, 88 ff.
[2] Zosimus, V, 13, *init.*
[3] Claudian, *In Eutrop.*, 2, 177 f.; 191. f.
[4] Zosimus, 262, 11 ff. Claudian, *In Eutrop.*, 2, 275 ff.
[5] Zosimus, 262, 20 ff.
[6] Claudian, *In Eutrop.*, 2, 304–316.
[7] *Op. cit.*, 2, 316–325.
[8] *Op. cit.*, 2, 325–405.
[9] Zosimus, 263, 3 ff.
[10] *Op. cit.*, 264, 10 ff.

Gainas, the rebel was devastating Asia with impunity, and the alarm at Constantinople increased. Finally Tribigild fell unexpectedly upon the undisciplined Leo and utterly routed him.[1] Eutropius and his followers had placed all their reliance in Leo, and his defeat was a severe blow, for they had no other defence. The palace was filled with wild and terrifying rumors, which Gainas augmented by sending exaggerated reports of the prowess and exploits of Tribigild, and of his probable intention to attack the city.[2] To increase the dismay there came the rumor that the Persians were preparing an invasion.[3]

It was now generally recognized that all hope lay in Gainas. Seizing the opportunity for the revenge he desired, the Master of the Soldiers affected great doubt as to the outcome of the war, and intimated that he could do nothing unless Eutropius, the cause of all the Empire's distress, should be handed over to him for punishment. For once Arcadius acted promptly. The eunuch was summoned into his presence, stripped of his honors, and ejected from the palace.[4]

The abruptness of the fall of Eutropius suggests some reason other than those here given for his loss of favor. It does not seem probable that he would be held responsible for Leo's defeat, and the simple demand of the Gothic Master of the Soldiers that a trusted minister be dismissed is not enough to explain the Emperor's rancor as displayed in his edict against the Grand Chamberlain.[5]

There is some evidence that the young Empress may have been instrumental in bringing about the deposition of Eutropius. She was, as has been stated, the daughter of the Frankish general Bauto, and was possessed of no small amount of the spirit and independence of her race.[6] It must have roused her indignation to see her stolid husband bend in the hands of the despicable eunuch, and there can be little doubt that her opposition caused the Grand Chamberlain many moments of uneasiness. But Eudoxia had reasons of her own also for hating Eutropius. It was he who had persuaded Arcadius to withhold from her the title of Augusta until she should bear him a male heir.[7]

It is small wonder, therefore, that there is occasional slight evidence that the Empress and the Grand Chamberlain were not in harmony,

[1] Claudian, *In Eutrop.*, 2, 432–455. [2] Zosimus, 268, 5 ff. Claudian, *In Eutrop.*, 2, 462–473.
[3] Claudian, *In Eutrop.*, 2, 473 ff. [4] Zosimus, 268, 16 to 269, 5.
[5] See pp. 283 f. [6] Philostorgius, 11, 6.
[7] This is the not improbable conjecture of Thierry (*Les trois ministres des fils de Theodose*, p. 107), based on the fact that Eudoxia was not elevated to the rank of an Augusta until the year 400. (Cf. *Chron. Pasch.*, 307.) The withholding of this title, which was Eudoxia's due, can have been caused by no other influence than that of the jealousy of Eutropius. Cf. Tillemont, *Histoire des Empereurs*, vol. V, p. 465 f.

and it is not difficult to believe that she was secretly hoping for his overthrow. If she accomplished her desire in this matter, it was because Eutropius offered the opportunity.

Philostorgius states that Eutropius had insulted Eudoxia, threatening soon to eject her from the palace, and that she, with a child in either arm, at once sought out her husband and told of the insult, holding before him the two children, breaking into tears, and, as Philostorgius slyly says, "doing other things such as angry women are wont to do with a woman's art to move their husbands' minds more strongly to pity." Arcadius's anger was aroused, and "then, indeed, he appeared an Emperor." Eutropius was straightway dealt with as has been related.[1]

Here again it is difficult to judge the merits of the two versions. The account given by Philostorgius is convincing, and receives some support from references to "insults to the Emperor" by Chrysostom, though the Emperor's anger had so far subsided before the preacher uttered these words that he had begged the soldiers to spare the culprit's life.[2] The version given by Zosimus and Claudian also demands credence, and finds support in the anger of the soldiers against Eutropius.[3] Whatever may have been the immediate cause of the eunuch's downfall, it is safe to conclude that the demands of Gainas and his own overbearing attitude contributed to his ruin.

Eutropius's greed and his injustice, his presumption and his incompetency had not been without result, and he was no sooner deposed than he found himself surrounded by enemies of his own making. A few moments before he had been master of the Eastern Empire, now he was a fugitive. There was but one place in the city of Constantinople where there was any chance of safety, and that was within the church. Thither he fled, and, clinging to the altar table, craved protection.[4]

This is precisely what many an unfortunate had done during the years of the Grand Chamberlain's power. The church had long maintained that secular officials had no authority within its walls, and therefore claimed for itself the right of giving asylum. This it had offered to many of the victims of the oppression of Eutropius, among them to Pentadia, the wife of Timasius, of whom mention has been made.[5]

[1] Philostorgius, II, 6. [2] Chrysostom, *In Eutrop.*, I, 4 *sub fine.* [3] *Ibidem.*
[4] Zosimus, 269, 3 ff. Claudian, *In Eutrop.*, 2, *Prolog.*, 25 ff. [5] Sozomen, VIII, 7.

Eutropius could ill brook this defiance on the part of the church, and had finally obtained the passage of a law forbidding any fugitive to take refuge in the church, and giving authority to the magistrates to take thence any who should do so in contravention of the law.[1] Chrysostom had stoutly defended the church's right, and had vigorously attacked Eutropius for his action.[2] It was, therefore, a slender hope on which the eunuch relied when he fled to the altar of Chrysostom's church; but the Archbishop refused to permit the church's right of asylum to be questioned even when it was her enemy who sought its benefit.

The news of the overthrow of Eutropius seems to have spread rapidly, and in a short time a turbulent band of soldiers presented itself at the church and demanded the surrender of the refugee. Chrysostom refused to comply and the soldiers, abashed probably by his intrepid defence, dragged him off to give an explanation of his actions to the Emperor.[3] His eloquence must have moved the Emperor strangely, for he appeared before the irate mob and strove to allay their rage by a long speech, and when they brandished their swords and still demanded the life of the eunuch, the Emperor, with tears streaming from his eyes, begged them to respect the Holy Table, and so succeeded in appeasing their wrath.[4]

The following day was Sunday, and a great throng pressed into the church to hear what Chrysostom would say.[5] The Archbishop took his accustomed place in the *ambon* or high reading-desk and, pointing to the shaking form of Eutropius, which was now seen prostrate at the foot of the altar table,[6] broke forth, "Vanity of vanities, all is vanity," and using the striking example before their eyes, preached to his hearers on his favorite theme.[7]

At this time the fate of Eutropius had not been decided, for Chrysostom urged his auditors to pray God to move the Emperor to compassion that he might grant the whole of their request,[8] which probably was that the eunuch's life be spared. A day or two later appeared the edict by which Eutropius was officially stripped of all honors, his acts as consul made void, the title of the year changed, and his property confiscated. It was also commanded that all statues or other representations of the degraded consul should be broken in pieces,

[1] Sozomen, VIII, 7; Socrates, VI, 5.
[2] Socrates, *loc. cit.*
[3] Chrysostom, *De Capto Eutropio*, chap. 3.
[4] Chrysostom, *In Eutrop.*, chap. 4.
[5] *Op. cit.*, chap. 3.
[6] Socrates, VI, 5.
[7] Chrysostom, *In Eutropium.*
[8] *In Eutrop.*, chap. 4.

and that he be safely conveyed to the island of Cyprus, there to live in custody.[1]

Eutropius remained in the protection of the church for a few days, but at the end of that time fell into the hands of his enemies. Chrysostom declared that he would never have been given up if he had not abandoned the church; that he was not surrendered from within the church, but outside its walls, and that if one were so pusillanimous as to leave the fold, he must expect to become the wild beast's prey.[2] It seems probable that Eutropius thought he could escape, trusting possibly in some supposed friend, but that he had no sooner left the sanctuary than he was seized and taken to Cyprus. Only thus can be explained Chrysostom's care to make it known that the church had not surrendered the fugitive, and Zosimus's contradictory statement that the right of asylum was violated by the secular authorities.[3]

Though he had obtained a promise that he would not be put to death, the unhappy eunuch was not allowed to remain long in Cyprus. Gainas desired to put him out of the way, and he was presently accused of having worn imperial regalia. A court, sitting at Pantichium, found him guilty and condemned him to death. He was taken to Chalcedon and there executed.[4]

The deceit, the trickery, the rapacity, the cruelty of Eusebius and Eutropius seem to have been characteristic, in some degree, of most eunuchs, and it is easy to understand, after following the careers of these intriguers, the exasperation with which a once famous Chrysaorius exclaimed, "If you have a eunuch, kill him; if you haven't, buy one and kill him!"[5]

IV. The Grand Chamberlain Narses

The story of Narses, the famous minister of Justinian, is less that of a Grand Chamberlain than that of a successful general, and if told in detail would almost constitute a history of the Gothic Wars of Justinian's reign. Only a brief sketch of the eunuch's life can be given here. For a fuller account of his military exploits the Gothic War of Procopius and the History of Agathias, or the fourth volume of Hodgkin's *Italy and her Invaders*, may be consulted.

Narses, an Armenian by birth, was, as has been said, a eunuch.[6]

[1] *Codex Theodosianus*, IX, 40, 17.

[2] Chrysostom, *De Capto Eutropio*, chap. 1.

[3] Zosimus, 269, 7 ff.

[4] *Op. cit.*, 269, 9 ff. Philostorgius, 11, 6.

[5] Cedrenus, vol. II, 29, 8 ff.: *ὥστε Χρυσαόριον τὸν πάλαι θαυμασιώτατον εἰπεῖν πρός τινα τῶν μεγάλων ὅτι εἰ μὲν ἔχεις εὐνοῦχον, φόνευσον, εἰ δ' οὐκ ἔχεις, ἀγόρασον καὶ φόνευσον.*

[6] Procopius, *De Bello Persico*, 79, 7.

He was a man of exceptional prudence, industry, and adaptability, not very well educated or very eloquent, but a clear and forceful speaker. Short of stature, frail, of elegant manners, he was nevertheless energetic and equal to the greatest tasks.[1] He first appears in history about the year 530, shortly after the battle of Dara, when he treated so liberally certain of his own countrymen who had deserted to the imperial army that the hope of similar reward induced one of their kinsmen to surrender an important outpost to the soldiers of Justinian. On this occasion Narses is said to have been an imperial treasurer.[2] Perhaps he was in charge of the funds which belonged to the Emperor personally, the forerunner of the later Sakellarios.[3] In 532 he was a Chamberlain and Spathar,[4] and by 563 had been made a Protospathar.[5] At a somewhat later date he is described as a Chartulary of the Sacred Bedchamber.[6]

In the year 531, Narses, described in this connection as a Chamberlain, was sent into Armenia to take, in the Emperor's name, the rich spoil which was found in a certain Persian town which had fallen into the hands of the Byzantines.[7]

A year later his prompt action in a crisis won him the enduring esteem of the Emperor and his consort, the clever, haughty Theodora. In January of the year 532 there was some turbulence in the streets, caused by the Greens and the Blues, the unruly factions of the circus. The leaders were executed, but the bungling work of the executioner incensed the mob, and the famous Nika riot broke out. For six days the streets of Constantinople were filled with turmoil and violence. The Senate House, the Church of St. Sophia, and a number of other imperial edifices were burned. The mob controlled the city, and the palace alone was left to the Emperor. The police force had been helpless from the first, and Belisarius, the Master of the Soldiers, with the few troops in the city had failed to quell the riot. The Greens were threatening to proclaim a new Emperor. The situation appeared hopeless, and Justinian was about to flee from the city by boat, but the imperious Theodora refused to leave. "Empire," said she, "is the best winding-sheet." There was nothing to do but to attempt a last assault on the rebels, and Belisarius prepared to lead out his forces.

Meanwhile the mob had thronged to the hippodrome and were on the point of proclaiming Hypatius, the nephew of Anastasius, Emperor.

[1] Agathias, I, 16, *init.* [2] Procopius, *op. cit.*, 79, 7: Ναρσῆς ὁ βασιλέως ταμίας.
[3] See p. 247. [4] Malalas, 476, 3 f. [5] Theophanes, 376, 9.
[6] Marcellinus Comes, *sub anno* 552. Marius Aventicensis, 798 B. [7] Malalas, 469, 15 ff.

Belisarius proposed to attack them by breaking in at the gates, but the rival factions, now united in a common undertaking, constituted a formidable force, which had already shown itself a match for the soldiery. While Belisarius was organizing his attack, Narses made his way into the hippodrome and by lavish gifts won over the leaders of the Blues, who raised the loyalist cry of "Long live Justinian and Theodora." Dissension sprang up immediately, and in the midst of the confusion the soldiers forced their way in at the gates and cut down the trapped rioters without mercy. The riot was ended and the Empire was saved. The soldiers had done good work, but it was Narses, Chamberlain and Spathar, who broke the back of the Nika sedition.[1]

In the summer of 535, after the Vandals in North Africa had been subdued, Justinian declared war on the Goths in Italy. Belisarius with a very small force at once got possession of Sicily, and passing to Italy marched steadily northward, paused for a short time to take the city of Naples, and in December of 536, with a force of about 5,000 men, captured Rome. The following spring the Gothic King Witiges began a blockade of the city with an army of more than 100,000. The odds were enormous, but Belisarius and his insignificant force withstood every assault and foiled every scheme of the besiegers. The Gothic king, indeed, showed little knowledge of warfare, and after blundering for more than a year withdrew his sadly depleted army.

In the early summer of 538 Justinian sent Narses with 5,000 men to Italy.[2] It seems strange that a palace eunuch with but little experience, probably, in warfare should be sent on a military expedition, and now that Rome had been free from siege for three months and the pressing need of reinforcements had passed, the expedition itself seems strange. Its purpose is nowhere disclosed, and it can be deciphered, if at all, only from subsequent events. Hodgkin concludes that Justinian was somewhat uneasy over the brilliant successes and growing popularity of Belisarius, fearing that he might become an aspirant to the purple, and that he therefore sent his trusted minister from a half conviction that the general ought to be closely watched, but not seriously hampered, in his military activities, and that it was perhaps for reasons of diplomacy that a saving clause was inserted in the commission of Narses which relieved him from the necessity of absolute obedience to Belisarius.[3] No more satisfactory explanation

[1] Malalas, 476, 3 ff.; *Chronicon Paschale*, 626, 4 ff. [2] Procop., *De Bello Gothico*, 199, 4 ff.
[3] *Italy and her Invaders*, vol. IV (2d ed.), pp. 274–275, 287.

of the eunuch's really puzzling expedition seems to have been offered.

Belisarius and Narses joined forces in Picenum and deliberated on the course of action to be pursued. Rimini was under siege by the Goths, but Belisarius, courageous as he was, was sometimes overcautious, and now opposed going to the relief of the city, on the ground that his force was not large enough to venture so far into hostile territory. Narses, on the contrary, urged the move, influenced no doubt by the fact that his bosom friend, John, was in command of the threatened city. His counsels finally prevailed and the army prepared to move northward.[1]

The fleet which bore a large detachment of the Byzantine army appeared off Rimini one morning, and the Goths, terrified by reports that a large army was approaching, fled precipitately. When Belisarius arrived at mid-day he remarked to John that he ought to thank the commander of the fleet for the relief of the city, but John answered, "Not him, but Narses." Jealousy may have existed between Belisarius and Narses since the time of the Nika riot; at any rate it now developed rapidly. Some of the soldiers suggested to Narses that it was not fitting that he, who knew all the Emperor's secret purposes, should be second in command, and assured him that the larger part of their number would prefer to win glory under him rather than under Belisarius. The eunuch's vanity was touched, and when a letter from the Emperor was read to him, stating that he was to obey Belisarius in all things, he pointed out the words, "for the good of the state," and thereafter coöperated with the Master of the Soldiers only when he wished to consider his plans as consonant with these words.[2]

With the leadership thus divided, especially since Narses often followed an obstructionist policy, no general campaign could be conducted, and local operations met with varying success; the Byzantines sustained a severe loss in the capture of the city of Milan, which probably would not have befallen them had the army been under a single leader. Finally a report of this condition of affairs reached Justinian, and he ordered the immediate return of Narses.[3]

It would be but natural to suppose that Narses was punished in some manner for his marked insubordination, but this was not the case. He seems to have lost none of his favor at court, but to have remained the most trusted servant and minister of the Emperor and his consort. That the events in Italy had done nothing to impair the

[1] Procop., *De Bello Gothico*, II, 16. [2] *Op. cit.*, II, 18. [3] *Op. cit.*, 235, 5 f.

trust in his loyalty is clear from the fact that it was he who was chiefly intrusted with the securing of evidence against the aspiring Pretorian Prefect, John of Cappadocia, in 541. Marcellus, the commander of the Palace Guard, seems to have been sent with his band of soldiers on this occasion merely for the purpose of putting the ambitious culprit to death.[1] Narses was also employed on other imperial missions of more or less importance.[2]

Of the career of Narses during the ten years following the attempt on the life of the Prefect almost nothing is known. He remained in high favor at court, however, retaining the position of Grand Chamberlain, and wisely avoided the dangerous intrigues and the soaring ambition which had brought about the downfall of Eusebius and Eutropius.

In 549, after five years of desultory warfare against the Goths in Italy, Belisarius was relieved of his second command in that field, and a little later, in 551, Narses was appointed to succeed him, for reasons which no one clearly understood.[3] The new commander-in-chief extorted from the parsimonious Emperor the support which Belisarius never had, and with a strong army and a well-stocked purse started for the Adriatic.[4]

Narses had previously given evidence of his generosity, and officers and soldiers of all nationalities offered him their services, remembering his past favors or relying on his future bounty.[5] Indeed, no motive but the hope of rich rewards and spoils could have induced so motley an army to attempt to regain Italy for the "Roman" Empire. Byzantines, Thracians and Illyrians, Lombards, Herulians and Huns, Gepids, and even Persians followed the Grand Chamberlain. Harangues about patriotism could not move such a mercenary host, but the display of armlets, collars and bridles of gold could and did.[6]

Except for a preliminary sea-fight by which the Goths were compelled to raise the siege of Ancona, and some minor engagements by which the last remnants of the Gothic nation were driven from their isolated strongholds and out of Italy, the campaign of Narses was marked by but two important battles. The first took place near the little town of Tadinum, high up in the Apennines, and though Totila and his Goths showed great bravery, the superior numbers of the Byzantine army decided the fortunes of the day. The battle

[1] Procop., *De Bello Persico*, 134, 2 ff.
[2] Malalas, 481, 13 ff.
[3] Procop., *De Bello Gothico*, 570, 2 ff.
[4] Procop., *op. cit.*, 571, 19 ff.; 597, 13 ff.; 598, 5 ff.
[5] *Op. cit.*, 598–600.
[6] *Op. cit.*, 619, 4 ff.

continued till evening, when the Goths broke and fled, and learned a little later that their gallant king had been fatally wounded. Descending into the plains of Campania, they reformed their army under a chieftain named Teia.

Narses and his generals marched rapidly against the new leader, giving him small opportunity to prepare for defence, but he chose a favorable location near the base of Mt. Vesuvius and there withstood his enemies for two months until, in a heroic attempt to rout the army which had checkmated him, he fell at the front of his troops. His followers then begged and received permission to pass unmolested out of Italy.[1]

There were still a few Goths in Italy. Aligern, the brother of Teia, held the ancient citadel of Cumae, where was deposited the Gothic hoard, and Narses at once set himself to reduce this stronghold. It was very well fortified and stoutly defended, however, and the eunuch was forced to fall back on the tedious process of starving the garrison into submission.[2]

Meanwhile his generals entered Etruria, and the cities which had acknowledged Gothic sovereignty readily opened their gates on receiving promises of immunity. Lucca alone held out, encouraged by the report that Frankish troops were on their way from the north. Narses grew impatient. He tried promises and threats to no avail, and even resorted to the comic ruse of cutting off the heads of the Luccan hostages in full sight of the defenders of the town and then promising the wailing citizens to restore their kinsmen unhurt, if they would surrender. They gave their word that they would open their gates if the eunuch should perform such a miracle, but when Narses brought the unharmed hostages to the walls, and it became clear that the heads which the citizens had seen roll on the ground at the strokes of the executioner were false heads, they changed their minds about their promised surrender. This odd story illustrates the unswerving fidelity of Narses to his word, for he sent the hostages back to Lucca in safety, in spite of the failure of the city to perform its part of the contract.[3] Narses renewed his attacks on Lucca's fortifications with more desperate energy than before, and soon wrought such havoc that the inhabitants willingly surrendered.[4]

While these things were happening, Aligern, shut up in the fortress of Cumae, was meditating on the probable course of future events,

[1] Procop., *op. cit.*, IV, 28–35.
[2] Agathias, *Hist.*, I, 8–11.
[3] Agathias, *op. cit.*, I, 12–13.
[4] *Op. cit.*, I, 17–18.

and becoming convinced that he had no more to hope from Frankish aid than from surrender to the Byzantines, he carried the keys of the city to Narses, and himself entered the service of Justinian.[1]

The rumors about the approach of the Frankish hordes had not been idle, and Narses knew that he must meet a new foe. Answering the appeals of a remnant of the northern Goths, two brothers, Leuthar and Butilin, led their Frankish and Alemannic bands down from the Alps into the plain of Italy. Narses first crossed swords with these invaders in a skirmish near Rimini. Two thousand Franks were wasting the countryside, and the eunuch, unable to endure the sight, mounted his remarkably trained war-horse and rode against them with only three hundred followers. The Franks, forming in close array, were too strong to be successfully attacked. Perceiving this, Narses feigned flight, but when he saw that the pursuers were streaming after him in disorder across the plain, he ordered his men to wheel about and attack. The enemy was utterly routed and retired, leaving many dead on the field.[2] After this Narses set affairs in order at Ravenna, then returned to Rome where he spent the winter months drilling his troops.[3]

Meanwhile the Franks poured down into southern Italy. Butilin ravaged all the southwestern coast to the very straits of Messina, and Leuthar laid waste the southern part of the Adriatic coast. Loaded down with captives and spoil, he decided to carry his booty back to the north before continuing the pillaging of Italy. He had gone as far as Fanum in safety, when two of the generals of Narses fell on his disorderly line and dealt it a severe blow. Many of the Franks were slain, the captives made off with much of the booty, and Leuthar continued his northward march by a road which would not bring him into contact with imperial garrisons. When he reached Venetia a terrible pestilence fell upon his army, and he himself met a miserable death.[4]

Butilin's army also suffered from disease, which was aggravated by the fact that they were unable to procure wholesome food; this difficulty resulted from the prudence of Narses, who had ordered all the crops destroyed. Butilin desired to attack Narses before his army should be too greatly weakened, and marched north to Capua. Here he fortified himself as if for a siege, though his force greatly outnumbered that of the eunuch.[5]

When the conflict could no longer be avoided, the Franks formed

[1] *Op. cit.*, I, 20. [2] *Op. cit.*, I, 21–22. [3] *Op. cit.*, I, 22, end; II, 1. [4] *Op. cit.*, II, 1–3. [5] *Op. cit.*, II, 4.

a great wedge the point of which should pierce the centre of Narses's army. This was, in fact, the weakest point of his line, being composed of rather unstable foot-soldiers, while the wings were made up of the mounted archers who gave so good an account of themselves in all the Italian campaigns. When the Franks made their attack, their wedge pierced deep into the centre of the Byzantine line, but at Narses's command the wings of the imperial army folded in upon the sides of the wedge, and the archers discharged their arrows, not at the men who were directly opposing them and whose heavy shields and breastplates afforded them protection, but at the soldiers on the other side of the wedge, whose unprotected backs made them easy victims. Finally the point of the Frankish wedge was driven back upon its weakened centre, and in the resulting disorder and confusion the soldiers of Narses inflicted terrible slaughter upon their foes. The Frankish host was destroyed and Butilin himself killed.[1]

Just before the battle began, there occurred another incident which disclosed something of the character of Narses. A Herulian chieftain had murdered with great cruelty one of his slaves, because of some slight negligence. Narses learned of the case, and although he had already mounted his horse to begin the battle, he sought out the man, and charged him with his deed. The Herulian retorted that he had acted within his rights, and would treat another slave so if the occasion should arise. Indignant at such cruelty and insolence, Narses commanded his guardsmen to slay the Herulian, and he fell at once with a fatal wound. The Herulians resented this killing of their kinsman, and were not in line at the beginning of the conflict. It was their tardy aid, however, which forced back the point of the Frankish wedge.[2]

After the defeat of Butilin, the Byzantines returned to Rome flushed with victory, and abandoned themselves to sensual delights. Here again Narses's unusual qualities were evident. He realized the danger of this demoralization, and addressed his soldiers, telling them that they might soon have to face other perils, and that their present conduct was not worthy of their Roman forefathers. The magic name brought them to their senses.[3]

One small garrison of Goths still held out in the Apennine town of Campsa, under the leadership of a Hun by the name of Ragnaris. The strong position of the fortress made it necessary to resort to a blockade. This was maintained through the winter of 554, but in the

[1] *Op. cit.*, II, 8–9. [2] *Op. cit.*, II, 7. [3] *Op. cit.*, II, 11–12.

early spring Ragnaris, when leaving a colloquy with Narses, turned and shot an arrow at him, but his aim was untrue. Narses's guards let fly a volley of arrows and Ragnaris fell mortally wounded. The town willingly surrendered at once.[1]

Few details are given of the life of Narses after his defeat of the Franks and Goths. In the year 555, the clergy of Rome made a request to the Emperor, through Narses, that the banished Pope, Vigilius, be returned to them. The request was granted, and Vigilius and his fellow exiles started on their return to Italy, but the Pope never again saw Rome, for he died on the way at Syracuse.[2]

The Emperor had made it clear that it was his desire that the Archdeacon Pelagius should succeed Vigilius,[3] but the superstitious Italians, believing that he had in some way been the cause of the suffering of Vigilius, were not at once reconciled to his ordination. To overcome their hostility, a solemn procession was arranged, in which Narses, the representative of the Byzantine Empire, and Pelagius, the head of the church, attended by priests who chanted litanies, marched from the church of St. Pancratius to St. Peter's. Here Pelagius mounted the pulpit, and with the gospels in his hand and a cross over his head, solemnly asserted that he had had no part in the misfortunes of Vigilius, and so mollified the people.[4]

About the year 561, a new danger confronted Narses. The Gothic Count, Widin, led a revolt against the Byzantine rulers of Italy, and was aided by Aming, a Frank. The rebellious leaders were successfully opposed by Narses; Widin was captured and sent to Constantinople, and Aming fell "by Narses' sword." [5]

The details of this revolt are not known, but the first encounter may have occurred on the banks of the Adige, for there Aming placed his army in the path of Narses, and declared that he would not move "so long as hand could hurl a javelin," although the eunuch had urged him not to break the treaty then in force between the Franks and Romans.[6]

In 563 messengers arrived in Constantinople to announce that Narses had taken the two Gothic strongholds of Verona and Brescia.[7] The capture of Verona by Narses seems to be referred to by Agnellus, who states that it occurred on July 20.[8] It is not improbable that

[1] *Op. cit.*, II, 13–14.
[2] *Liber Pontificalis, Vita Vigilii,* VIII.
[3] *Ibidem.*
[4] *Op. cit., Vita Pelagii.*
[5] Paulus Diaconus, *Historia Langobardorum*, 2, 2.
[6] Menander Protector (*F. H. G.*), *frag.* 8.
[7] Theoph., 367, 6 ff.
[8] *Liber Pontificalis, Pars II, Vita S. Maximiani,* V, end.

the capture of these important cities constituted a part of the campaign against Aming and Widin.[1]

Shortly after the suppression of the Frankish insurrection, Narses was called upon to crush the revolt of the Heruli under Sinduald. The Heruli had marched under the Emperor's standards, and had given Narses valuable assistance on more than one occasion, but they were an unreliable and unruly people. Sinduald had become their chief in 553, through the aid of Narses,[2] and had received many favors at the hands of the eunuch, but soon became haughty and rebellious, and finally sought to win the mastery of Italy for himself. Narses met him in battle, defeated his army, and hung the traitorous leader from a high gallows.[3] These events occurred in 565, the year of Justinian's death.[4] The reconquest of the Italian peninsula was now completed. Narses held "all the borders of Italy,"[5] and "all Italy rejoiced."[6]

Narses was now faced by economic problems no less grave than the military problems had been. By years of devastating warfare, barbarian armies had spread in Italy a desolation which was rendered more terrible by the havoc of the bubonic plague, which appeared in the peninsula in 565, and ravaged all the country, but especially the district of Liguria.[7]

The immediate task before the people of Italy was the rebuilding of their ruined towns and the renewed cultivation of their abandoned fields. To this task Narses applied himself, worthily restoring Milan and other cities which had been destroyed by the Goths,[8] and repairing the churches ruined by time or the enemy.[9] The poverty which met his sight on every hand roused his compassion also, and he was generous in his relief of the needy.[10]

This work of restoration and relief was laudable, but as it necessitated the collection of large sums of money from the more fortunate sections of the country, it engendered much ill-will toward the eunuch.[11] At last the Romans made complaint to the Emperor Justin and his wife Sophia. "It had been better," said they, "for the Romans to serve the Goths than the Greeks. Where Narses, the eunuch, rules he

[1] Suggested by Hodgkin, *Italy and her Invaders*, vol. V, p. 55.

[2] Agathias, *op. cit.*, I, 20.

[3] Paul. Diac., *op. cit.*, 2, 3.

[4] Marius Aventicensis, *Chronicon*, 799 C. On the chronology of Marius, see Clinton, *Fasti Romani*, years 566, 567.

[5] Paul. Diac., *op. cit.*, 2, 3.

[6] *Lib. Pont.* (Duchesne), vol. I, p. 305, 8.

[7] Paul. Diac., *op cit.*, 2, 4.

[8] Marius Aventicensis, *Chronicon*, 799 D. *C.I.L.*, VI, 1199, records the reconstruction of a bridge over the Anio by Narses.

[9] Paul. Diac., *op. cit.*, 2, 3.

[10] Paul. Diac., *op. cit.*, 2, 3.

[11] *Op. cit.*, 2, 5.

has reduced us even to slavery." Hearing of this protest, Narses said, "If I have done the Romans wrong, may I suffer an evil fate."[1]

The representations of the Romans probably constituted the immediate cause of the recall of Narses in 567,[2] and the appointment of the Prefect Longinus in his stead,[3] but later writers make much of the Empress Sophia's contemptuous treatment of the eunuch, implying that there had previously been ill-feeling between them. According to the account of Paul the Deacon, Narses did not dare to return to Constantinople, for the Empress had informed him that, as he was a eunuch, she would make him serve in the women's apartments, portioning out to the girls the wool for the day's spinning; to which the insulted eunuch replied, that he would lay her such a web as she could not finish while she lived.[4] Fearing for his life, Narses withdrew to the vicinity of Naples, and, carrying out his threat against the Empress, sent to the Langobards, who were eking out their existence in unproductive Pannonia, an invitation to enter Italy and possess themselves of its abundance.[5]

It is an astounding charge that would make Narses, the faithful, responsible for the invasion of Italy by Alboin, but it has good, though not unquestionable, support. The mention of this accusation in the *Life* of Pope John III, which was written shortly after the death of the eunuch, during the life of the Pope Pelagius II,[6] indicates that such a report was current almost in Narses's own day.

The story is repeated in the first part of the following century by Isidore of Seville,[7] in the middle of that century by the so-called Fredegarius,[8] about the year 671 by the author of the *Origo gentis Langobardorum*,[9] and toward the middle of the eighth century by Paul the Deacon.[10] Its picturesqueness grew as it was told. Fredegarius says that the insulting message of the Empress was accompanied by a golden distaff, and Paul the Deacon states that Narses's messengers to the Langobards bore many kinds of fruits and samples of other produce in which Italy abounds, for the purpose of enticing the barbarians into the country.

[1] *Lib. Pont.*, *Vita Iohannis III.* The text is too corrupt to admit of certainty in translation.

[2] Marius Avent., *Chron.*, 799 D. Cf. Agnellus, *Lib. Pont.*, *Pars II*, *Vita S. Agnelli*, III.

[3] Paul. Diac., *op. cit.*, 2, 5.

[4] Paul. Diac., *op. cit.*, 2, 5. Given in slightly different form by Fredegarius, *Historia Francorum Epitomata*, LXV.

[5] *Lib. Pont.*, *Vita Iohannis III.*

[6] Cf. Hodgkin, *Italy and her Invaders*, vol. V, p. 60, n. 1.

[7] *Chronicon*, 116.

[8] *Gregorii Historia Francorum Epitomata*, LXV.

[9] *Scriptores Rerum Langobardicarum* (*Monumenta Germaniae Historica*), p. 4.

[10] *Hist. Lang.*, 2, 5.

These details have the appearance of having been embroidered upon the plain story of the earlier historians. Especially is this true of the display of fruit, for the Langobard warriors had been serving in Italy in the army of Narses only a little more than a decade earlier, and knew the country well. There would, therefore, have been no necessity for such proofs of its fertility.

These later versions of the accusation against Narses may be rejected, and even the statement regarding the treachery of the eunuch will be tinged with doubt. The very earliest version, that of the *Liber Pontificalis*, is not beyond suspicion. If Narses wished to betray Italy, it is probable that fear of detection and punishment would have led him to await the arrival of the invaders in the north, that he might enjoy their protection at the earliest possible moment; but according to the account of the *Liber Pontificalis*, as well as that of Paul the Deacon, he deliberately withdrew to Naples before sending the embassy to Pannonia. The element of improbability which is thus introduced brings the whole story into doubt.

This doubt is increased by the fact that although Marius Aventicensis and Gregory of Tours, who are contemporary authorities for the time of the Langobard invasion, both mention the entry of Alboin into Italy, neither of them implicates Narses in any way, and the *Excerptum Sangallense* is as silent. It can only be concluded that the story of Narses's invitation to the Langobards was not widely known in the years immediately succeeding his death, or that Marius and Gregory and the author of the *Excerptum Sangallense* rejected it as apocryphal. Certainly there is nothing either in the previous acts of the eunuch or in the accounts of his treacherous dealings with the Langobards which could be considered convincing evidence of his duplicity, and were it not for the early mention of the story in the biography of Pope John III, it could hardly be considered worthy of serious discussion.

It is obvious, however, that there was a report, which had some currency in the days of the papal biographer, that Narses was implicated in the Langobard invasion. This, as Hodgkin has pointed out,[1] might well arise from the fact that the invasion occurred almost immediately after Narses's deposition, and might, therefore, easily be attributed to his desire for revenge. Further plausibility would attach to such a supposition if some temporary ill-feeling were actually

[1] *Italy and her Invaders*, vol. V, p. 64 f. The criticism of the sources which is given here is largely repeated from Hodgkin.

known to exist between the eunuch and the Empress.[1] It may be impossible to free Narses of suspicion in this matter, but it is obviously impossible to convict him of treachery on the evidence which we possess.

Further details of the later life of Narses become even more uncertain. The account given by the biographer of Pope John III includes the mention of an odd meeting of that Pope and the eunuch. "The Pope goes in haste to Naples and asks the ex-governor to return to Rome. Narses says, 'Tell me, most holy Pope, what mischief have I done to the Romans? I will go to the feet of him that sent me, that all Italy may know how I have labored in its behalf.' The Pope answered, 'I will go more quickly than thou canst return from this land.' Therefore Narses returned to Rome with the most holy Pope John, and, after a considerable time, he died there; his body was placed in a leaden chest, and all his riches were brought back to Constantinople. At the same time Pope John died also." [2]

Any attempt to divine the cryptic meaning of this narrative must be well-nigh hopeless. Obviously the Pope made complaint to Narses regarding some real or fancied wrong he had done the Romans. Narses, with the air of one innocent of guilt and grieved that his innocence should be questioned, offered to go to the Emperor and in his presence disprove the charges which had been made against him. The sincerity of this proposal is not without doubt, for when the Pope, not to be put off by such a proposal, threatened to precede the eunuch to the court of the Emperor, there to prefer his charges in person, Narses appears to have capitulated. He went not to Constantinople, but to Rome, and appears to have lived on terms of amity with John.

The threatening tone of the Pope's words is unmistakable; the admission of Narses that he could not defend himself against the charges seems equally clear. Why, then, did the eunuch accompany the Pope to the city of Rome, where there was probably great hostility toward him, and how did he come to enjoy the protection of his chief accuser? Can it be that John undertook to perform for Narses the service that Narses had performed for Pelagius, and to stand sponsor for him in the presence of the Romans? What moved John to accept this rôle; gratitude either for Narses's espousal of the cause of Pelagius or for his past generosity toward the church; or was his menacing atti-

[1] That there was no permanent hostility between Narses and Sophia seems probable in view of the presence of the Empress at the burial of the eunuch. See p. 299.

[2] *Lib. Pont.*, *Vita Iohannis III*.

tude during the interview designed to wring from the opulent eunuch the promise of a rich reward in return for his protection? These questions appear unanswerable — in view of the uncertainty of the text upon which they are based, perhaps they should not even be asked.

The sojourn of Narses in the neighborhood of Naples, and his return to Rome in the year 571 are recorded in the *Excerptum Sangallense*, with the further statement that he plundered the city.[1]

From this account and the statement in the *Life* of Pope John III that on their return from Naples the Pope remained outside the walls, dwelling in the cemetery of Saints Tiburtius and Valerianus, while Narses entered the city, De Rossi concludes that the Pope and Narses did not live harmoniously, and that the Pope, in remonstrance against the rapaciousness of the eunuch, refused to live within the city. He apparently accepts as credible the tradition that Narses invited the Langobards to enter Italy, and explains that his plundering of the city was carried on under the protection of the invaders.[2] Duchesne is of the opinion that the Pope's dwelling outside the city is significant, but is careful to avoid an interpretation of it.[3] Few, probably, would wish to be as specific in the interpretation of the statements as De Rossi.

The historians are almost unanimous in describing Narses as possessed of much wealth, which they seem to have regarded as the plunder of Italy. Agnellus says: "Now in the third year of the Emperor Justin II, Narses the Patrician, being recalled from Ravenna, departed with all the wealth of Italy;"[4] and again: "Narses the Patrician died at Rome after he had won many victories in Italy, and had stripped all the Romans of Italy (*cum denudatione omnium Romanorum Italiae*)."[5] The *Excerptum Sangallense* is more specific in its charge: "Narses entered Rome and plundered the statue (statues?) of its *palatium*, and the *capitolium* (*Narses ingressus Romam et deposuit palatii eius statuam et capitolium*)."[6] According to the *Liber Pontificalis* Narses's wealth was sent with his body to Constantinople.[7]

In the earlier acts of Narses there was nothing to suggest that he was avaricious. In fact, his generosity toward the mercenaries in his army and toward unfortunate subjects is mentioned more than once, and throughout the accounts of his exploits in Italy, power rather than wealth seems to have been the goal of his ambition. It is quite

[1] De Rossi, *Bullettino di Archeologia Cristiana*, vol. V (1867), p. 22. De Rossi computes this date from the consular year.

[2] *Op. cit.*, vol. V, p. 23.

[3] *Liber Pontificalis*, vol. I, 307.

[4] *Lib. Pont., Pars II, Vita S. Agnelli*, III.

[5] *Op. cit., Vita Petri Senioris*, III.

[6] *Bull. di Arch. Crist.*, vol. V (1867), p. 22.

[7] *Vita Iohannis III.*

possible that the belief that Narses was extremely wealthy arose from the fact that he levied heavy taxes upon all Italy for the rehabilitation of the desolated regions. His construction of churches and public buildings with the money thus obtained, and his generosity toward the destitute would only serve to add conviction to this belief.

No doubt the eunuch was possessed of a considerable amount of this world's goods — it would be strange if any governor of a district as large as Italy, in the time of Justinian, were not. It may readily be granted also that much of this wealth had been derived from Italian sources. Probably, however, statements to the effect that he had plundered all Italy are to be taken as gross exaggerations. In the imaginations and on the tongues of the credulous Italians Narses's wealth developed into a fabulous treasure.

Gregory of Tours relates the following picturesque tale: "Since Narses, the famous commander of Italy, had a great house in a certain city, he set forth to Italy [1] with many treasures, and came to the afore-mentioned city. There in his own house he secretly had dug a great cistern, in which he placed many hundred thousand pounds of gold and silver, and then, putting to death those who shared his secret, he intrusted his hidden wealth, on oath, to but a single old man. After the death of Narses the treasure lay undiscovered in the earth. But when the aforesaid old man observed the daily charities of the Emperor, forthwith he went to him and said, 'If I shall gain any advantage thereby, I shall make known to you a great matter, O Caesar.' And he replied, 'Speak out, what you will, for you shall be rewarded if what you say is to our advantage.' Said he, 'I have the secret of Narses's hidden treasure, but being at the end of my life I cannot keep it concealed.' Then Caesar Tiberius, being overjoyed, straightway sent his servants to the place, and as the old man led them they followed in amazement. Arriving at the cistern they opened it and entered, and found therein so much gold and silver that it was scarcely removed although they carried it forth for many days." [2]

The date of the death of Narses can be determined with fair accuracy. It has already been indicated that he moved from Naples to Rome in the year 571. The *Life* of Pope John III states that he

[1] MSS. — *Italiam* (or *in Italiam*) *cum multis thesauris egressus*. Hodgkin (*Italy and her Invaders*, vol. V, p. 66) translates, "went forth from Italy . . . and came to the aforesaid city of Constantinople." He has violated the Latin needlessly. The disregard of considerations of time and space in the latter part of the narrative is characteristic of wonder-tales, and even to Gregory this is plainly nothing more.

[2] Gregory of Tours, *Historia Francorum*, 5, 20.

died there after a considerable time, and that at the same time Pope John also died. The statements of the *Liber Pontificalis* are not very accurate, but apparently Narses died shortly before the Pope.

The Pope's death occurred July 13, 574,[1] and the conclusion may therefore be drawn that Narses died in 573 or 574. He died at Rome, according to the statement of the biographer of Pope John, and that of Agnellus, who adds that he died in his ninety-fifth year.[2] His body was taken back to Constantinople, and then, in the presence of the Emperor and Empress, was deposited in a splendid monastery which he himself had built,[3] in Bithynia.[4]

Narses was a very pious Catholic. Evagrius says that those who were intimate with him stated that he so worshipped God with prayers and other religious offices, and was so zealous in paying due honors to the Virgin, that she revealed to him clearly the time when he should commence battle, and that Narses never made an attack until he had received a sign from her.[5] Paul the Deacon describes him briefly as follows:

"He was a very pious man, in religion a Catholic, generous toward paupers, quite zealous in repairing churches, so earnest in vigils and prayers that he won his victories more by entreaties which he poured forth to God than by warlike arms." [6] He was withal a stern general, for his lieutenants feared his rebuke more than the sword,[7] and in modern times his military genius has been rated higher than that of his famous contemporary and rival, Belisarius.[8]

[1] Duchesne, *Lib. Pont.*, vol. I, p. cclxi.

[2] *Lib. Pont.*, *Pars II*, *Vita Petri Senioris*, III.

[3] John of Ephesus, *Ecclesiastical History*, 1, 39. (Translation by R. Payne Smith, Oxford, 1860, p. 75.) Theodosius Melitenus, *Chronographia* (ed. Tafel), p. 95.

[4] John of Ephesus, *op. cit.*, p. 160.

[5] *Hist. Eccl.*, 4, 24. Cf. Agathias, *op. cit.*, 79, 9 f.

[6] *De Gestis Langobardorum*, 2, 3.

[7] Agathias, *op. cit.*, 45, 7 ff.

[8] Diehl, *Justinien et la Civilisation Byzantine*, p. 167.

CHAPTER V

SUMMARY

In the preceding chapters there has been presented as full an account as it seems possible to give, at the present time, of the office of Grand Chamberlain from the time of its inception, under Diocletian, to its disappearance in the eleventh century. The time and circumstances of the origin of the office have been discussed, the stages of its growth have been marked, and probable dates for a number of changes have been determined.

The honors which were accorded to the Grand Chamberlain, the titles by which he was addressed, and the privileges which were granted to him have been given consideration, as have also the various duties, whether of an administrative, juridical, ceremonial, or other nature, which seem to have been assigned to him. The reasons for the decline of the office and the probable date of its abolishment have been discussed. In order to give a complete account of the administrative activities of the Grand Chamberlain, it has been found necessary to include a rather full treatment of the various departments which were under his supervision, and of the subordinate officials who directed those departments.

It has been shown that the importance and influence of the office of Grand Chamberlain increased steadily until the time of Justinian; that during that Emperor's reign the office reached the culmination of its administrative importance; that thereafter the administrative competence of the Grand Chamberlain was reduced almost to insignificance, while his ceremonial activities became increasingly conspicuous and important until the tenth century, when they began to suffer eclipse by new offices which were rapidly rising into prominence; that in the reorganization of the court, which was in gradual progress during the tenth and eleventh centuries, the Grand Chamberlain's office became superfluous and was finally discontinued. Some account has been given, furthermore, of the ceremonial activities of the Grand Chamberlain; and finally, by means of four biographical sketches, an attempt has been made to illustrate the importance which attaches to the figure of the Grand Chamberlain because of his unofficial activities.

The material for this paper has been drawn from a wide range of authors — from Cicero, in 70 B.C., to Cedrenus, in the fourteenth century — and its interpretation has been aided by modern works ranging in date from 1602 to 1919. The difficulties encountered in surveying so broad a field have been great, especially because of the lack of adequate indices and lexica of the writers of the Byzantine period, and the author fears that, in spite of the most painstaking endeavor to make this study complete, he may have overlooked some significant point.

BIBLIOGRAPHY

I. Greek and Latin Texts

Acta Apostolorum.

Acta Sanctorum. Collegit Joannes Bollandus (et alii). Paris, 1883–.

Ammianus Marcellinus, *Rerum Gestarum Libri Qui Supersunt.* Recensuit rhythmiceque distinxit C. U. Clark. Berlin, 1910–1915.

Translation by C. D. Yonge. London, 1862.

Anonymus Valesianus. Edidit V. Gardthausen. Leipzig, 1875.

Cicero, *Orationes Verrinae.* Recognovit brevique adnotatione critica instruxit W. Peterson. Editio altera, Oxford, 1916.

Epistulae ad Atticum. Recognovit brevique adnotatione critica instruxit L. C. Purser. Oxford, 1903.

Claudianus, *Carmina.* Recognovit J. Koch. Leipzig, 1893.

Codex Theodosianus. Edidit Th. Mommsen. Berlin, 1905.

Corippus, *Libri Qui Supersunt.* Recensuit J. Partsch, in *Monumenta Germaniae Historica, Auctores Antiquissimi,* vol. III. Berlin, 1879.

Corpus Inscriptionum Latinarum. Berlin, 1863–.

Corpus Iuris Civilis:

I. *Digesta.* Recognovit Th. Mommsen. Berlin, 1872.

II. *Codex Justinianus.* Recognovit P. Krueger. Editio stereotypa sexta. Berlin, 1895.

III. *Novellae* (including the *Edicta* and *Appendix Constitutionum Dispersarum*). Recognoverunt R. Schoell, W. Kroll. Editio stereotypa secunda. Berlin, 1899.

Corpus Scriptorum Historiae Byzantinae. Editio emendatior et copiosior consilio B. G. Niebuhr C. f. instituta, auctoritate academiae litterarum regiae Borussicae continuata. Bonn, 1828–1897.[1]

Agathias, *Historiae.* Recensuit B. G. Niebuhr, 1828.

Anna Comnena, *Alexias,* vol I. Recensuit L. Schopen, 1839.

Breves Enarrationes Chronographicae, Incerti Auctoris. Ex recognitione I. Bekkeri, 1843.

Cedrenus, *Compendium Historiarum a Mundo Condito ad Imperatorem Isaacum Comnenum.* Ioannis Scylitzae ope ab I. Bekkero suppletus et emendatus, 1838–1839.

Chronicon Paschale. Recensuit L. Dindorf, 1832.

[1] Citations from this *Corpus* are sometimes by book and chapter, when Roman and Arabic numerals are used, thus, V, 27; generally, however, they are by page and line, in which case Arabic numerals alone are employed, thus, 227, 18.

Codinus Curopalates, *De Officialibus Palatii Constantinopolitani.* Ex recognitione I. Bekkeri, 1839.
Codinus, Georgius (Pseudo-), *Excerpta de Antiquitatibus Constantinopolitanis* (cited as *De Originibus Constantinopolitanis, De Signis, De Aedificiis*). Ex recognitione I. Bekkeri, 1843.
Constantine Porphyrogenitus, *De Caerimoniis Aulae Byzantinae.* Recensuit J. J. Reiske, 1830.
Genesius, *Reges.* Ex recognitione C. Lachmanni, 1834.
Georgius Monachus, *Vitae Recentiorum Imperatorum.* Ex recognitione I. Bekkeri, 1838.
Luitprand, *Legatio.* Ex Muratorii scriptoribus rerum Italicarum sumpta, 1828.
Lydus, Joannes, *De Magistratibus Populi Romani.* Ex recognitione I. Bekkeri, 1837.
Malalas, Joannes, *Chronographia.* Recensuit L. Dindorf, 1831.
Michael Attaliota, *Historia.* Recognovit I. Bekker, 1853.
Nicephorus Bryennius, *Commentarii.* Recognovit A. Meineke, 1836.
Olympiodorus, *Excerpta.* Edidit B. G. Niebuhr, 1829.
Περὶ ταξειδίων (Appendix to Constantine Porphyrogenitus, *De Caerimoniis Aulae Byzantinae*, Book I).
Petrus Patricius, sections of Constantine Porphyrogenitus, *De Caerimoniis Aulae Byzantinae.*
Philotheos, *Kletorologion*, sections of Constantine Porphyrogenitus, *De Caerimoniis Aulae Byzantinae.*
Procopius, *Opera.* Ex recensione G. Dindorfii, 1833–1838.
Scylitzes. See Cedrenus.
Symeon Magister, *Chronographia.* Ex recognitione I. Bekkeri, 1838.
Theophanes, *Chronographia.* Ex recensione J. Classeni, 1839–1841.
Theophanes Continuatus, *Chronographia.* Ex recognitione I. Bekkeri, 1838.
Theophylactus Simocatta, *Historiae.* Recognovit I. Bekker, 1834.
Zonaras, *Epitome Historiarum*, vol. III. Ex recensione M. Pinderi edidit Th. Büttner-Wobst, 1897.
Zosimus, *Historiae.* Ex recognitione I. Bekkeri, 1837.

Dio Cassius, *Historiarum Romanarum Quae Supersunt.* Edidit U. P. Boissevain. Berlin, 1895–1901.
Diodorus Siculus, *Bibliotheca Historica.* Recognoverunt F. Vogel, E. T. Fischer. Leipzig, 1888–1906.
Eutropius, *Breviarium Historiae Romanae.* Editio altera. Curavit H. R. Dietsch. Leipzig, 1877.
Excerptum Sangallense. Edidit G. B. De Rossi, in *Bullettino di Archeologia Cristiana* (first series), vol. V (1867), pp. 17–23.
Fragmenta Historicorum Graecorum. Ediderunt C. et Th. Mueller. Paris, 1841–1883.
Eunapius of Sardis.
Menander Protector.
Herodianus, *Ab Excessu Divi Marci Libri Octo.* Ab I. Bekkero recogniti. Leipzig, 1855.

Herodotus, *Historiae*. Recognovit brevique adnotatione critica instruxit C. Hude. Oxford, 1912.

John of Ephesus, *Ecclesiastical History*. Translated by R. Payne Smith. Oxford, 1860.

Julian. *The Works of the Emperor Julian, with an English translation* by W. C. Wright. London, 1913– (*Loeb Classical Library*).

Justini II, *Novellae*. Cited from Bury, *Imperial Administrative System in the Ninth Century*, p. 79.

Leges Novellae ad Theodosianum Pertinentes. Edidit P. M. Meyer. Berlin, 1905.
Novellae Marciani.
Novellae Valentiniani.

Liber Pontificalis. Edidit l'Abbé Duchesne. Paris, 1886–1892.

Marcus Diaconus, *Vita Porphyrii Episcopi Gazensis*. Edidit M. Haupt, in *Abhandlungen der königliche Akademie der Wissenschaften zu Berlin*, 1874. Pp. 171–215.

Martialis, *Epigrammata*. Recognovit brevique adnotatione critica instruxit W. M. Lindsay. Oxford, 1902.

Notitia Dignitatum Utriusque Imperii. Edidit O. Seeck. Berlin, 1876.

Origo Gentis Langobardorum. Edidit G. Waitz, in *Monumenta Germaniae Historica, Scriptores Rerum Langobardicarum*. Hannover, 1878.

Papiri Diplomatici. Edidit G. L. Marini. Rome, 1805.

Patrologiae Cursus Completus. Accurante J.-P. Migne. Paris, 1844–1866.

Series Graeca:

Athanasius Alexandrinus, vols. XXV, XXVI.
Chrysostomus, Joannes, vol. LII.
Eusebius Caesariensis, vol. XX.
Palladius Helenopolitanus, vol. XXXIV.
Philostorgius, vol. LXV.
Socrates Scholasticus, vol. LXVII.
Sozomenus, vol. LXVII.
Synesius, vol. LXVI.
Theodoretus, vol. LXXXII.
Theodorus Lector, vol. LXXXVI.

Series Latina:

Agnellus, vol. CVI.
Ambrosius Milanensis, vols. XVI, XVII.
Cassiodorus Senator, vol. LXIX.
Fredegarius (Pseudo-), vol. LXXI.
Gregorius Turensis, vol. LXXI.
Idatius, vol. LI.
Isidorus Hispalensis, vol. LXXXIII.
Marcellinus Comes, vol. LI.
Marius Aventicensis, vol. LXXII.
Prosper Aquitanus, vol. LI.
Symmachus, vol. XVIII.

Paulus Diaconus, *Historia Gentis Langobardorum*. Ediderunt L. Bethmann, G. Waitz, in *Monumenta Germaniae Historica, Scriptores Rerum Langobardicarum*. Hannover, 1878.

Phaedrus, *Fabulae Aesopiae*. Recognovit brevique adnotatione critica instruxit J. P. Postgate. Oxford, 1919.

Philo Judaeus, Tauchnitz edition. Leipzig, 1851–1853.

Plinius Secundus, *Naturalis Historia*. Recognovit et edidit C. Mayhoff. Leipzig, 1875–1906.

Plinius Caecilius Secundus, *Opera*. Recensuit R. C. Kukula. Leipzig, 1912.

Plutarch, *Moralia*. Recognovit G. N. Bernardakis. Leipzig, 1888–1896.

Vitae Parallelae. Iterum recognovit C. Sintenis. Leipzig, 1864–1883.

Sacrorum Conciliorum Nova et Amplissima Collectio, vol. XVI. Evulgavit G. D. Mansi. Venice, 1771.

Scriptores Historiae Augustae. Iterum recensuit H. Peter. Leipzig, 1884.

Capitolinus, *Gordiani Tres*.

Lampridius, *Commodus Antoninus*.

Vopiscus, *Carus*.

Seneca, *Dialogi*. Edidit E. Hermes. Leipzig, 1905.

Epistulae Morales. Iterum edidit O. Hense. Leipzig, 1914.

Suetonius, with an English Translation by J. C. Rolfe. London, 1914 (*Loeb Classical Library*).

Suidas, *Lexicon*. Recensuit J. Bernhardy. Halle, 1853.

Τακτικὸν ἐν ἐπιτόμῳ γενόμενον ἐπὶ Μιχαὴλ . . . καὶ Θεοδώρας. Edidit Th. Uspenski, in *Izviestiia Russkago Arkheologicheskago Instituta v Konstantinopolie*, vol. III (1898), pp. 109 ff.

Theodosius Melitenus. Edidit Theoph. Tafel. Munich, 1859.

Velleius Paterculus, *Historia Romana*. Edidit R. Ellis. Oxford, 1898.

II. Modern Works

Bethmann-Hollweg, M. A., *Der römische Civilprozess*. Bonn, 1865–1866.

Boak, A. E. R., *The Master of the Offices*, in *University of Michigan Studies, Humanistic Series*, vol. XIV; Part I of this volume.

Roman Magistri, in *Harvard Studies in Classical Philology*, vol. XXVI (1915), pp. 73–164.

Böcking, E., *Notitia Dignitatum*. Recensuit . . . commentariis indicibusque illustravit E. Böcking. Bonn, 1839–1853.

Bulletin de Correspondance Hellénique, vol. IV.

Bury, J. B., *The Ceremonial Book of Constantine Porphyrogennetos*, in *English Historical Review*, vol. XXII (1907), pp. 209–227, 417–439.

The Imperial Administrative System in the Ninth Century, with a Revised Text of the Kletorologion of Philotheos, British Academy Supplemental Papers, I. London, 1911.

The Treatise De Administrando Imperio, in *Byzantinische Zeitschrift*, vol. XV (1906), pp. 517–577.

Cesano, L., in De Ruggiero, *Dizionario Epigrafico*, s.v. *cubiculum*.

Clinton, H. F., *Fasti Romani*. Oxford, 1845.

Daremberg et Saglio, *Dictionnaire des Antiquités Grecques et Romaines.* Paris, 1877–1919.

De Ruggiero, E., *Dizionario Epigrafico di Antichità Romane.* Rome, 1895–.

De Sanctis, G., in De Ruggiero, *Dizionario Epigrafico*, s.v. *castrensis.*

De Villafosse, A. Heron, in Daremberg et Saglio, *Dictionnaire des Antiquités*, s.v. *castrensis.*

Diehl, Ch., *Justinien et la Civilisation Byzantine au VI*[e] *Siècle.* Paris, 1901.

De Rossi, G. B., *Excerptum ex Chronica Horosii*, in *Bullettino di Archeologia Cristiana* (first series), vol. V (1867), pp. 17–23.

Du Cange, D., *Glossarium Mediae et Infimae Latinitatis.* Digessit G. A. L. Henschel. Paris, 1840–1850.

Fairon, E., *La Ratio Castrensis*, in *Musée Belge*, vol. II (1898), pp. 241–266.

L'Organisation du Palais Impérial à Rome, in *Musée Belge*, vol. IV (1900), pp. 5–25.

Friedlaender, L., *Darstellungen aus der Sittengeschichte Roms*, seventh edition. Leipzig, 1901.

Gatti, G., *Del Caput Africae nella Seconda Regione di Roma*, in *Annali dell' Instituto di Corrispondenza Archeologica di Roma*, vol. LIV (1882), pp. 191–220.

Gibbon, E., *The Decline and Fall of the Roman Empire.* Edited by J. B. Bury. London, 1896–.

Gothofredus, J. L. - Ritter, J. D., *Codex Theodosianus cum Perpetuis Commentariis.* Leipzig, 1736–1745.

Grossi-Gondi, F., in De Ruggiero, *Dizionario Epigrafico*, s.v. *comes.*

Gwatkin, H. M., *Studies of Arianism.* Cambridge, 1882.

Hastings, *Encyclopaedia of Religion and Ethics*, vol. V.

Hirschfeld, O., *Die kaiserliche Verwaltungsbeamten bis auf Diocletian.* Berlin, 1905.

Rangtitel der römischen Kaiserzeit, in *Sitzungsberichte der königlichen-preussichen Akademie der Wissenschaft*, 1901, pp. 579–610.

His, R., *Die Domänen der römischen Kaiserzeit.* Leipzig, 1896.

Hodgkin, Th., *Italy and her Invaders:*

Vol. IV, *The Imperial Restoration*, second edition. Oxford, 1896.

Vol. V, *The Lombard Invasions.* Oxford, 1895.

Jullian, C., in Daremberg et Saglio, *Dictionnaire des Antiquités*, s.v. *illustris.*

Karlowa, O., *Romische Rechtsgeschichte:* vol. I, *Staatsrecht und Rechtsquellen.* Leipzig, 1885.

Koch, P., *Die byzantinischen Beamtentitel von 400 bis 700.* Jena, 1903.

Lambeck, P., Commentary on Codinus. See Codinus.

Mansi, G. D. See *Sacrorum Conciliorum Nova et Amplissima Collectio*, under Greek and Latin Texts.

Marini, G. L. See *Papiri Diplomatici*, under Greek and Latin Texts.

Marquardt, J., *Das Privatleben der Römer*, second edition. Leipzig, 1886.

Michiels, J., *Les Cubicularii des Empereurs Romains d'Auguste à Diocletien*, in *Musée Belge*, vol. VI (1902), pp. 364–387.

Mommsen, Th., *Ostgothische Studien*, in *Neues Archiv*, vol. XIV (1889), pp. 225 ff., 453 ff.

Oman, C. W. C., *The Byzantine Empire.* New York, 1892.

Pancirolus, G., *Notitia Utraque Dignitatum . . . et in eam C. Panciroli . . . commentarium.* Venice, 1602.

Pauly-Wissowa, *Real-Encyclopädie der klassischen Altertumswissenschaft.* Stuttgart, 1894–.

Pelham, H. F., *The Imperial Domains and the Colonate*, in *Essays on Roman History*, edited by F. Haverfield. Oxford, 1911.

Reid, J. S., *The Reorganization of the Empire*, in *The Cambridge Medieval History*, vol. I, chapter ii. Cambridge, 1911.

Rostowzew, M., in Pauly-Wissowa, *Real-Encyclopädie*, s.v. *cubicularius, a cubiculo.*

Schiller, H., *Geschichte der römischen Kaiserzeit.* Gotha, 1883–1887.

Schlumberger, G., *Sigillographie de l'Empire Byzantin.* Paris, 1884.

Seeck, O., *Geschichte des Untergangs der antiken Welt.* Berlin, 1898–1913.

Quaestiones de Notitia Dignitatum. Berlin, 1872.

Articles in Pauly-Wissowa, *Real-Encyclopädie*, s.v. *comites, canonicarii, castrensis, cursus publicus.*

Smith, Wm., *Dictionary of Greek and Roman Biography and Mythology*, vol. II. Boston, 1867.

Thierry, Amédée, *Nouveaux Récits de l'Histoire Romaine aux IVe et Ve Siècles — Les Trois Ministres des Fils de Theodose.* Paris, 1865.

Tillemont, Lenain, *Histoire des Empereurs*, vol. V, second edition. Paris, 1723.

Waltzing, A. P., *Étude Historique sur les Corporations Professionelles chez les Romains.* Louvain, 1895–1900.

APPENDIX A

THE GRAND CHAMBERLAINS OF THE LATER ROMAN AND BYZANTINE EMPIRES

Under Constantine the Great, 324–337:
Urbicius, Codinus, *De Originibus Constantinopolitanis*, 18, 3; 23, 2.
Olybrius, *op. cit.*, 18, 3.
Hilarion, *op. cit.*, 63, 1.
Festus, *Liber Pontificalis* (ed. Duchesne), vol. I, 174, 19.

Under Constans, 335–350:
Valentinianus, *Incerti Auctoris, Breves Enarrationes Chronographicae*, 173, 11.

Under Constantius, 335–361:
Eusebius, for references, see pp. 260–270.

Under Gallus, Caesar, 351–353:
Gorgonius, Ammianus Marcellinus, 15, 2.

Under Julian, 361–363:
Eutherius, *op. cit.*, 16, 7; 20, 8.

Under Valentinian, 364–375:
Rhodanus, *Chronicon Paschale*, 558, 2; Malalas, 340, 1; Leo Grammaticus, 97, 14; Georgius Cedrenus, 544, 6
Calligonus, Ambrose, *Epistolae*, 20, 28.

Under Valens, 364–378:
Heliodorus, Ammianus Marcellinus, 29, 2.
Mardonius, Socrates, *Historia Ecclesiastica*, 3, 1; Sozomen, *Historia Ecclesiastica*, 7, 21; Cassiodorus, *Historia Tripartita*, 6, 1; 9, 43.

Under Maximus, 383–388:
. . . . (οὐκ εὐνοῦχός τις ὤν), Zosimus, 217, 14.

Under Honorius, 395–423:
Deuterius, Zosimus, 296, 20.
Terentius, *op. cit.*, 300, 18; 313, 17.
Eusebius, *op. cit.*, 314, 4; Olympiodorus, 452, 8.
Lauricius, Agnellus, *Liber Pontificalis, Pars I, Vita S. Iohannis Angelopti*, chap. 1.

Under Arcadius, 395–408:
  Eutropius, for references, see pp. 272–284.
  Lausus, Palladius, *Historia Lausiaca*, inscription and *ad finem;* Codinus, *De Signis Constantinopolis*, 37, 16.
  Antiochus, Suidas, *Lexicon*, s.v.

Under Theodosius II, 408–450:
  Antiochus, Suidas, *Lexicon*, s.v.; Theophanes, 125, 9; 148, 12; Malalas, 361, 1; Codinus, *De Aedificiis Constantinopolitanis*, 94, 18; Cedrenus, 586, 13; 587, 9; 600, 11.
  Musellius, *Codex Theodosianus*, XI, 28, 9.
  Macrobius, *op. cit.*, VI, 8.
  Artaxis, *Codex Justinianus*, III, 26, 11.
  Chrysaphius, Priscus, 1, 5.

Under Marcian, 450–457:
  Maximinus, *Novellae Marciani*, II, *subscript.*
  Gratesimus, Theophanes, 175, 5; Theodorus Lector, *Ecclesiastica Historia*, 1, 17.

Under Zeno, 474–491:
  Cosmas, *Codex Justinianus*, XII, 16, 4.
  Chryserotes, *op. cit.*, XI, 69, 1.
  Urbicius, Constantine Porphyrogenitus, *De Caerimoniis*, 421, 20.

Under Anastasius, 491–518:
  Antiochus, *Codex Justinianus*, V, 62, 25; XII, 16, 5.
  Amantius, Theophanes, 253, 3; 255, 11; *Chronicon Paschale*, 610, 16; 611, 19; Malalas, 408, 19; 409, 1; 409, 8; 410, 9; Evagrius, *Historia Ecclesiastica*, 6, 2; Procopius, *Historia Arcana*, 46, 12; Marcellinus Comes, *Chronicon*, *an.* 519; Codinus, *De Aedificiis Constantinopolitanis*, 105, 2; Leo Grammaticus, 123, 5; Cedrenus, 636, 2; 637, 23.

Before the sixth century, probably:
  Antiochus, *C.I.L.*, XV, 7131.
  Parthenius, *ibid.*

Under Justinian, 527–565:
  Calopodius, Theophanes, 360, 13.
  Narses, for references, see pp. 284–299.
  Leo, *Acta Sanctorum*, 27 June, vol. V, p. 271.

Under Justin II, 565–578:
  . . . . (τοῦ πραιποσίτου κουβικουλαρίων), Theophanes, 380, 1.

Under Mauricius, 582–602:
  Margarites (Marites?), Theophylactus Simocatta, *Historiae*, 52, 14; Theophanes, 388, 20.

Under Phocas, 602–610:
  Smaragdus, *C.I.L.*, VI, 1200.

Under Justinian II, 685–695:
Stephanus, πρωτοευνοῦχος,[1] Theophanes, 562, 2.

Under Theophilus, 829–842:
Nicephorus, Codinus, *De Aedificiis Constantinopolitanis*, 80, 9.

Under Michael III, 842–867:
Michael Angoures, Georgius Monachus, *De Michaele et Theodora*, 832, 10.
Iohannes, *op. cit.*, 838, 15; Symeon Magister, *De Michaele et Theodora*, 686, 4; Leo Grammaticus, 252, 14.

Under Basil I, 867–886:
Bahanes, Constantine Porphyrogenitus, *De Caerimoniis*, 503, 9; Mansi, *Sacrorum Conciliorum Nova Collectio*, vol. XVI, 18 B; 18 D; 19 D; 19 E; 27 C; 30 C; 36 C; 54 B; 55 A; 56 D; 80 B; 80 E; 97 E; 309 E; 316 D; etc.
Theophilus, Mansi, *op. cit.*, vol. XVI, 84 C.
Theodorus, Mansi, *op. cit.*, vol. XVI, 18 B.

Of the eighth or ninth century:
Basilius, Schlumberger, *Sigillographie*, p. 568.

Under Constantine VII, Porphyrogenitus, 912–958:
Joseph Bringas, Theophanes Continuatus, 466, 14.

Under Romanus II, 958–963:
Joseph Bringas, *op. cit.*, 469, 17 ff.

Under Basil II, Bulgaroctonus, 963–1025:
Symeon (elevated 1009), Cedrenus, vol. II, 455, 16 ff.

Under Nicephorus II, Phocas, 963–969:
Iohannes, Constantine Porphyrogenitus, *De Caerimoniis*, 437, 22.
Christophorus, Luitprand, *Legatio*, p. 362.

Under Romanus III, Argyrus, 1028–1034:
Iohannes, Cedrenus, vol. II, 498, 19.

Under Michael IV, Paphlagonian, 1034–1042:
Basilius Pediadites, Cedrenus, vol. II, 523, 10.
Constantinus, Michael Attaliota, 33, 22.

Under Isaac Comnenus, 1057–1059:
Stephanus, mentioned by Schlumberger, *Sigillographie*, p. 111.

Under Constantine X, Ducas, 1059–1067, or

Under Michael VII, Ducas, 1067–1078:
Stephanus Katydites, Schlumberger, *op. cit.*, p. 634.

Of the eleventh or twelfth century:
Basilius Strobilos, Schlumberger, *op. cit.*, p. 568.

[1] None but a Grand Chamberlain would have dared to beat the Emperor's mother! Cf. Theophanes, 562, 6 ff.

Of the twelfth or thirteenth century(?):
Nicetas, Schlumberger, *op. cit.*, p. 567.[1]

Of unknown date:
Joseph, *Revue Archéologique*, 1887, vol. I, p. 87.
. . . . (Unnamed), Schlumberger, *op. cit.*, p. 257.

[1] Nicetas and the three preceding Grand Chamberlains are known only by the evidence of seals. The dating of seals is a matter of such difficulty that the periods to which these officials have been assigned by Schlumberger must be considered as only approximately determined. Especially doubtful is the date given for Nicetas, since no mention of a Grand Chamberlain in the twelfth or thirteenth centuries has been found in the general literature of that period.

APPENDIX B

EXPRESSIONS EMPLOYED TO DESIGNATE THE GRAND CHAMBERLAIN

Occasional mention has been made in these pages of the great variety of expressions employed by ancient writers to designate the Grand Chamberlain. Very frequently these expressions are ambiguous, and it becomes necessary to read very closely the context in which they occur, in order to determine whether they refer to the Grand Chamberlain or to some other eunuch official. Occasionally it is impossible to arrive at any certain conclusion in the matter. No claim is made that the following list of expressions is complete, but it will give some idea of the multiplicity of periphrases which are to be met, and an appreciation of one of the difficulties which it has been necessary to overcome in studying the office of the Grand Chamberlain.

I. Latin Titles:

praepositus sacri cubiculi, *Codex Theodosianus*, VI, 8.
praepositus cubiculi, Ammianus Marcellinus, 16, 7, etc.
cubiculariis officiis praepositus, *op. cit.*, 29, 2.
praepositus imperatoris, Cassiodorus, *Historia Tripartita*, 10, 4.
cui erat thalami Caesariani cura commissa, Ammianus Marcellinus, 15, 2.
praesidentem imperiali cubiculo, Cassiodorus, *op. cit.*, 6, 1.
maiordomus imperialis, *op. cit.*, 9, 43.[1]
maiore cubiculi imperatoris, Agnellus, *Vita S. Iohannis Angelopti*, chap. 1.
sacri palatii cubicularius, Marcellinus Comes, *Chronicon*, *anno* 396.
palatii praepositus, *op. cit.*, *anno* 519.
cubicularius, *op. cit.*, *anno* 562.

II. Greek Titles:

πραιπόσιτον τοῦ εὐσεβεστάτου κοιτῶνος, Palladius, *Historia Lausiaca*, end.
τὸν πραιπόσιτον τοῦ παλατίου, *Chronicon Paschale*, 558, 1.
ὁ πραιπόσιτος, Codinus, *De Originibus Constantinopolitanis*, 18, 3.
πρωτότυπος τῶν κοιτώνων τοῦ βασιλέως εὐνοῦχος, Socrates, *Historia Ecclesiastica*, 2, 2.
προειστήκει δὲ τότε τῆς βασιλικῆς οἰκίας, Sozomen, *Historia Ecclesiastica*, 3, 1.

[1] Mention may be made of a dissertation by H. E. Bonnell, *De Dignitate Maioris Domus Regum Francorum a Romano Sacri Cubiculi Praeposito Ducenda*. Berlin, 1858.

ὁ τοῦ βασιλείου οἴκου προεστὼς εὐνοῦχος, Sozomen, *Historia Ecclesiastica*, 6, 16.
τοῦ τῶν εὐνούχων πρωτεύοντος, Theophanes, 53, 14.
τοῦ πρώτου τῶν εὐνούχων, Theophanes, 61, 12.
τὸν προεστῶτα τοῦ βασιλικοῦ κοιτῶνος, Socrates, *Historia Ecclesiastica*, 3, 1.
τὸν μείζονα τῆς βασιλικῆς αὐλῆς, Sozomen, *Historia Eccelsiastica*, 5, 5.
τὸν πρῶτον τῶν βασιλικῶν εὐνούχων, Theophanes, 71, 15.
πρῶτον τὸν βασίλειον εὐνοῦχον, Leo Grammaticus, 94, 8.
τῆς βασιλικῆς οἰκίας μείζων εὐνοῦχος, Sozomen, *Historia Ecclesiastica*, 7, 21.
ὁ τοὺς βασιλικοὺς φυλάττειν ἐπιτεταγμένος κοιτῶνας, Zosimus, 217, 13.
ὁ τῆς φυλακῆς τοῦ βασιλικοῦ κοιτῶνος προεστώς, Zosimus, 296, 20.
Τερέντιον ἔταξεν ἀρχεῖν τοῦ βασιλικοῦ κοιτῶνος, Evagrius, *Historia Ecclesiastica*, 6, 2.
τὸν τῶν βασιλικῶν προεστῶτα κοιτώνων, Zosimus, 313, 17.
φύλακα τοῦ κοιτῶνος, Zosimus, 314, 5.
ἀφηνητὴς τῶν βασιλικῶν κοιτώνων, Palladius, *Vita S. Iohannis Chrysostomi*, chap. 5.
εἷς τῶν περὶ τὴν βασιλικὴν θεραπείαν εὐνούχων, Zosimus, 249, 11.
τῶν ἐν τῇ αὐλῇ πραττομένων κύριος, Zosimus, 256, 6.
τὴν ἡγεμονίαν πάντων τῶν βασιλικῶν εἶχε κοιτώνων, Zosimus, 257, 13.
τὸν προεστῶτα τοῦ βασιλέως οἴχου, Sozomen, 8, 2.
μείζων τοῦ βασιλέως εὐνούχων, Sozomen, 8, 7.
τὸν εὐνοῦχον, Theophanes, 121, 11.
εὐνοῦχος τοῦ τε παλατίου καὶ τοῦ βασιλέως κρατῶν, Evagrius, *Historia Ecclesiastica*, 1, 9.
τὸν κουβικουλάριον, Malalas, 363, 4.
τὸν κουβικουλάριον καὶ πραιπόσιτον, Malalas, 408, 19.
τὸν τῶν ἐν παλατίῳ εὐνούχων ἄρχοντα, Procopius, *Historia Arcana*, 46, 13.
τοῦ πραιποσίτου κουβικουλαρίων, Theophanes, 308, 1.
ὁ τοῦ βασιλέως νυμφευτής, Theophylactus Simocatta, 52, 12.
εὐνοῦχος τοῦ παλατίου μέγας ὑπάρχων, Theophanes, 389, 1.
πρωτοευνοῦχον, Theophanes, 562, 3.
ὁ κατακοιμιστής, Julian, *Epistola ad Athenaios*, 274 A.

INDEX

T

U

V

University of Michigan Studies

HUMANISTIC SERIES

General Editors: **FRANCIS W. KELSEY** and **HENRY A. SANDERS**

Size, 22.7 × 15.2 cm. 8°. Bound in cloth

VOL. I. ROMAN HISTORICAL SOURCES AND INSTITUTIONS. Edited by Henry A. Sanders, University of Michigan. Pp. vii + 402. $2.50 net.

CONTENTS

1. THE MYTH ABOUT TARPEIA: Henry A. Sanders.
2. THE MOVEMENTS OF THE CHORUS CHANTING THE CARMEN SAECULARE: Walter Dennison.
3. STUDIES IN THE LIVES OF ROMAN EMPRESSES, JULIA MAMAEA: Mary Gilmore Williams, Mt. Holyoke College.
4. THE ATTITUDE OF DIO CASSIUS TOWARD EPIGRAPHIC SOURCES: Duane Reed Stuart, Princeton University.
5. THE LOST EPITOME OF LIVY: Henry A. Sanders.
6. THE PRINCIPALES OF THE EARLY EMPIRE: Joseph H. Drake, University of Michigan.
7. CENTURIONS AS SUBSTITUTE COMMANDERS OF AUXILIARY CORPS: George H. Allen.

VOL. II. WORD FORMATION IN PROVENÇAL. By Edward L. Adams, University of Michigan. Pp. xvii + 607. $4.00 net.

VOL. III. LATIN PHILOLOGY. Edited by Clarence Linton Meader, University of Michigan. Pp. vii + 290. $2.00 net.

Parts Sold Separately in Paper Covers:

Part I. THE USE OF IDEM, IPSE, AND WORDS OF RELATED MEANING. By Clarence L. Meader. Pp. 1–112. $0.75.

Part II. A STUDY IN LATIN ABSTRACT SUBSTANTIVES. By Manson A. Stewart, Yankton College. Pp. 113–78. $0.40.

Part III. THE USE OF THE ADJECTIVE AS A SUBSTANTIVE IN THE DE RERUM NATURA OF LUCRETIUS. By Frederick T. Swan. Pp. 179–214. $0.40.

Part IV. AUTOBIOGRAPHIC ELEMENTS IN LATIN INSCRIPTIONS. By Henry H. Armstrong, Beloit College. Pp. 215–86. $0.40.

THE MACMILLAN COMPANY

Publishers **64–66 Fifth Avenue** **New York**

University of Michigan Studies — *Continued*

VOL. XII. STUDIES IN EAST CHRISTIAN AND ROMAN ART. By Charles R. Morey, Princeton University, and Walter Dennison. With 67 plates (10 colored) and 91 illustrations in the text. Pp. xiii + 175. Bound in cloth. $4.75 net.

Parts Sold Separately:

Part I. EAST CHRISTIAN PAINTINGS IN THE FREER COLLECTION. By Charles R. Morey. With 13 plates (10 colored) and 34 illustrations in the text. Pp. xiii + 86. Bound in cloth. $2.50 net.

Part II. A GOLD TREASURE OF THE LATE ROMAN PERIOD FROM EGYPT. By Walter Dennison. With 54 plates and 57 illustrations in the text. Pp. 89–175. Bound in cloth. $2.50 net.

VOL. XIII. DOCUMENTS FROM THE CAIRO GENIZAH IN THE FREER COLLECTION. Text, with Translation and an Introduction by Richard Gottheil, Columbia University. (*In press.*)

VOL. XIV. TWO STUDIES IN LATER ROMAN AND BYZANTINE ADMINISTRATION. By Arthur E. R. Boak and James E. Dunlap, University of Michigan. Pp. x + 324. Bound in cloth. $2.25 net.

Parts Sold Separately in Paper Covers:

Part I. THE MASTER OF THE OFFICES IN THE LATER ROMAN AND BYZANTINE EMPIRES. By Arthur E. R. Boak. Pp. x + 160. Paper covers. $1.00 net.

Part II. THE OFFICE OF THE GRAND CHAMBERLAIN IN THE LATER ROMAN AND BYZANTINE EMPIRES. By James E. Dunlap. Pp. 161–324. $1.00 net.

VOL. XV. GREEK THEMES IN MODERN MUSICAL SETTINGS. By Albert A. Stanley, University of Michigan. With 10 plates. Pp. xxii + 385. Bound in cloth, $4.00 net.

Parts Sold Separately in Paper Covers:

Part I. INCIDENTAL MUSIC TO PERCY MACKAYE'S DRAMA OF SAPPHO AND PHAON. Pp. 1–68. $.90 net.

Part II. MUSIC TO THE ALCESTIS OF EURIPIDES WITH ENGLISH TEXT. Pp. 71–120. $.80 net.

Part III. MUSIC TO THE IPHIGENIA AMONG THE TAURIANS BY EURIPIDES, WITH GREEK TEXT. Pp. 123–190. $.75 net.

Part IV. TWO FRAGMENTS OF ANCIENT GREEK MUSIC. Pp. 217–225. $.30 net.

Part V. MUSIC TO CANTICA OF THE MENAECHMI OF PLAUTUS. Pp. 229–263. $.50 net.

Part VI. ATTIS: A SYMPHONIC POEM. Pp. 265–383. $1.00 net.

THE MACMILLAN COMPANY

Publishers **64–66 Fifth Avenue** **New York**

University of Michigan Studies — *Continued*

VOL. XVI. NICOMACHUS OF GERASA: INTRODUCTION TO ARITHMETIC. Translated into English by Martin Luther D'Ooge, with Studies in Greek Arithmetic by Frank Egleston Robbins and Louis C. Karpinski. (*In preparation.*)

VOLS. XVII, XVIII, XIX, XX. ROYAL CORRESPONDENCE OF THE ASSYRIAN EMPIRE. Translated into English, with a transliteration of the Text and a Commentary. By Leroy Waterman, University of Michigan. (*In press.*)

FACSIMILES OF MANUSCRIPTS

Size, 40.5 × 35 cm.

FACSIMILE OF THE WASHINGTON MANUSCRIPT OF DEUTERONOMY AND JOSHUA IN THE FREER COLLECTION. With an Introduction by Henry A. Sanders. Pp. x; 201 heliotype plates. The University of Michigan. Ann Arbor, Michigan, 1910.

Limited edition, distributed only to Libraries, under certain conditions. A list of Libraries containing this Facsimile is printed in *University of Michigan Studies, Humanistic Series*, Volume VIII, pp. 351–353.

Size, 34 × 26 cm.

FACSIMILE OF THE WASHINGTON MANUSCRIPT OF THE FOUR GOSPELS IN THE FREER COLLECTION. With an Introduction by Henry A. Sanders. Pp. x; 372 heliotype plates and 2 colored plates. The University of Michigan. Ann Arbor, Michigan, 1912.

Limited edition, distributed only to Libraries, under certain conditions. A list of Libraries containing this Facsimile is printed in *University of Michigan Studies, Humanistic Series*, Volume IX, pp. 317–320.

SCIENCE SERIES

Size, 28 × 18.5 cm. 4°. Bound in cloth

VOL. I. THE CIRCULATION AND SLEEP. By John F. Shepard, University of Michigan. Pp. ix + 83, with an Atlas of 63 plates, bound separately. Text and Atlas, $2.50 net.

VOL. II. STUDIES ON DIVERGENT SERIES AND SUMMABILITY. By Walter B. Ford, University of Michigan. Pp. xi + 194. $2.50.

University of Michigan Publications

General Editor: EUGENE S. McCARTNEY.

Size, 22.7 × 15.2 cm. 8°. Bound in cloth

THE LIFE AND WORKS OF GEORGE SYLVESTER MORRIS: A CHAPTER IN THE HISTORY OF AMERICAN THOUGHT IN THE NINETEENTH CENTURY. By Robert M. Wenley, University of Michigan. Pp. xv + 332. $1.50 net.

THE MACMILLAN COMPANY

Publishers **64–66 Fifth Avenue** **New York**

University of Michigan Publications — *Continued*

LATIN AND GREEK IN AMERICAN EDUCATION, WITH SYMPOSIA ON THE VALUE OF HUMANISTIC STUDIES. Edited by Francis W. Kelsey. Pp. x + 396. $1.50. (*Out of print; new edition in preparation.*)

THE PRESENT POSITION OF LATIN AND GREEK, THE VALUE OF LATIN AND GREEK AS EDUCATIONAL INSTRUMENTS, THE NATURE OF CULTURE STUDIES.

SYMPOSIA ON THE VALUE OF HUMANISTIC, PARTICULARLY CLASSICAL, STUDIES AS A PREPARATION FOR THE STUDY OF MEDICINE, ENGINEERING, LAW AND THEOLOGY.

A SYMPOSIUM ON THE VALUE OF HUMANISTIC, PARTICULARLY CLASSICAL, STUDIES AS A TRAINING FOR MEN OF AFFAIRS.

A SYMPOSIUM ON THE CLASSICS AND THE NEW EDUCATION.

A SYMPOSIUM ON THE DOCTRINE OF FORMAL DISCIPLINE IN THE LIGHT OF CONTEMPORARY PSYCHOLOGY.

THE SENATE AND TREATIES, 1789–1817: THE DEVELOPMENT OF THE TREATY-MAKING FUNCTIONS OF THE UNITED STATES SENATE DURING THEIR FORMATIVE PERIOD. By Ralston Hayden, University of Michigan. Pp. xvi + 237. Cloth. $1.50 net.

Size, 23.5 × 15.5 cm. 8°. Bound in cloth

WILLIAM PLUMER'S MEMORANDUM OF PROCEEDINGS IN THE UNITED STATES SENATE, 1803–1807. Edited by Everett Somerville Brown, University of Michigan. Pp. xi + 673. Cloth. $3.50.

PAPERS OF THE MICHIGAN ACADEMY OF SCIENCE, ARTS AND LETTERS, submitted at the Annual Meetings. Edited by Paul S. Welch and Eugene S. McCartney.

VOL. I. Papers submitted at the Annual Meeting of 1921. With 38 plates and 5 maps. Pp. xi + 424. Bound in cloth. $2.00 net.

VOL. II. Papers submitted at the Annual Meeting of 1922. With 11 plates. Pp. xi + 226. Bound in cloth. $2.00 net.

Size, 18 × 12 cm.

THE MENAECHMI OF PLAUTUS. The Latin Text, with a Translation by Joseph H. Drake, University of Michigan. Pp. xi + 129. $.60 net.

This edition of the Menaechmi was prepared, with stage directions, as a libretto for the presentation of the play at the University of Michigan in 1890. It was revised and republished in 1916.

THE MACMILLAN COMPANY

Publishers **64–66 Fifth Avenue** **New York**